Lecture Notes of the Institute for Computer Sciences, Social Informatics and Telecommunications Engineering 441

More information about this series at https://link.springer.com/bookseries/8197

Pavel Gladyshev · Sanjay Goel · Joshua James ·
George Markowsky · Daryl Johnson (Eds.)

Digital Forensics
and Cyber Crime

12th EAI International Conference, ICDF2C 2021
Virtual Event, Singapore, December 6–9, 2021
Proceedings

Springer

Editors
Pavel Gladyshev
School of Computer Science
University College Dublin
Dublin, Ireland

Sanjay Goel
State University of New York
University at Albany
Albany, NY, USA

Joshua James
DFIR Science
Champaign, IL, USA

George Markowsky
Missouri University
Rolla, MO, USA

Daryl Johnson
Rochester Institute of Technology
Rochester, NY, USA

ISSN 1867-8211 ISSN 1867-822X (electronic)
Lecture Notes of the Institute for Computer Sciences, Social Informatics
and Telecommunications Engineering
ISBN 978-3-031-06364-0 ISBN 978-3-031-06365-7 (eBook)
https://doi.org/10.1007/978-3-031-06365-7

This Springer imprint is published by the registered company Springer Nature Switzerland AG
The registered company address is: Gewerbestrasse 11, 6330 Cham, Switzerland

Preface

We are delighted to introduce the proceedings of the 12th edition of the European Alliance for Innovation (EAI) International Conference on Digital Forensics and Cyber Crime (ICDF2C 2021). This conference brought together researchers and practitioners around the world who are developing and using digital forensic technologies and techniques for a variety of applications in criminal investigations, incident response, and broader information security. The focus of ICDF2C 2021 was on various applications of digital evidence and forensics beyond "traditional" cyber crime investigations and litigation.

The technical program of ICDF2C 2021 consisted of 22 full papers presented over three days at the main conference track. Aside from the high-quality technical paper presentations, the technical program also featured three keynote speeches and two technical workshops. The three keynote speeches were given by Joe Weiss, the author of Protecting Industrial Control Systems from Electronic Threats, Vitaly Kamluk, the lead threat researcher for Kaspersky APAC, and Jonathan Pan, the head of the Disruptive Technologies Office of the Home Team Science and Technology Agency (HTX), Singapore. The two workshops were Password Cracking and Rainbow Tables, organized by George Markowsky, and Intelligence Gathering Through the Internet and Dark Web, organized by Lu Liming, Jacob Abraham, Selvakulasingam Thiruneepan, and James Ng Hian from the Singapore Institute of Technology and Feixiang He from Group-IB.

Coordination with EAI was essential for the success of the conference. We sincerely appreciate their constant support and guidance. We are grateful to Conference Managers Natasha Onofrei and Lenka Ležanská, Managing Editor Lucia Sedlárová, and all the authors who submitted their papers to the ICDF2C 2021 conference.

March 2022

Pavel Gladyshev
Sanjay Goel
Joshua James
George Markowsky
Daryl Johnson

Organization

Steering Committee

Imrich Chlamtac   University of Trento, Italy
Sanjay Goel   University at Albany, SUNY, USA

Organizing Committee

General Chair

Pavel Gladyshev   University College Dublin, Ireland

General Co-chair

Sanjay Goel   University at Albany, SUNY, USA

Vice-Chair

Alexey Chilikov   Bauman Moscow State Technical University, Russia

Technical Program Committee Chairs

Daryl Johnson   Rochester Institute of Technology, SUNY, USA
George Markowsky   Missouri University of Science and Technology, USA
Joshua Isaac James   DFIR Science, LLC, USA

Sponsorship and Exhibit Chair

Nikolay Akatyev   Horangi Cyber Security, Singapore

Local Chair

Nikolay Akatyev   Horangi Cyber Security, Singapore

Workshops Chair

Paulo Roberto Nunes de Souza   Federal University of Espírito Santo, Brazil

Outreach Co-chairs

Afrah Almansoori   Dubai Police, UAE
Emil Tan   Division Zero, Singapore

Publications Chair

Xiaoyu Du   University College Dublin, Ireland

Web Chair

Pavel Gladyshev   University College Dublin, Ireland

Technical Program Committee

Ahmed Shosha   Microsoft, UK
Ahmed Hamza   Rochester Institute of Technology, USA
Ambika N.   SSMRV College, India
Anca Delia Jurcut   University College Dublin, Ireland
Anthony Cheuk Tung Lai   VX Research Limited, Hong Kong
Babak Habibnia   University College Dublin, Ireland
Bill Stackpole   Rochester Institute of Technology, USA
Bo Chen   Michigan Technological University, USA
David Lillis   University College Dublin, Ireland
Ding Wang   Nankai University, China
Fahim Khan   University of Tokyo, Japan
Farkhund Iqbal   Zayed University, UAE
Glenn Dardick   Longwood University, USA
John Sheppard   Waterford Institute of Technology, Ireland
M. P. Gupta   Indian Institute of Technology Delhi, India
Mengjun Xie   University of Tennessee at Chattanooga, USA
Nhien An Le Khac   University College Dublin, Ireland
Nickkisha Farrell   Concordia University of Edmonton, Canada
Omid Mirzaei   Elastic, Boston, USA
Pavol Zavarsky   Concordia University College of Alberta, Canada
Pradeep Atrey   University of Albany, USA
Prakash G.   Amrita Vishwa Vidyapeetham University, India
Sai Mounika Errapotu   University of Texas at El Paso, USA
Seungjoo Kim   Korea University, South Korea
Shaikh Akib Shahriyar   Rochester Institute of Technology, USA
Spiridon Bakiras   Hamad Bin Khalifa University, Qatar
Stig Mjolsnes   Norwegian University of Science and Technology,
                                      Norway
Umit Karabiyik   Purdue University, USA

Vinod Bhattathiripad   G J Software Forensics, India
Vivienne Mee   VMGroup, Ireland
Xianzhi Wang   University of Technology Sydney, Australia
Xiaochun Cheng   Middlesex University London, UK

Contents

Quantifying Paging on Recoverable Data from Windows User-Space Modules

Miguel Martín-Pérez and Ricardo J. Rodríguez[✉]

Department of Computer Science and Systems Engineering,
University of Zaragoza, Zaragoza, Spain
{miguelmartinperez,rjrodriguez}@unizar.es

Abstract. Memory forensic analysis enables a forensic examiner to retrieve evidence of a security incident, such as encryption keys, or analyze malware that resides solely in memory. During this process, the current state of system memory is acquired and saved to a file denoted as *memory dump*, which is then analyzed with dedicated software for evidence. Although a memory dump contains large amounts of data for analysis, its content can be inaccurate and incomplete due to how an operating system's memory management subsystem works: page swapping, on-demand paging, or page smearing are some of the problems that can affect the data that resides in memory. In this paper, we evaluate how these issues affect user-mode modules by measuring the ratio of modules that reside in memory on a Windows 10 system under different memory workloads. On Windows, a module represents an image (that is, an executable, shared dynamic library, or driver) that was loaded as part of the kernel or a user-mode process. We show that this ratio is particularly low in shared dynamic library modules, as opposed to executable modules. We also discuss the issues of memory forensics that can affect scanning for malicious evidences in particular. Additionally, we have developed a Volatility plugin, dubbed `residentmem`, which helps forensic analysts obtain paging information from a memory dump for each process running at the time of acquisition, providing them with information on the amount of data that cannot be properly analyzed.

Keywords: Digital forensics · Memory forensics · Windows modules · Paging · Malware

1 Introduction

Incident response aims to find out what happened in a security incident and, more importantly, preserve *evidence* related to the incident that can then be used to take legal action, trying to respond to the known 6 W (*what, who, why, how, when* and *where*) [12]. An important activity performed during the incident response process is digital forensics, which in the event of a computer incident is performed on the computers or network where the incident occurred [20]. While

© ICST Institute for Computer Sciences, Social Informatics and Telecommunications Engineering 2022
Published by Springer Nature Switzerland AG 2022. All Rights Reserved
P. Gladyshev et al. (Eds.): ICDF2C 2021, LNICST 441, pp. 1–19, 2022.
https://doi.org/10.1007/978-3-031-06365-7_1

computer forensics attempts to find evidence on computers and digital storage media, network forensics deals with the acquisition and analysis of network traffic.

Computer forensics is divided into different branches, depending on the digital evidence that is analyzed. In particular, this paper focuses on memory forensics, which deals with the retrieval of digital evidence from computer memory rather than from computer storage media, as disk forensics does. Memory forensics is useful in scenarios where encrypted or remote storage is used, improving on traditional forensic techniques more focused on non-volatile storage [28]. For instance, memory forensic analysis enables a forensic examiner to retrieve encryption keys or analyze malicious software (*malware*) that resides solely in RAM. In addition, triage in memory forensic is faster since the amount of data to be analyzed is less than in disk forensics.

The memory of a computer system can be acquired by different means, which are highly dependent on the underlying operating system and the hardware architecture of the system. A recent and comprehensive study of the latest memory acquisition techniques is provided in [26]. The memory acquisition process retrieves the current state of the system, reflected as it is in memory, and dumps it into a snapshot file (known as *memory dump*). This file is then taken off-site and analyzed with dedicated software for evidence (such as Volatility [57], Rekall [44], or Helix3, to name a few).

A memory dump contains data relevant to the analysis of the incident. In forensic terminology, these items are called *memory artifacts* and include items such as running processes, open files, logged in users, or open network connections at the time of memory acquisition. Additionally, a memory dump can also contain recently used items that have been freed but not yet zeroed, such as residual IP packets, Ethernet frames, or other associated data structures [6]. Many of these artifacts are more likely to reside in memory than on disk, due to their volatile nature.

Malware is currently one of the biggest security threats for both businesses and home users. Malware analysis is the process of determining whether a software program performs harmful activity on a system. The malware analysis methodology comprises two steps [48]: (1) *static analysis*, where the binary code of the suspicious software program is analyzed without executing it; and (2) *dynamic analysis*, where the program is executed and its interaction with operating system resources (other processes, persistence mechanisms [54], file system and network) is monitored.

As the rootkit paradox states [25], whenever code wants to run on a system, it must be visible to the system in some way. Therefore, running malware will leave traces of its nefarious activity, which are then useful for finding out what happened during a security incident. These traces, as digital artifacts, can reside in memory or on disk. For instance, fileless malware exists exclusively as a memory-based artifact, unlike file-based malware. According to recent industry security reports, this type of malware is increasing every year, especially taking advantage of PowerShell to launch attacks [5]. Fileless attacks grew 265% in

2019 [4], and Symantec detected a total of 115,000 malicious PowerShell scripts (on average) each month during that year [40]. In this regard, there is more likely evidence of malicious activity from sophisticated malware or fileless malware in memory than on disk. In this paper, we focus on the Windows operating system (Windows for short), as at the time of this writing is still the most predominant target of malware attacks [2].

On Windows, an executable, shared dynamic library, or driver file that was loaded as part of the kernel or a user-mode process is named *image*, while the file is named *image file*. Finally, an image as well as a process are internally represented by a *module* [33]. In what follows, we adhere to this terminology.

In the event of a malware-related security incident, it is likely that malicious modules exist in a memory dump, as the malicious image file and its dependent images were loaded into memory for execution. However, *to what extent can we trust the contents of a memory dump?* This content may be inaccurate due to the way the memory management subsystem works. This inaccuracy problem, called *page smearing*, is particularly visible when we acquire memory on a live system: while the operating system is running, the references to memory in the running processes are constantly updated and, therefore, memory inconsistencies can occur since the acquisition process is usually carried out non-atomically [41].

Additionally, some optimization methods performed by the memory management subsystem can also affect the data in a memory dump. For example, *page swapping*, which refers to copying pages from the process's virtual address space to the swap device (which is typically non-volatile secondary memory storage), or vice versa. In the same way, *on-demand paging* (also known as deferred paging) delays loading a page from disk until it is absolutely necessary. Both methods affect the contents of a memory dump since parts of memory are likely to be swapped or not loaded at the time of acquisition. Therefore, false negative results are likely to occur when looking for evidence of malware exclusively in memory.

The contribution of this work is twofold. First, a detailed analysis of how these paging issues affect the user-mode modules that reside in memory on a Windows system with different memory workloads. In particular, we studied them on a Windows 10 64-bit system (build 19041) as at the time of this writing this is the predominant version on the market worldwide, with the 78% share [19]. Second, a thorough discussion on the issues to detect malware artifacts in memory forensics. As a side product of our research, we have developed a Volatility plugin, dubbed `residentmem`, which allows us to extract the number of resident pages (that is, in memory) of each image and each process within a memory dump. This tool therefore provides forensic analysts with information on the amount of binary data that cannot be analyzed correctly.

The outline of this paper is as follows. To provide a better understanding of this paper, we first give some background on the Windows memory subsystem in Sect. 2. Then we review the related work in Sect. 3. Section 4 presents the experiments performed to quantify the effect of paging on the Windows system under study. Next, we discuss how these issues can affect the analysis of malware artifacts in Sect. 5. Finally, Sect. 6 concludes the paper and highlights future directions.

2 Background

A Windows process has a private memory address space that cannot be accessed by other processes and cannot be exceeded. The *virtual address space* of a process (also known as the *page table*) defines the set of virtual addresses available to that particular process. Page tables are only accessible in kernel-mode, and therefore a user-space process cannot modify its own address space layout.

By default, the size of the virtual address space of a 32-bit Windows process is 2 GiB (before Windows 8). This size can be expanded to 3 GiB (or 4 GiB on 64-bit versions of Windows) in certain configurations [60]. The size of the virtual address space of a process in Windows 8.1 64-bit (and later) is 128 TiB, although the maximum amount of physical memory supported by Windows at the time of this writing is less than 24 TiB.

The memory unit by which Windows manages memory is called *memory page* [23]. A memory page defines a contiguous block of virtual memory of fixed length. Page sizes can be small or large. The small page size is 4 KiB, while the large page size ranges from 2 MiB (on x86 and x64 architectures) to 4 MiB (on ARM) [60]. The relationship between virtual memory and physical memory is made through the *page table entries* (PTE), which map a page of process virtual memory to a page of physical memory.

Since the virtual address space of the process can be larger than the physical memory on the machine, the Windows memory subsystem must maintain these page table entries to ensure that when a thread in the context of a process reads/write to addresses in its virtual memory space, they refer to the correct physical addresses [34]. Likewise, when the memory required by running processes exceeds the available physical memory, it also sends some pages to disk that are later retrieved by returning them to physical memory when necessary.

A page of a virtual address space of a process can be in different states [35]: *free*, when the page has never been used or is no longer used (initial state of all pages of a process). A free page is not accessible for the process but can be reserved, committed or simultaneously reserved and committed; *reserved*, when the process has reserved some memory pages within its virtual address space for future use. These pages are not yet accessible to the process, but their address range cannot be used by other memory allocation functions; *committed*, when the page has been allocated from RAM and paging files on disk, ready to be used by the process. Committed pages are also known as private pages, as they cannot be shared with other processes, unlike shareable pages, which are shared but can only be in use by a single process at a time. When a process accesses committed or shareable pages, the memory page is said to have been "touched". This is when the Windows memory manager finally allocates a page of physical memory via a page table entry.

3   Related Work

Forensic analysis of user-space memory has been approached in different ways. The work in [59] introduces an approach based on Virtual Address Descriptors (VAD) [14] that identifies all user allocations and then determines their purpose using kernel and user-space metadata sources. Based on an extensive analysis of the Windows XP SP3 32-bit and Windows 7 SP1 32-bit operating systems, the authors created two Volatility plugins to describe the content of allocations within user-space memory and to verify whether a virtual address of a process not described by a VAD is assigned to a page of physical memory. Paging is an important issue for this approach, as some metadata sources can be paged to disk, thus preventing extraction of their related metadata. Our work complements this approach by providing insight into the internals of the Windows memory manager with regard to paging.

A utility dubbed `PageDumper` that captures traces of attacks based on run-time memory protection tampering in the Linux operating system is proposed in [42]. Implemented as a kernel module, it helps analyze kernel and user-process address spaces, parsing page table entries in both kernel and user contexts. Rather, we focus on Windows and a post-mortem analysis of a complete memory dump. In any case, `PageDumper` can be a good complement to our plugin when analyzing a Linux operating system memory dump. More research is needed to extend our plugin to Linux and integrate it with the output of `PageDumper`.

With regard to malware detection in memory forensics, most works use Virtual Machine Introspection (VMI) techniques to avoid inaccuracy due to memory acquisition on live systems. The fundamental papers in this area are [22,38]. In [16], the authors demonstrated that the memory forensic community can develop tools using VMI and proceed much more quickly with memory analysis. In this regard, in [53] the authors introduce a VMI-based system on top of Xen that can detect malware in virtual machines using Volatility by comparing memory dumps acquired before and after executing a suspicious image file.

Other work focuses on using memory forensics as the basis for malware analysis. The differences between applying YARA signatures to disk or in-memory files and how these can be improved to effectively search for malware in memory are discussed in [13]. YARA is a very popular open-source and multi-platform tool to identify and classify malware samples. In [1], the effectiveness of different machine-learning classifiers is evaluated using information from VADs, registry hives, and other internal process structures such as `EPROCESS`. However, the software used to recover these memory artifacts is unclear. The work in [18] uses the prevalence of certain dynamic link libraries in processes contained in a memory dump as a characteristic of malicious behavior. The work in [37] presents a machine learning model that uses some features (such as registry keys, imported shared libraries, and called operating system functions) extracted from the reports provided by Cuckoo Sandbox to obtain information about a memory dump. Similarly, the work in [43] presents an analysis system composed of Cuckoo Sandbox and Volatility in which, as a final analysis step, the results obtained are compared with the results of VirusTotal. The work in [10] introduces `hooktracer_messagehooks`, a Volatility plugin that helps analyze hooks in a Windows memory dump to determine if they are associated with a malicious keylogger or with benign software. Finally, the authors introduce a system in [8] that first uses the Procdump tool, a Microsoft command line tool, to dump processes from memory in Windows 10 version 1903 systems and then converts them into RGB images for classification using machine learning algorithms.

With regard to malware focused on hiding its presence, in [7] an approach is presented to discover executable pages despite the use of stealthy techniques so that they are not reported by current detection tools. The authors implement it in a plugin for the `Rekall` memory forensic framework and evaluate it against own implementations of different stealthy techniques, as well as against real-world malware samples. Instead of VAD, this approach relies on PTE that are listed through paging structures to avoid certain (advanced) stealthy techniques. However, as before this approach does not work if the page tables are paged and the paging file is not provided. A similar work is [3], which introduces different techniques that malware can adopt to hide its presence using GPU memory. This work is very interesting, since the malware that resides in that memory cannot leave a trace in the physical memory. The analysis of another type of memory instead of the physical memory, though, is beyond the scope of this article.

To the best of our knowledge, we are the first to study in detail and quantify the effect of paging in Windows user-space modules. Our work is complementary to all those presented, as it provides information on how paging works in Windows, which is a problem for detecting malware by memory forensic analysis when paging files are not used. Unfortunately, this lack of paging files is common as Volatility does not support analyzing a dump alongside its paging file, despite being the most widely used and powerful memory forensic framework currently available.

4 Quantification and Characterization of the Windows Paging Mechanism

In this section, we first describe the experiments carried out to quantify and characterize the effect of paging on the Windows system under study and then discuss the results.

4.1 Description of Experiments

As an experimental scenario, we use a virtual machine with a base installation of Windows 10 64-bit version 19041 running on the VirtualBox 6.1.18 hypervisor with default paravirtualization and large paging disabled. Note that in the default paravirtualization, VirtualBox only supports paravirtualized clocks, APIC frequency reporting, guest debugging, guest crash reporting, and relaxed timer checks. Therefore, the behavior of the guest memory management unit is not affected by paravirtualization. Furthermore, we use a virtual machine to avoid the problem of page smearing, since we are interested in quantifying paging, which is affected by page swapping and on-demand paging. We consider two configurations of physical memory, 4 GiB and 8 GiB, with an Intel Core i7-6700 3.40 GHz dual-core processor. The Internet has been disconnected after updating the machines.

As memory workloads, we consider 25%, 50%, 75%, 100%, 125%, and 150% of the total physical memory. We have developed a simple C tool to allocate the amount of memory needed to reach the specified percentage of memory used (that is, the tool allocates between 1 GiB and 6 GiB and between 2 GiB and 12 GiB, for the memory configurations of 4 GiB and 8 GiB, respectively). In particular, the tool allocates memory and writes a random byte every 4KiB to ensure that pages are constantly used and avoid their paging as much as possible. Note that this tool will consume a large chunk of memory and will leave less space for the pages of other user-space processes, regardless of the use of these pages (recall that both anonymous mappings and file mappings are backed by the system paging file [11]).

Under these conditions, the system memory has been acquired at various runtimes for each memory workload. First, we initialize the virtual machine and wait 5 min for the machine to reach a stable state. Immediately after, we pause the virtual machine and acquire the *initial* dump. Then we launch the memory allocator tool explained above and dump the memory every 15 s for one minute, pausing and resuming the execution of the virtual machine before and after memory acquisition. After the first minute, we continue to capture the memory every minute for 4 more minutes, also pausing and resuming the execution of the virtual machine between memory acquisitions. These memory dumps make up the *first observation moment*. We then stop the memory allocator process, pause the execution of the virtual machine, and dump the memory using the same pattern: every 15 s for the first minute and every 1 min for the next 4 min. These memory dumps are part of the *second observation moment*. Finally, we shut down and reboot the virtual machine to restart the dump process with another memory workload.

For each memory dump, we get the number of recoverable modules and how many resident pages are in each module. The process of memory acquisition and computation of recoverable data has been replicated 10 times in order to increase the reliability of the evaluation. We finally took into account the average of the 10 independent repeats for each recoverable module. To help us obtain the recoverable data of modules, we have implemented a tool, dubbed `residentmem`, as a Volatility plugin released under GNU/GPL version 3 license and publicly available at https://github.com/reverseame/residentmem. The plugin iterates through the processes contained in the memory dump and, for each process, it checks the memory pages assigned to each module associated with that process through internal Volatility structures. As input, the plugin needs a memory dump. As output, it returns a list of the recoverable modules with the resident pages and the total pages of each module, the process to which the module belongs, the path where is stored in the file system, and other information of interest related to the module (such as its version, base address, and its process identifier, among other information). In addition, it allows obtaining the specific list of physical pages for each resident page of a recoverable module.

The plugin analysis workflow is as follows. We first obtain the list of processes that were running at the time of memory acquisition through Volatility's internal structures. We then iterate through this list, accessing its memory address space and validating with a 4096-byte step (the size of a small page) if each memory address is resident. This gives us the number of resident and total memory pages for each process and its related modules.

4.2   Discussion of Results

We only discuss the 75%, 100%, and 125% memory workloads because we have empirically observed that experiments below 75% and above 125% behave equal to 75% and 125%, respectively. Likewise, we do not plot all the instants of time because otherwise the graphs are overloaded and difficult to understand. For this reason, we only show the *Initial (before execution)* (before any interaction with the system), 0 min (just after interacting with the system, that is, starting or stopping the memory allocator tool); and *0.5, 1, 3,* and 5 min, a subset of the observed instants of time that faithfully represent the complete behavior.

In addition, for the graphs relative to the second observation moment one more moment, *Initial (just before ending)*, has been incorporated to show how the system is just before interacting with it. This instant of time is actually the same as the 5 min instant of the first observation moment. The graphs of both observation moments show *Initial (before execution)* to have a common reference that allows comparing the results.

Modules of Executable Image Files. Figure 1 shows the resident pages of the recoverable modules of executable files under different memory workloads for 4 GiB and 8 GiB of physical memory (Figs. 1a and 1b, respectively), for both observation moments. Every plot shows the distributions of two variables (the size of a module file in log-base 10, on the x-axis, and the percentage of resident pages, on the y-axis) through color intensity. The darker the region, the more data is in that region. The subplots on the top and right of the main plots show a smoothed version of the frequencies of the size and resident pages data, revealing the distribution of resident pages and module file sizes.

Looking at the first observation moment, the initial conditions show that almost 80% of the executable module pages are resident in memory. With a memory workload of 75%, there are no significant changes to the resident pages because there is still enough free memory, regardless of the size of the physical memory. A slight reduction in recoverable modules is observed throughout the acquisition time points, which may be motivated by the paging of unused modules, while the resident pages remain constant. Note that the colored areas are mostly identical. With regard to 100% memory workload, in 0.5 min most modules are expelled and the number of resident pages for recoverable modules is drastically reduced. With the 125% memory workload, there is again a large

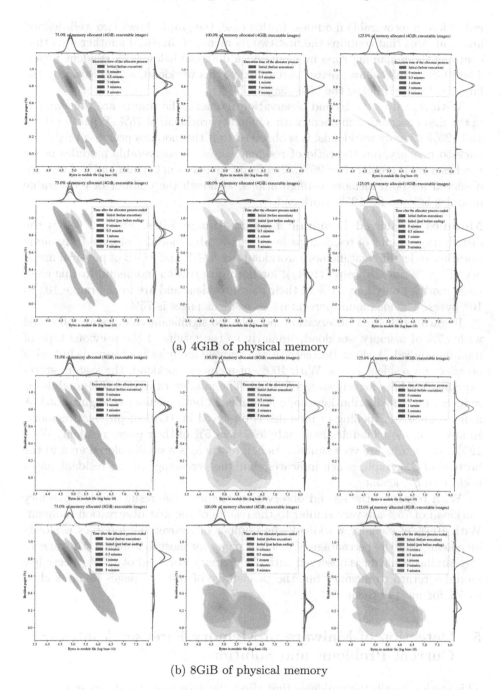

(a) 4GiB of physical memory

(b) 8GiB of physical memory

Fig. 1. Resident pages of recoverable executable modules at the first (first and third row) and at the second observation moments (second and fourth), with memory workloads of 75%, 100%, and 125% (first, second, and third column, respectively).

reduction in recoverable modules. In this case, the graph shows two well-defined areas, an area that contains the first two moments of time and another area that contains the remaining rime moments on a diagonal below 60% resident pages. The 8 GiB results show greater variability in this workload, as indicated by the larger color areas below the 60% diagonal.

With regard to the second observation moment, the results are the same as in the first observation moment with a memory workload of 75%. With the 100% and 125% memory workloads, it is observed that the modules progressively come back to memory, but the ratio of resident pages for recoverable modules never reaches a value greater than 25%. Significant increases in 0.5 min and in 3 min are observed for both memory configurations, although the number of recoverable modules is lower for 125% workload.

Modules of Shared Dynamic Library Image Files. Figure 2 shows the distribution graphs of resident pages of recoverable modules of shared dynamic libraries under different memory workloads for 4 GiB and 8 GiB of physical memory (Figs. 2a and 2b, respectively), for both observation moments. In this case, most modules only have 20% of their pages resident and are in the range 10^5 to 10^6 bytes. The maximum percentage of resident pages is 75%.

Regarding the first observation moment, no significant changes are observed with 75% of memory workload, similarly to the results of the previous type of module studied. A slight decrease in recoverable modules is observed, but with no effect on resident pages. With 100% of memory workload, the system starts expelling modules for any size in 0.5 min. The number of recoverable modules is reduced, but the distribution shape is similar in both memory configurations. A more aggressive expelling of modules is observed in 8 GiB of physical memory. In any case, most modules have only less than 5% of their pages resident. With 125%, the results are very similar. As before, there is a small colored area in the bottom of the graph, which indicates that the percentage of the resident pages is close to 5% again.

With regard to the second observation moment, the results with a memory workload of 75% are very similar to the results of the first observation moment. With 100% of memory workload, the number of recoverable modules is slowly increasing, but the percentage of resident pages for most modules is still close to 5%. Similar behavior is observed with the memory workload of 125%, where few modules return to memory but the percentage of resident pages remains close to 5% for most of them.

5   Detection of Malware in Memory Forensic Analysis: Current Problems and Solutions

This section details the problems that affect the detection of malware in memory forensic analysis, as well as some solutions to overcome them.

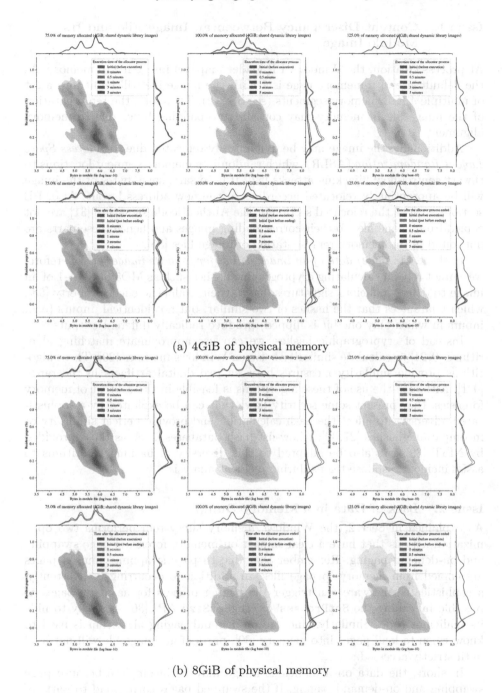

(a) 4GiB of physical memory

(b) 8GiB of physical memory

Fig. 2. Resident pages of recoverable shared dynamic library modules at the first (first and third row) and at the second observation moments (second and fourth), with memory workloads of 75%, 100%, and 125% (first, second, and third column, respectively).

Issue 1.   Content Discrepancy Between an Image File and Its Module Image

At process creation, the Windows PE loader maps an image file to memory. As the default size of a memory page is 4 KiB, the image file will be fit into a set of multiple 4 KiB memory segments (see Sect. 2). Therefore, the representation of the image file in memory may contain zero-padding bytes due to memory alignment.

Additionally, the image may be dynamically relocated due to *Address Space Layout Randomization* (ASLR), which randomizes memory segment locations to thwart control-flow hijacking attacks [52]. If necessary, some bytes of the image will be appropriately relocated according to the new address layout. Also, PE sections such as the relocated section or the Authenticode signature [31] are not copied from image files to their corresponding images and hence these parts are not found in the memory representation of image files [55].

In short, *the (byte) data of an image will differ from its image file*. Therefore, we cannot rely on calculating cryptographic hashes such as MD5 or SHA-1 of an image to detect malicious signatures due to their avalanche effect property [58], which guarantees that the hashes of two similar, but not identical, inputs (e.g., inputs in which only one bit is flipped) produce radically different outputs.

Instead of cryptographic hashes, we can use approximate matching algorithms [9,21] to calculate similarity between Windows modules [29]. These algorithms provide similarity measures between two digital artifacts in the range [0, 1]. Although the use of these algorithms is feasible in the context of memory forensics, they present some security flaws that can be exploited by a sophisticated adversary to affect the hash calculation and provide perfect similarity or incomparable hashes [27,30]. Allow-list hash databases, such as those provided by NIST [39], can also be adapted to this diversity of hashing algorithms to assist incident response teams during incident analysis.

Issue 2.   Lack of Data in a Memory Dump

As explained in Sect. 2, the Windows memory subsystem performs two optimization actions that have a clear impact on memory forensics: page swapping and on-demand paging. Remember that due to page swapping, unused pages are copied from memory to page files. In addition to occurring inadvertently, a sophisticated malware can trigger the paging process for as many pages as possible by calling the SetProcessWorkingSetSize API [36] as a way to hide its malicious code. Similarly, since an on-demand paging algorithm is used to know when to load pages into memory [60], parts of an image file will not load until strictly accessed.

In short, the data on a malicious image may be incomplete because page swapping and on-demand paging. If the swapped pages correspond to parts of the module header, the module will not be recoverable. Similarly, if the malicious code has not yet been loaded, it will remain undiscovered in the memory dump.

Also, as part of its life cycle, malware often uses a persistence strategy to ensure that it will persist on the system upon restart [49]. A feature commonly used by malware to achieve persistence is based on the Windows Registry [54], which is a hierarchical database divided into tree-like structures (called hives) that contain data critical to the operation of Windows and other applications [60].

As shown in Dolan-Gavitt's seminal work on memory forensics and the Windows Registry [15], some of these hives are volatile while others reside on disk (mapped to memory during Windows startup). Therefore, as a consequence of the paging issues highlighted above, unused portions of the Windows Registry may be on disk.

In summary, the Windows Registry of a memory dump cannot be treated as reliable evidence for detecting the persistence of malware, as the contents of the registry hives are incomplete. Additionally, the malware can still use other persistence methods that are not based on the Windows Registry and are also not detected by memory forensics [54].

Page swapping is really hard to beat when working with only memory artifacts. One possibility is to use disk forensics to first recover the page files and then use them together with the memory dump to complete the analysis. However, from Windows 8.1 onwards, the pages are swapped to disk in a compressed form, using Microsoft's Xpress algorithm [32], making content access a major challenge for current forensic tools. A recent publication in BlackHat USA 2019 presents a method to recover Windows 10 compressed pages and rebuild memory artifacts regardless of their storage location [47,51]. This method is a promising approach that has yet to be integrated with memory analysis frameworks like Volatility or Rekall.

A similar problem occurs with on-demand paging. In this regard, the best solution that we envision is to also combine memory forensics with disk forensics. Regarding the memory forensic analysis of persistence methods used by malware, we can again combine memory and disk forensics to extract the files on disk that represent the registry hives and get a complete and accurate overview of the Windows Registry.

In any case, we argue that these problems evidence that memory forensics cannot be seen as a single process but as a complementary process during an incident response activity.

Issue 3. Inaccuracy of a Memory Dump

When the memory is acquired in a live system, inaccuracies are highly likely to occur because memory is continually updated and acquired non-atomic. This page smearing problem is particularly relevant as kernel-space structures can be affected and lead to possible parsing errors, as some PTE can refer to wrong addresses (*pointer inconsistency*). Similarly, if a data object spans multiple physical pages, this fragmentation also affects the memory acquisition process, as the content may not be consistent over time (*fragment inconsistency*). These types of problems are commonly found in live memory acquisition on systems with large RAM or under heavy load [41].

Additionally, a rootkit or other sophisticated malware can detect when the memory acquisition is taking place to deliberately produce these inconsistencies through Direct Kernel Object Manipulation (DKOM) attacks, thus avoiding detection [45].

In summary, the data contained in a memory dump is likely to be inaccurate or unreliable if the memory acquisition process was performed on a live system. As possible solutions to avoid inaccuracies in the data, other acquisition techniques can be used [26] (for example, based on DMA or system management mode level). Invasive acquisition processes can also be used to acquire memory, such as cooling RAM modules (using liquid nitrogen or cold sprays) or forcing non-recoverable hardware errors to cause a *Blue Screen of Death* and generate a crash dump (which contains not only the RAM but also other data about the state of the system). These methods, however, can lead to the loss of important and unrecoverable data during the process.

In this regard, a recent contribution in memory forensics is the introduction of temporal dimension [41], which refers to the temporal consistency of the data stored in a memory dump. In [41], the authors present a Volatility plugin that accurately records time information while the memory dump is acquired. This time information is then used to construct a timeline that is displayed during memory dump analysis, suggesting to a forensic analyst the probability of inconsistencies and therefore taking appropriate action, such as additional data validation.

Issue 4.   Stealthy Malware

Common signature-based methods of detecting malware artifacts in each process virtual address space in a memory dump can be problematic, as the page containing the searched signature may be non-resident at the time of memory acquisition. Additionally, sophisticated malware and advanced persistent threats can incorporate features to remain stealthy and hidden after infecting a computer [46].

For example, injected code can be hidden from forensic tools such as the Volatility plugin `malfind` because they are typically based on information provided by VAD, which are unfortunately an unreliable source of information. Remember that Windows uses VAD to store information about the memory regions of a process [14]. However, important information such as page permissions are not updated when changed. On this matter, a malware only needs to allocate memory initially with a protection without the write or execute permission and then add any of these permissions to the pages containing the malicious code [7,50]. In addition, as explained above, the malware can trigger the paging process for as many pages as possible by calling the `SetProcessWorkingSetSize` API to increase the likelihood of swapping pages that contain malicious code [36].

In short, stealthy malware can incorporate different features to remain stealthy and hidden on the infected system. To detect them, we can rely on malware signatures. A recent enhancement to `malfind` is the Volatility plugin `malscan`, which integrates `malfind` with Clam-AV antivirus signatures to reduce the number of false positives [56]. Robust kernel signatures can also be used to detect sophisticated attacks, such as DKOM attacks [17].

Another technique widely used by malware to stay hidden is process hollowing, which occurs when a malware creates a process in a suspended state, then unmaps its memory and replaces it with malicious code. In this regard, the Volatility plugin `impfuzzy` allows malware to be detected in a memory dump based on the hash values generated from the import functions of the processes [24].

6 Conclusions and Future Directions

Memory forensics relies on memory dump analysis to look for evidence of security incidents. However, the content of dumps can be inaccurate and incomplete due to page smearing, page swapping, and on-demand paging. This lack of reliable data becomes particularly relevant when looking for evidence of malware exclusively in memory, as false negative results are likely to occur. This issue also shows that memory dumps are unreliable partial sources of evidence.

In this paper, we have studied the effect of paging in Windows modules of the user-space processes. In particular, we have focused on Windows 10 build 19041. At different observation moments and under memory workloads, the number of recoverable modules and the number of resident pages have been quantified considering two sizes of physical memory. Our experimental results show that paging behave different depending on the type of module. At first, almost 80% of the executable module pages and 20% of the shared dynamic library module pages are resident. These values are drastically reduced when the operating system needs memory, as most modules are expelled from memory and then unrecoverable. Once the memory load is no longer high, the system recovers some of the paged modules but very slowly, never returning to the initial conditions (25% and 5% for executable and shared library image files, respectively).

Furthermore, we also describe the problems for malware detection in memory forensics, discussing some solutions to overcome them as well. These issues cause the data in an image to differ from its image file and to be incomplete, inaccurate, and unreliable. Additionally, malware can incorporate features to remain stealthy and hidden from memory forensics.

As future work, we plan to extend our study to other versions of Windows (such as server editions) and to better characterize paging distributions under different system workloads. In addition, we also intend to investigate new methods to detect stealthy malware in memory forensics and quantify the effects of paging on the kernel space.

Acknowledgments. This work was supported in part by the Spanish Ministry of Science, Innovation and Universities under grant MEDRESE-RTI2018-098543-B-I00, by the University, Industry and Innovation Department of the Aragonese Government under *Programa de Proyectos Estratégicos de Grupos de Investigación* (DisCo research group, ref. T21-20R), and by the University of Zaragoza and the *Fundación Ibercaja* under grant JIUZ-2020-TIC-08. The research of Miguel-Martín Pérez was also supported by Spanish National Cybersecurity Institute (INCIBE) "Ayudas para la excelencia de los equipos de investigación avanzada en ciberseguridad", grant numbers INCIBEC-2015-02486 and INCIBEI-2015-27300.

References

1. Aghaeikheirabady, M., Farshchi, S.M.R., Shirazi, H.: A new approach to malware detection by comparative analysis of data structures in a memory image. In: 2014 International Congress on Technology, Communication and Knowledge (ICTCK), pp. 1–4 (2014)
2. AV-TEST GmbH: AV-TEST Security Report 2019/20, August 2020. https://www.av-test.org/fileadmin/pdf/security_report/AV-TEST_Security_Report_2019-2020.pdf. Accessed 15 Apr 2021
3. Balzarotti, D., Di Pietro, R., Villani, A.: The impact of GPU-assisted malware on memory forensics: a case study. Digit. Investig. **14**, S16–S24 (2015). The Proceedings of the Fifteenth Annual DFRWS Conference
4. Barnes, E.: Mitigating the risks of fileless attacks. Comput. Fraud Secur. **2021**(4), 20 (2021)
5. Beek, C., et al.: McAfee Labs Threats Report, June 2018. https://www.mcafee.com/enterprise/en-us/assets/reports/rp-quarterly-threats-jun-2018.pdf. Accessed 15 Apr 2021
6. Beverly, R., Garfinkel, S., Cardwell, G.: Forensic carving of network packets and associated data structures. Digit. Investig. **8**, S78–S89 (2011). The Proceedings of the Eleventh Annual DFRWS Conference
7. Block, F., Dewald, A.: Windows memory forensics: detecting (un)intentionally hidden injected code by examining page table entries. Digit. Investig. **29**, S3–S12 (2019)
8. Bozkir, A.S., Tahillioglu, E., Aydos, M., Kara, I.: Catch them alive: a malware detection approach through memory forensics, manifold learning and computer vision. Comput. Secur. **103**, 102166 (2021)
9. Breitinger, F., Guttman, B., McCarrin, M., Roussev, V., White, D.: Approximate Matching: Definition and Terminology. Techreport NIST Special Publication 800-168, National Institute of Standards and Technology, May 2014. https://doi.org/10.6028/NIST.SP.800-168
10. Case, A., et al.: Hooktracer: automatic detection and analysis of keystroke loggers using memory forensics. Comput. Secur. **96**, 101872 (2020)
11. Chen, R.: The source of much confusion: "backed by the system paging file", March 2013. https://devblogs.microsoft.com/oldnewthing/20130301-00/?p=5093. Accessed 24 Apr 2021
12. Cichonski, P., Millar, T., Grance, T., Scarfone, K.: Computer Security Incident Handling Guide. Techreport SP 800-61 Rev. 2, National Institute of Standards and Technology (NIST), September 2012. Special Publication (NIST SP)
13. Cohen, M.: Scanning memory with Yara. Digit. Investig. **20**, 34–43 (2017)
14. Dolan-Gavitt, B.: The VAD tree: a process-eye view of physical memory. Digit. Investig. **4**, 62–64 (2007)
15. Dolan-Gavitt, B.: Forensic analysis of the windows registry in memory. Digit. Investig. **5**, S26–S32 (2008). The Proceedings of the Eighth Annual DFRWS Conference

16. Dolan-Gavitt, B., Payne, B., Lee, W.: Leveraging forensic tools for virtual machine introspection. Technical report, Georgia Institute of Technology (2011)
17. Dolan-Gavitt, B., Srivastava, A., Traynor, P., Giffin, J.: Robust signatures for kernel data structures. In: Proceedings of the 16th ACM Conference on Computer and Communications Security, CCS 2009, pp. 566–577. Association for Computing Machinery, New York (2009)
18. Duan, Y., Fu, X., Luo, B., Wang, Z., Shi, J., Du, X.: Detective: automatically identify and analyze malware processes in forensic scenarios via DLLs. In: 2015 IEEE International Conference on Communications (ICC), pp. 5691–5696 (2015)
19. GlobalStats: Desktop Windows Version Market Share Worldwide, April 2021. https://gs.statcounter.com/os-version-market-share/windows/desktop/worldwide. Accessed 15 Apr 2021
20. Granc, T., Chevalier, S., Scarfone, K.K., Dang, H.: Guide to Integrating Forensic Techniques into Incident Response. Techreport 800-86, National Institute of Standards and Technology (NIST), August 2006. Special Publication (NIST SP)
21. Harichandran, V.S., Breitinger, F., Baggili, I.: Bytewise approximate matching: the good, the bad, and the unknown. J. Digit. Forensics Secur. Law **11**(2), 4 (2016)
22. Hay, B., Nance, K.: Forensics examination of volatile system data using virtual introspection. SIGOPS Oper. Syst. Rev. **42**(3), 74–82 (2008)
23. Huffman, C.: Process memory. In: Huffman, C. (ed.) Windows Performance Analysis Field Guide, pp. 93–127. Syngress, Boston (2015)
24. JPCERT/CC: A New Tool to Detect Known Malware from Memory Images - impfuzzy for Volatility, December 2016. https://blogs.jpcert.or.jp/en/2016/12/a-new-tool-to-d-d6bc.html. Accessed 23 Apr 201
25. Kornblum, J.D.: Exploiting the rootkit paradox with windows memory analysis. Int. J. Digit. EVid. **5**(1), 1–5 (2006)
26. Latzo, T., Palutke, R., Freiling, F.: A universal taxonomy and survey of forensic memory acquisition techniques. Digit. Investig. **28**, 56–69 (2019)
27. Lee, A., Atkison, T.: A comparison of fuzzy hashes: evaluation, guidelines, and future suggestions. In: Proceedings of the SouthEast Conference, ACM SE 2017, pp. 18–25. Association for Computing Machinery, New York (2017)
28. Ligh, M.H., Case, A., Levy, J., Walter, A.: The Art of Memory Forensics: Detecting Malware and Threats in Windows, Linux, and Mac Memory. Wiley, Hoboken (2014)
29. Martín-Pérez, M., Rodríguez, R.J., Balzarotti, D.: Pre-processing memory dumps to improve similarity score of windows modules. Comput. Secur. **101**, 102119 (2021)
30. Martín-Pérez, M., Rodríguez, R.J., Breitinger, F.: Bringing order to approximate matching: classification and attacks on similarity digest algorithms. Forensic Sci. Int. Digit. Investig. **36**, 301120 (2021)
31. Microsoft Corporation: Windows Authenticode Portable Executable Signature Format, March 2008. http://download.microsoft.com/download/9/c/5/9c5b2167-8017-4bae-9fde-d599bac8184a/authenticode_pe.docx. Accessed 25 Sept 2019
32. Microsoft Corporation: [MS-XCA]: Xpress Compression Algorithm, March 2020. https://docs.microsoft.com/en-us/openspecs/windows_protocols/ms-xca/a8b7cb0a-92a6-4187-a23b-5e14273b96f8. Accessed 15 Apr 2021
33. Microsoft Docs: Modules, May 2017. https://docs.microsoft.com/en-us/windows-hardware/drivers/debugger/modules. Accessed 15 Feb 2020
34. Microsoft Docs: Memory Management, May 2018. https://docs.microsoft.com/en-us/windows/win32/memory/memory-management. Accessed 15 Feb 2020

35. Microsoft Docs: Page State, May 2018. https://docs.microsoft.com/en-us/windows/win32/memory/page-state. Accessed 15 Feb 2020
36. Microsoft Docs: SetProcessWorkingSetSize function (winbase.h), May 2018. https://docs.microsoft.com/en-us/windows/win32/api/winbase/nf-winbase-setprocessworkingsetsize. Accessed 25 Apr 2021
37. Mosli, R., Li, R., Yuan, B., Pan, Y.: Automated malware detection using artifacts in forensic memory images. In: 2016 IEEE Symposium on Technologies for Homeland Security (HST), pp. 1–6 (2016)
38. Nance, K., Bishop, M., Hay, B.: Investigating the implications of virtual machine introspection for digital forensics. In: 2009 International Conference on Availability, Reliability and Security, pp. 1024–1029 (2009)
39. National Institute of Standards and Technology: National Software Reference Library (NSRL) - Approximate Matching, July 2017. https://www.nist.gov/itl/ssd/software-quality-group/national-software-reference-library-nsrl/technical-information-0. Accessed 15 Apr 2021
40. O'Gorman, B., et al.: Internet Security Threat Report - volume 24, February 2019. https://www.symantec.com/content/dam/symantec/docs/reports/istr-24-2019-en.pdf. Accessed 15 Apr 2021
41. Pagani, F., Fedorov, O., Balzarotti, D.: Introducing the temporal dimension to memory forensics. ACM Trans. Priv. Secur. **22**(2), 9:1–9:21 (2019)
42. Parida, T., Das, S.: PageDumper: a mechanism to collect page table manipulation information at run-time. Int. J. Inf. Secur. **20**(4), 603–619 (2020). https://doi.org/10.1007/s10207-020-00520-9
43. Rathnayaka, C., Jamdagni, A.: An efficient approach for advanced malware analysis using memory forensic technique. In: 2017 IEEE Trustcom/BigDataSE/ICESS, pp. 1145–1150 (2017)
44. Rekall: The Rekall memory forensic framework (2014). http://www.rekall-forensic.com/. Accessed 15 Apr 2021
45. Rodionov, A.M.E., Bratus, S.: Rootkits and Bootkits: Reversing Modern Malware and Next Generation Threats, 1st edn. No Starch Press Inc., San Francisco (2019)
46. Rudd, E.M., Rozsa, A., Günther, M., Boult, T.E.: A survey of stealth malware attacks, mitigation measures, and steps toward autonomous open world solutions. IEEE Commun. Surv. Tutor. **19**(2), 1145–1172 (2017)
47. Sardar, O., Andonov, D.: Paging All Windows Geeks - Finding Evil in Windows 10 Compressed Memory. BlackHat USA (2019)
48. Sikorski, M., Honig, A.: Practical Malware Analysis: The Hands-On Guide to Dissecting Malicious Software. No Starch Press, San Francisco (2012)
49. Sood, A.K., Bansal, R., Enbody, R.J.: Cybercrime: dissecting the state of underground enterprise. IEEE Internet Comput. **17**(1), 60–68 (2013)
50. Srivastava, A., Jones, J.H.: Detecting code injection by cross-validating stack and VAD information in windows physical memory. In: 2017 IEEE Conference on Open Systems (ICOS), pp. 83–89, November 2017
51. Stancill, B., Vogl, S., Sardar, O.: Finding Evil in Windows 10 Compressed Memory, Part One: Volatility and Rekall Tools, July 2019. https://www.fireeye.com/blog/threat-research/2019/07/finding-evil-in-windows-ten-compressed-memory-part-one.html. Accessed 15 Apr 2021
52. Szekeres, L., Payer, M., Wei, T., Song, D.: SoK: eternal war in memory. In: 2013 IEEE Symposium on Security and Privacy, pp. 48–62, May 2013
53. Tien, C., Liao, J., Chang, S., Kuo, S.: Memory forensics using virtual machine introspection for malware analysis. In: 2017 IEEE Conference on Dependable and Secure Computing, pp. 518–519 (2017)

54. Uroz, D., Rodríguez, R.J.: Characteristics and detectability of windows auto-start extensibility points in memory forensics. Digit. Investig. **28**, S95–S104 (2019)
55. Uroz, D., Rodríguez, R.J.: On challenges in verifying trusted executable files in memory forensics. Forensic Sci. Int. Digit. Investig. **32**, 300917 (2020)
56. Uroz, D., Rodríguez, R.J.: malscan plugin (2020). https://github.com/reverseame/malscan. Accessed 23 Apr 2021
57. Walters, A., Petroni, N.: Volatools: Integrating Volatile Memory Forensics into the Digital Investigation Process. BlackHat DC (2007)
58. Webster, A.F., Tavares, S.E.: On the design of S-boxes. In: Williams, H.C. (ed.) CRYPTO 1985. LNCS, vol. 218, pp. 523–534. Springer, Heidelberg (1986). https://doi.org/10.1007/3-540-39799-X_41
59. White, A., Schatz, B., Foo, E.: Surveying the user space through user allocations. Digit. Investig. **9**, S3–S12 (2012). The Proceedings of the Twelfth Annual DFRWS Conference
60. Yosifovich, P., Ionescu, A., Russinovich, M.E., Solomon, D.A.: Windows Internals, Part 1: System Architecture, Processes, Threads, Memory Management, and More, 7th edn. Microsoft Press, Redmond (2017)

Forensic Investigations of Google Meet and Microsoft Teams – Two Popular Conferencing Tools in the Pandemic

M. A. Hannan Bin Azhar[(⊠)], Jake Timms, and Benjamin Tilley

School of Engineering, Technology and Design, Canterbury Christ Church University,
Canterbury, UK
{hannan.azhar,jt472,bt145}@canterbury.ac.uk

Abstract. The Covid-19 pandemic has created unprecedented challenges in the technology age. Previous infrequently used applications were pushed into the spotlight and had to be considered reliable by their users. Applications had to evolve to accommodate the shift in normality to an online world quickly, predominantly for businesses and educational purposes. Video conferencing tools like Zoom, Google Hangouts, Microsoft Teams, and WebEx Meetings can make communication easy, but ease of online communications could also make information easier for cybercriminals to access and to use these tools for malicious purposes. Forensic evaluation of these programs is important, as being able to easily collect evidences against the threat actors will aid investigations considerably. This paper reports how artefacts from two popular video conferencing tools, Microsoft Teams and Google Meet, could be collected and analysed in forensically sound manners. Industry standard cyber forensics tools have been reported to extract artefacts from range of sources, such as memory, network, browsers and registry. The results are intended to verify security and trustworthiness of both applications as an online conferencing tool.

Keywords: Google Meet · MS Teams · Digital forensics · Memory forensics · Network forensics · Video conferencing

1 Introduction

Due to the Covid-19 pandemic, there has been a substantial increase in video calling/conferencing software being utilised. Reference [1] revealed that in March 2020 in the UK, popular applications such as 'Google Hangout/Meet', 'Houseparty', 'Microsoft Teams', and 'Zoom' were downloaded on average 19 times more than in Q4 of 2019. This spike in usage derives solely from the lockdowns and restrictions forced by the pandemic and can be correlated to both an increase in employees working from home and home-schooling. The UK's Office for National Statistics [2] published data that showed 46.6% of people in employment conducted some form of work at home, with 86% of these people doing so because of Covid-19. Similarly, between the months of

© ICST Institute for Computer Sciences, Social Informatics and Telecommunications Engineering 2022
Published by Springer Nature Switzerland AG 2022. All Rights Reserved
P. Gladyshev et al. (Eds.): ICDF2C 2021, LNICST 441, pp. 20–34, 2022.
https://doi.org/10.1007/978-3-031-06365-7_2

May and June 2020, it was discovered that 87% of parents with a child in education had undertaken some form of home-schooling. Whilst video conferencing apps are usually used for work and school meetings, there can also be a darker side to these programs. It might not be as common as work meetings, but video conferencing programs can be used for criminal uses. 'Zoombombing' has become an issue in recent times, according to Wiltshire Police [3]. 'Zoombombing' has been defined as the act of interrupting a zoom call, often with disturbing images of child abuse. This has been allowed by a security flaw in zoom that allows people to join without a password, using a zoom call code that has been posted publicly, such as by pages on Facebook. Whilst there are mitigations for this sort of issue, such as using the "waiting room" feature, and only sending the room code to the people involved, the fact that 'Zoombombing' is happening shows that there is the risk for people to be snooping on calls, or even using them to distribute illegal and disturbing images. As video conferencing has only recently had a boom in popularity, therefore there are not many researches regarding their forensic findings and artefacts. This paper reports how forensic evidence from Microsoft Teams and Google Meet could be collected by forensic examiners, and how these artefacts can be used as evidence. This study will forensically analyse both applications in order to assess their security and provide a detailed review of the features associated with the applications, including any forensic artefacts that could be of interest to investigators or alternatively be used maliciously against users.

The remainder of the paper is organised as follows: Sect. 2 describes existing literature on forensic analysis of similar video conferencing tools and reports the gaps. Section 3 discuses experimental setups for the investigations. Section 4 and 5 reports artefacts recovered for MS Teams and Google Meet respectively. For both applications, various sources of artefacts are reported in detail, including memory, network, registry, etc. Finally, Sect. 6 concludes the paper and give directions to future works.

2 Literature Review

Considering a variety of applications that allow users to make conference calls for social, business, or educational purposes, whether individual or in a group, this section of the literature review intends to uncover and discuss any relevant studies on forensic investigation on similar applications. Acknowledgement of security and privacy issues were first discussed by 'Zoom' in 2020 at the beginning of the first UK lockdown, before the release of 'Zoom 5.0'. The application was understood to have been sending users' device data to 'Facebook' without user permission, wrongfully claiming the application was end-to-end encrypted and unintentionally allowing meeting hosts to track attendees [4]. At this stage also, 'Zoombombing' was at its highest, which is where uninvited guests crashed meetings, including in at least one case displaying pornographic images and shouting profanities [5]. 'Zoom' is not the only application to fall under scrutiny in recent times. 'McAfee' conducted research on Microsoft Teams [6]; with use of more than forty million 'McAfee MVISION Cloud' users worldwide. This research formulated ten prominent security concerns with regards to Microsoft Teams, with issues such as malware being uploaded via Teams, data loss through file sharing in the application and the inclusion of guest users, potentially being inadvertently added to calls where sensitive content may be included.

External security concerns are not the only prevalent issue. However, in 2020, 'Consumer Reports' evaluated the privacy policies of Google Meet, Microsoft Teams and 'Webex' and discovered that these applications may be collecting data whilst in a videoconference to combine with information from data brokers to build consumer profiles and even access video calls in order to train facial recognition systems [7]. Reference [8] conducted a forensic analysis of the 'Zoom' application during the Covid-19 pandemic, when usage statistics were at some of their highest, and discovered that it is possible to find user's data both encrypted and in plain text with information such as chat logs, names, email addresses and passwords. The study involved analysing network traffic and included disk and memory forensics in attempts to obtain notable artefacts that could be of use in an investigation or potentially abused by a malicious user.

The usage of group video calling software has been available for many years. Early applications such as 'Skype', which was released in 2003, quickly utilised better performing networks to allow users to video call. It was from this stage that the importance of security of these applications became prevalent. The Common Vulnerabilities and Exposures or CVE [9], who work alongside some of the biggest software vendors globally is a list of free, publicly disclosed, cybersecurity vulnerabilities found in all forms of software. One such CVE regarding Skype details how attackers could remotely execute arbitrary code on targeted systems by manipulating '.dll' files that Skype loads [10]. Reference [11] analysed 'Skype' on a mobile phone running Android OS 5.5 and discovered that records stored could contain user data and other noteworthy metadata in plain-text format that could be easily accessed by anyone with the physical device.

Aside from Skype and Zoom, existing literature lacks technical investigations of similar popular applications that are widely used and may pose security and privacy threats. This paper contributes to fill this gap by reporting experimental results of forensic investigations of two popular video conferencing applications: MS Teams and Google Meet, both of which have been widely used during the pandemic in a variety of sectors, particularly in business and education.

3   Experimental Setup

To conduct forensic investigation for MS Team, a Windows based virtual machine (VM) was used to capture evidence. With VMs, snapshots can be taken so that any changes can be rolled back if necessary, for instance, when a clean install is needed before any software or files have contaminated the evidence. The choice of Microsoft Windows was based on its popularity in the world with more than three fourths of the global desktop market share [12].

Three test accounts ('is20user1@outlook.com', 'is20user2@outlook.com' and 'is20user3@outlook.com') were created in order to conduct investigations with MS Teams. These accounts were added to join an organisation called 'IS20 Testing'. After the Teams application was installed in the VM, messages were sent from a phone (Samsung Galaxy S8+) with Microsoft Teams installed. Voice calls were used as one of the artefacts. Conducting these calls would show how Teams logs and stores information about them. Testing was done by exploiting the application in the way people would use it on a daily basis.

A similar setup was used to investigate the Google Meet. Four devices were used: two computers (one desktop PC and one laptop) with clean Windows 10 VM installed, one Oracle VM VirtualBox, and finally a Samsung Galaxy S7 mobile phone. In addition to this, a VPN ('NordVPN') was utilised on two of the three devices all times to ensure different IP addresses were assigned to each device during the analysis of network traffic, providing a testing environment mimicking a standard conference call on Google Meet. Scenarios were created and examined, including setups where only the host remained active in the call, one-to-one calls, and group calls with three users. Setups comprised three test accounts created specifically for the experiment, and scenarios were created by connecting meetings using a one-time hyperlink and alternatively through the 'Google Calendar'.

4   Experimental Findings on MS Teams

Microsoft Teams can be used in a web browser, but it is more often used as an installed desktop application. Different types of investigations were performed, including disk, memory and network forensics. Disk forensics examines the artefacts left behind on a device, such as log and cache files. These artefacts could include information such as IP addresses, email addresses, and even messages between users. Since data in use by programs is held in memory, it is likely that there is information in memory could be of use to an investigation. The network is another possible medium in which artefacts might be found. The network traffic can be captured for analysis, such as searching for unencrypted information, and how Teams makes connections, such as whether it uses P2P connections or always connects to Microsoft servers.

4.1   Disk Forensics for MS Teams

During the investigation, the FTK imager was used to capture forensically sound images of both the hard drive. Once the tests were completed and the images captured, the disk drive evidence was placed into the forensic software Autopsy 4.17. Several ingest modules within the Autopsy were run to ensure data integrity and to verify that the evidences have not been tampered with. Also, Autopsy can create a timeline of events and file type identification, which checks for a files MIME type. Checking for MIME types allows for easier finding of files that may not have the correct file extension, such as images and databases. In Autopsy, the disk image was searched for known phrases that have been sent in a channel, as well as using private messages.

Disk forensics revealed that some data such as emails could be found in logs and cache. Windows registry also only held a small number of artefacts, the most useful of which was email addresses. Also, while looking at the Window's registry it was found that MS Teams added the email address to other programs, such as OneDrive and parts of the Windows Security Center.

To explore anti-forensics the program was uninstalled, and search was done to find any artefacts left. This is the usual way some suspects would try to hide their activities. One example of a deleted file recovered after uninstallation was an email address used in a call, as shown in Fig. 1. This shows that Teams can leave behind fairly important information about previous contacts, even after uninstallation.

/img_Uninstalled.E01/vol_vol3/Users/Forensics/AppData/R...   @canterbury.ac.uk

Fig. 1. Recovery of email address after uninstallation of MS Teams.

4.2 Memory Forensics for MS Teams

At several points during the investigation, memory captures were performed. This was due to the fact that memory was constantly changing and would have significantly differed based on the actions of the user, such as sending or receiving a message. For memory forensics, images were searched for relevant files and connections. This included files such as images sent in the channel and by direct message. It also involved network connections that were established. For analysis of memory, 'volatility3' was used, as it is one of the most commonly used tools in memory forensics. Volatility enables searching of any strings open in memory, as well as internet connections, using the command shown in Fig. 2.

```
python3 .\vol.py -f '..\Shared Drive\Images\voiceCall2.mem' windows.netscan
```

Fig. 2. Command in Volatility to show network connections.

Column1	Column2	Column3	Column4	Column5	Column6	Column7	Column8	Column9	Column10
Offset	Proto	LocalAddr	LocalPort	ForeignAddr	ForeignPort	State	PID	Owner	Created
0xe70da7bc2a20	TCPv4	192.168.1.171	62843	52.170.57.27	443	ESTABLISHED	8308	Teams.exe	2021-05-10 15:24:04.000000
0xe70da7f4c010	TCPv4	192.168.1.171	62834	13.107.18.11	443	CLOSED	8308	Teams.exe	2021-05-10 15:19:10.000000
0xe70da7f89700	TCPv4	192.168.1.171	62839	51.140.157.153	443	CLOSED	6924	Teams.exe	2021-05-10 15:23:59.000000
0xe70da808c010	TCPv4	192.168.1.171	62635	52.113.199.54	443	ESTABLISHED	8308	Teams.exe	2021-05-10 15:13:22.000000
0xe70da8204260	TCPv4	192.168.1.171	62841	52.111.242.2	443	ESTABLISHED	8308	Teams.exe	2021-05-10 15:24:03.000000
0xe70da86ed370	TCPv4	192.168.1.171	62849	52.114.128.75	443	ESTABLISHED	8308	Teams.exe	2021-05-10 15:24:27.000000
0xe70da8ae62b0	TCPv4	192.168.1.171	62659	52.113.205.20	443	ESTABLISHED	5980	Teams.exe	2021-05-10 15:13:27.000000
0xe70da90e3b10	TCPv4	192.168.1.171	62838	52.114.88.83	443	ESTABLISHED	5980	Teams.exe	2021-05-10 15:23:58.000000
0xe70da9187010	TCPv4	192.168.1.171	62831	52.113.199.99	443	ESTABLISHED	8308	Teams.exe	2021-05-10 15:16:33.000000
0xe70da96e3010	TCPv4	192.168.1.171	62837	52.113.194.132	443	ESTABLISHED	8308	Teams.exe	2021-05-10 15:23:21.000000
0xe70da1e7b570	UDPv4	192.168.1.171	50018	*	0		5980	Teams.exe	2021-05-10 15:15:40.000000
0xe70da1e7c380	UDPv4	192.168.1.171	50035	*	0		5980	Teams.exe	2021-05-10 15:15:40.000000
0xe70da22f7e30	UDPv4	0.0.0.0	50995	*	0		5980	Teams.exe	2021-05-10 15:13:27.000000
0xe70da6c95730	UDPv4	0.0.0.0	0	*	0		5980	Teams.exe	2021-05-10 15:13:26.000000
0xe70da9b8ed50	UDPv4	192.168.1.171	50014	*	0		5980	Teams.exe	2021-05-10 15:23:58.000000
0xe70da9dbc700	UDPv4	0.0.0.0	50808	*	0		5980	Teams.exe	2021-05-10 15:13:26.000000
0xe70daa0574e0	UDPv4	0.0.0.0	0	*	0		5980	Teams.exe	2021-05-10 15:13:26.000000
0xe70da22f7e30	UDPv6	::	50995	*	0		5980	Teams.exe	2021-05-10 15:13:27.000000
0xe70da6c95730	UDPv6	::	0	*	0		5980	Teams.exe	2021-05-10 15:13:26.000000
0xe70da9dbc700	UDPv6	::	50808	*	0		5980	Teams.exe	2021-05-10 15:13:26.000000

Fig. 3. Network connections carved from memory. (Color figure online)

Volatility revealed that there were multiple TCP and UDP network connections from the Teams program. The output of volatility was saved into a text file to facilitate easy viewing of the data in Excel. Figure 3 shows the output of a memory capture during a voice call, Teams has a number of TCP connections established with Microsoft servers over port 443, showing the use of encrypted traffic, shown in red. It also shows a number of UDP connections referring to calls made using the App, shown in blue.

The memory image can also be scanned for open files, and strings of information. Using the volatility 'filescan' module, files in use by windows were revealed, and the only files related to Teams were databases, logs, and assets in use by Teams. String analysis revealed that there are email addresses held in RAM. The strings command placed the output in a file, which can then be searched for either specific email

```
Ben@Dream-Machine:/mnt/c/Users/tille/OneDrive/Documents/Uni/Year 3/IS20/Shared Drive/Images$
soyakim@eastman.com
Presence-Away-Taskbar@2x.png
Presence-DND-Taskbar@2x.png
Error-Systray16x16@2x.png
Presence-Busy-Taskbar@2x.png
ransomware@sj.msr
mail@substack.net
tutanota.com2021FIRST@protonmail.com
30b0b758-f40b-41e3-af46-9b1c1ddb30a5_4ffa2a66-03d2-4d8a-834e-b7323207b1a9@unq.gbl.spaces
accv@accv.es
support@moblize.it
Presence-Offline-Systray16x16@2x.png
Presence-OnShift-Systray16x16@2x.png
30b0b758-f40b-41e3-af46-9b1c1ddb30a5_4ffa2a66-03d2-4d8a-834e-b7323207b1a9@unq.gbl.spaces
30b0b758-f40b-41e3-af46-9b1c1ddb30a5_4ffa2a66-03d2-4d8a-834e-b7323207b1a9@unq.gbl
30b0b758-f40b-41e3-af46-9b1c1ddb30a5_4ffa2a66-03d2-4d8a-834e-b7323207b1a9@unq.gbl
30b0b758-f40b-41e3-af46-9b1c1ddb30a5_4ffa2a66-03d2-4d8a-834e-b7323207b1a9@unq.gbl.spaces
30b0b758-f40b-41e3-af46-9b1c1ddb30a5_4ffa2a66-03d2-4d8a-834e-b7323207b1a9@unq.gbl.spaces
is20user1@outlook.com
x@mail.ru
is20user1@outlook.com
is20user1@outlook.com
is20user1@outlook.com
30b0b758-f40b-41e3-af46-9b1c1ddb30a5_4ffa2a66-03d2-4d8a-834e-b7323207b1a9@unq.gbl.spaces
30b0b758-f40b-41e3-af46-9b1c1ddb30a5_4ffa2a66-03d2-4d8a-834e-b7323207b1a9@unq.gbl.spaces
30b0b758-f40b-41e3-af46-9b1c1ddb30a5_4ffa2a66-03d2-4d8a-834e-b7323207b1a9@unq.gbl.spaces
30b0b758-f40b-41e3-af46-9b1c1ddb30a5_4ffa2a66-03d2-4d8a-834e-b7323207b1a9@unq.gbl.spaces
30b0b758-f40b-41e3-af46-9b1c1ddb30a5_4ffa2a66-03d2-4d8a-834e-b7323207b1a9@unq.gbl.spaces
support@auth0.com
y@window.location.href
30b0b758-f40b-41e3-af46-9b1c1ddb30a5_4ffa2a66-03d2-4d8a-834e-b7323207b1a9@unq.gbl.spaces
30b0b758-f40b-41e3-af46-9b1c1ddb30a5_4ffa2a66-03d2-4d8a-834e-b7323207b1a9@unq.gbl.spaces
30b0b758-f40b-41e3-af46-9b1c1ddb30a5_4ffa2a66-03d2-4d8a-834e-b7323207b1a9@unq.gbl.spaces
30b0b758-f40b-41e3-af46-9b1c1ddb30a5_4ffa2a66-03d2-4d8a-834e-b7323207b1a9@unq.gbl.spaces
@canterbury.ac.uk
@canterbury.ac.uk
```

Fig. 4. Strings analysis revealing emails.

addresses, or for an email pattern. Figure 4 shows email addresses related to Teams, such as "is20user1@outlook.com". It also shows email address that were used for testing from outside of the testing organisation, as well as various other emails perhaps used by other programs. Emails that are of use to this investigation are highlighted in red.

The memory was also searched for password strings used for accounts logged in, and none were found. Memory analysis of the captures taken at different times revealed similar artefacts, so only those discovered during a voice call are reported here.

4.3 Network Forensics for MS Teams

By capturing network traffic using Wireshark, investigation of transmitted and received packets can be performed, giving access to any user information, such as log-in details and messages transmitted. Wireshark is a popular network protocol analyser that captures live traffic as it is sent and received on the host machine. The 'Whois' command will also be used to determine ownership of domain names and websites visited.

For network forensic analysis in Teams, a Virtual Machine was created with an IP address 192.168.1.171. When a phone was connected to the same network, it had IP address of 192.168.50.6. As for the phone tested via a 4G mobile network, the IP address was 92.40.175.11. Logging into the Teams client on Windows resulted in a lot of internet traffic. Many of the DNS queries were to obvious places such as login servers owned by Microsoft, however there were a few servers that did not belong to Microsoft. One of these requests is for 'oneclient.sfx.ms', but a 'whois' lookup shows it belongs to 'Akami Technologies', a globally operating caching company, so the use of this server is perhaps not so surprising.

When examining the traffic used for logging in and general communication between the client and the Teams' online service, it was clear that the data exchange was encrypted. The network capture of Fig. 5 and Fig. 6 shows a TLS exchange defining key exchange mechanisms, as well as which cipher suite to be used. Between the client and the server, it was found that Ecliptic Curve Diffie Hellman was used for key exchange, and AES 256 GCM as the encryption. This shows that Microsoft Teams used stronger encryption for data transmission.

1031 2021-04-18 21:01:42…	192.168.1.171	52.152.110.14	TCP	54 50030 → 443 [ACK] Seq=1 Ack=1 Win=262656 Len=0
1032 2021-04-18 21:01:42…	192.168.1.171	52.152.110.14	TLSv1.2	265 Client Hello
1040 2021-04-18 21:01:42…	52.152.110.14	192.168.1.171	TCP	1494 443 → 50030 [ACK] Seq=1 Ack=212 Win=525312 Len=1440 [TCP segment of a reassembled PDU]
1041 2021-04-18 21:01:42…	52.152.110.14	192.168.1.171	TLSv1.2	1050 Server Hello, Certificate, Server Key Exchange, Server Hello Done
1042 2021-04-18 21:01:42…	192.168.1.171	52.152.110.14	TCP	54 50030 → 443 [ACK] Seq=212 Ack=2437 Win=262656 Len=0
1043 2021-04-18 21:01:42…	192.168.1.171	52.152.110.14	TLSv1.2	212 Client Key Exchange, Change Cipher Spec, Encrypted Handshake Message

Fig. 5. Wireshark key exchange.

Cipher Suite: TLS_ECDHE_ECDSA_WITH_AES_256_GCM_SHA384 (0xc02c)

Fig. 6. Wireshark cipher suite.

Further network forensics involved searching the packet capture for phrases that are known to be used in the test organisation, such as "IS20", "Networking", and "general Channel". When Wireshark was used to search in the packet details for those strings, no results were found, indicating that they were not in plain text. Another important network forensics exercise was capturing packets sent during a phone call. Capturing this specific traffic provided a better understanding of how Teams was able to create connections and what type of architecture was used. The main discovery from monitoring the voice call was that Teams utilised a Peer To Peer (P2P) connection between devices. When connecting to a one-on-one call, it was clear that the two clients are talking directly to each other.

1295 2021-05-10 16:23:57.536275	92.40.175.11	192.168.1.171	UDP	140 20585 → 50014 Len=98
1296 2021-05-10 16:23:57.537414	192.168.1.171	92.40.175.11	UDP	140 50014 → 20585 Len=98
1298 2021-05-10 16:23:57.556042	192.168.1.171	92.40.175.11	UDP	78 50014 → 20585 Len=36
1299 2021-05-10 16:23:57.564377	92.40.175.11	192.168.1.171	UDP	141 20585 → 50014 Len=99
1300 2021-05-10 16:23:57.575335	192.168.1.171	92.40.175.11	UDP	78 50014 → 20585 Len=36

Fig. 7. Voice call P2P conncetion on WAN.

9900 2021-05-07 22:03:31.584854	192.168.1.171	192.168.50.6	UDP	77 50012 → 50006 Len=35
9901 2021-05-07 22:03:31.591660	192.168.50.6	192.168.1.171	UDP	74 50006 → 50012 Len=32
9902 2021-05-07 22:03:31.604931	192.168.1.171	192.168.50.6	UDP	78 50012 → 50006 Len=36
9903 2021-05-07 22:03:31.610996	192.168.50.6	192.168.1.171	UDP	74 50006 → 50012 Len=32
9904 2021-05-07 22:03:31.625674	192.168.1.171	192.168.50.6	UDP	77 50012 → 50006 Len=35
9905 2021-05-07 22:03:31.627564	192.168.50.6	192.168.1.171	UDP	82 50006 → 50012 Len=40

Fig. 8. Voicecall P2P connection on LAN.

As shown in the Fig. 7 and Fig. 8, the two devices have established a UDP stream that appears to circumvent Microsoft's servers. The traffic appears to be streaming directly between devices, both over LAN and WAN. However, when examining the Wireshark

2021-05-10 17:54:34.770423	52.112.97.9	192.168.1.171	UDP	111 plethora(3480) → 50004 Len=69
2021-05-10 17:54:34.794288	192.168.1.171	52.112.97.9	STUN	158 ChannelData TURN Message
2021-05-10 17:54:34.794317	192.168.1.171	52.112.97.9	STUN	158 ChannelData TURN Message
2021-05-10 17:54:34.794892	52.112.97.9	192.168.1.171	UDP	111 plethora(3480) → 50004 Len=69
2021-05-10 17:54:34.810893	52.112.97.9	192.168.1.171	UDP	84 plethora(3480) → 50004 Len=42
2021-05-10 17:54:34.827356	192.168.1.171	52.112.97.9	STUN	93 ChannelData TURN Message

Fig. 9. Wireshark capture of Teams meeting.

⊘ 52.112.97.9

cloud

City	Amsterdam
Country	Netherlands
Organization	Microsoft Corporation
ISP	Microsoft Corporation

Fig. 10. Microsoft server location.

55411 2021-05-07 21:33:52.783032…	192.168.50.6	52.114.132.73	TCP	158 55796 → https(443) [ACK] Seq=16162 Ack=8877 Win=122368 Len=0
55536 2021-05-07 21:33:53.104935…	192.168.50.6	52.114.76.58	TLSv1.2	482 Application Data
55549 2021-05-07 21:33:53.121031…	52.114.76.58	192.168.50.6	TLSv1.2	200 Application Data
55553 2021-05-07 21:33:53.123124…	192.168.50.6	52.114.76.58	TLSv1.2	1400 Application Data
55584 2021-05-07 21:33:53.139493…	192.168.50.6	52.113.205.254	TLSv1.2	200 Application Data
55586 2021-05-07 21:33:53.139724…	52.114.76.58	192.168.50.6	TLSv1.2	200 Application Data
55600 2021-05-07 21:33:53.180742…	52.114.76.58	192.168.50.6	TLSv1.2	317 Application Data
55604 2021-05-07 21:33:53.182178…	192.168.50.6	52.114.76.58	TCP	158 33492 → https(443) [ACK] Seq=15976 Ack=53694 Win=244096 Len=0
55608 2021-05-07 21:33:53.182193…	192.168.50.6	52.114.76.58	TCP	158 33492 → https(443) [ACK] Seq=15976 Ack=53853 Win=244096 Len=0

Fig. 11. Encrypted WiFi traffic.

capture of a meeting (Fig. 9), it appeared to go through a Microsoft server from Amsterdam (Fig. 10), rather than communicating directly. As shown in the Fig. 10, the VM is contacting a Microsoft server, rather than the other clients in the meeting. However, all call traffic was encrypted before being sent through UDP. Additionally, WiFi was monitored for any forensic artefacts, such as transmitting credentials in cleartext. The phone was tested both by logging into Teams and by making an audio call, and all traffic was encrypted between the application and the server, as shown in Fig. 11.

4.4 Registry Forensics for MS Teams

The Windows registry is an important place to check for forensic artefacts, as many of the settings used by Windows and other installed programs are stored in registry hives. This allows forensic investigators to get a good idea of how a computer was set up and used. It also contains history of network interfaces and USB devices, again giving a good idea of how the device was used.

In searching the registry for relevant data before uninstallation, artefacts such as logged in emails, install dates, and locations were found, but no personal data, such as passwords or messages, was located. Figure 12 displays a registry key related to Teams showing the logged in email.

After the uninstallation of the application, used or created emails could be still found in the registry, although these were found when looking for known emails. An interesting

HKCU\SOFTWARE\Microsoft\Office\Teams   HomeUserUpn   REG_SZ   is20user1@outlook.com

Fig. 12. Registry key showing logged in email.

HKCU\SOFTWARE\Microsoft\OneDrive\Accounts\Personal   UserEmail   REG_SZ   IS20user1@outlook.com
HKLM\SOFTWARE\Microsoft\Security Center\Provider\CBP\10bd9a11-c7bd-4f16-83b6-e933f3c8d6f9   ACCOUNTNAME   REG_SZ   IS20user1@outlook.com
HKU\S-1-5-21-2972868649-818311016-2888665685-1001\SOFTWARE\Microsoft\OneDrive\Accounts\Personal   UserEmail   REG_SZ   IS20user1@outlook.com

Fig. 13. Remnants in registry.

find was that the email address used by Teams was also linked to OneDrive, as shown in Fig. 13. OneDrive is also a Microsoft product, so it is not too surprising, but it might be worth noting in an investigation.

4.5 Evaluation of Findings for MS Teams

Email addresses and IP addresses are the most common artefacts left by Teams, however a lot of the artefacts that can be recovered from Teams require prior investigation. This means that network activity must already be in the process of being captured, however this cannot be guaranteed. It is similar to memory capture, as this process requires the suspect's computer to be on and running Teams.

Memory analysis revealed some emails and network connections that might be of value. Finding emails might lead to other pieces of evidence in other areas. Network connections in memory may also be useful, however volatility was unable to recover the endpoints of UDP connections. Teams used UDP for activities like calls, so not being able to retrieve that information may negatively impact the investigation. On the other hand, a network monitoring tool such as Wireshark was able to capture the P2P connection during a call. Wireshark captured a lot of information that could be useful for a forensic investigation, such as encryption handshakes and connected IP addresses. Being able to see the IP addresses of devices connected to Teams provides insight into how it works. However, monitoring a suspect's internet traffic is not always possible, and cannot be done after the act has occurred.

5 Experimental Findings on Google Meet

Google Meet is a web-only application, with no options to download the software onto a machine. Additionally, no chat logs, call/meeting history or contact list is available on the application and to set up meetings. It must be simply created instantly with the use of a hyperlink, or created for a future meeting using 'Google Calendar'. Because of the data not being stored locally on the file system, and the application is only being available on a web browser, methods were shifted to attain information surrounding the memory, network, and browser forensics.

5.1 Memory Forensics for Google Meet

We captured the memory on two occasions. The first occurred during an active call between three of the test accounts created for this study, and the second occurred moments after a call ended. To capture the memory, like before the FTK Imager was used live on the 'Windows 10 Virtual Machine' and saved to an external USB-drive. It creates an image of the memory used on the machine that allows further analysis to be conducted without risking altering the memory being used on the live machine accidentally.

To capture memory with the FTK Imager, the option 'Capture Memory' was used. When this option is selected, a new window appears which requests a destination path to save the memory dump, the filename, whether or not to include the 'pagefile' - a reserved portion of the hard-drive that RAM uses, and finally an option to create an 'AD1 file' - a compressed and hashed version of the memory dump, allowing forensic approval of hash correlation to occur.

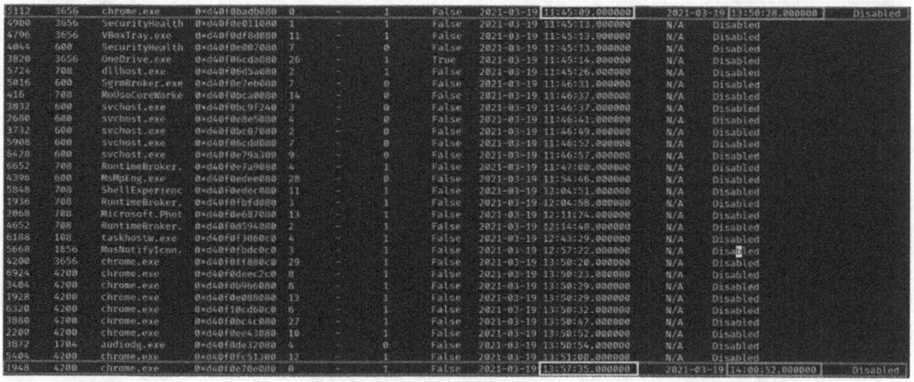

Fig. 14. Memory processes.

After capturing the memory during Google Meet sessions, when analysed in 'Volatility3' with the 'windows.pslist.Pslist' command, a process list was formed. With the example of 'Chrome' being used, this process list outlines multiple "chrome.exe" processes. 'Chrome' creates a separate process for every single web-app, plug-in, tab and extension, explaining the large number of "chrome.exe" processes present. Each process lists a creation time and an exit time, as shown in Fig. 14.

Fig. 15. Volatility Netscan.

Furthermore, when the "windows.netscan" command is used, network connections both live and recently terminated can be recovered. Figure 15 shows two connections with the owner of "chrome.exe". When further analysed, the IP addresses highlighted link to 'Google Cloud' servers located in North America.

5.2 Network Forensics for Google Meet

Like before, again Wireshark was used to capture packet information during Google Meet sessions both a meeting consisting of only an individual test account participating in a call, as well as a call consisting of all three test accounts. On both occurrences, the packet information was the same. The 'shark-fin' icon in Wireshark must be selected once to capture packets and can be paused or stopped at any time (see Fig. 16). The duration of packet capture was approximately thirty seconds on both occasions.

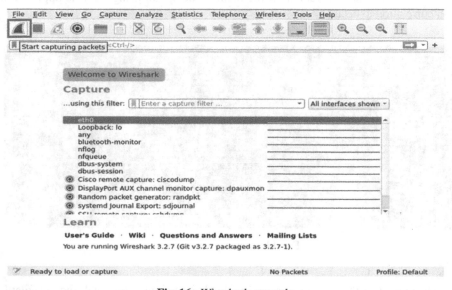

Fig. 16. Wireshark example.

Once packets were captured, a saved log was created for further analysis. The search for keywords or filters to find packets of notability can then be analysed further with a description-style section detailing information about each packet. 'Wireshark' clearly shows the use of TLSv1.2 both when sending and receiving packets (Fig. 17).

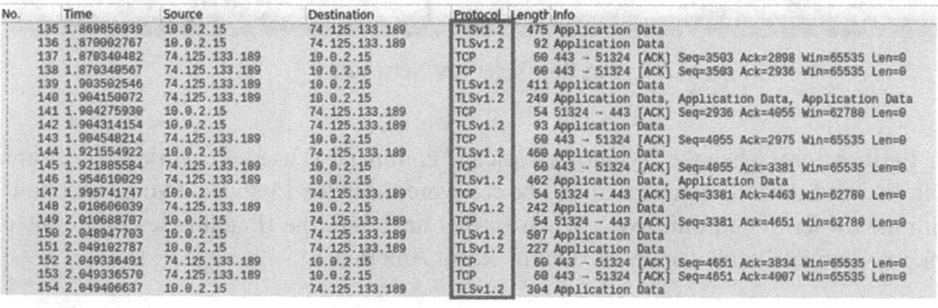

Fig. 17. Wireshark results.

Figure 17 outlines a smooth connection between the virtual machine host (IP: 10.0.2.15) and the 'Google Cloud' server (IP: 74.125.133.189). Hence, it can be inferred that the Google servers sit in the middle between connected parties to prevent private network information from being passed between guests in a call. The same test was conducted on different days and from different host IP addresses with similar results, except the 'Google Cloud' server IP address would change. Knowing that 'Firefox' on 'Kali Linux' utilised TLSv1.2, an SSL review was conducted to ascertain TLS versions on older browsers in contrast to the most recent. The review used a hyperlink generated from Google Meet, which could be used to invite participants to a conference call. The results of the review showed that older browser versions utilising TLS 1.0, a protocol with several published vulnerabilities.

5.3 Browser Forensics for Google Meet

Browser forensics analyses the files stored locally on a system that correlate with the independent browsers. As a result, the disk image acquisition covers all files for each browser, permitting analyses in 'Autopsy'. An example of the 'Chrome' file storage system in 'Autopsy' can be shown in Fig. 18.

Cookies	2021-03-18 16:14:09 GMT	2021-03-18 16:14:09 GMT	2021-03-18 16:14:09 GMT	2021-03-18 15:22:34 GMT	32768
Cookies-journal	2021-03-18 16:14:09 GMT	2021-03-18 16:14:09 GMT	2021-03-18 16:14:09 GMT	2021-03-18 15:22:34 GMT	0
Favicons	2021-03-18 15:55:56 GMT	2021-03-18 15:55:56 GMT	2021-03-18 15:55:56 GMT	2021-03-18 15:22:27 GMT	49152
Favicons-journal	2021-03-18 15:55:56 GMT	2021-03-18 15:55:56 GMT	2021-03-18 15:55:56 GMT	2021-03-18 15:22:27 GMT	0
Google Profile Picture.png	2021-03-18 15:23:50 GMT	2021-03-18 15:23:50 GMT	2021-03-18 15:23:50 GMT	2021-03-18 15:23:50 GMT	1989
Google Profile.ico	2021-03-18 15:23:50 GMT	2021-03-18 15:23:50 GMT	2021-03-18 15:23:50 GMT	2021-03-18 15:22:29 GMT	181072
heavy_ad_intervention_opt_out.db	2021-03-18 15:23:21 GMT	2021-03-18 15:23:21 GMT	2021-03-18 15:23:21 GMT	2021-03-18 15:23:01 GMT	16384
heavy_ad_intervention_opt_out.db-journal	2021-03-18 15:23:21 GMT	2021-03-18 15:23:21 GMT	2021-03-18 15:23:21 GMT	2021-03-18 15:23:01 GMT	0
History	2021-03-18 15:55:56 GMT	2021-03-18 15:55:56 GMT	2021-03-18 15:55:56 GMT	2021-03-18 15:22:26 GMT	135168
History Provider Cache	2021-03-18 15:23:28 GMT	2021-03-18 15:23:28 GMT	2021-03-18 15:23:28 GMT	2021-03-18 15:23:28 GMT	1450
History-journal	2021-03-18 15:56:28 GMT	2021-03-18 15:56:28 GMT	2021-03-18 15:56:28 GMT	2021-03-18 15:22:26 GMT	8720
Login Data	2021-03-18 15:22:27 GMT	2021-03-18 15:22:27 GMT	2021-03-18 15:22:27 GMT	2021-03-18 15:22:26 GMT	40960
Login Data For Account	2021-03-18 15:22:27 GMT	2021-03-18 15:29:03 GMT	2021-03-18 15:29:02 GMT	2021-03-18 15:22:26 GMT	40960
Login Data For Account-journal	2021-03-18 15:22:27 GMT	2021-03-18 15:22:27 GMT	2021-03-18 15:22:27 GMT	2021-03-18 15:22:26 GMT	0
Login Data-journal	2021-03-18 15:22:27 GMT	2021-03-18 15:22:27 GMT	2021-03-18 15:22:27 GMT	2021-03-18 15:22:26 GMT	0
Media History	2021-03-18 15:34:36 GMT	2021-03-18 15:34:36 GMT	2021-03-18 15:34:36 GMT	2021-03-18 15:22:26 GMT	143360
Media History-journal	2021-03-18 15:34:36 GMT	2021-03-18 15:34:36 GMT	2021-03-18 15:34:36 GMT	2021-03-18 15:22:26 GMT	0

Fig. 18. Chrome file system in Autopsy.

The image file generated with the FTK Imager contained data for each of the tested browsers: 'Chrome', 'Firefox' and 'Edge'. When analysed with 'Autopsy', several arte-facts were found. First, in the "History" SQLite database file, it is clear that "meet" was searched on Google, as shown in Fig. 19. After this has been searched, a result approx-imately ten minutes later in the "History" file shows that Google Meet was accessed (Fig. 20).

Furthermore, in the History file, a link that appears to be an invitation code can be found moments before Google Meet was accessed. It can be deduced that this is the invitational link used to access the specific meeting, as seen in Fig. 21. Also, remnants of information regarding the 'Google Calendar' can be found in the 'History' file. This tells us the calendar was accessed and contains information on potential future events that might occur within a specific week, as illustrated in Fig. 22. Within the "Web Data"

Result: 1 of 51	Result ← →
Type	Value
URL	https://www.google.com/search?q=meet&oq=meet&aqs=chrome..69i57.1950j0j4&sourceid=chrome&ie=UTF-8
Date Accessed	2021-03-18 15:23:04
Referrer URL	https://www.google.com/search?q=meet&oq=meet&aqs=chrome..69i57.1950j0j4&sourceid=chrome&ie=UTF-8
Title	meet - Google Search
Program Name	Google Chrome
Domain	www.google.com
Source File Path	/img_Windows Gmeet 2.E01/vol_vol3/Users/User/AppData/Local/Google/Chrome/User Data/Default/History
Artifact ID	-9223372036854774944

Fig. 19. Chrome – "meet" searched.

Result: 7 of 51	Result ← →
Type	Value
URL	https://meet.google.com/
Date Accessed	2021-03-18 15:34:42
Referrer URL	https://meet.google.com/
Title	Google Meet
Program Name	Google Chrome
Domain	meet.google.com
Source File Path	/img_Windows Gmeet 2.E01/vol_vol3/Users/User/AppData/Local/Google/Chrome/User Data/Default/History
Artifact ID	-9223372036854774938

Fig. 20. Google Meet accessed.

Result: 19 of 51	Result ← →
Type	Value
URL	https://meet.google.com/_meet/vsc-hcbk-kez?hs=187&jlm=16160814863698adhoc=1
Date Accessed	2021-03-18 15:31:30
Referrer URL	https://meet.google.com/_meet/vsc-hcbk-kez?hs=187&jlm=16160814863698adhoc=1
Title	Meet – vsc-hcbk-kez
Program Name	Google Chrome
Domain	meet.google.com
Source File Path	/img_Windows Gmeet 2.E01/vol_vol3/Users/User/AppData/Local/Google/Chrome/User Data/Default/History
Artifact ID	-9223372036854774924

Fig. 21. Google Meet invitation code.

file in the browser files, an email address can be identified. This is the email address that was used to access the Google Meet call and can be seen being accessed shortly before using the 'Meet' application, this can be shown in Fig. 23.

Result: 44 of 51	Result ← →
Type	Value
URL	https://calendar.google.com/calendar/u/0/r?hl=en-GB&pli=1
Date Accessed	2021-03-18 15:36:57
Referrer URL	https://calendar.google.com/calendar/u/0/r?hl=en-GB&pli=1
Title	Google Calendar - Week of 14 March 2021
Program Name	Google Chrome
Domain	calendar.google.com
Source File Path	/img_Windows Gmeet 2.E01/vol_vol3/Users/User/AppData/Local/Google/Chrome/User Data/Default/History
Artifact ID	-9223372036854774897

Fig. 22. Chrome – 'Google Calendar' artefact.

Result: 1	of 1	Result ← →	
Type		Value	
Name		identifier	
Value		jt472test1@gmail.com	
Count		1	
Date Created		2021-03-18 15:23:39	
Date Accessed		2021-03-18 15:23:39	
Program Name		Google Chrome	
Source File Path		/img_Windows Gmeet 2.E01/vol_vol3/Users/User/AppData/Local/Google/Chrome/User Data/Default/Web Data	
Artifact ID		-9223372036854774820	

Fig. 23. Chrome – Email artefact.

The artefacts that have been obtained by 'Chrome' were also found in the browser files for both 'Firefox' and 'Edge'. In 'Firefox', the browsing history was located in an SQLite database labelled 'defaultplaces.sqlite' file and the email used to login to Google Meet was located in the 'defaultlogins.json' file. Similarly, for the Edge, browsing history was located in a file labelled 'History' and the email used to login to 'Meet' was located in 'Web Data'.

5.4 Evaluation of Findings in Google Meet

Two important findings emerged from the investigation of Google Meet. In the first finding, a collection of artefacts indicates that a user accessed and circumstantially used the Google Meet application. This information can be gathered from artefacts such as the "History" file, which shows when the web application was accessed. Additionally, this information can be backed up with data retrieved from the memory surrounding the networking activity, producing a time-labelled artefact that can be correlated with the "History" file data. Furthermore, the 'Web data' file contains the login email address, potentially identifying the user active at the time Google Meet was accessed.

The second finding relates to the hyperlinks recovered from the "History" file. With the hyperlink being unique to a specific call, there is a possibility of proving a person was involved in the Google Meet call without further proof required, as the retrieved link alone would be sufficient to show that the machine was used to access the specific call. Additionally, the hyperlinks obtained can be used to rejoin existing calls. Therefore, if a malicious person gained access to this artefact in the browser files, they could potentially gain access to a Google Meet call that they were not supposed to be on.

6 Conclusions

The Covid-19 pandemic introduced some difficult times for businesses and education to remain connected. With technology such as videoconferencing assisting in replicating some form of connection, this study examines the security of two popular applications for this purpose: Google Meet and MS Teams. After working through the stages of this study chronologically, beginning with the extensive research phase to identify gaps in the literature, this study can conclude that whilst Google Meet and MS Teams may be more cybersecure than similar applications in studies, it still presents a number of important cyber forensic artefacts that can be used to aid investigations or perhaps in a malicious manner. Results do reveal several key artefacts, including suspects' email addresses, as well as email addresses of other parties who may have been involved. Finding out that these artefacts exist and knowing where to look for them could be key information for investigators, since it would save them time and resources.

Considering the scope of the study focused on only the 'Windows 10' operating system, the evidence may be limited. Therefore, it could be suggested that the use of different operating systems may present more, less or simply different artefacts. Future work should include testing the application on other popular platforms, such as, but not limited to, 'macOS', 'iOS', 'Linux' and 'Android'. By applying this study to alternative platforms, a full picture of the forensic soundness of both Google Meet and MS Teams can be created.

References

1. Statista: Growth in downloads of select video conferencing apps as of March 2020 vs. weekly average for Q4 2019, by country (2021). https://www.statista.com/statistics/1109875/dow nload-growth-video-conferencing-apps/. Accessed 02 September 2021
2. Office for National Statistics: Coronavirus and homeschooling in Great Britain: April to June 2020 (2020). https://www.ons.gov.uk/peoplepopulationandcommunity/educationand childcare/articles/coronavirusandhomeschoolingingreatbritain/apriltojune2020. Accessed 02 September 2021
3. Wiltshire Police: Incidents of 'zoom-bombing' reported in Wiltshire - Wiltshire Police (2020). https://www.wiltshire.police.uk/article/6136/Incidents-of-zoom-bombing-reported-in-Wiltshire. Accessed 02 September 2021
4. BBC News: 'Zoombombing' targeted with new version of app' (2020). https://www.bbc.com/news/business-52392084. Accessed 02 September 2021
5. Sky News: Coronavirus: FBI investigating after pornography used to 'Zoombomb' video conferences (2020). https://news.sky.com/story/coronavirus-fbi-investigating-after-pornog raphy-used-to-zoombomb-video-conferences-11966712. Accessed 02 September 2021
6. Hawthorn, N.: McAfee Blogs -Top 10 Microsoft Teams Security Threats (2020). https://www.mcafee.com/blogs/enterprise/cloud-security/microsoft-teams-top-ten-security-thr eats/. Accessed 02 September 2021
7. John, A.S.: It's Not Just Zoom. Google Meet, Microsoft Teams, and Webex Have Privacy Issues, Too (2020). https://www.hawaii.edu/its/wp-content/uploads/sites/2/2020/05/Google-Meet-Microsoft-Teams-Webex-Privacy-Issues-Consumer-Reports.pdf. Accessed 02 September 2021
8. Mahr, A., Cichon, M., Mateo, S., Grajeda, C., Baggili, I.: Zooming into the pandemic! A forensic analysis of the Zoom Application. Foren. Sci. Int. Dig. Invest. **36**, 301107 (2021). https://doi.org/10.1016/j.fsidi.2021.301107
9. CVE - Request CVE IDs (2021). https://cve.mitre.org/cve/request_id.html#cna. Accessed 02 September 2021
10. CVE-2017–6517: Vulnerability Details: CVE-2017–6517 (2019). https://www.cvedetails.com/cve/CVE-2017-6517/. Accessed 02 September 2021
11. Idowu, S., Dominic, D., Okolie, S.O., Goga, N.: Security vulnerabilities of skype application artifacts: a digital forensic approach. Int. J. Appl. Inf. Syst. **12** (2019). https://doi.org/10.5120/ijais2019451784
12. StatCounter GlobalStats: Mobile Operating System Market Share Worldwide (2021). https://gs.statcounter.com/os-market-share/mobile/worldwide. Accessed 02 September 2021

On Exploring the Sub-domain of Artificial Intelligence (AI) Model Forensics

Tiffanie Edwards[(✉)], Syria McCullough, Mohamed Nassar,
and Ibrahim Baggili

University of New Haven Cyber Forensics Research and Education Group
(UNHcFREG) and Connecticut Institute of Technology (CIT),
West Haven, CT 06516, USA
{tedwa4,smccu1}@unh.newhaven.edu, {mnassar,ibaggili}@newhaven.edu

Abstract. AI Forensics is a novel research field that aims at providing techniques, mechanisms, processes, and protocols for an AI failure investigation. In this paper, we pave the way towards further exploring a sub-domain of AI forensics, namely AI model forensics, and introduce AI model ballistics as a subfield inspired by forensic ballistics. AI model forensics studies the forensic investigation process, including where available evidence can be collected, as it applies to AI models and systems.

We elaborate on the background and nature of AI model development and deployment, and highlight the fact that these models can be replaced, trojanized, gradually poisoned, or fooled by adversarial input.

The relationships and the dependencies of our newly proposed sub-domain draws from past literature in software, cloud, and network forensics. Additionally, we share a use-case mini-study to explore the peculiarities of AI model forensics in an appropriate context. Blockchain is discussed as a possible solution for maintaining audit trails. Finally, the challenges of AI model forensics are discussed.

Keywords: Digital forensics · Artificial Intelligence · AI forensics

1 Introduction

The rapid integration of Artificial Intelligence (AI) in modern technologies, services, and industries is leading AI to become a fundamental part of daily life. AI applications are found in video games [23], autonomous vehicles [18], healthcare [13], and cybersecurity [19]. While AI exists to benefit society, it is not without its challenges, which led to the development of the AI safety field [2]. Further exploration is necessary in the realm of forensics concerning AI, particularly how forensics will apply to the AI domain, to contribute to overall AI safety. This new discipline has been coined as AI Forensics [3].

AI Forensics is a subfield of digital forensics and is defined as *"Scientific and legal tools, techniques, and protocols for the extraction, collection, analysis, and reporting of digital evidence pertaining to failures in AI-enabled systems"*

© ICST Institute for Computer Sciences, Social Informatics and Telecommunications Engineering 2022
Published by Springer Nature Switzerland AG 2022. All Rights Reserved
P. Gladyshev et al. (Eds.): ICDF2C 2021, LNICST 441, pp. 35–51, 2022.
https://doi.org/10.1007/978-3-031-06365-7_3

[3]. Within this domain is the subdomain of AI Model Forensics, which narrows the forensic focus of failures in AI-enabled systems to information linked to AI models, usually stored in model files. Before, during, or after model deployment, AI models may suffer from malicious attacks ranging from physical adversarial samples [26], backdoors [6], malware injection [40], active learning, gradual poisoning, or replacing the authentic model by a malicious one, compromising an AI-enabled system.

For instance, [3] coined AI model authentication forensics as a subfield of AI model forensics. Recent work identified watermarking techniques to authenticate the ownership of AI models. Behzadan et al. [4] proposed a novel scheme for the watermarking of Deep Reinforcement Learning (DRL) policies. In [20,41], watermarks are generated samples, almost indistinguishable from their origins, and infused into the deep neural network model by assigning specific labels to them. The specific labels are the basis for copyright claims.

However, watermarked models can still be tampered with or forged [3], which impedes AI model authentication and verification. In addition, watermarking in itself does not hinder an adversary from publishing or deploying a new model under the name of an authentic model provider or creator. The possibility of such events leads to the need for procedures and protocols that help determine the forensic soundness of AI model digital evidence.

Within the new field of AI model forensics, we ask the questions: "What evidence is left behind in terms of AI model artifacts such as files, examined samples, label predictions, logs, etc.?", "How to examine such evidence?", and "What conclusions can be made about the type of event that occurred and its source?". We propose to establish AI model ballistics as a subfield of AI Model Forensics, focusing on digital forensic investigations that involve AI systems [3]. In general, the study of forensic ballistics refers to examining evidence left behind from firearms which would lead to conclusions about the type of firearm and its owner. Model ballistics could possibly help investigators identify information, such as the intention of the AI model, whether or not the output of the model differs from the creator's intention, the framework the model was created on, and any other relevant information that can be used in a digital forensic investigation.

Our work provides the following contributions:

- We provide the primary in-depth discussion of AI model forensics.
- We provide an overview of digital forensic practices for domains that are strongly connected to AI and are useful in initiating protocols and procedures tailored for AI investigations.
- We provide a primary case study to motivate the sub-domain of AI model forensics.
- We share a cohesive view of the intersection of AI model forensics with software forensics, cloud forensics, and network forensics.
- We enumerate primary challenges in AI model forensics.

The remainder of this paper is divided into the following sections: Sect. 2 describes the basic principles of digital forensics and establishes the motivation. Work from related forensic areas is discussed in Sect. 3. An example case study is presented in Sect. 4. Section 5 discusses the use of Blockchain technology in AI model forensics. The subfield AI model ballistics is formally introduced in Sect. 6. Section 7 explores the challenges and limitations of AI model forensics. Lastly, we conclude our work in Sect. 8 and discuss future directions.

2   Background and Motivation

2.1   Principles of Digital Forensics Overview

Digital forensics (DF) is formally defined by the National Institute of Standards and Technology (NIST) as *the application of science to the identification, collection, examination, and analysis, of data while preserving the integrity of the information and maintaining a strict chain of custody for the data* [15]. Under this definition, many subfields exist such as cloud forensics [31], software forensics [37], and network forensics [14]. Digital forensics and its subfields come with continuously evolving policies and procedures that protect the forensic soundness of digital data during investigations. Digital data is forensically sound when the scientific process follows the five major principles [12]:

1. Authenticity: Digital data is proved to be unchanged after collection and analysis; if necessary, only minimal changes are made to the data.
2. Error: All known errors in the forensic process are thoroughly documented.
3. Reliability: All utilized procedures must be published and accepted within the scientific community.
4. Reproducibility: All procedures should produce consistent results on the digital data each time the procedure(s) is performed.
5. Experience: All investigators handling the digital data should have a sufficient amount of experience or knowledge.

AI Forensics aims at replicating these principles when creating policies and procedures that are suitable for investigating failures in AI-enabled systems. AI model forensics, considered a subset of the AI forensics, focuses on how to address AI model artifacts, such as files, logs, model authenticity, classification history, etc., and how to promote the forensic soundness of these artifacts.

AI-related crime has two major categories: *AI as a tool crime* and *AI as a target crime* [12]. *AI as a tool crime* implies that AI systems or services are used to commit physical crimes or aid in cybercrimes. [34] conducted experiments related to *AI as a tool crime* from an AI forensic standpoint. The research viewed a "malicious by design" AI system and set out to determine if an AI system caused a malicious incident and why the incident was caused. From their perspective, *AI as a tool* can become "malicious by design" through methods of tampering and then be used as a malicious tool by a perpetrator.

In contrast, *AI as a target crime* implies that vulnerabilities in AI-enabled systems are exploited or hijacked. Potential threats include but are not limited to: manipulation of training data, malicious code change or replacement, and tricking AI systems into improper operation.

With any forensic approach, the collected evidence should answer questions related to the when and where of the crime, who is the criminal, what was the crime's target, and how the crime occurred. Defining a forensic approach for model ballistics will help investigators answer these key questions about AI systems, whether it falls under the category of *AI as a tool crime* or *AI as a target crime.*

To gain a clear picture of what investigators will encounter when dealing with AI models, model files, and artifacts, it is imperative to provide insights and a general understanding about how model files are generated and how AI models are deployed in production.

2.2   Model Generation and Deployment Overview

Deploying, or serving, a model simply means to turn it into a usable model to host in a production platform. For example, the macro steps leading to the deployment of a typical Machine Learning (ML) model are depicted in Fig. 1. The outlined steps are data collection and preparation, feature selection, model training and testing, model packaging, and deployment.

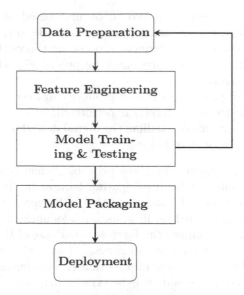

Fig. 1. Simplistic pipeline of the development and deployment of an AI model

Usually an AI model, a machine/deep learning one in particular, is saved to a single file containing the architecture and the parameters of the model, e.g. layers and weights (deep learning), support vectors (SVM), cluster centroids (K-means clustering), etc. The file is the output of the three first steps of the pipeline. Usually an inner loop that goes back to the first step may take place here if the model performance was not sufficiently satisfying.

Creators have the option to save the entire AI model, or some specific parts of it, into a file, known as the model file. Saving an AI model is useful for restoring it at any time in the future without having to repeat any previous training and parameter tuning. The saved model can be used for transfer learning, to train over new datasets, packaging, distribution, hosting, and deployment. Examples of frameworks using this approach are TensorFlow [38] and PyTorch [30]. For instance, we can restore only the architecture of a deep learning (DL) network (layers, nodes, layer types, activation functions, etc.), or the architecture along with the parameters (e.g. weights, biases, dropout, etc.).

We collected in Table 1 information about popular AI and ML platforms along with model file format, model file extension and other options of model saving. We also note that some frameworks allow models to be imported/exported from/to different formats.

Table 1. Popular AI/ML frameworks and their model formats

Framework	File format	File extension	Saving options
Tensorflow	tf or HDF5	.tf or .h5	weights & checkpoints, or entire model
Scikit-Learn	Pickled Python	.pkl	Compression
Keras	tf or HDF5	.tf or .h5	checkpoints, optimizer state, whole model
PyTorch	Torchscript	.pt or .pth	state_dict
iOS Core ML	Apple ML Model	.mlmodel	Add to App.
SparkML	model: JSON, data: Parquet	.json, .parquet	Save a Pipeline
spaCy	model:Config, metadata: JSON	.cfg, .json	Save a Pipeline and its metadata

AI and ML models are usually deployed as cloud services, and not necessarily in form of model files. Cloud deployment helps in connecting the AI model to clients and mobile applications, either for further data collection and improvement, such as in the case of federated learning [16], or for providing prediction and recommendation services for the model clients, whether they are AI agents, IoT devices, mobile applications, or browser-based users. Prediction services can be provided in batch mode or in single mode.

3 Literature Review

AI model forensics is strongly tied to other forms of forensics, and is useful when examining and analyzing model files and model deployments. We estimate that three areas in particular, namely cloud, software, and network forensics, are related to AI model forensics and may support the creation of its standards and procedures.

3.1 Cloud Forensics

The NIST defines Cloud Computing Forensic Science as "the application of scientific principles, technological practices and derived and proven methods to reconstruct past cloud computing events through identification, collection, preservation, examination, interpretation and reporting of digital evidence [11]". Cloud forensics [32] has emerged from both the digital forensics and the cloud computing fields. Cloud forensics is in high demand today because of the importance of these two emerging fields. The Market Research Firm report [8] classifies cloud forensics as a type of digital forensics and estimates the global digital forensics market to grow to 9.68 billion by year 2022. The report correlates the prolific spread of cloud-based applications in North America with an increase in cyber-attacks and a growing sophistication of these attacks.

Challenges of Cloud Forensics. Since cloud forensics is a fairly new field, compared to its predecessors cloud computing and digital forensics, there are still many challenges in the field. Different challenges can be attributed based on the cloud service model. Three service models are identified in [22]:

- Infrastructure as a service (IaaS): Delivery of bare metal and virtual machines, e.g. AWS;
- Platform as a service (PaaS): serves application development and deployment, e.g. AWS Elastic Beanstalk;
- Software as a service (SaaS): provides packaged software such as office apps or an AI engine.

Many of these challenges are identified in [35]. Cloud resources are virtualized and shared in nature. Cloud data is described as "fragile and volatile," which makes correct data extraction a very sensitive process. Remote data collection and preservation is more difficult than its standardized counterpart for collecting physical evidence at a crime scene. The remote collection requires contact and agreements with the cloud service provider. [10] suggests using a separate cloud to store collected data due to its large amount and the peculiarities of the cloud storage structure. Maintaining the chain of custody within cloud forensics is another challenge. For instance, logs can be located within different layers of the cloud, and are sometimes volatile in nature. Lastly, during presentation, it may be difficult for the members of a jury to understand the concepts and technicalities of the cloud. We expect AI model forensics to inherit these challenges. Nevertheless, cloud forensics may help answer some of the essential questions related to AI model forensics.

3.2 Software Forensics

Software forensics is another branch of digital forensics that specifically focuses on "areas of author discrimination, identification, and characterization, as well as intent analysis" based on software source code [21]. One of the original motives for software forensics was disabling the authorship anonymity of distributed malicious code. Any remnants of the malware code left behind on the target system may point back to the author(s). Inspired by handwriting analysis techniques, software forensics adapted new methods to uniquely identify a source code author based on distinguishing features, such as programming language, coding style, level of expertise, etc.

Source Code Analysis and Authorship Attribution. The four principal applications of software forensics according to [21] are author discrimination, author identification, author characterization, and author intent determination. *Author discrimination* is the task of deciding whether the code was written by a single author or by a number of authors. *Author identification* is the process of attributing authorship to software code, sometimes based on extracted statistics and similarity measures to other compiled code samples. *Author characterization* is similar to suspect profiling in criminal investigations. Its task is to determine personal characteristics of the software creator, such as educational background and personality traits. *Author intent determination* is the principle of determining whether or not software code failures or unexpected behaviours were written purposefully by the software developer or were the result of a human-error during the software development process. The same principles apply to AI model forensics, even though the techniques may be different. AI software is a special case of general-purpose software. Malicious AI software is, however, very different in nature than malicious general-purpose software, such as rootkits and worms. For instance, maliciousness can be hidden in the model parameters rather than being manifested in the flow control directives.

The feasibility of software forensics is questioned in [37]. Author identification may be subject to false positives due to insufficient amounts of data or recurring anti-forensic techniques, such as code reuse from other authors to increase the similarity to legitimate code. However, it has been shown that, with a sufficient amount of data and a careful choice of appropriate and distinctive characteristics, software forensics proves useful in reverse engineering and authorship attribution. [33] later proposed to build an *author profile* based on measurable authorship identifiers, namely program layout, program style, and program structure metrics. [33] also stated that combining techniques from software metric analysis and computational linguistics may lead to a more accurate plagiarism detection and author identification.

The applications of source code analysis and software forensics were extended in [9] to include plagiarism detection. The paper outlined new methods of analysis, such as discriminant analysis, neural network classification, code-based reasoning, and similarity calculation. [5] emphasized on clone detection, debugging, reverse engineering, and the visualization of analysis results. New application areas of source code analysis include middleware, software reliability engineering, and model checking in formal analysis. The paper also outlined the future challenges of software code analysis. Code written by a small number of software engineers is widely reusable by other programmers and can be combined into custom applications and model-based programming. This requires a new approach to source code analysis based on both the models itself and source codes. In a way, the need for AI model forensics was predicted in [5].

More recently, approaches to source code analysis and authorship attribution started utilizing ML and DL techniques. [1] achieved state-of-the-art results in source code authorship attribution based on automatic learning of efficient representations for Abstract Syntax Tree (AST) features. The representation learning is implemented through two types of DL models: Long Short-Term Memory (LSTM) and Bidirectional Long Short-Term Memory (BiLTSM). DL models that were deemed successful in natural language processing (NLP) tasks show good performance for authorship attribution in [17].

Challenges of Software Forensics. Source code such as notebooks, scripts, and model files can be found left after an attack event. Software forensics based on the analysis of source code files may prove difficult in the special case of AI programs because of code reuse. Moreover, AI model files eliminate the need to have access to the original source code. None of the code written by a programmer is actually stored in the model files. Without the source code, it is difficult to tie a model file to a specific author using the current software forensic approaches. This presents a research opportunity for the forensics community.

3.3   Network Forensics

Network forensics is "the use of scientifically proven techniques to collect, fuse, identify, examine, correlate, analyze, and document digital evidence from multiple, actively processing and transmitting digital sources for the purpose of uncovering facts related to the planned intent, or measured success of unauthorized activities meant to disrupt, corrupt, and or compromise system components as well as providing information to assist in response to or recovery from these activities [29]."

Similar to the digital forensics model, network forensics follows the process of preservation, collection, examination, analysis, and reporting. Evidence can be found within the network or outside of the network. Evidence that can be seized from within the network includes device logs, network traffic, and the volatile memory from the devices in question. Evidence processed from outside the network can include internet archives and logs from the domain hosting provider, domain name controller, and internet service providers [7]. The staggering amount of the evidence that can be collected from within and outside the network alludes to some of the challenges within this field. [25] acknowledges that the analysis of log data is extensive because the system has to account for all actions performed. Additionally, those logs must be processed, converted, and compared against a set of accepted misuse and attack patterns.

The future direction of network forensics corresponds to the rise of cloud-based applications and the importance of cloud forensics. [36] recommends that instead of only using packet capture files of network segments for analysis, the investigation needs to include packet capturing and analysis in cloud environments.

4 Case Study: Model Forensics of an Autonomous Need-for-Surgery Classifier

To better understand the context of AI model forensics, we present a case study where an AI-based model decides on surgery, based on patient information. Examples of patient information are: age, life quality, symptoms, past medical records, past family history, medical tests results, etc. In this scenario, the system has to decide on the need for a surgery, whether it is microsurgery, radiosurgery, or just active observation. The system helped medical staff make good decisions. Suddenly, the system started outputting bad decisions, which led to the confusion of medical staff and the occurrence of several deaths. An investigation has to take place.

A digital forensic investigator is hired to examine the system. Some of the hypotheses an investigator may consider are:

- The model has been completely replaced (Malicious). For example, a simple *wget* or *git clone* command in the system logs (or network traces) may reveal that a replacement model has been downloaded. The investigator may find the actual source code and other useful information in the git repository.
- The model has been gradually modified and poisoned (Malicious).
- The model was always malicious, but the malicious aspects remained dormant (Malicious).
- The problem occurred after an update of the libraries or some of the dependencies (Benign).
- A problem in feature extraction and prepossessing occurred following a recent code pull (Benign).
- The addition of new features to the model decreased its accuracy (Benign).

To begin, the investigator needs to determine the following:

- Where the model is hosted: locally in the internal network, or deployed as a web service on a cloud platform?
- What is the access control policy (who has access to the model, and who has access to the hosting system)?
- In the case of cloud deployment, what is the service model (e.g. PaaS, SaaS, or IaaS)?
- Is the hosting system properly protected, patched and updated?

If the model is deployed from the local system, forensic evidence about the model may reside in memory. If the model is served and deployed from the cloud, most of the evidence resides in the cloud; however, some residual evidence may also reside on the end-user machine. Methods of cloud forensics are applicable to collect evidence about the model. Figure 2 depicts possible locations where forensic evidence pertaining to AI model forensics is likely to reside.

It is also important to identify the model's framework and libraries used in order to gather information about the author's intent. The model file has to be examined to determine this information. Typically, most model files have

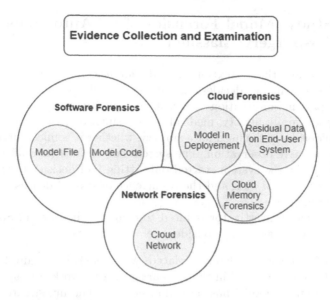

Fig. 2. Diagram of where evidence and information related to AI model forensics is likely to be located

plaintext framework information within the first few lines of the file; however, sometimes this information may not be as easy to find. For example, Fig. 3 depicts the contents of the saved iris classification model in PyTorch. From the files contents, we can see PyTorch libraries that help us correctly identify the model framework. Other information, such as parameters and function calls, can also be seen in the file.

In cases where plaintext is not found within a saved model file, we should still not only rely on the file extension or the header information. Additional fingerprinting is required to provide a clear answer. Figure 4 displays some of the most popular *AI platforms*, *AI tools & frameworks*, and *Model deployment & services*. Popular cloud providers such as Amazon AWS and Microsoft Azure have different paradigms for storing and serving AI models. The diversity, interoperability, and heterogeneity of the AI sphere is in the challenge list of AI model forensics.

The investigator has to check when the model file was last modified, and figure out whether the modification is performed by an adversary or a legitimate user. A typical defense against unsolicited model modification is to create a read-only database of cryptographic hashes for production-plan AI models, store these hashes offline, and regularly compare hashes of the active models to the stored hashes looking for changes.

The more important questions our investigator will face are determining the original intent of the model, who made the modification, was the modification authorized, what exactly was the modification, and to what degree did it alter the model's intent. Software forensic methods and techniques, such as author

```
archive/data.pklFB ZZZZZZZZZZZZZZ
_parametersq ccollections
OrderedDict
_non_persistent_buffers_setq
_backward_hooksq _forward_hooksq _forward_pre_hooksq _state_dict_hooksq _load_state_dict_pre_hooksq layer1q
ctorch.nn.modules.linear
Linear
weightq ctorch._utils
_rebuild_parameter
q ctorch._utils
_rebuild_tensor_v2
storageq"ctorch
FloatStorage
105455744q$X cpuq%K 105462944q0h%K2tq1QK )Rq4tq5Rq6
in_featuresqDK out_featuresqEK2ubX layer2qFh 132915008qJh%M tqKQK )RqNtqORqP 132915168qTh%K tqUQK )RqXtqYRqZ
)RqghDK2hEK 132915488qlh%K<tqmQK )RqptqqRqr 105462544qvh%K tqwQK
archive/data/105455744FB2 ZZZZZZZZZZZZZZZZZZZZZZZZZZZZZZZZZZZZZZZZZZZZZZZZ
archive/data/105462544FB ZZZZZZZZZZZZZZZZZZZZZZZZZ
archive/data/105462944FB, ZZZZZZZZZZZZZZZZZZZZZZZZZZZZZZZZZZZZZZZZZZ
archive/data/132915008FB0 ZZZZZZZZZZZZZZZZZZZZZZZZZZZZZZZZZZZZZZZZZZZZ
archive/data/132915168FB ZZZZZZZZZZZZZZZZZZZZZZZZZv: archive/data/132915488FB(
ZZZZZZZZZZZZZZZZZZZZZZZZZZZZZZZZZZZZZZZZZZ
archive/versionFB ZZZZZZZZZZZZZZ3
archive/data.pklPK archive/data/105455744PK archive/data/105462544PK archive/data/105462944PK
archive/data/132915008PK archive/data/132915168PK archive/data/132915488PK archive/versionPK
```

Fig. 3. Contents of the saved model file for the iris classification system written in PyTorch

identification, characterization, and intent, may help the investigator find some of the answers to the above questions. Model files offer the internal architecture, parameters of the model, and input features; however, the investigator might not have access to the training and testing dataset, the source code that generated the model, or previous versions of the same model. A list of non-comprehensive techniques that may help the investigation are:

Malware Check whether the host was infected by any kind of malware or was the target of offensive black-hat penetration testing.

Adversarial Samples The investigator may test the sensitivity of the model to adversarial samples generated by well known algorithms. If the model is vulnerable to these samples, the investigator may test logged input vectors to check if they are adversarial as well.

Visualization Techniques such as t-distributed stochastic neighbor embedding (t-SNE) and Uniform Manifold Approximation & Projection (UMAP) may help determine whether the classifier is a poor one or whether the input data is noisy and inconsistent.

XAI The investigator may employ well-known eXplainable AI (XAI) techniques to generate explanations for the inquiry decisions. The explanations can be checked by experts to see if they make sense or not. Good explainers tell a lot about possible model overfitting, underfitting, or adversarial behaviour. In case the explanations are incoherent with human expert reasoning given the input features, the investigator has to turn back to earlier parts in the AI pipeline such as data inputting and feature extraction.

Fig. 4. Diagram of popular AI platforms, AI tools & frameworks, and model deployment & services

Note that the above list is not comprehensive. Digital forensics, in general, is a domain requiring a lot of innovation and where new techniques continuously arise. The overall goal of using these techniques in AI model forensics are to distinguish factors, such as author identification, author characterization, and author intent, if possible. The exact methods for utilizing these techniques and answering the aforementioned investigative questions need to be established. Storing and arbitrating AI models using Blockchain helps preemptively solve a lot of issues for AI model forensics. We discuss this context in the next section.

5   Blockchain and AI Model Forensics

Blockchain systems provide properties of transparency, visibility, immutability, traceability, nonrepudiation, and smart contracts. These properties reveal important information for AI model forensics; it makes it straightforward to answer questions about who is responsible for the inquired model behaviour.

All the transactions taking place within a Blockchain are stored in a public, decentralized, and append-only ledger. The ledger is accessible to anyone with access to the Blockchain and is secure and tamper-proof. Each transaction in the Blockchain is cryptographically signed by all involved parties. The signed transactions must be verified by a majority of the Blockchain users before being officially added to the ledger. The Blockchain provides an ecosystem where AI developers, utility providers, deployment engineers, and other participants can interact. This allows AI models to be tracked back to their origins. Such an ecosystem supporting both AI and XAI is described in [27].

With Blockchain support, the causes of misconduct of an AI model and the liability for bad behaviour become easily identified. During investigation, the AI model left over is compared to the one stored in the Blockchain. If there is no match, the model has been modified without the consent of the participants. If there is a match, the investigation may trace the source of the buggy behavior causing the deficit. Examples include a library update, a previously committed buggy version, a shortage in training data, or a misconfiguration in the number of training epochs. Using Blockchain in this way can offer potential solutions to author identification, which can further lead to author characterization. That said, we cannot expect that a wide adoption of Blockchain for arbitrating AI models is occurring anytime soon. AI model forensics must not solely rely on the existence of cryptographic ledgers.

Intellectual Property or copyright can be managed through transactions and smart contracts. Privacy of the entities involves the life-cycle of the AI model, which can be achieved by using public keys instead of real identities. For instance, identities such as the forensic investigator, a witness, or an AI expert can be masked using public keys. Of course, the topic of blockchain for AI forensics can be further developed and detailed in a future research. Blockchain as a solution is promising but needs more investigation in future work.

6   AI Model Ballistics

The first documented use of ballistics in forensics occurred in 1835 [39]. Matching the unique bullet mold to one in the possession of the suspect led to a confession and eventual conviction. Forensic ballistics has evolved and now the microscopic indentations on the bullet and cartridge case after a gun is fired can be used to create a ballistic fingerprint [28]. When the term ballistics is used in relation to forensics, conventionally, it implies firearm analysis. However, in recent years some areas have adapted this term, in particular, camera ballistics. Camera ballistics uses the camera sensor to match a photo to a camera, like a bullet to a gun [24]. In a similar fashion, AI model ballistics is needed to match a creator to an AI model.

The motivation behind AI model ballistics is to identify and manipulate AI model artifacts in a crime scene investigation in a forensically sound manner. The goal of AI model ballistics is to identify relevant information for the investigation, such as: the type and creator of an AI model, the intention of an AI model, the compliance of the model's behaviour with the creator's intended behaviour, the framework, tools and datasets used in model creation, and more. Fingerprinting a model is another way to view AI model ballistics. To acquire the *fingerprint* of a model, an investigator would need to interrogate a model, such as passing various inputs and analyzing the outputs.

For this reason, we tentatively define AI model ballistics as the subfield of AI model forensics pertaining to the processing and analysis of AI model artifacts left behind. These artifacts could potentially lead to the identification of the model's creation framework, creator's intent (benign or malicious), and any other relevant identifiers or information that can be extracted.

7   Challenges of AI Model Forensics

While incorporating methods from cloud, software, and network forensics, AI model forensics inherit their challenges and manifest unprecedented ones. For example, an AI model stored in the cloud inherits a major limitation of cloud forensics, which is the inability to physically acquire and seize evidence. In standard digital forensic investigations, the digital device in question is collected for analysis; however, in cloud forensics the evidence cannot be physically collected and the data can be dispersed through numerous servers and architectures. The AI model service may be dependent on other web micro services or federated learning. Investigation relies on help from cloud service providers, which makes the chain of custody and the validity of the evidence less credible.

Other challenges include legal issues, such as jurisdictional boundaries and obtaining a search warrant. AI models are generated by AI code that is linked to different developers, researchers, and providers. AI models are also typically located in shared storage and use shared computational resources. User privacy in these settings is an additional challenge. It is difficult investigating one user's data without accessing and violating the privacy of other users.

Applying methods of software forensics are not directly applicable to AI models and source code. The swift development in AI frameworks and deployment models makes the search space even larger. AI model forensics must be able to determine as much information as possible about the development frameworks and libraries, authorship attribution, training and testing history or logs, adversarial behaviour, or intentionally designed malicious backdoors.

In addition, adversarial attacks and anti-forensics are always a concern in any form of digital forensics. We expect adversaries to perform anti-forensics in many different ways and hinder the investigation.

8   Conclusion

In this paper, we sketched the motivation and the description for a sub-domain of AI forensics that we dubbed AI model forensics. We elaborated on the background and nature of AI model development and deployment, and highlighted the fact that these models can be replaced, trojanized, gradually poisoned, or fooled by adversarial input. We suggested an extended definition of AI model forensics, namely examining left-behind AI models, and their surrounding artifacts, such as logs, traces, service code, source code, datasets, and input samples with the goal of helping an investigation reach correct conclusions about a security incident. In particular, we focus on the identity of the model creator and the intention of the model, which is our motivator for the new subfield AI model ballistics.

We explored the relationships and the dependencies of the newly arising sub-domain with the literature work from software forensics, highlighting the importance of author identification, characterisation, and intent and cloud and network forensics, focusing on the challenges faced in the field. The use-case showed the peculiarities of AI model forensics in a proper context. Blockchain is a possible solution to support AI model forensics, but we cannot assume that AI models are tracked and managed by a Blockchain in all cases. AI model ballistics is a new topic as it relates to identifying the type, owner, and intent of a AI system. Finally, we approached the challenges of this novel field. Our work is a step towards further exploring and defining AI model forensics and model ballistics as an interesting and fascinating subfield under the umbrella of AI forensics.

Future work should explore applying and creating scenarios to show how to apply a sound methodology for AI model ballistics in end-to-end investigation use-cases and exploring their artifacts. Each scenario should address both malicious and benign incidents of model files to find an appropriate solution. For instance, each hypothesis presented in the case-scenario will be further explored to find resolutions. Future work should also explore the contents of a model file in depth for a better understanding of how software forensic techniques can be applied.

Acknowledgements. This material is based upon work supported by the National Science Foundation under Grant Number 1921813. Any opinions, findings, and conclusions or recommendations expressed in this material are those of the author(s) and do not necessarily reflect the views of the National Science Foundation.

References

1. Alsulami, B., Dauber, E., Harang, R., Mancoridis, S., Greenstadt, R.: Source code authorship attribution using long short-term memory based networks. In: Foley, S.N., Gollmann, D., Snekkenes, E. (eds.) ESORICS 2017. LNCS, vol. 10492, pp. 65–82. Springer, Cham (2017). https://doi.org/10.1007/978-3-319-66402-6_6
2. Amodei, D., Olah, C., Steinhardt, J., Christiano, P., Schulman, J., Mané, D.: Concrete Problems in AI Safety (2016)
3. Behzadan, V., Baggili, I.M.: Founding the domain of AI forensics. In: SafeAI@ AAAI, pp. 31–35 (2020)
4. Behzadan, V., Hsu, W.: Sequential triggers for watermarking of deep reinforcement learning policies. arXiv preprint arXiv:1906.01126 (2019)
5. Binkley, D.: Source code analysis: a road map. In: Future of Software Engineering (FOSE 2007), pp. 104–119 (2007). https://doi.org/10.1109/FOSE.2007.27
6. Chen, X., Liu, C., Li, B., Lu, K., Song, D.: Targeted backdoor attacks on deep learning systems using data poisoning. arXiv preprint arXiv:1712.05526 (2017)
7. Datt, S.: Learning Network Forensics. Community Experience Distilled. Packt Publishing, Birmingham (2016)
8. Digital Forensics Market: Market Research Firm (2018). https://www.marketsandmarkets.com/Market-Reports/digital-forensics-market-230663168.html
9. Frantzeskou, G., MacDonell, S., Stamatatos, E.: Source code authorship analysis for supporting the cybercrime investigation process. In: Proceedings of the 1st International Conference on E-Business and Telecommunications Networks, pp. 85–92 (2004)

10. Grispos, G., Storer, T., Glisson, W.B.: Calm before the storm: the challenges of cloud computing in digital forensics. Int. J. Digit. Crime Forensics (IJDCF) **4**(2), 28–48 (2012)
11. Herman, M., et al.: NIST cloud computing forensic science challenges. Technical report, National Institute of Standards and Technology (2020)
12. Jeong, D.: Artificial intelligence security threat, crime, and forensics: taxonomy and open issues. IEEE Access **8**, 184560–184574 (2020)
13. Jiang, F., et al.: Artificial intelligence in healthcare: past, present and future. Stroke Vasc. Neurol. **2**(4), 230–243 (2017). https://doi.org/10.1136/svn-2017-000101
14. Karpisek, F., Baggili, I., Breitinger, F.: Whatsapp network forensics: decrypting and understanding the whatsapp call signaling messages. Digit. Investig. **15**, 110–118 (2015). https://doi.org/10.1016/j.diin.2015.09.002. https://www.sciencedirect.com/science/article/pii/S1742287615000985
15. Kent, K., Chevalier, S., Grance, T., Dang, H.: Guide to integrating forensic techniques into incident response. NIST Special Publication 800–86 10(14) (2006)
16. Konečný, J., McMahan, H.B., Yu, F.X., Richtárik, P., Suresh, A.T., Bacon, D.: Federated learning: strategies for improving communication efficiency. CoRR abs/1610.05492 (2016). http://arxiv.org/abs/1610.05492
17. Kurtukova, A., Romanov, A., Shelupanov, A.: Source code authorship identification using deep neural networks. Symmetry **12**(12) (2020). https://doi.org/10.3390/sym12122044. https://www.mdpi.com/2073-8994/12/12/2044
18. Levinson, J., et al.: Towards fully autonomous driving: systems and algorithms. In: 2011 IEEE Intelligent Vehicles Symposium (IV), pp. 163–168 (2011). https://doi.org/10.1109/IVS.2011.5940562
19. Li, J.: Cyber security meets artificial intelligence: a survey. Front. Inf. Technol. Electron. Eng. **19**(12), 1462–1474 (2018). https://doi.org/10.1631/FITEE.1800573
20. Li, Z., Hu, C., Zhang, Y., Guo, S.: How to prove your model belongs to you. In: Proceedings of the 35th Annual Computer Security Applications Conference (2019). https://doi.org/10.1145/3359789.3359801
21. MacDonell, S.G., Buckingham, D., Gray, A.R., Sallis, P.J.: Software forensics: extending authorship analysis techniques to computer programs. JL Inf. Sci. **13**, 34–69 (2002)
22. Mell, P., Grance, T., et al.: The NIST definition of cloud computing. NIST Special Publication 800–145 (2011)
23. Mnih, V., et al.: Human-level control through deep reinforcement learning. Nature **518**, 529–33 (2015). https://doi.org/10.1038/nature14236
24. MOBILedit: Camera Ballistics. https://www.mobiledit.com/camera-ballistics
25. Mukkamala, S., Sung, A.H.: Identifying significant features for network forensic analysis using artificial intelligent techniques. Int. J. Digit. Evid. **1**, 1–17 (2003)
26. Nassar, M., Itani, A., Karout, M., El Baba, M., Kaakaji, O.A.S.: Shoplifting smart stores using adversarial machine learning. In: 2019 IEEE/ACS 16th International Conference on Computer Systems and Applications (AICCSA), pp. 1–6. IEEE (2019)
27. Nassar, M., Salah, K., ur Rehman, M.H., Svetinovic, D.: Blockchain for explainable and trustworthy artificial intelligence. Wiley Interdiscip. Rev. Data Mining Knowl. Discov. **10**(1), e1340 (2020)
28. NIST: Ballistics (2021). https://www.nist.gov/ballistics
29. Palmer, G.: A road map for digital forensic research. Technical report. DFRWS (DTRT0010-01) (2001)

30. PyTorch: PyTorch tutorials: saving and loading models (2017). https://pytorch.org/tutorials/beginner/saving_loading_models.html#saving-loading-model-for-inference

31. Ruan, K., Carthy, J., Kechadi, M.T., Baggili, I.: Cloud forensics definitions and critical criteria for cloud forensic capability: an overview of survey results. Digit. Investig. **10**, 34–43 (2013)

32. Ruan, K., Carthy, J., Kechadi, T., Crosbie, M.: Cloud forensics. In: Peterson, G., Shenoi, S. (eds.) Advances in Digital Forensics VII (2011). https://doi.org/10.1007/978-3-642-24212-0_3

33. Sallis, P., Aakjaer, A., MacDonell, S.: Software forensics: old methods for a new science. In: Proceedings 1996 International Conference Software Engineering: Education and Practice, pp. 481–485. IEEE (1996)

34. Schneider, J., Breitinger, F.: AI forensics: did the artificial intelligence system do it? Why? (2020)

35. Shah, J.J., Malik, L.G.: Cloud forensics: issues and challenges. In: 6th International Conference on Emerging Trends in Engineering and Technology, pp. 138–139 (2013). https://doi.org/10.1109/ICETET.2013.44

36. Sikos, L.F.: Packet analysis for network forensics: a comprehensive survey. Forensic Sci. Int. Digit. Investig. **32**, 200892 (2020). https://doi.org/10.1016/j.fsidi.2019.200892. https://www.sciencedirect.com/science/article/pii/S1742287619302002

37. Spafford, E.H., Weeber, S.A.: Software forensics: can we track code to its authors? Comput. Secur. **12**(6), 585–595 (1993)

38. TensorFlow: TensorFlow core: save and load models (2021). https://www.tensorflow.org/tutorials/keras/save_and_load#save_the_entire_model

39. Tilstone, W., Tilstone, W., Savage, K., Clark, L.: Forensic Science: An Encyclopedia of History, Methods, and Techniques. ABC-CLIO (2006). https://books.google.com/books?id=zIRQOssWbaoC

40. Wang, Z., Liu, C., Cui, X.: Evilmodel: hiding malware inside of neural network models. arXiv preprint arXiv:2107.08590 (2021)

41. Zhang, J., et al.: Protecting intellectual property of deep neural networks with watermarking. In: Proceedings of the 2018 on Asia Conference on Computer and Communications Security, ASIACCS 2018, pp. 159–172. Association for Computing Machinery (2018). https://doi.org/10.1145/3196494.3196550

Auto-Parser: Android Auto and Apple CarPlay Forensics

Andrew Mahr(✉), Robert Serafin, Cinthya Grajeda, and Ibrahim Baggili

Connecticut Institute of Technology, University of New Haven Cyber Forensics
Research and Education Group (UNHcFREG), West Haven, USA
amahr1@unh.newhaven.edu, {rsera1,cgrajedamendez,ibaggili}@newhaven.edu

Abstract. Mobile device features like Apple CarPlay and Android Auto
provide drivers safer hands-free navigation methods to use while driving.
In crash investigations, understanding how these applications store data
may be crucial in determining the what, when, where, who and why.
By analyzing digital artifacts generated by Android Auto and Apple
CarPlay, investigators can determine the last application displayed on the
head unit, the application layout of the user's home display screen, and
other evidence which points to the utilization of the mobile device and
its features while driving. Additionally, usage data can be found within
other applications compatible with Android Auto and Apple CarPlay. In
this paper, we explore the digital evidence produced by these applications
and propose a proof of concept open source tool to assist investigators
in automatically extracting relevant artifacts from Android Auto and
Apple CarPlay as well as other day-to-day essential applications.

Keywords: Android auto · Apple CarPlay · Mobile forensics ·
Artifacts

1 Introduction

Digital evidence acquired from mobile devices supporting vehicular hands-free
navigation and communication may prove useful in crash investigations. According to the Centers for Disease Control and Prevention (CDC), a distraction while
driving could simply be using one's cell phone to send a text message or place a
call, etc. Unfortunately, in 2019, texting or emailing while driving was a common-
ality seen more in older teens than younger teens. The consequences of driving
while being distracted could be fatal. In fact, in 2018, the CDC reported that
over 2,800 people died as a result of distracted driving [7], while in 2019, this
number increased by 9.9% [1]. The advancement, and increased consumption of
mobile and vehicular technology is growing exponentially [9,14,34]. This caused
the need for safer and tighter integration between mobile devices and cars.

Apple's CarPlay[1] was introduced in 2014 and is native to iOS. Once enabled
by the user, it can only .be paired to the vehicle via a USB connection or

---

[1] https://www.apple.com/ios/carplay/.

P. Gladyshev et al. (Eds.): ICDF2C 2021, LNICST 441, pp. 52–71, 2022.
https://doi.org/10.1007/978-3-031-06365-7_4

Bluetooth, however, only a few cars support the Bluetooth feature [31]. On the other hand, Android Auto[2] is a non-native application that was created in 2015 and can be downloaded from the Google Play store. Android Auto must also be paired via USB and Bluetooth. Since the development of these mobile applications, car manufacturers have been working to integrate them into their frameworks. Today, over 600 car models offer support for CarPlay[3], while close to 60 manufacturers offer or will soon offer support for Android Auto [3].

Consequently, our work provides a forensic analysis of the Android Auto and Apple CarPlay applications. We also present an open source Python tool, *Auto-Parser*, to extract relevant data from digital artifacts and present them in an HTML report. To the best of our knowledge, this tool is the first of its kind. *Auto-Parser* may be added as part of an investigator's forensic workflow to shed light on actions taken when using these services and applications while driving.

Our work provides the following contributions:

- A primary review of the forensic disk analysis of Apple CarPlay and Android Auto applications.
- A collection of Android Auto and Apple CarPlay digital forensic artifacts publicly shared on the Artifact Genome Project[4] [15].
- An open-source tool for the automated retrieval, analysis, and reporting of relevant digital artifacts acquired from forensic images of the mobile devices.[5]

The remainder of this paper includes related work found in Sect. 2. Section 3 discusses the approach and methodology for this work. Section 4 outlines the experimental results, while Sect. 5 explains the creation and usage of the parsing tool. Lastly, Sect. 6 concludes the paper and presents future work.

2 Related Work

At the time of writing, no peer reviewed work existed on the forensic analysis of Android Auto and Apple CarPlay applications. Moreover, to the best of our knowledge, there has not been an open source tool developed to address the type of evidence that could be collected from these applications.

Nevertheless, some blogs and presentations explored this topic [12,19–21,29]. Our work was initially motivated by posts made by Joshua Hickman on his personal blog "The Binary Hick" [19,21]. We expand on past work and provide a first of its kind open source tool to automate the forensic analysis process and present relevant data in a report. In the next sections, we highlight related work on vehicular infotainment systems, and small scale digital device forensics.

---

[2] https://www.android.com/auto/.
[3] https://www.apple.com/ios/carplay/.
[4] https://agp.newhaven.edu.
[5] The tool may be downloaded from https://github.com/unhcfreg/Auto-Parser-Android-Auto-Apple-CarPlay.

2.1   Vehicular Forensics

Vehicle infotainment systems may offer digital evidence related to driving activities, phone calls, and mobile messaging [26]. Past work provided a structure of embedded vehicle systems and discussed the long-term information that could be found and recovered to better understand the system's end users [26].

Other work explored the challenges of Vehicle Ad-Hoc Networks and the forensic potential of entertainment systems were discussed [27]. The authors then captured forensic images of a Ford F-150 vehicle's infotainment system and described the data that could be recovered. Another case study noted the challenges in conducting vehicle forensics and contributed a case study on a Volkswagen Golf [24]. It also important to note that the Berla Corporation specializes in the development of tools and techniques for vehicle infotainment forensics[6].

2.2   Mobile and Application Forensics

The field of small scale digital device forensics is vast. There have been numerous studies that forensically explored applications and devices. Since Android Auto and Apple CarPlay interact with mobile devices and their applications (such as WhatsApp), prior work in this domain is of relevance.

Past work examined the data stored in vehicle assistant applications for notable car manufacturers and discussed digital artifacts that could be extracted [11]. Relevant to our work is also an extensive study related to mobile GPS applications. The work was conducted on both Android and iOS mapping applications such as Waze, MapQuest and Google Maps. A tool was created based on the findings of the study to parse data found in the applications [32]. Likewise, [18] provided an analysis and algorithm for the automated retrieval of data from health and fitness applications. Their work discovered health information, passwords, geo-location data, and other private information that could be useful in an investigation.

Let us not forget that car systems also interact with mobile messaging applications. Relevant work explored the forensics of social-messaging applications such as WhatsApp, Tango, Viber, and ooVoo to determine their security and forensic footprints. This work concluded that Personally Identifiable Information (PII) could be found within application data folders as well as on servers publicly accessible [35]. Similar work and results were also conducted recently on the Zoom application concluding that PII such as chat messages, contacts, profile images, and passwords could be recovered from devices [30].

Other work purely focused on network traffic analysis of the WhatsApp call signaling protocol by decrypting its associated network traffic. The researchers uncovered the codec used for call transfer. Metadata related to the call such as phone numbers and duration can also be forensically found [25].

In a different domain of device forensics, [8] investigated the DJI Phantom III Drone and the research resulted in a tool which could recover flight data

---

[6] https://berla.co/.

taken from the suspect device. This work provided insight into GPS locations, speeds, flight time, and other critical information that could be recovered and used by investigators.

Additional research on social media and mobile applications on iPhones and Androids has been conducted [2,4,5,22,37]. Similarly, forensic analysis of Android vault applications was conducted [38]. Other relevant work explored the forensics of IoT devices [10], gaming consoles [33], tablets [23] and Virtual Reality headsets [6,36].

3 Methodology

We conducted our research in four main phases: scenario/case creation, data acquisition, data analysis, and the creation of a tool to parse, extract and report on all relevant artifacts stored in an acquired forensic disk image for use in an investigation. Table 1 outlines the apparatus used in our methodology. Details of these four phases and results are elaborated on.

3.1 Setup and Scenario Creation

Fig. 1. Alpine stereo internal setup (Key - Red: Belkin Battery Supply, Blue: Rockford Fosgate R14X2 Speakers, Green: Alpine iLX-W650 Head Unit, Pink: USB Cable for Device Connection, Yellow: Wiring for power, speaker channels, etc.) (Color figure online)

In this phase, a stereo head unit was constructed (Figs. 1 and 2) to conduct testing in a controlled environment. At the time, a vehicle that supported these features was not available to the researchers. For some tests, this engineered,

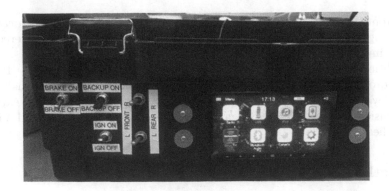

Fig. 2. Front of alpine unit

Table 1. Apparatus

Hardware/Software	Use	Version
Galaxy S6	Android Auto	Nougat 7.0
iPhone 5s	Apple CarPlay	iOS 12.4.5, 12.4.6
Android Auto	Android Auto	5.1, 5.4, 6.0
Alpine ILX-W650	Simulated Car Stereo Unit	V1.014_1206
BELKIN Battery Backup Unit	Battery Supply	N/A
(2) Rockford Fosgate R14X2	Stereo Speakers	N/A
2020 Subaru Crosstrek	Real World Tests	Rel_UA.19.01.70
Magnet Acquire	Full Image Creator (Android/iOS)	2.25.0.20236
Autopsy	Full Image Viewer	4.17.0
Android Debug Bridge (ADB)	Android Data Extraction Tool	1.0.41, Version 29.0.6-6198805
DB Browser for SQLite	View Sqlite/ DB files	3.11.2
Xcode	View pList & XML Files	12.5 (12E262)
iBackup Viewer	pList & XML Files	4.1583
Hex Fiend	Hex Editor	Version 2.14 (1613443925)
checkra1n	iOS Jailbreak Tool	0.9.7 BETA
SuperSU	Android Jailbreak Tool	V2.82
Filza File Manager	File System Manager	3.7 Build 7

portable, stereo unit was placed inside a vehicle to simulate a real world experience. Specifically, an Alpine[7] stereo head unit was used to serve as the interface for the Android Auto and Apple CarPlay applications. The backup battery supply and speaker units served to power the device and simulate normal car interaction (Fig. 1). Once a compatible vehicle was available, the tests were also conducted with a 2020 Subaru Crosstrek Premium[8] to note any forensic differences between devices.

---

[7] https://www.alpine-usa.com/.

[8] https://www.subaru.com/.

To control the experiment, and obtain the most amount of data possible, communication was kept between two rooted mobile phones (Table 1). In the case of the iPhone, it was only connected via USB cable as neither head units supported Apple CarPlay connection via Bluetooth. It is important to note that Bluetooth for Apple CarPlay is supported on other vehicles. On the other hand, the Android device had to be connected via both, Bluetooth, and a USB cable for the Android Auto application to function with the head units. Additionally, to mimic other possible distractions like listening to music, the Spotify application was installed on both mobile devices. It is important to note that during the course of this research, the Android Auto application versions changed and updating the application was necessary to continue testing.

In order to simulate normal user actions with these systems, and create the most relevant data possible, the experiments listed below were conducted with both the custom built stereo head unit, and the Subaru's stereo head unit.

- Sent and received text messages between testing devices.
- Sent and received phone calls between testing devices.
- Asked Siri (iOS) and Google Assistant (Android) for driving directions to an specific address.
- Asked Siri (iOS) and Google Assistant (Android) to place phone calls and send text messages.
- Played music through the Spotify music application and interacted with the application's features on the head units.

3.2 Data Acquisition

In this phase, data was acquired from the two different mobile devices. Magnet Acquire[9] was used to obtain forensic images of each device. For the rooted Samsung, initially a full forensic image was taken, resulting in the acquisition of a RAW data file. After additional tests, logical acquisitions of the Samsung were taken as full physical images were not necessary. For the iPhone, it is important to note that while the iPhone was jailbroken, Magnet Acquire only supported the acquisition of logical images [28].

4 Experimental Results

To analyze all experimental results and extract relevant artifacts, different tools shown in Table 1 were utilized along with manual analysis. The next subsections discuss all artifacts of interest identified per device. Appendix B, Table 2, references those significant artifacts and their data directory paths.

---

[9] https://www.magnetforensics.com/resources/magnet-acquire/.

4.1 Major Artifacts Found - Apple CarPlay

CarPlay Data Structure: To identify artifacts related to the Apple CarPlay feature, understanding how data is stored on an iOS device is critical. Apple CarPlay is part of Apple's SpringBoard framework that manages the screen of an iOS (or macOS) device [13]. Thus, unlike the Android Auto application, the hands-free features of CarPlay are built in the main settings of the phone rather than being compiled in a sole separate application. Therefore, the settings files associated with CarPlay are spread out throughout the phone and not compartmentalized like a normal application. If the iPhone is connected to more than one head unit that supports Apple CarPlay, the feature names the settings' files with a Globally Unique Identifier (GUID) associated with each head unit that can later be used to correlate data found in the settings' files [16]. Throughout our research, it was determined that data pertaining to other applications or features used while implementing CarPlay was not found within the CarPlay settings. CarPlay simply serves as a projection feature to assist users in viewing and accessing every day items such as music, messages, and phone calls and any other application with support for CarPlay. However, we realized there were still relevant pieces of information that are recoverable that can help investigators gain a glimpse into what was being displayed or used while an individual was driving. The following subsections denote the relevant files where this information can be found.

cache.plist: This artifact contained data pertaining to timestamps associated with core phone settings and other location calibration information unrelated to CarPlay (Appendix B, Table 2, File ID 1). The most important data i n this artifact is the "Last Vehicle Connection" entry which provides the connect and disconnect timestamps in Cocoa Core Data format for the last time the device was connected to a vehicle. This entry also notes the name of the vehicle the iPhone was last connected to. The latter is relevant in an investigation to confirm a timeline of events and that in fact the user's phone was connected to the vehicle.

com.apple.carplay.plist: This pList file contained information about the vehicle pairings associated with the car (Appendix B, Table 2, File ID 2). Since the device was connected to two car audio head units, one custom built and one with an actual car, two GUIDs were found, along with strings that identify the model of the units: iLX-W650 and Subaru respectively (Fig. 3). This information uniquely identifies and confirms pairings to different devices. Additionally, the file contains "carPlayProtocols" which were found to be additional applications that come as part of the standard head unit's settings. In the case of the Subaru, the head unit comes with support for Aha, a road map software, Pandora, and Subaru's global infotainment application.

com.apple.celestial.plist: This pList file contained settings for many different features of the phone (Appendix B, Table 2, File ID 3). Among these

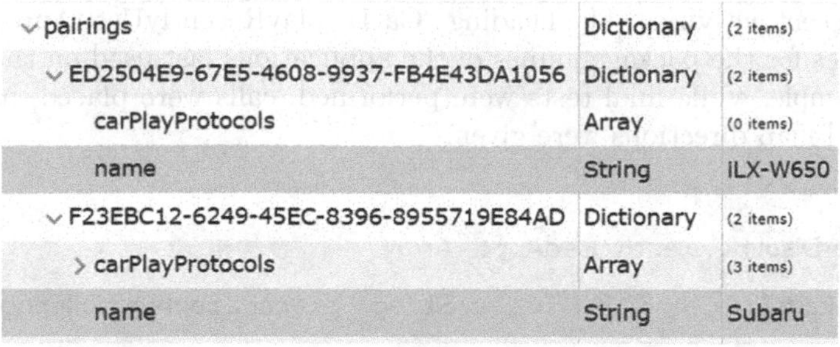

pairings	Dictionary	(2 items)
∨ ED2504E9-67E5-4608-9937-FB4E43DA1056	Dictionary	(2 items)
carPlayProtocols	Array	(0 items)
name	String	iLX-W650
∨ F23EBC12-6249-45EC-8396-8955719E84AD	Dictionary	(2 items)
> carPlayProtocols	Array	(3 items)
name	String	Subaru

Fig. 3. Head unit pairings

features are volume settings for different connections, information about the camera, and IDs for the applications on the display when CarPlay was disconnected. Data of interest in this file includes, the strings "nowPlayingAppWasPlayingUponCarPlayDisconnect" and "nowPlayingAppDisplayIDUponCarPlay-Disconnect" which denote the App ID associated with the last app running on CarPlay (Fig. 4). It is interesting to note that for some tests, the string "now-PlayingApp" noted Apple's "Music" app was playing although this app was not used during the tests. Conclusions as to why this occurred were not formally reached but in some instances the values for the "nowPlayingApp" matched that of the strings related to the application last being used upon disconnect from the car. Additionally, there was a "CarAudioOutput-"Car ID"" entries with a unique identifier for each car which denoted what appeared to be the volume level for when the phone is connected to the car.

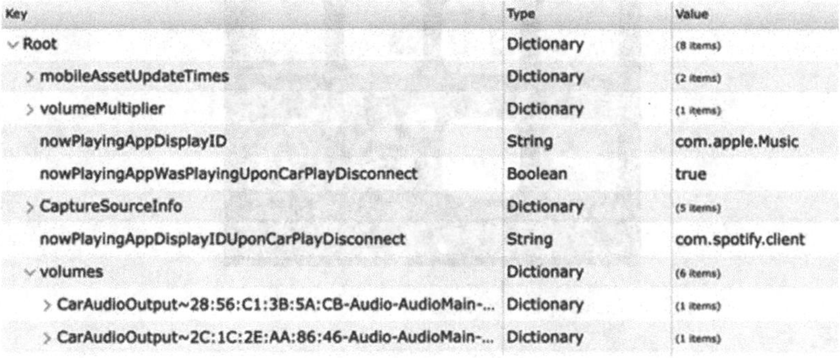

Key	Type	Value
∨ Root	Dictionary	(8 items)
> mobileAssetUpdateTimes	Dictionary	(2 items)
> volumeMultiplier	Dictionary	(1 items)
nowPlayingAppDisplayID	String	com.apple.Music
nowPlayingAppWasPlayingUponCarPlayDisconnect	Boolean	true
> CaptureSourceInfo	Dictionary	(5 items)
nowPlayingAppDisplayIDUponCarPlayDisconnect	String	com.spotify.client
∨ volumes	Dictionary	(6 items)
> CarAudioOutput~28:56:C1:3B:5A:CB-Audio-AudioMain-...	Dictionary	(1 items)
> CarAudioOutput~2C:1C:2E:AA:86:46-Audio-AudioMain-...	Dictionary	(1 items)

Fig. 4. CarPlay com.apple.celestial.plist

com.apple.springboard.plist: This file contained general and user settings for the SpringBoard application which manages the home screen for iOS devices [17] (Appendix B, Table 2, File ID 4). While many of the entries in this file are not relevant to CarPlay, there is an entry which provides potential insight into the most recent activities. The heading "CarDisplayRecentlyUsedApps" (Fig. 5) shows values for the package names of the applications last used on the display. In this example, while final tests were performed, calls were placed, music was played, and map directions were given.

⌄ CarDisplayRecentlyUsedApps	Array	(3 items)
item 0	String	com.apple.mobilephone
item 1	String	com.spotify.client
item 2	String	com.apple.Maps
CarDisplayStartApp	String	com.apple.springboard

Fig. 5. CarPlay recently used applications

"Car GUID"-CarPlay[Desired/Display]IconState.plist: These pList files contained data pertaining to the Icon Layout on the CarPlay display (Appendix B, Table 2, File IDs 5, 6). Each car had its own unique application layout for the applications installed on the phone. A user can change this by visiting the CarPlay settings located within the General settings of the iPhone (Figs. 6 and 7).

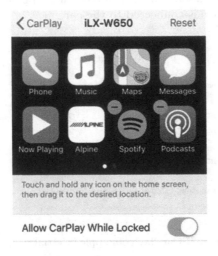

Fig. 6. CarPlay application settings

Fig. 7. CarPlay headunit apps

carplay_connect_timestamp and carplay_success_timestamp: It is important to note that these artifacts did not contain any data but their name and timestamps may be relevant to an investigation (Appendix B, Table 2, File IDs 7, 8). These files were found in the Assistant directory, associated with Siri, and the timestamps are associated with actions completed between CarPlay and Siri. The "carplay_connect_timestamp" is the timestamp for the last initial connection to the vehicle (i.e. turning the vehicle on at the start of a drive and connecting the phone). The "carplay_success_timestamp" is associated with the last time Siri was used while using CarPlay. This was verified after comparing testing notes for asking Siri for directions to the timestamp associated with the file.

4.2 Major Artifacts Found - Android Auto

Android Auto Data Structure: The structure of the data files stored by Android Auto follows that of a normal application on the phone. Unlike Apple CarPlay, Android Auto is an application that can be downloaded from the Google Play Store. The important data files were found within the "com.google.android.projection.gearhead" folder within the /data/data directory and are broken into XML and SQLite databases. The most important artifacts found are discussed in the following sub-sections.

carservicedata.db: This database (Appendix B, Table 2, File ID 9) included information verifying the stereo head units the mobile device has connected to. It had two tables which separated the "allowedcars" and "rejectedcars". Both tables contained data about the manufacturer, the vehicle ID, Bluetooth addresses and allowed connections. It is interesting to note that the first twelve characters of the Subaru's vehicle ID are the same used for its Bluetooth address. The "connectiontime" value is the timestamp associated with the first time the phone was connected to the car within a given driving session (i.e., initially turning on vehicle and connecting to the car). To approximate the accuracy of that timestamp, the "app_state_shared_preferences.xml" file (Appendix B, Table 2,

File ID 12) stored a "pref_lastrun" value that depicted the date and time the Android Auto application was last run. The timestamp in the carservicedata.db will always be a few seconds ahead of the other as the application is opened first before connecting to Bluetooth.

Additionally, the database made a distinction if the head unit was "After Market", which refers to the custom built head unit, or associated with a brand model such as Subaru. Finally, the table had four more columns pertaining to WiFi information such as the WiFi Service Set Identifier (SSID), Basic service set identifier (BSSID), password and security for vehicles that have WiFi. Note, the latter was not tested.

common_user_settings.xml: This XML file (Appendix B, Table 2, File ID 10 and Fig. 8) contained information about the preferred settings for each head unit the device has connected to. For instance, enabled messaging notifications, visual preview of messages, auto reply messages while driving and more. Furthermore, for every vehicle, there is a section identified by the Bluetooth Address pertaining to each vehicle and a "USB" value denoting the device was also connected via a USB cable. It is interesting to note that for the Subaru, one could assign a custom name to the vehicle's Bluetooth connection. In this research, the Subaru's connection name was "Bluebaru."

```
<string name="key_settings_carmode_screen_on">SCREEN_ON_POLICY_ALWAYS_ON</string>
<boolean name="key_settings_autolaunch_delay_proximity" value="true"/>
<string name="key_settings_notifications_auto_reply_message">I'm driving right now</string>
<set name="AndroidAutoBluetooth_28:56:C1:3B:5A:CB">
    <string>USB</string>
```

Fig. 8. Android auto common user settings

default_app.xml: This file (Appendix B, Table 2, File ID 11) provided a method to verify package names of the default applications that were displayed on the Android Auto Interface of the stereo head unit (Fig. 9).

auto_launch_prompt.xml: This artifact (Appendix B, Table 2, File ID 12) is associated with the application's auto launch feature. It contains the Bluetooth Addresses to the vehicles the device has ever connected to.

carservice.xml: This file (Appendix B, Table 2, File ID 13) contained car_module_feature_set values which define settings and information for the connections to the car. It is important to note when the Samsung device was first connected to the custom built stereo, this file contained minimal settings. However, after connecting to the Subaru vehicle's head unit, this file supported additional settings such as "car night mode" and enabling/disabling "connection to known cars only" among other settings.

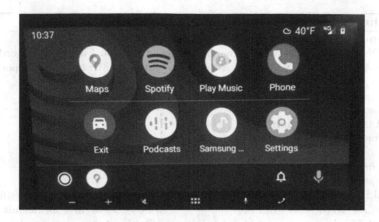

Fig. 9. Default displayed applications

5 Tool Creation and Usage

Overview: The purpose of this tool is to assist the forensic community in automatically identifying relevant artifacts within Apple and Android smartphone forensic disk images. The artifacts created while using these applications paired to the vehicle, could possibly aid in determining causes of different incidents, including car crashes.

A Python tool was constructed using a wordlist to search through the forensic tar images of Apple and Android smartphones. Note, that only tar formats are supported now, however, support for other types may be added in the future. Based on our manual analysis and identification of relevant forensic artifacts and their storage locations on the devices, default wordlists were created. The "words" used in this case could be full file paths and their file names, solely artifact file names, or other useful keywords. For a complete list, see Appendix B, Table 2. A default wordlist containing all relevant and important paths for an investigation is provided if the user does not add a custom one themselves. For the default wordlist, once the critical files are extracted, they are parsed to return specific data in the form of an HTML report. Note, if the default wordlist is edited to add more files, these files will be extracted but will not be included in the report. This also applies to the custom wordlist option. The high level algorithm for this tool is shown in Algorithm 1.

For Apple devices, wav, pList and SQLite file types were the focus within the report. The wav files store a user's voice commands when using Apple's Siri. The pList files store information about the Apple device settings and the vehicle's head unit identifiers. The SQLite files hold information on recent phone calls and text messages. For the Android devices Binarypb, XML, and SQLite file types were focused on to extract and parse. The Binarypb files store a user's voice commands using Android Assistant. The XML and SQLite files store information about the Androids device settings and the vehicle's head unit identifiers. The SQLite databases also store information on recent phone calls and text messages.

Algorithm 1. High-level Automation Algorithm

Requirements: Python3 and a TAR image of a device.
Input: iPhone or Android Mobile tar image, (optional) inputFile with keywords
Output: Apple Carplay & Android Auto artifacts and HTML Forensics Report
Select image type:
if *Apple option* **then**
| iPhone_artifact();
else if *Android option* **then**
| Android_artifact();

Specified image analysis
if *Wordlist option not set* **then**
| initial_hashing();   ▷ Obtain hashes of images for verification
| search_archive(default wordlist);   ▷ Searches archive for default values
| extract_found();   ▷ Extracts files located during search to folder
| analyze_files();   ▷ Parses data
| check_hashing();   ▷ Verification of hashes
| generate_report();   ▷ Generates HTML report detailing findings

else
| initial_hashing();   ▷ Obtain hashes of images for verification
| search_archive(user wordlist);   ▷ Searches archive for user values
| extract_found();   ▷ Extracts files located during search to folder
| check_hashing();   ▷ Verification of hashes
| generate_report();   ▷ Generates HTML report header

Usage: The tool is portable and designed to be used with the command line terminal (Fig. 10). The user may want to use either an Apple or an Android forensic disk image and there are two flags to denote these options. There is also an option to select a custom user created wordlist. Since the parsing/grouping analysis is specific to the default wordlist, if a user chooses their own wordlist an examination will not be done to produce an actual HTML report. Instead, the tool will only extract files or file paths that match words in the wordlist. When the tool is run, the case number and examiners name can be entered.

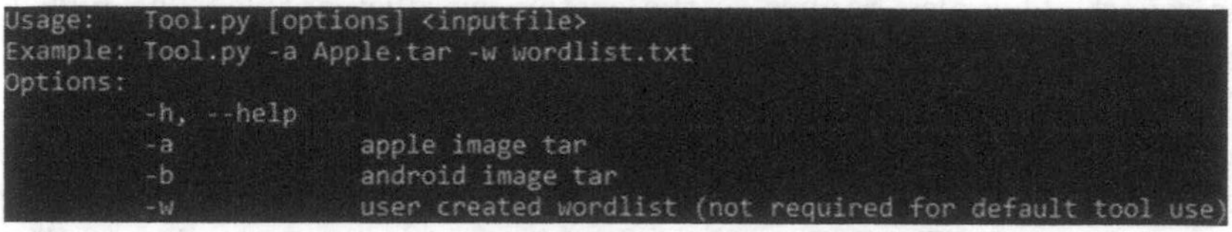

```
Usage:    Tool.py [options] <inputfile>
Example:  Tool.py -a Apple.tar -w wordlist.txt
Options:
          -h, --help
          -a              apple image tar
          -b              android image tar
          -w              user created wordlist (not required for default tool use)
```

Fig. 10. Tool's usage help menu

Output: The tool will organize the recovered files into a generated folder. The first part of the name being the timestamp the program ran and the second part being either "Apple" or "Android" depending on the type of image being used. The results of the analysis will output in table form. This will be displayed to the user on the console as well as an HTML report. Along with the data the output will contain the timestamp taken, examiner's name, and case number. Both the md5 and sha256 hashes will be taken of the image before and after its analysis to ensure changes were not made during processing. It is important to note that this report will only be generated when the default wordlists are used. Figures 11 and 12 in Appendix A demonstrate sample generated output from cases that have Apple and Android forensic images as input.

6 Conclusion and Future Work

The world is heavily reliant on vehicles and mobile phones now more than ever. Understanding the interaction between phones and vehicles can be important to investigators. While this research confirmed that Android Auto and Apple CarPlay only serve as projection methods for the applications that offer support for these features, we concluded there is still relevant information that can be acquired for use in crash investigations. By determining any vehicles that a device has been connected to, investigators can link suspects to cars left at crime scenes or to other investigations. Additionally, investigators can determine possible areas of distraction when examining the default home application settings for the Apple CarPlay or Android Auto interfaces. These areas of data provide a greater insight into how the phone was connected to the vehicle and the way in which a user interacts with it. The tool presented offers a fast and compact solution for obtaining the relevant information such as vehicles the device has been connected to, timestamps, text message and phone call histories, and other relevant information investigators may need.

Future work must be focused on maintaining the tool to adapt to how the applications' files change over time and as new features are added to the applications and the vehicle head units. Additionally, some examiners may not have imaging software that supports tar outputs, thus, support for additional forensic image file types would increase the usability of the tool.

Acknowledgement. This material is based upon work supported by the National Science Foundation under Grant Numbers 1900210 and 1921813. Any opinions, findings, and conclusions or recommendations expressed in this material are those of the author(s) and do not necessarily reflect the views of the National Science Foundation. Additionally, the authors would like to thank Mark Morton for his help in designing and building the stereo head unit.

A   Appendix - Sample Tool Reports

Android Auto Forensics Report

Filename: 001.01-Android
Case: 001.01
Timestamp: 05/07/2021-17:36:24 UTC
Examiner: John Doe
Before Analysis:
MD5: 5640adff284e0e4a1e678413049213a6
SHA256: 1af53c7495022a3a6f1f357c7ef84b00d6a8c7a7b6cffadd65829515e5b06134
After Analysis:
MD5: 5640adff284e0e4a1e678413049213a6 : Matched
SHA256: 1af53c7495022a3a6f1f357c7ef84b00d6a8c7a7b6cffadd65829515e5b06134 : Matched

Recent Android Assistant Voice Commands

File	User_commands	In Car
ce00000000000000000100.binarypb	['call Ann', 'Andrew']	No
ce00014866982783350581.binarypb	['call Andrew iPhone']	Yes
ce00022018206419064429.binarypb	['send a message', 'Andrew iPhone', 'good morning', 'send']	Yes

Android Auto

manufacturer	vehicle id	last connection	bluetooth address
Subaru	2856C13B5ACB8AD7	2021-02-20 19:02:09 UTC	28:56:C1:3B:5A:CB
Alpine	2C:1C:2E:AA:86:46	2021-02-19 19:48:56 UTC	18:6D:99:C1:F8:98

Contacts

Name	Number
IPhone 2.0	(203) 809-9848
Andrew IPhone	(203) 435-1505

Recent Phone Calls

timestamp_duration	type	contact	number
2021-02-20 19:15:25 - 2021-02-20 19:16:03 UTC	Incoming	IPhone 2.0	2038099848
2021-02-20 19:10:04 - 2021-02-20 19:10:31 UTC	Outgoing	IPhone 2.0	2038099848
2021-02-18 16:41:58 - 2021-02-18 16:42:56 UTC	Incoming	IPhone 2.0	2038099848

Recent SMS

timestamp	number	origin	text
2021-02-20 18:37:38 UTC	+12038099848	Received	It is a beautiful day! What are you up to today?
2021-02-20 18:34:18 UTC	2038099848	Sent	Good morning. It's a beautiful day.
2021-02-18 16:41:16 UTC	+12038099848	Received	Ok see you soon

Fig. 11. Sample android auto output

Apple Carplay Forensics Report

Filename: 001.01-Apple
Case: 001.01
Timestamp: 03/22/2021-19:48:55 UTC
Examiner: John Doe
Before Analysis:
MD5: 9fe5cfd3a3b7b89cd91b421112d4d86b
SHA256: df73ffd582c3121630531feeabadf2ce29315ba42c7791646bf47c8ff20cb071
After Analysis:
MD5: 9fe5cfd3a3b7b89cd91b421112d4d86b : Matched
SHA256: df73ffd582c3121630531feeabadf2ce29315ba42c7791646bf47c8ff20cb071 : Matched

Recent Siri Voice Commands

timestamp	command
2021-05-14 15:46:48.868510 UTC	play some music
2021-05-14 15:46:48.868510 UTC	send a message
2021-05-14 15:46:48.837267 UTC	set a timer for 3 minutes
2021-05-14 15:46:48.837267 UTC	how's the weather today

Carplay Pairings

Paired To	Apps
Alpine iLX-W650	['com.apple.mobilephone', 'com.apple.Music', 'com.apple.Maps', 'com.apple.MobileSMS', 'com.apple.cardisplay.nowplaying', 'com.apple.cardisplay.OEM', 'com.spotify.client', 'com.apple.podcasts', 'com.apple.iBooks']
SUBARU	['com.apple.mobilephone', 'com.apple.Maps', 'com.apple.MobileSMS', 'com.apple.cardisplay.nowplaying', 'com.apple.cardisplay.OEM', 'us.zoom.videomeetings', 'com.spotify.client', '', '']

Carplay Apps

Recent Apps	App Used Upon Disconnect
['com.apple.mobilephone', 'com.spotify.client', 'com.apple.Maps']	com.spotify.client

Contacts

Name	Number
Samsung 2.0	(203) 640-7875
Andrew Samsung	+12033935613

Recent Phone Calls

timestamp_duration	received	origin	address
2020-03-30 13:39:53 - 13:39:53 UTC	Missed Call	Outgoing	+12033935613
2020-03-30 13:39:06 - 13:39:06 UTC	Missed Call	Outgoing	+12033935613
2020-03-30 13:34:20 - 13:34:28 UTC		Outgoing	+12033935613

Recent SMS

time_received	time_read	origin	text
2021-02-20 18:37:35 UTC		Sent	It is a beautiful day! What are you up to today?
2021-02-20 18:34:50 UTC	2021-02-20 18:34:54 UTC	Recieved	Good morning. It's a beautiful day.
2021-02-18 19:08:37 UTC		Recieved	once you watch his clip you will totally Get it https://9o4m.s3.eu-west-3.amazonaws.com/c5uj.html

Fig. 12. Sample apple CarPlay output

B   Appendix - Table 2 - Relevant Artifacts

Table 2. Important data path directories and files found in disk

File ID	Path	OS	Description
1	/private/var/root/Library/Caches/locationd/cache.plist	iOS	Last Vehicle Connection Timestamps & vehicle name
2	XXX/Preferences/com.apple.carplay.plist	iOS	CarPlay Pairings & Protocols
3	XXX/Preferences/com.apple.celestial.plist	iOS	Volume Settings, Camera, Last App Displayed on CarPlay
4	XXX/Preferences/com.apple.springboard.plist	iOS	SpringBoard Settings & CarPlay Recently Used Apps
5	XXX/SpringBoard/"Car GUID"-CarPlayDesiredIconState.plist	iOS	User Display Icons Layout
6	XXX/SpringBoard/"Car GUID"-CarPlayDisplayIconState.plist	iOS	User Display Icons
7	XXX/Assistant/carplay_connect.timestamp	iOS	No Data but interesting
8	XXX/Assistant/carplay_success.timestamp	iOS	No Data but interesting
9	***/databases/carservicedata.db	Android	Accepted/Rejected Car Connections
10	***/shared_prefs/common.user.settings.xml	Android	User Settings
11	***shared_prefs/default.app.xml	Android	Default Screen App Layouts
12	***shared_prefs/auto.launch.prompt.xml	Android	Auto Launch Prompt Count for Vehicle Connections
13	***shared_prefs/carservice.xml	Android	Car Feature Settings

Base iOS Path: XXX = /private/var/mobile/Library — Base Android Path: *** = vol_vol20/data/com.google.android.projection.gearhead

References

1. National Highway Traffic Safety Administration: Overview of motor vehicle crashes in 2019. Traffic Safety Facts Research Note. Report No. DOT HS 813 060, December 2020. https://crashstats.nhtsa.dot.gov/Api/Public/ViewPublication/813060
2. Al Mutawa, N., Baggili, I., Marrington, A.: Forensic analysis of social networking applications on mobile devices. Digit. Investig. **9**, S24–S33 (2012)
3. Android: Android auto compatibility. https://www.android.com/auto/compatibility-/#compatibility-vehicles
4. Anglano, C., Canonico, M., Guazzone, M.: Forensic analysis of telegram messenger on android smartphones, September 2017. https://www.sciencedirect.com/science/article/abs/pii/S-1742287617301767
5. Bader, M., Baggili, I.: iphone 3GS forensics: logical analysis using apple itunes backup utility (2010)
6. Casey, P., Baggili, I., Yarramreddy, A.: Immersive virtual reality attacks and the human joystick. IEEE Trans. Dependable Secure Comput. 1 (2019)
7. CDC: Distracted driving, March 2021. https://www.cdc.gov/transportationsafety/distracted_driving/index.html
8. Clark, D.R., Meffert, C., Baggili, I., Breitinger, F.: Drop (drone open source parser) your drone: forensic analysis of the DJI phantom III. Digit. Investig. **22**, S3–S14 (2017)
9. Statista Research Department: Worldwide - connected car shipments, August 2021. https://www.statista.com/statistics/743400/estimated-connected-car-shipments-globally/
10. Dorai, G., Houshmand, S., Baggili, I.: I know what you did last summer: your smart home internet of things and your iphone forensically ratting you out. In: Proceedings of the 13th International Conference on Availability, Reliability and Security, ARES 2018. Association for Computing Machinery, New York (2018). https://doi.org/10.1145/3230833.3232814
11. Ebbers, S., Ising, F., Saatjohann, C., Schinzel, S.: Grand theft app: digital forensics of vehicle assistant apps. CoRR abs/2106.04974 (2021). https://arxiv.org/abs/2106.04974
12. Edwards, S., Mahalik, H.: They see us rollin'; they hatin': Forensics of iOS carplay and android auto. SANS DIFR Summit (2019). https://www.youtube.com/watch?v=IGhXsfZXL6g
13. iPhone FAQ, T.: What is the iphone iOS springboard? April 2015. https://www.iphonefaq.org/archives/971473
14. Graham, J.: Apple iphone again best tech seller of the year, thanks to the working-from-home trend, December 2020. https://www.usatoday.com/story/tech/2020/12/28/apple-iphone-best-selling-tech-device-year-work-home-helped/4048111001/
15. Grajeda, C., Sanchez, L., Baggili, I., Clark, D., Breitinger, F.: Experience constructing the artifact genome project (AGP): managing the domain's knowledge one artifact at a time. Digit. Investig. **26**, S47–S58 (2018)
16. guid.one: what is a GUID? http://guid.one/guid
17. Hamilton, D.: Corrupt iCloud data causes iOS springboard home screen crash (with fix!), April 2013. https://www.macobserver.com/tmo/article/corrupt-icloud-data-can-cause-ios-springboard-home-screen-crash

18. Hassenfeldt, C., Baig, S., Baggili, I., Zhang, X.: Map my murder. In: Proceedings of the 14th International Conference on Availability, Reliability and Security - ARES 2019 (2019). https://doi.org/10.1145/3339252.3340515
19. Hickman, J.: Ka-chow!!! Driving android auto (2019). https://thebinaryhick.blog/2019/01/30/ka-chow-driving-android-auto/
20. Hickman, J.: Ka-chow!!! Driving android auto. DFIR Review (2019). https://dfir.pubpub.org/pub/716tlra7/release/2
21. Hickman, J.: Ridin' with apple carplay, May 2019. https://thebinaryhick.blog/2019/05/08/ridin-with-apple-carplay/
22. Husain, M.I., Baggili, I., Sridhar, R.: A simple cost-effective framework for iphone forensic analysis. In: Baggili, I. (ed.) ICDF2C 2010. LNICST, vol. 53, pp. 27–37. Springer, Heidelberg (2011). https://doi.org/10.1007/978-3-642-19513-6_3
23. Iqbal, A., Alobaidli, H., Marrington, A., Baggili, I.: Amazon kindle fire HD forensics. In: Gladyshev, P., Marrington, A., Baggili, I. (eds.) ICDF2C 2013. LNICSSITE, vol. 132, pp. 39–50. Springer, Cham (2014). https://doi.org/10.1007/978-3-319-14289-0_4
24. Jacobs, D., Choo, K.K.R., Kechadi, M.T., Le-Khac, N.A.: Volkswagen car entertainment system forensics. In: 2017 IEEE Trustcom/BigDataSE/ICESS (2017). https://doi.org/10.1109/trustcom/bigdatase/icess.2017.302
25. Karpisek, F., Baggili, I., Breitinger, F.: Whatsapp network forensics: decrypting and understanding the whatsapp call signaling messages (2015)
26. Lacroix, J.: Vehicular infotainment forensics: collecting data and putting it into perspective (2017)
27. Lacroix, J., El-Khatib, K., Akalu, R.: Vehicular digital forensics: what does my vehicle know about me? In: DIVANet 2016: Proceedings of the 6th ACM Symposium on Development and Analysis of Intelligent Vehicular Networks and Applications, pp. 59–66 (2016)
28. Magnet Forensics: Magnet acquire (2020). https://www.magnetforensics.com/resources/magnet-acquire/
29. Mahalik, H.: How android bluetooth connections can determine if a driver had their hands on the wheel during an accident. DFIR Review (2020). https://dfir.pubpub.org/pub/6ysxvhvc/release/1
30. Mahr, A., Cichon, M., Mateo, S., Grajeda, C., Baggili, I.: Zooming into the pandemic! a forensic analysis of the zoom application. Forensic Sci. Int. Digit. Investig. **36**, 301107 (2021)
31. Mays, K.: Wireless apple carplay and android auto: Where are they now?: news from cars.com, December 2020. https://www.cars.com/articles/wireless-apple-carplay-and-android-auto-where-are-they-now-407297/
32. Moore, J., Baggili, I., Breitinger, F.: Find me if you can: mobile GPS mapping applications forensic analysis & SNAVP the open source, modular, extensible parser. J. Digit. Forensics Secur. Law **12**(1), 7 (2017)
33. Moore, J., Baggili, I., Marrington, A., Rodrigues, A.: Preliminary forensic analysis of the xbox one. Digit. Investig. **11**, S57–S65 (2014)
34. Statista: Samsung smartphone sales 2020, March 2021. https://www.statista.com/statistics/299144/samsung-smartphone-shipments-worldwide/
35. Walnycky, D., Baggili, I., Marrington, A., Moore, J., Breitinger, F.: Network and device forensic analysis of android social-messaging applications, August 2015. https://www.sciencedirect.com/science/article/pii/S1742-287615000547
36. Yarramreddy, A., Gromkowski, P., Baggili, I.: Forensic analysis of immersive virtual reality social applications: a primary account. In: 2018 IEEE Security and Privacy Workshops (SPW), pp. 186–196 (2018). https://doi.org/10.1109/SPW.2018.00034

37. Zhang, S., Wang, L.: Forensic analysis of social networking application on iOS devices. In: Sixth International Conference on Machine Vision (ICMV 2013), vol. 9067, p. 906715. International Society for Optics and Photonics (2013)
38. Zhang, X., Baggili, I., Breitinger, F.: Breaking into the vault: privacy, security and forensic analysis of android vault applications, August 2017. https://www.sciencedirect.com/science/article/pii/S01674-04817301529

Find My IoT Device – An Efficient and Effective Approximate Matching Algorithm to Identify IoT Traffic Flows

Thomas Göbel[1]([✉]), Frieder Uhlig[2], and Harald Baier[1]

[1] Research Institute CODE, Universität der Bundeswehr München,
Munich, Germany
{thomas.goebel,harald.baier}@unibw.de
[2] Technical University Darmstadt, Darmstadt, Germany
frieder.uhlig@stud.tu-darmstadt.de

Abstract. Internet of Things (IoT) devices has become more and more popular as they are limited in terms of resources, designed to serve only one specific purpose, and hence cheap. However, their profitability comes with the difficulty to patch them. Moreover, the IoT topology is often not well documented, too. Thus IoT devices form a popular attack vector in networks. Due to the widespread missing documentation vulnerable IoT network components must be quickly identified and located during an incident and a network forensic response. In this paper, we present a novel approach to efficiently and effectively identify a specific IoT device by using approximate matching applied to network traffic captures. Our algorithm is called `Cu-IoT` and is publicly available. `Cu-IoT` is superior to previous machine-learning approaches because it does not require feature extraction and a learning phase. Furthermore, in the case of 2 out of 3 datasets, `Cu-IoT` outperforms a hash-based competitor, too. We present an in-depth evaluation of `Cu-IoT` on different IoT datasets and achieve a classification performance of almost 100% in terms of accuracy, recall, and precision, respectively, for the first dataset (*Active Data*), and almost 99% accuracy and 84% precision and recall, respectively, for the second dataset (*Setup Data*), and almost 100% accuracy and 90% precision and recall, respectively, for the third dataset (*Idle Data*).

Keywords: Internet of Things (IoT) · IoT device · Device classification · Device identification · Network forensics · Network traffic fingerprinting · Approximate matching · Multi Resolution Hashing (MRSH) · Cuckoo filter

1 Introduction

Typically, Internet of Things (IoT) devices have limited security capabilities, because their hardware is often too weak and their software is often too focused on a specific use case. There have been many documented security flaws found

P. Gladyshev et al. (Eds.): ICDF2C 2021, LNICST 441, pp. 72–92, 2022.
https://doi.org/10.1007/978-3-031-06365-7_5

in the past on consumer IoT devices such as baby monitors, security cameras, doorbells or smart thermostats [31]. As patching is practically impossible, IoT devices are a primary target for attackers, especially considering that many of these devices have an extremely long lifetime (e.g., smart home devices such as a coffee maker or washing machine). After a successful attack, compromised IoT devices are often used as relays for further attacks. For instance, IoT devices have been used in the past to build large-scale botnets such as Mirai or Bashlite [18,21]. The malware targets unprotected IoT devices and turn them into bots. The attacker is then able to launch the actual attack (e.g., a distributed denial-of-service (DDoS) attack) by commanding all bots through a central Command-and-Control (C&C) server.

A well-known target of such an IoT-based DDoS attack was the website Krebs on Security[1]. According to Akamai (the digital security service provider of the website Krebs On Security), the DDoS attack was close to 620 Gbps (Gigabits of traffic per second). A second prominent victim of such an attack paradigm was the French WebHost and cloud service provider OHV[2], where the DDoS attack traffic peak using Mirai malware was 1.1 Tbps (Terabits of traffic per second). These massive attacks highlight the risks resulting from inadequate security mechanisms in IoT devices.

However, besides the missing patching ability and the ease with which the security mechanisms of IoT devices typically can be circumvented, the topology of networks comprising IoT network devices are often documented poorly [14]. Hence it is important to support the network forensic process to efficiently and effectively identify IoT devices in a network on base of their network traffic fingerprint. The findings of the survey [32] show that there is still a general lack of IoT forensics tools. The authors state that further research should focus on developing tools in IoT forensics to identify and acquire relevant IoT data.

In this paper, we show the efficiency and effectiveness of approximate matching to identify common IoT devices using their network captures. We present our algorithm Cu-IoT, which is an adapted version of the mrsh-cf algorithm [13] (the name Cu reminds on both the use of Cuckoo filters to represent the approximate hash and the task "See you" to find an IoT device). We show that Cu-IoT is superior to previous machine-learning approaches [1,20], because it does not require feature extraction and a learning phase. Furthermore, Cu-IoT outperforms its hash-based competitor LSIF [8], which is based on the Nilsimsa hash, in 2 out of 3 cases. We present an in-depth evaluation of Cu-IoT on three different datasets that include network traffic collected of a variety of different IoT devices. The captures include data of three different device states, specifically in their setup-phase [20], on an idle state [25], or on an active-state [9]. We achieve between 83% and almost 100% classification performance in terms of accuracy, recall, and precision, depending on the respective dataset. Our evaluation shows that the classification performance of Cu-IoT is at least as good as related work

---

[1] https://krebsonsecurity.com/2016/09/krebsonsecurity-hit-with-record-ddos/.

[2] https://arstechnica.com/information-technology/2016/09/botnet-of-145k-cameras-reportedly-deliver-internets-biggest-ddos-ever/.

algorithms without the computational overhead for feature extraction and model training typically associated with machine learning algorithms.

In detail the contributions of this paper are as follows:

1. Detailed presentation of our own approach Cu-IoT, an adapted version of the approximate matching algorithm mrsh-cf, to efficiently and effectively identify an IoT device based on the approximate hash of its network traffic capture.
2. Full publication of Cu-IoT including its source code to the digital forensics community via the website https://github.com/dasec/Cu-IoT.
3. Evaluation of Cu-IoT on three different IoT device traffic datasets containing many different IoT devices in different device states, such as setup-, idle-, and active-phase.
4. Comparison of Cu-IoT with its competitors from both the field of Locality-Sensitive Hashing, i.e., LSIF and TLSH, as well as from feature-extraction based approaches.

The remainder of this paper is organized as follows. Section 2 presents related work focusing on IoT device identification. Section 3 provides background information on approximate matching in general as well as information on the IoT device datasets used for our evaluation. Section 4 describes our selection process to find an appropriate classical approximate matching method for IoT device identification. Section 5 then shows how Cu-IoT works in detail. Moreover, this section presents the results of our experimental evaluation of Cu-IoT and provides a comparison with its competitors. Section 6 summarizes this paper and points to tasks for future work.

2   Related Work

In this section, we present related work to identify an IoT device based on its network capture. Identifying IoT devices based only on their MAC address and DHCP negotiation is an unreliable solution on a large scale, as stated by Sivanathan et al. [29], since these can be faked, spoofed, or changed easily. Therefore, many different approaches in natural language processing, multiclass machine learning classifiers, one-class classifiers, and neural networks have been published recently. We first turn to the class of machine learning-based approaches and then discuss an approximate hash-based method.

We first turn to machine learning approaches. Aksoy proposes in his Ph.D. thesis an IoT identification method called SysID [2], which was later published jointly with Gunes [1]. SysID can classify an IoT device using machine learning and genetic algorithms. SysID extracts features of submitted TCP/IP packet headers based on genetic algorithms and then applies machine learning algorithms (e.g., Decision Trees) to classify the device based on the protocol features selected by the genetic algorithm. Miettinen et al. published IoT Sentinel [20]. IoT Sentinel follows a similar approach to SysID, i.e. it uses packet headers for identification and subsequent security measures of IoT devices. It identifies device types by its device signature using a machine learning-based classification model. Another interesting approach was published by Bezerra et al., who proposed the Internet of Things Detection System (IoTDS) [4], which generates a device signature by extracting features from the device's CPU utilization and temperature, memory consumption, and the number of running tasks, meaning that it does not make use of network traffic data. This approach was evaluated using four different one-class classification algorithms (Elliptic Envelope (EE), Isolation Forest, Local Outlier Factor, and One-class Support Vector Machine (OSVM)). Other approaches, like that of Dong et al. [10] and Bai et al. [3], use neural networks for IoT traffic fingerprinting. Unlike these supervised machine learning algorithms, our approach Cu-IoT does not require feature extraction, training, and multiple adjustments of a machine learning model, which typically requires expert knowledge and high computational power.

On the other hand, an algorithm similar to established approximate matching methods was used to identify IoT devices. Charyyev and Gunes introduced Locality-Sensitive IoT Fingerprinting (LSIF) [9], which is described as a framework and makes use of the Nilsimsa algorithm [30] for the detection of devices in networks. Nilsimsa is a Locality-Sensitive Hashing algorithm originally proposed for spam detection. In contrast to our algorithm Cu-IoT, LSIF is not publicly available. Nevertheless, based on the datasets used in [9] and public implementation of Nilsimsa, we can show that our approach is superior to LSIF concerning run time efficiency and detection performance, respectively. Furthermore, our algorithm comes with a publicly available implementation.

3   Approximate Matching and IoT Device Datasets

This section introduces approximate matching algorithms and then turns to IoT device datasets, which we will use for our evaluation.

3.1   Approximate Matching Algorithms

Approximate matching is called fuzzy hashing or similarity hashing, too. It has already been used in a variety of contexts, its baseline, however, is to identify a known digital artefact from a given dataset automatically. A typical use case is the matching of binary data, such as documents, executables, memory dumps and network traffic, against the filter of the approximate matching algorithm. For example, approximate matching has been used for file recognition [5], for malware detection [16,24] and as a data loss prevention solution [12].

Compared to cryptographic hashes, fuzzy hashes are robust to changes in the input. While cryptographic hashes change entirely when a single bit is flipped (so-called avalanche effect), fuzzy hashes account for this change with a hash similar to the unchanged original.

Multi Resolution Similarity Hashing (MRSH) is a well-established 'classical' approximate matching algorithm. It comprises three steps: (i) selecting features from the input, (ii) generating a digest, and (iii) comparing that digest with another. During the comparison in the third step MRSH, as well as other approximate matching algorithms, rely on a specific filter to look up familiar hashes. Several iterations of the original MRSH algorithm [26] have been published in the past, such as mrsh-v2 [6], mrsh-net [7], and mrsh-hbft [17], all using different filters and the most efficient ones at the time of their release. The latest version of the MRSH algorithms is known as mrsh-cf [13]. It is equipped with a Cuckoo filter which is considered the fastest lookup filter and is superior to the Bloom filter of previous versions of the algorithm [11]. While other approximate matching algorithms are built to compare a specific file or data types, MRSH can compare data regardless of its context, but only based on its content at the byte-level, making it universally applicable.

Further, besides the previously mentioned MRSH family, other well-known approximate matching algorithms exist, such as the sdhash [27] algorithm and the de-facto standard algorithm ssdeep [15] which is known to be used on Google's VirusTotal platform together with Trendmicros' TLSH as a representative of Locality Sensitive Hashing algorithms.

3.2 IoT Device Datasets

We evaluate our algorithm Cu-IoT on three different publicly available datasets containing 22 IoT devices that are on an active state [9], 31 IoT devices that are being set up [20], and 81 IoT devices that are on an idle state [25], respectively. All three IoT datasets originate from the network activities of various illumination devices, smart plugs, doorbells, cameras, coffeemakers, radios, TVs, smart speakers (e.g., Amazon Echo, or Google Home), and other smart home appliances. The same devices from all three datasets that we used for our research are shown in Table 1.

The traffic flow data of the first IoT dataset [9] was collected over 20 days, i.e., it contains measurements for each of the 22 devices over a period of 20 days. The data within this dataset represents network traffic collected when users actively interacted with the IoT devices. Charyyev and Gunes assembled this dataset for testing their IoT traffic flow identification approach using Locality-Sensitive Hashes.

The second IoT dataset [20] represents the traffic emitted during the initial setup phase of 31 smart home IoT devices in a network of 27 different device types (4 types are represented by two devices each) and different vendors (e.g., D-Link, Edimax Plug, Hue, TP-Link Plug, etc.). However, only 23 of these devices have at least 20 recorded traces from their setup phase available. Therefore, we used precisely these 23 devices in our research.

The third IoT dataset [25] consists of 82 overall smart home IoT devices (including duplicates) that are in an idle state, i.e., when there is no interaction with the device. These IoT devices are deployed in two testbeds, one at the Northeastern University, US, and in the Imperial College London, UK. The dataset consists of traces for 56 unique devices (including two TP-Link Plugs for fair comparison). For 26 devices, these traces are available twice. However,

Table 1. List of IoT devices in the three datasets used in our evaluation.

#	First dataset [9] (Active data)	Second dataset [20] (Setup data)	Third dataset [25] (Idle data)
1	Chime_Doorbell	D-Link WiFi Day Camera DCS-930L	Allure Speaker with Alexa
2	D-Link_Cam936L	D-Link Door & Window sensor	Amazon Cloud Cam
3	Gosuna_LightBulb	D-Link Connected Home Hub DCH-G020	Amcrest Cam
4	Gosuna_Socket	D-Link HD IP Camera DCH-935L	Anova Sousvide
5	Goumia_Coffemaker	D-Link Smart plug DSP-W215	Apple TV
6	LaCrosse_AlarmClock	D-Link Water sensor DCH-S160	Behmor Brewer
7	Lumiman_Bulb600	D-Link Siren DCH-S220	Blink Cam
8	Lumiman_Bulb900	D-Link WiFi Motion sensor DCH-S150	Blink Hub
9	Lumiman_SmartPlug	Philips Hue Bridge model 3241312018	Bosiwo Cam
10	Minger_LightStrip	Philips Hue Light Switch PTM 215Z	D-Link Cam
11	Ocean_Radio	SmarterCoffee coffee machine SMC10-EU	D-Link Mov Sensor
12	Renpho_SmartPlug	Smarter iKettle 2.0 water kettle SMK20-EU	Echo Dot
13	Ring_Doorbell	TP-Link WiFi Smart plug HS110	Echo Plus
14	Smart_Lamp	TP-Link WiFi Smart plug HS100	Echo Spot
15	Smart_LightStrip	Edimax SP-1101W Smart Plug Switch	Fire TV
16	Tenvis_Cam	Edimax SP-2101W Smart Plug Switch	Flux Bulb
17	Wans_Cam	Fitbit Aria WiFi-enabled scale	GE Microwave
18	Wemo_SmartPlug	Homematic pluggable switch HMIP-PS	Google Home
19	itTiot_Cam	Osram Lightify Gateway	Google Home Mini
20	oossxx_SmartPlug	Ednet.living Starter kit power Gateway	Honeywell T-stat
21	tp-link_LightBulb	MAX! Cube LAN Gateway for MAX! Home automation sensors	Insteon Smart Hub
22	tp-link_SmartPlug	WeMo Link Lighting Bridge model F7C031vf	Invoke Speaker with Cortana
23		Withings Wireless Scale WS-30	Lefun Cam
24			LG TV
25			Lightify Smart Hub
26			Luohe Cam
27			Magichome Strip
28			Microseven Cam
29			Nest T-stat
30			Netatmo Weather
31			Philips Bulb
32			Philips Hue Smart Hub
33			Ring Doorbell
34			Roku TV
35			Samsung Dryer
36			Samsung Fridge
37			Samsung TV
38			Samsung Washer
39			Sengled Smart Hub
40			Smarter Brewer
41			Smarter iKettle
42			Smartthings Smart Hub
43			TP-Link Bulb
44			TP-Link Plug
45			TP-Link Plug 2
46			Wansview Cam
47			WeMo Plug
48			WiMaker Spy Camera
49			Wink 2 Smart Hub
50			Xiaomi Cam
51			Xiaomi Cleaner
52			Xiaomi Smart Hub
53			Xiaomi Rice Cooker
54			Xiaomi Strip
55			Yi Cam
56			ZModo Doorbell

we use them only once because using both capture sets would bias the results in favor of the 26 duplicate devices. The captures of the devices on idle state cover an average of 8 hours per night for one week for both labs, i.e., 112 per devices which results in roughly 6272 h in total of idle experiments.

4   Suitable Approximate Matching Algorithms

This section shows our selection process to find the best suitable classical approximate matching method for IoT device identification. We compare the mrsh approximate matching algorithm using three different representations of the approximate hashes (Bloom filter, Cuckoo filter, Hierarchical Bloom filter), ssdeep, and TLSH.

As a first general test, which approximate matching algorithm shows a promising performance, we used the so-called All-vs-All test, which sets a baseline for the algorithm's performance with data-at-rest. Every examined algorithm generates its filter of the well-known *t5-corpus* [28] in a first step. In a second step, the algorithm with this filter is given the complete *t5-corpus* (1.8 GB). The time it takes for every algorithm to generate the filter and to apply it onto every file in the corpus is shown in Table 2.

We assume that speed is a key indicator of the suitability of an algorithm for the quick identification of a specific IoT device in a large network. This is why we tested five of the prevalent algorithms for their performance when matching the *t5-corpus* with itself. Due to its good performance, we chose mrsh-cf for our further evaluation steps. Another candidate that performed well in our All-vs-All test is ssdeep. However, it was already shown that this approximate matching algorithm does not perform good with small fragments, i.e., it only performs well when fragments contain at least 25%–50% of the original file [22], which is why we did not consider ssdeep further. To analyze not only an algorithm of the MRSH family but also a maintained, efficient and optimized algorithm of the LSH family, we also consider the TLSH algorithm in our further evaluation. Further, to be able to compare the performance of these algorithms with the results of our competitor LSIF, which is based on Nilsimsa, we also use the Nilsimsa algorithm in our evaluation.

Table 2. Time for filter generation and application.

	mrsh-cf	mrsh-net	mrsh-hbft	ssdeep·	TLSH
Filter Gen. (in sec)	12.51	32.90	274	14.90	17.18
All-vs-All (in sec)	12.94	67.84	300	27.37	78.29

It is important to understand that TLSH is one of the best performing algorithms for similarity hashing out-of-the-box, but it has a certain limitation in the input of data to be compared. As far as we know, the algorithm can only compare "1 to n" but not "n to n" efficiently. A "1 to n" test with TLSH has to be through comparing the "1" consecutively with every "n," which means a slight loss in performance compared to the other algorithms. This is why the All-vs-All test in Table 2 is slightly slower for TLSH. In detail, this means you can give the algorithm the hashes of several files to compare them with one file. Also, reverse order works, i.e., compare the hash of one file vs. multiple files. Furthermore, it is possible to compare all files of a directory, each with each, by the algorithm. However, it is not intuitively possible to give the algorithm the hash values of several files and compare them with several other distinct files unless you do this outside the algorithm code in a script (as was done for our modified **All-vs-All** test in Table 2). However, as we will see in our further evaluations, TLSH is still a valid option for hashing IoT traces.

For a rough estimation of the performance of the most promising algorithms (mrsh-cf, TLSH, and Nilsimsa) with IoT device data, we performed a trivial test. We tested the algorithms' performance for the simple task of hashing a pcap-file and comparing it to itself. Note that Charyyev and Gunes [8] evaluated their LSIF method against TLSH in greater detail, but since LSIF is not open source we relied on a well documented Go version of the Nilsimsa algorithm for our initial performance tests[3]. The size of the input trace file used in our first test was 6160 KB.

Table 3. Naive benchmark for IoT device network capture.

	Hashing (in ms)	Comparison (in ms)
mrsh-cf	12	0.3
Nilsimsa	44	0.6
TLSH	10	0.2

Table 3 shows that TLSH performs best in this limited scenario. The algorithm's codebase is well maintained due to its use in commercial products, such as Google's VirusTotal, which accounts for its fast execution. mrsh-cf is positioned in the midfield, whereas Nilsimsa takes a comparatively long time to hash. It is important to note that Nilsimsa examines strings for their similarity, and input must first be converted into string form, whereas the other two algorithms can perform direct-byte-wise comparisons. Given the possible use of the algorithm in a highly automated network scenario, this point should be considered. mrsh-cf relies on SHA-1 and Murmurhash for hashing, which have a better runtime performance than Nilsimsa.

For further understanding, it is essential to know that Cu-IoT is fundamentally different from the other two algorithms in terms of its recognition of the

---

[3] https://github.com/tsaost/nilsimsa/.

difference between input and filter. Compared to other similarity hashing algorithms, both the `mrsh-cf` and the `Cu-IoT` algorithm based on it do not have a static similarity score. The result of a hash comparison performed by `mrsh-cf` is a comparison of the total chunks, that the input item has, and the number of chunks that where detected. This means that the results have to be interpreted as relational matching results. The file that was recognized for the most part also matches the previously unidentified input file with the utmost certainty.

Table 4. Performance metrics of `mrsh-cf` compared to `Nilsimsa` and `TLSH`.

	Model size	Feature size	Response time	Processing speed
`mrsh-cf`	16.4 MB	8.9 KB	97 ms	8.327×10^8 bits/s
`Nilsimsa`	8.24 MB	4.12 KB	112.0 ms	5.886×10^8 bits/s
`TLSH`	258 KB	0.129 KB	57 ms	0.3621×10^8 bits/s

The results of a second, more reliable test, are summarized in Table 4, where the processing costs for `mrsh-cf` compared to `Nilsimsa` (on which `LSIF` is based) are shown with regards to the model size (size of the signature database), feature size (size of the one hash generated from flow), the response time (the time required to identify the flow), and processing speed (speed of generating the digest of the flow). In this test, we assume that the filter consists of 20 devices with 100×10-min traces per device. Table 4 shows that `mrsh-cf` works more efficiently than its competitors. Crucial for the efficiency of any matching process is the underlying lookup mechanism. Assuming that `LSIF` works with a hash database that is not designed for lookup-efficiency, the time complexity is at worst $(O(n))$, while Cuckoo filters guarantee a time complexity of at worst $O(1)$. `TLSH` is very space-efficient, so its model size is only a fraction of that of its competitors. `TLSH`'s response time might be faster, but in terms of processing speed, `mrsh-cf` takes the lead. Based on `mrsh-cf`'s good performance and its flexibility, we chose to use it as the basis of our approach to IoT device fingerprinting, namely `Cu-IoT`.

5 Evaluation

In this section, we present our evaluation methodology as well as our evaluation setup for the three different datasets and show how `Cu-IoT` works in detail on our setup and the datasets. Moreover, this section presents the results of our experimental evaluation of `Cu-IoT` and provides a comparison with its competitors `TLSH` and `LSIF`.

5.1 Evaluation Setup of the First and Third Dataset

The first (*Active Data*) and third (*Idle Data*) dataset consist of relatively large device records that vary in size but were all collected over a more extended period compared to the second (*Setup Data*) dataset. As already mentioned in Sect. 3.2, the first dataset represents 20 days, and the third dataset represents approximately 2.33 days overall. However, the second dataset represents only a shorter time interval, namely the setup phase of each device, so the filter for the second dataset must be different, as shown in Sect. 5.2.

For the first and third datasets, we divide all traces into 10-min segments. One hundred of these segments are randomly selected and form the filter for a device, which is used to find the remaining traces of the device among all the others. The traces are ranked according to their detected proportion. For the first dataset, the apparatus for which a higher relative proportion was detected are ranked higher. This behavior is shown in Fig. 1. For the third dataset, the highest-ranking is given to those files from which the most "chunks" were found regardless of how much of the total trace this represents. The different approaches yield better results with the respective data (operational data - relational ranking; idle data - non-relational ranking).

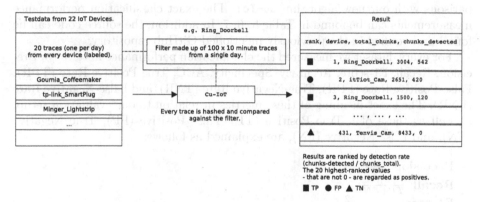

Fig. 1. Evaluation setup of the first and third dataset: Testrun with Ring_Doorbell as filter device. For the third dataset the calculation (chunks detected/chunks total) is ignored and results are ranked according to how much of their chunks were recognized overall.

5.2 Evaluation Setup of the Second Dataset

In contrast to the first (*Active Data*) and the third (*Idle Data*) dataset, the second dataset (*Setup Data*) consists of comparatively little data from the actual lifecycle of IoT devices. Since we are working with network captures of relatively similar but short duration, namely those of the setup phase, the tests with the algorithms on these data must also be handled differently than on the first and third datasets. For each device, 20 setup phases were recorded. One of them (i.e., 5% of the total data) serves as a filter to identify the other 19 among the traces of other devices. The results are ranked according to the devices from which the most chunks were found, and thus the same evaluation methodology is used for the third dataset. The top 19 traces are considered positives (either true positives or false positives), and the rest are considered negatives (either true negatives or false negatives).

5.3 Evaluation Methodology

In the following, we discuss the results of the devices traffic matching using `Cu-IoT` on three different datasets. We compare the results of `Cu-IoT` with the results of `LSIF` and `TLSH` for each of the three IoT datasets in Table 5, 6, 7, respectively. It is important to mention that based only on the information given in the paper by Charyyev and Gunes [8], it is not clear which exact implementation of the `Nilsimsa` algorithm was used for their `LSIF` approach. However we were in close contact with the original authors of `LSIF` and were able to rebuild Charyyev's algorithms in the Go programming language. Therefore, with the only exception of the `TLSH` values in Table 7[4], we were able to do our own measurements using our own implementation of `LSIF` using `Nilsimsa` and our own `TLSH` implementation. These measurements helped us to conduct fair comparisons with our new algorithm `Cu-IoT`. The exact classification performance measurements can be found in Table 5, 6, 7. In addition, the source code can be found and verified in the previously mentioned GitHub repository.

For every dataset we measured the classification performance in terms of Precision, Recall, F1-score, Accuracy, Specificity, AUC, True-Positive Rate (TPR), False-Positive Rate (FPR), True-Negative Rate (TNR), and False-Negative Rate (FNR). The exact meaning of these metrics in relation to our evaluation setup, as well as those of a True Positive (TP), False Positive (FP), True Negative (TN), and False Negative (FN), are explained as follows:

- **Precision:** $\frac{TP}{TP+FP}$
- **Recall:** $\frac{TP}{TP+FN}$
- **F1-score:** $\frac{2}{\frac{1}{Precision}+\frac{1}{Recall}}$
- **Accuracy:** $\frac{TP+TN}{TP+FP+TN+FN}$
- **Specificity:** $\frac{TN}{FP+TN}$
- **AUC:** $\frac{1}{2} \cdot (\frac{TP}{TP+FN} + \frac{TN}{TN+FP})$
- **True Positive (TP):** Is a trace in the top 20 ranked traces that belongs to the same device that is used for the filter.
- **False Positive (FP):** Is a trace in the top 20 ranked traces that does not belong to the same device that is used for the filter.
- **True Negative (TN):** Is a trace that is not ranked in the top 20 traces that does not belong to the same device that is used for the filter.
- **False Negative (FN):** Is a trace that is not ranked in the top 20 traces that belongs to the same device that is used for the filter
- **TPR:** $\frac{TP}{TP+FN}$
- **FPR:** $\frac{FP}{FP+TN}$

---

[4] Since in the case of `TLSH` on *Idle Data* without the original source code, we were not able to rebuild the data preprocessing and had to rely on the existing measurements.

- **TNR:** $\frac{TN}{TN+FP}$
- **FNR:** $\frac{FN}{FN+FP}$

5.4 Evaluation Results on Active Data

For the first dataset, i.e., based on the *active data*, in Table 5 we can see the slightly better performance of `Cu-IoT` compared to `LSIF` in almost all metrics. How much of a device's traces were matched on average given a filter from a device (a) or (b) (while (a) stands for the same device, or (b) stands for a different one) are presented in Fig. 2. Overall `Cu-IoT` matches the correct traces given a filter of the same device very accurately. However, it is noteworthy that devices, that emit little data during their active phase (e.g., *Goumia_Coffeemaker* or *tpLink_LightBulb*), still are well detected by `Cu-IoT`. This clearly distinguishes it from its competitor `LSIF`, where the authors claim that simple traffic flows may hurt the classification performance of `LSIF` [9]. Figure 2 represents the average recognition of a specific device given a filter from the same or another device. As we can see, the traces from the devices *Goumia_Coffeemaker* and *tpLink_LightBulb* are usually only detected to a small extent, but on average still identified correctly. The traces of these two devices are probably never completely recognized, as is the case with other devices with a low similarity score, too. Meaning that a trace of these two devices is never fully recognized in its entirety. Nevertheless, it is always correctly identified as belonging to the correct device. What we try to illustrate with this example is that `Cu-IoT` does not need to recognize a trace in its entirety to connect it to the correct device.

While the first dataset is quite heterogeneous and we achieve overall an average precision, recall, and accuracy of 97.5%, 98.4%, and 99.8% on *Active Data*, respectively, it remains to be validated how well the identification works on a more homogeneous dataset. However, in a larger dataset with more devices from the same vendor (as it is the case in the second dataset), which might also rely on similar transmission protocols, these devices might become indistinguishable for `Cu-IoT`. We will examine the algorithm's behaviour on such a homogeneous dataset in Sect. 5.5.

Table 5. Average evaluation results of `Cu-IoT` and `TLSH` compared to `LSIF` for the first dataset (*Active Data*).

	Precision	Recall	F1-Score	Accuracy	Specificity	AUC	TPR	FPR	TNR	FNR
`Cu-IoT`	97.5%	98.4%	97.9%	99.8%	99.9%	95.5%	98.4%	0.16%	99.8%	1.5%
`LSIF`	92.4%	90.8%	92.1%	99.8%	98.5%	95.2%	90.0%	0.03%	99.6%	0.1%
`TLSH`	90.1%	85.3%	85.2%	99.0%	99.2%	92.1%	84.8%	0.03%	99.6%	1.5%

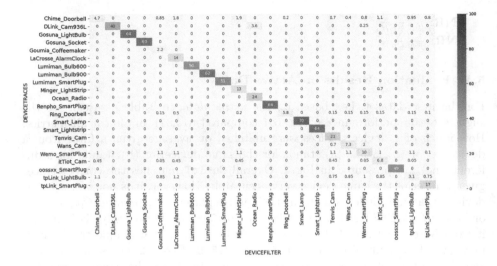

Fig. 2. Average similarity scores calculated by `Cu-IoT` for the 22 IoT devices of the first dataset (*Active Data*) (Relational similarity score on a scale from 0 to 100 (0 means that nothing was found and 100 means that the entire trace was found)).

5.5   Evaluation Results on Setup Data

We now evaluate the algorithms behavior in case of the *setup data*, i.e., on traffic captures of IoT devices performing their setup phase. For each device, we have 20 traces that represent the devices setup phase. The evaluation was done by using one measurement as the filter for the device and the other 19 traces together with all the traces from all the other devices form the test data so that the filter represents only 5% of the overall data from a respective device, and we have no bias with respect to a specific device. Our measurements for `Cu-IoT` are shown in Table 6 together with the corresponding measurements for `LSIF` by Charyyev and Gunes. However, it should be mentioned that according to [8], the filter for their `LSIF` algorithm consists of 14 traces instead of 1 (as in our case) for each device. Therefore, their filter represents 70% of the overall data for a single device, which is a huge difference from our approach. The reason we still chose to built the filter from a single trace rather than from 14 traces is that we can compare our results to those of feature extraction-based methods in terms of accuracy, as is depicted in Fig. 5.

However, despite these serious differences in the structure of the filter, our measurements for `Cu-IoT` and `TLSH` still hold up very well against `LSIF`. Overall the average precision, recall, and accuracy of `Cu-IoT` on *Setup Data* is 83.3%, 83.9%, and 98.6%, respectively.

Table 6. Average evaluation results of `Cu-IoT` compared to `LSIF` for the second dataset (*Setup Data*).

	Precision	Recall	F1-Score	Accuracy	Specificity	AUC	TPR	FPR	TNR	FNR
Cu-IoT	83.3%	83.9%	83.6%	98.6%	99.2%	91.6%	81.5%	0.8%	99.0%	18.5%
LSIF	80.2%	79.9%	80.5%	97.6%	99.1%	89.3%	87.9%	0.1%	98.0%	20.1%
TLSH	80.8%	80.8%	80.8%	98.5%	99.2%	89.9%	80.8%	0.9%	99.4%	19.3%

Figure 3 shows the average similarity score assigned by `Cu-IoT` to all devices, i.e. we can see the average matching results of the device traces given a certain filter. Figure 4 represents the confusions between filter-device and input-device. Especially the high confusion rate for devices from the vendor D-Link is striking. This is due to the number of similarities in the setup protocols of those devices. While for some devices, the setup phase might accumulate only a few kilobytes, for others (especially those from the vendor D-Link) the setup phase might produce a few hundred kilobytes of traces. However, suppose we pay attention to the highest similarity scores per device. In that case, almost all of them are correctly identified on average, with the only exception of the *D-LinkSwitch*, which was confused with the devices *D-LinkSiren* and *D-LinkWaterSensor*, which have a higher similarity score.

Please note, that the results in Fig. 3 cannot be derived directly from the values in Table 6. The table shows how many traces of the devices were detected correctly on average, while the graph shows how much of them was detected on average.

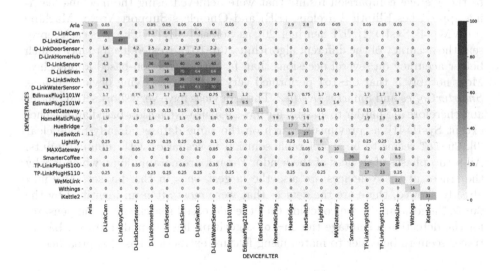

Fig. 3. Average similarity scores calculated by `Cu-IoT` for the 23 IoT devices of the second dataset (*Setup Data*) (Relational similarity score on a scale from 0 to 100 (0 means that nothing was found and 100 means that the entire trace was found)).

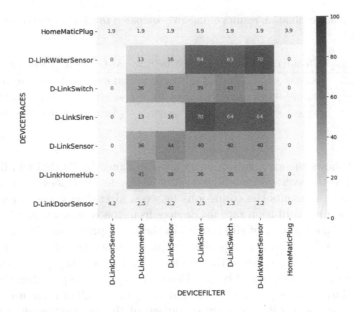

Fig. 4. Average `Cu-IoT` similarity scores for IoT devices in the second dataset (*Setup Data*) that were most often misidentified (Relational similarity score on a scale from 0 to 100 (0 means that nothing was found and 100 means that the entire trace was found)).

Figure 5 shows the relation of `Cu-IoT`'s device matching results compared to the average comparison results that were achieved using the machine learning approaches Elliptic Envelope (EE) and One-class Support Vector Machine (OSVM) [4], SysID [1], IoT Sentinel [20], as well as LSIF [9]. The bars each represent the accuracy of the different algorithms. `Cu-IoT` revealed itself to have much better accuracy on several occasions than feature extraction-based approaches. Most notably is that `Cu-IoT` performed very well at classifying devices such as *SmarterCoffee* and Smarter *iKettle2*. These devices have very short setup phases and therefore are harder to classify for most feature extraction-based approaches except SysID [1], as previous research on the same dataset already made clear [9]. `Cu-IoT` seems to be a preferable solution in scenarios with minimal inputs. All setup phases of devices of the vendor D-Link are notably long, which is why the traces of these devices are also the largest ones in the dataset. As Fig. 4 already showed, these are the devices that were most often misidentified by the `Cu-IoT` algorithm. So we conclude that the increased search space compensates for the detection advantage the `Cu-IoT` algorithm has at smaller traces. Larger traces seem to be easier to match using feature extraction-based approaches.

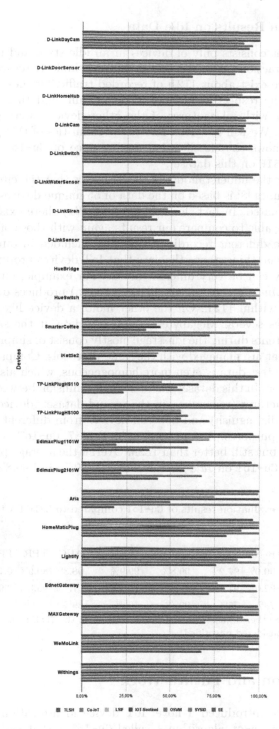

Fig. 5. Accuracy achieved per device on the second dataset (*Setup Data*). The metrics for EE, OSVM and SYSID in this chart are taken from the work of Charyyev et al. [9]. All other metrics are based on the measurements of our own algorithms.

5.6   Evaluation Results on Idle Data

The third dataset consists only of devices in an idle state and thus is isolated from human interactions. This test was performed similarly to our first test. For each device, there exist about 112 h of recorded traffic. Of these, 100 × 10 min were taken for the respective filter of an algorithm, and then the remaining capture, together with all captures of the other devices, were evaluated as a test environment. We will now look into the peculiarities of this particular test. Again, Table 7 shows the classification performance of Cu-IoT in comparison with TLSH and LSIF on this dataset.

Important for the understanding of the results is that the cited results from Charyyev and Gunes [8] is based on the data of 55 unique devices, but 56 device results were evaluated. In fact, for the *TP-Link Plug* there exist two different recordings. To be able to compare our results again with those of Charyyev and Gunes, these two different recordings were also included in our evaluation of Cu-IoT. The special thing about the data that IoT devices produce in their idle state is that they can be very different in size. For example, on the one hand, a device like *D-Link Camera* (a surveillance camera) produces only a few bytes of network data within 112 h. On the other hand, a device like the *Wansview Webcam* produces several Megabytes of network data at the same time. The transmission contents during the idle stage mostly consist of simple heartbeats or update checks that are managed with the same protocols. Compared to the first two datasets, the test data is even more homogeneous, which also increases the chance of confusion. In this dataset, there is much confusion between devices from the same manufacturer (remember, in the second dataset, devices from D-Link were difficult to distinguish) and between devices from different manufacturers and for different purposes. As can be seen in Table 7, Cu-IoT performs slightly worse than LSIF but still better than TLSH. Overall the average precision, recall, and accuracy of Cu-IoT on *Idle Data* is 90.1%, 90.0%, and 99.8%, respectively.

Table 7. Average evaluation results of Cu-IoT compared to LSIF for the third dataset (*Idle Data*).

	Precision	Recall	F1-Score	Accuracy	Specificity	AUC	TPR	FPR	TNR	FNR
Cu-IoT	90.1%	90.0%	97.2%	99.8%	99.9%	98.3%	89.9%	0.1%	99.0%	9.7%
LSIF	91.5%	92.0%	91.1%	99.8%	99.2%	97.4%	95.3%	0.9%	99.0%	4.1%
TLSH[a]	83%	78%	75%	99%	100%	89%	–	–	–	–

[a] In contrast to the other datasets, in the case of *Idle Data* the TLSH results are taken from [8] and must be considered unverified.

6   Conclusion and Future Work

In this paper, we introduced a novel IoT device identification method using a re-engineered mrsh-cf algorithm – called Cu-IoT – that can be applied on arbitrary IoT devices network captures. Unlike other existing approaches, our approach uses approximate matching and therefore does not require multiple iterations of feature extraction from traffic, tuning of model parameters, and re-training of the model. To the best of our knowledge, during the time of writing, Cu-IoT shares these benefits with only two other algorithms, which both rely on Locality-Sensitive Hashing instead of Multi-Resolution Similarity Hashing. Our evaluations have shown that Cu-IoT performs significantly better than its competitors on *Active Data* with a precision and recall of 97.5% and 98.4%, respectively (as shown in Sect. 5.4), and reaches higher precision (83.3%), higher recall (83.9%) and higher accuracy (98.6%) on *Setup Data* (as shown in Sect. 5.5). However, on *Idle Data* (as shown in Sect. 5.6), Cu-IoT performs slightly worse than LSIF in terms of precision (90.1% vs. 91.5%) and recall (90.0% vs. 92.0%), and equally in terms of accuracy (99.8% vs. 99.8%). All in all, Cu-IoT can keep up well with LSIF, while the latter - and thus also Cu-IoT - is competitive with typical machine learning approaches. Our work showed for the first time that a well-established 'classical' approximate matching algorithm applies to the task of IoT device identification. This was validated using three different data sets consisting of many different IoT devices. Therefore, the publicly available Cu-IoT algorithm is capable of supporting the network forensics process to efficiently and effectively identify IoT devices in a network during an incident. Since IoT devices pose a poor degree of security, tools like Cu-IoT, that focus on IoT forensics, in particular, will become increasingly important in the future.

Any future work could look into things like cross-testbed identification, since there are standard devices in the datasets used, and the issue of device confusion in case of the same vendor, as it is manifested in Subsect. 5.2, through the means of common block elimination. This technique could potentially benefit the precision and recall of the Cu-IoT with significant homogeneous traces originating from devices with very similar protocols. As was shown in Sect. 5, Cu-IoT performs well with small heterogeneous device traces but struggles with larger, more homogeneous ones. Through most common-block elimination, the larger traces can be reduced to smaller ones that could be easier to recognize.

In the future, we would like to perform the analysis using Cu-IoT on further, preferably larger, IoT datasets and examine the applicability of other prominent approximate matching algorithms for network device identification. We are optimistic that future research on IoT device identification can be enhanced by novel hash algorithms and more comprehensive test datasets. Additionally, we want to analyze how to approximate matching can be used to detect anomalies in the behavior of IoT devices and thus prevent prevalent attacks such as botnets or DDoS. It is feasible to extend Cu-IoT to reliably detect such anomalies since the signature generated by an anomalous traffic flow significantly differs from the signature of the benign traffic stored in its filter.

References

1. Aksoy, A., Gunes, M.H.: Automated IoT device identification using network traffic. In: Proceedings of the IEEE International Conference on Communications (ICC), Shanghai, China, pp. 1–7 (2019)
2. Aksoy, A.: Network traffic fingerprinting using machine learning and evolutionary computing automated IoT device identification using network traffic. Ph.D. thesis, University of Nevada (2019)
3. Bai, L., Yao, L., Kanhere, S.S., Wang, X., Yang, Z.: Automatic device classification from network traffic streams of internet of things. In: 2018 IEEE 43rd Conference on Local Computer Networks (LCN), pp. 1–9. IEEE, October 2018
4. Bezerra, V.H., da Costa, V.G.T., Barbon Junior, S., Miani, R.S., Zarpelão, B.B.: IoTDS: a one-class classification approach to detect botnets in internet of things devices. Sensors **19**, 3188 (2019). https://doi.org/10.3390/s19143188
5. Bjelland, P., Franke, K., Arnes, A.: Practical use of approximate hash-based matching in digital investigations. Digit. Investig. **11**(S1), 18–26 (2014)
6. Breitinger, F., Baier, H.: Similarity preserving hashing: eligible properties and a new algorithm. In: Rogers, M., Seigfried-Spellar, K.C. (eds.) ICDF2C 2012. LNICST, vol. 114, pp. 167–182. Springer, Heidelberg (2013). https://doi.org/10.1007/978-3-642-39891-9_11
7. Breitinger, F., Baggili, I.: File detection on network traffic using approximate matching. J. Digit. Forensics Secur. Law **9**(2), 23–36 (2014)
8. Charyyev, B., Gunes, M.H.: Locality-sensitive IoT network traffic fingerprinting for device identification. IEEE Internet Things J. **8**(3), 1272–1281 (2021). https://doi.org/10.1109/JIOT.2020.3035087
9. Charyyev, B., Gunes, M.H.: IoT traffic flow identification using locality sensitive hashes. In: ICC 2020–2020 IEEE International Conference on Communications (ICC), pp. 1–6 (2020). https://doi.org/10.1109/ICC40277.2020.9148743
10. Dong, S., Li, Z., Tang, D., Chen, J., Sun, M., Zhang, K.: Your smart home can't keep a secret: towards automated fingerprinting of IoT traffic with neural networks. arXiv preprint arXiv:1909.00104 (2019)
11. Fan, B., Andersen, D.G., Kaminsky, M., Mitzenmacher, M.D.: Cuckoo filter: practically better than bloom. In: Proceedings of the 10th ACM International on Conference on emerging Networking Experiments and Technologies (CoNEXT 2014), pp. 75–88. Association for Computing Machinery, New York (2014). https://doi.org/10.1145/2674005.2674994
12. Göbel, T., Uhlig, F., Baier, H.: Empirical evaluation of network traffic analysis using approximate matching algorithms. In: Peterson, G., Shenoi, S. (eds.) Advances in Digital Forensics XVII. Springer, Cham (2021). https://doi.org/10.1007/978-3-030-88381-2
13. Gupta, V., Breitinger, F.: How cuckoo filter can improve existing approximate matching techniques. In: James, J.I., Breitinger, F. (eds.) ICDF2C 2015. LNICST, vol. 157, pp. 39–52. Springer, Cham (2015). https://doi.org/10.1007/978-3-319-25512-5_4
14. Hossain, M.M., Fotouhi, M., Hasan, R.: Towards an analysis of security issues, challenges, and open problems in the internet of things. In: 2015 IEEE World Congress on Services, pp. 21–28 (2015). https://doi.org/10.1109/SERVICES.2015.12

15. Kornblum, J.: Identifying almost identical files using context triggered piecewise hashing. In: Proceedings of the Sixth Annual Digital Forensic Research Workshop, vol. 3, pp. 91–97 (2006)
16. Liebler, L., Baier, H.: Towards exact and inexact approximate matching of executable binaries. Digit. Investig. **28**, 12–21 (2019)
17. Lillis, D., Breitinger, F., Scanlon, M.: Expediting MRSH-v2 approximate matching with hierarchical bloom filter trees. In: Matoušek, P., Schmiedecker, M. (eds.) ICDF2C 2017. LNICST, vol. 216, pp. 144–157. Springer, Cham (2018). https://doi.org/10.1007/978-3-319-73697-6_11
18. Marzano, A., et al.: The evolution of Bashlite and Mirai IoT botnets. In: IEEE Symposium on Computers and Communications (ISCC) 2018, pp. 00813–00818 (2018). https://doi.org/10.1109/ISCC.2018.8538636
19. Oliver, J., Cheng, C., Chen, Y.: TLSH - a locality sensitive hash. In: Proceedings of the Fourth Cybercrime and Trustworthy Computing Workshop, pp. 7–13 (2013)
20. Miettinen, M., Marchal, S., Hafeez, I., Asokan, N., Sadeghi, A., Tarkoma, S.: IoT SENTINEL: automated device-type identification for security enforcement in IoT. In: Proceedings of the IEEE 37th International Conference on Distributed Computing Systems Workshops (ICDCS), pp. 2177–2184 (2017)
21. Kolias, C., Kambourakis, G., Stavrou, A., Voas, J.: DDoS in the IoT: Mirai and other botnets. Computer **50**(7), 80–84 (2017)
22. Lee, A., Atkison, T.: A comparison of fuzzy hashes: evaluation, guidelines, and future suggestions. In: Proceedings of the SouthEast Conference, pp. 18–25 (2017)
23. Meidan, Y., et al.: N-BaIoT-network-based detection of IoT botnet attacks using deep autoencoders. IEEE Perv. Comput. **17**(3), 12–22 (2018). https://doi.org/10.1109/MPRV.2018.03367731
24. Pagani, F., Dell'Amico, M., Balzarotti, D.: Beyond precision and recall: understanding uses (and misuses) of similarity hashes in binary analysis. In: Proceedings of the Eighth ACM Conference on Data and Application Security and Privacy, pp. 354–365. ACM (2018)
25. Ren, J., Dubois, D.J., Choffnes, D., Mandalari, A.M., Kolcun, R., Haddadi, H.: Information exposure from consumer IoT devices: a multidimensional, network-informed measurement approach. In: Proceedings of the Internet Measurement Conference (IMC 2019), pp. 267–279. Association for Computing Machinery, New York (2019). https://doi.org/10.1145/3355369.3355577
26. Roussev, V., Richard, G.G., Marziale, L.: Multi-resolution similarity hashing. Digit. Investig. **4**, 105–113 (2007)
27. Roussev, V.: Data fingerprinting with similarity digests. In: Chow, K.-P., Shenoi, S. (eds.) DigitalForensics 2010. IAICT, vol. 337, pp. 207–226. Springer, Heidelberg (2010). https://doi.org/10.1007/978-3-642-15506-2_15
28. Roussev, V.: An evaluation of forensic similarity hashes. Digit. Investig. **8**, 34–41 (2011)
29. Sivanathan, A., et al.: Classifying IoT devices in smart environments using network traffic characteristics. IEEE Trans. Mob. Comput. **18**(8), 1745–1759 (2018)
30. Damiani, E., De Capitani di Vimercati, S., Paraboschi, S., Samarati, P.: An open digest-based technique for spam detection. In: Proceedings of the Seventeenth International Conference on Parallel and Distributed Computing Systems, pp. 559–564 (2004)

31. Shwartz, O., Mathov, Y., Bohadana, M., Elovici, Y., Oren, Y.: Opening Pandora's box: effective techniques for reverse engineering IoT devices. In: Eisenbarth, T., Teglia, Y. (eds.) CARDIS 2017. LNCS, vol. 10728, pp. 1–21. Springer, Cham (2018). https://doi.org/10.1007/978-3-319-75208-2_1
32. Wu, T., Breitinger, F., Baggili, I.: IoT ignorance is digital forensics research bliss: a survey to understand IoT forensics definitions, challenges and future research directions. In: Proceedings of the 14th International Conference on Availability, Reliability and Security (ARES 2019), Article 46, pp. 1–15. Association for Computing Machinery, New York (2019). https://doi.org/10.1145/3339252.3340504

Accessing Secure Data on Android Through Application Analysis

Richard Buurke and Nhien-An Le-Khac(✉)

University College Dublin, Belfield, Dublin 4, Ireland
richard.buurke@ucdconnect.ie, an.lekhac@ucd.ie

Abstract. Acquisition of non-volatile or volatile memory is traditionally the first step in the forensic process. This approach has been widely used in mobile device investigations. However, with the advance of encryption techniques applied by default in mobile operating systems, data access is more restrictive. Investigators normally do not have administrative control over the device, which requires them to employ various techniques to acquire system data. On the other hand, application analysis is widely used in malware investigations to understand how malicious software operates without having access to the original source code. Hence, in this paper, we propose a new approach to access secure data on Android devices, based on techniques used in the field of malware analysis. Information gained through our proposed process can be used to identify implementation flaws and acquire/decode stored data. To evaluate the applicability of our approach, we analysed three applications that stored encrypted user notes. In two of the applications we identified implementation flaws that enabled acquisition of data without requiring elevated privileges.

Keywords: Android · Mobile device forensics · Application analysis · Secure data acquisition

1 Introduction

Mobile devices are becoming an increasingly important source of information in criminal investigations. These devices potentially store information about contacts, call logs, location history, images and other data which might be relevant to an investigation. Current forensic solutions aimed at mobile devices are primarily focused on post-mortem investigations. Often they are able to create a physical image of a device but are unable to process encrypted data from unsupported applications. This problem is quickly becoming more relevant since the use of encryption has become more widespread. In literature, most data acquisition techniques have their caveats in a practical environment. They are for example difficult to execute, require elevated privileges or are device specific [9, 24, 28, 29].

Besides, application analysis is widely used in the domain of malware analysis to understand how malicious software operates without having access to the original source code. It uses a combination of behavioural and static analysis to

© ICST Institute for Computer Sciences, Social Informatics and Telecommunications Engineering 2022
Published by Springer Nature Switzerland AG 2022. All Rights Reserved
P. Gladyshev et al. (Eds.): ICDF2C 2021, LNICST 441, pp. 93–108, 2022.
https://doi.org/10.1007/978-3-031-06365-7_6

map the characteristics of an application. Therefore, in this paper, we propose a new approach based on this technique to assist the investigator acquire data where traditional solutions are unable to. Application analysis is relatively easily to perform, will work cross-platform and does not require elevated privileges. It also seems to be practically viable since improper API usage is seen as a common security threat on mobile operating systems [8,14,18,21]. In this study, we have limited the scope of our research to the Android operating system. The general approach should however be transferable to other mobile operating systems.

To evaluate the applicability of our approach, we analysed three applications that focus on protecting user's data. In two of the applications we identified implementation flaws that enabled acquisition of data without requiring elevated privileges. We also show that our methodology can be applied to a wide range of applications. By looking at our experimental results, combined with the available literature, we expect other applications to exhibit the same behaviour. We have proven that by analysing individual applications it is possible to acquire application data without the need for elevated privileges.

The main contribution of this research can be listed as follows:

- We performed an extensive literature survey to identify Android security mechanisms and various data acquisition techniques.
- We propose an application-analysis based approach for data acquisition. Our approach can be used by forensic investigators to get a global understanding of the application features and identify possible opportunities for data acquisition.
- We evaluate our approach to demonstrate its feasibility with three popular applications that focus on securely storing user notes: Safe Notes, Private Notepad and Secure Notes.

The rest of this paper is organised as follows: Sect. 2 provides background information on related work on Android data acquisition. Section 3 describes our approach for Android application analysis, then we present our experiment results in Sect. 4. We discuss our results in Sect. 5 and finally Sect. 6 concludes this paper.

2   Related Work

Smartphone evidence acquisition is a challenge for investigators [1]. In this section, we review various methods for data acquisition on Android devices. The results of our review and comparison of the various methods are summarised in Table 1, where the first column lists relevant characteristics used to compare these methods.

Binary exploitation and CPU specific vulnerabilities can lead to full control over the device or escalation of privileges [7,22]. However these attacks are difficult to perform and binary exploitation depends on specific versions of software to be present on the device. The same is true for exploiting the Trusted Execution Environment (TEE), although common exploit mitigations are often missing in the secure world [3]. Another obstacle is the lack of publicly available basic tools such as a debugger for the secure world.

A cold boot attack requires flashing a custom recovery ROM onto the device and therefore needs an unlocked bootloader [25]. A copy of volatile memory can be created after quickly rebooting the device. Current versions of Android utilise the TEE for cryptographic operations, which makes it more complex to recover the disk encryption key [19]. Several other mitigations against cold boot attacks have been created but these are not currently implemented [13,20,30].

An evil maid attack is less difficult to execute and can also result in full control over the device. However this technique, just as the cold boot attack, requires an unlocked bootloader [12]. This makes it unlikely to be applicable in most real world scenarios. Using a duplicate device to trick the suspect into entering their code is still viable. Although it can also only be applied to devices for which the bootloader can be unlocked since a custom ROM is still required.

In the last few years we have seen various CPU specific attacks such as Spectre [17], DRAMMER [27] and TRRespass [11]. The aforementioned techniques can be leveraged to alter or leak information from volatile memory and affect the ARM architecture, which is used in the vast majority of smartphones [16]. This category of vulnerabilities enables the attacker to read or write arbitrary memory without the need for elevated privileges or existing software vulnerabilities. The lack of standardised tools and the required specialised skills make these techniques difficult to employ for the average forensic investigators.

Memory forensics has the most potential for gathering sensitive information, such as decrypted data and login credentials [4,6]. But it almost always requires elevated privileges on the device which must be obtained through exploitation [28]. Abusing the update protocol of a device can circumvent this restriction [29]. This technique requires a device of a specific brand. Also these vulnerabilities might be patched and public tools are unavailable. Migrating data using vendor specific tools can help to acquire a partial memory dump [9]. However it will not be possible to acquire data which only exists in volatile memory on the suspects device.

Network traffic analysis can be used to identify servers hosting information of interest. This information can then be acquired through legal procedures. In the vast majority of cases network traffic will be encrypted [15]. This will make it impossible to capture the plain text contents of packets without having elevated privileges on the device [10]. If the target application uses unencrypted connections, the investigator can acquire the data exchanged between the client and the server. Encrypted connections however still provide the investigator with relevant meta-data [6].

Authors in [2] proposed a wireless extraction of data for Android devices. However, it's only used for the logical extraction of the data from the Android file-system.

Table 1. Comparison of acquisition techniques (✓: Yes, X: No) - R: Required to apply this method; E: This method enables the investigator to do the following; P: A property of this method

		Improper API usage exploitation	Binary exploitation	TEE exploitation	Memory forensics			Update protocols	Data Migration	Cold boot attack	CPU Vulnerabilities		Evil maid attack		Network forensics
					Direct access	Loadable kernel modules	Kernel code injection				Fault induction	Branch prediction	Target device	Duplicate device	
R	Elevated privileges	X	X	X	✓	✓	✓	X	X	X	X	X	X	X	✓[a]
R	Unlocked bootloader	X	X	X	X	X	X	X	X	✓	X	X	✓	✓	X
R	Local code execution	X	✓[b]	✓	✓	✓	✓	X	X	X	✓	✓	X	X	X
R	Custom ROM	X	X	X	X	X	X	X	X	✓	X	X	✓	✓	X
E	Information leakage	✓	✓	✓	✓	✓	✓	✓	✓	✓	✓	✓	✓	✓	✓
E	Full control	X	✓[c]	✓[c]	N/A	N/A	N/A	X	X	X	✓[c]	✓[c]	✓[d]	✓[d]	X
E	Acq. non-volatile memory	Partial	✓[c]	✓[c]	N/A	N/A	N/A	X	X	✓[d]	✓[c]	✓[c]	✓[d]	✓[d]	Partial
E	Acq. volatile memory	Partial	✓[c]	✓[c]	✓	✓	✓	✓	Partial	✓	✓[c]	✓[c]	X	X	Partial
P	Difficulty	Med	High	High	Low	Med	Med	High	Low	Med	High	High	Med	Med	Low
P	Cross-platform	✓	X	X	✓	X	X	X	X	X	✓	✓	X	X	✓
P	Tools available	✓	✓	X	✓	✓	✓	X	✓	✓	✓	✓	✓	✓	✓

[a] Only required for decrypting encrypted network traffic on the target device
[b] Some exploits can be triggered remotely
[c] Different types of exploits exist, ranging from information leaks to full control over the target device
[d] Since the bootloader is unlocked, the investigator has full access to the device when the password is obtained

Improper API usage is seen as the number one category of vulnerabilities on the Android platform by the OWASP community [21]. By analysing applications and identifying these vulnerabilities it is possible to access sensitive information without the need for elevated privileges. This technique also works cross-platform and is less difficult to execute than techniques that rely on the binary exploitation. Application analysis generally will not result in local code executing or full control over the device and is usually limited to a single application.

3   Proposed Approach

To detect improper API usage in Android applications we propose an application analysis approach consisting of four phases (Fig. 1). Our approach combines concepts from the forensic field (repeatability) with concepts from the field of malware analysis (behavioural and static analysis). Its four phases can be summarised as in Table 2.

Table 2. Four phases for detecting improper API usage

Phase 1: Preparation	Reset the test device to a pre-defined state and check time and date settings for any deviations
Phase 2: Installation	Install the target application and start a network capture using a proxy or by hooking networking functions.
Phase 3: Behavioural analysis	Interact with the target application and collect relevant artifacts for later analysis. Capture volatile memory of the target process during it's lifetime. Copy the artifacts and base APK file to the investigative machine.
Phase 4: Static analysis	Examine phase 3 preliminary results and identify Points of Interests (POIs). Use the checklist (Table 3) to identify additional POIs in the manifest file and code base.
Repeat	If there are uncovered scenarios then hook any functions of interest and restart the network capture and behavioural analysis

The investigator should have access to a test device, which supports the target application. The test device should be rooted that usually requires that the bootloader can be unlocked. The device would then be configured to include any required tools (e.g. Frida/gdbserver/LiME) and self-signed CA certificates. A bit-for-bit image of the device can be created using a custom recovery ROM. The device should be reverted to an initial state before analysis commences by re-flashing the backup image. This ensures repeatability of the experiment. The target application is installed in phase two and networking interception techniques are employed to capture any network (meta-)data.

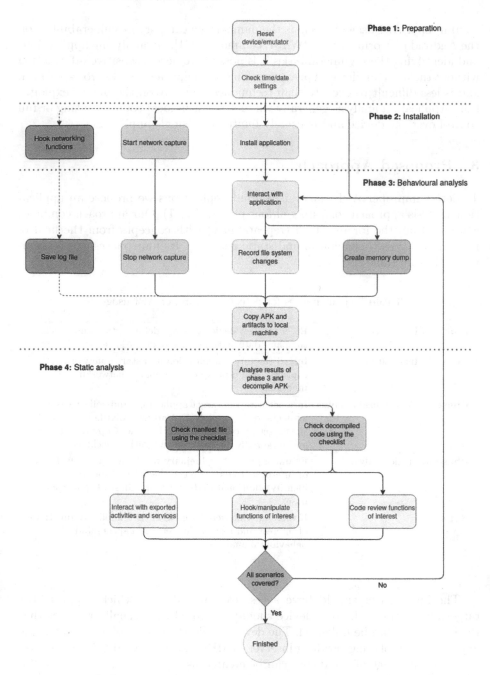

Fig. 1. Workflow for application analysis on Android

Dynamic analysis is a technique whereby we monitor the interaction between the application and other components such as the file system or remote servers. We first create a snapshot of the types of artifacts required for analysis, which will serve as our baseline. Then we run the application, perform some interactions and create another snapshot. Finally we compare the baseline with the application snapshot and determine which artifacts were created by our application. In our approach, we focus on the following locations:

- **File system** - We capture changes made to the file system by using standard Unix utilities.
- **API calls** - Systems calls made by the application are monitored using *strace* (if SELinux can be disabled) or they are hooked using *Frida*.
- **Volatile memory** - Application memory is captured by reading the */proc/<pid>/mem* block device. This process is automated by using the *PMDump* utility. We also use the GNU debugger to monitor live changes in process memory.
- **Network traffic** - Network traffic is captured through an HTTPS proxy using a self signed CA certificate. Analysis is performed using Wireshark and Moloch.

An example of behavioural analysis is determining file system changes using basic Unix tools such as "find". This enables identification of files that have been created or modified by the target application or operating system (Fig. 2):

```
FILE=$(mktemp); echo "Press any key to print file system changes ..."; read;
↪  find /data -newer $FILE
```

Fig. 2. Detect newly created or modified files in the /data folder

In Phase 4, we employed the well known tool "Frida" to hook or manipulate any functions of interest, which were detected using static analysis. This enables the investigator to follow the flow of data as the program runs or to trigger specific functionalities (such as a enabling a hidden debug menu). Static analysis is the process of analysing the compiled source code of an application. This can be achieved by using a decompiler such as "Jadx". Table 3 contains a non-exhaustive list of artifacts of interest. These artifacts are a great starting point for our static analysis. The manifest file of an Android application describes it's capabilities and is therefore also a valuable source of information.

The static analysis is aimed at identifying new code paths and to better understand previously observed behaviour. The behavioural analysis procedure should be repeated to trigger and analyse newly discovered functionality. The static analysis phase can be considered completed when no new code paths are identified. Figure 1 on page 6 contains a graphical representation of the procedure described in this section.

Table 3. Application analysis checklist - A: API Call; P: Permission; D: Directory; F: File; M: Manifest entry; V: Volatile memory; N: Network traffic

	Artifacts of interest	Description
A	.getExternalFilesDir()	Data is possibly stored in publicly accessible locations
A	.getExternalCacheDir()	
P	READ_EXTERNAL_STORAGE	
P	WRITE_EXTERNAL_STORAGE	
D	/sdcard	
A	.bindService()	The application might expose a public interface which could allow extraction of data or exploitation
A	.onStartCommand()	
A	.onBind()	
A	LocalSocket()	
A	.bind()	
M	<activity name=" exported"="true" />	The application exports an activity that can be started externally
A	MessageDigest.getInstance()	The application uses cryptographic operations. Check the hashing or encryption algorithm and determine if the developer uses static keys
A	Cipher.getInstance()	
A	Cipher.init()	
A	.digest()	
A	.doFinal()	
A	KeyStore.getInstance()	Encryption keys are possibly stored in a trusted execution environment (TEE)
A	KeyChain()	
A	isInsideSecureHardware()	
A	setIsStrongBoxBacked()	
A	.load()	
A	.getEntry()	
V	Encryption keys	Volatile memory can hold sensitive information such as decryption keys, login credentials, etc.
V	Login credentials	
V	Traces of unencrypted data	
A	Socket()	The application uses internet functionality. This could be an indication of cloud storage
A	HttpURLConnection()	
A	.connect()	
P	INTERNET	
A	FirebaseFirestore.getInstance()	The application uses Google Firebase as a backend. Check if a Mutual Legal Assistance Treaty (MLAT) exists
A	FirebaseAuth.getInstance()	
A	FirebaseStorage.getInstance()	
A	FirebaseDatabase.getInstance()	
N	Hostnames/IP-addresses	Network meta-data can identify servers that store application data. Check for use of TLS encryption
N	Authentication tokens	
N	User credentials	
N	Decrypted data	
A	ContentProvider()	The application provides a custom content provider which could be used to extract data
A	.query(); .insert(); .delete(); .update()	

4 Experiment Results

To validate our approach we tested it against three applications that were specifically designed to securely store user notes. We selected our target applications based on the position in the list of recommended applications, rating, approximate number of downloads and the total number of ratings (Table 4).

Table 4. Top three "secure notes" applications in the Google Play Store

Application	Position in recommendations	Rating	Approximate no. downloads	No. ratings
Safe notes	1	4.5	>100,000	8,239
Private notepad	3	4.5	>1,000,000	35,706
Secure notes	4	4	>100,000	3,486

To get an initial idea of the possible attack vectors we compared the functionality of the selected applications based upon their description. We limited our research to functionality which was provided free of charge (Table 5).

Table 5. Application features overview

	Safes notes	Private notepad	Secure notes
Encryption algorithm	AES	AES	AES[a]
Cloud synchronization	✓	✓	✓[b]
Multiple device synchronisation	✓	✓	✓[b]
PIN lock	✓	✓	X
Pattern lock	X	✓	✓
Fingerprint lock	X	✓	X
Password recovery	X	X	✓
Image support	X	✓	X
Intruder image	X	✓	X
Self destruct	X	✓	X
Data hiding	X	✓	X

[a] The application advertises using AES symmetric encryption but actually implements DES
[b] Online features did not function

For our experiment we used a Samsung SM-935F device with Android version 8.0, build number R16NW.935FXXS6ESI4 and root access. The device also uses a TWRP recovery image which is used to make a byte-for-byte copy of the system and user data partitions. Before we start our analysis procedure we will first restore the device backup. This ensures that the initial state of the device is the same for every application analysed. We then install the application and populate it with data. For every experiment we will be using the same dataset to ensure repeatability and consistency. Since we are creating notes we chose to define three standard messages:

- Message 1: This is just a test message!
- Message 2: How is this data stored?
- Message 3: I'm encrypted. Nothing to see here.

4.1   Safe Notes

Using behavioural analyses we determined that notes are stored in the directory */data/data/com.protectedtext.android/shared_prefs/* and use the naming convention *com.protectedtext.n[note-number].xml*. They are encrypted by default using one of the following static keys which are hard coded into the application:

1. **7igb2h048io6fyv8h92q3ruag09g8h** + <note-number>
2. **7igb2h048io6fyv98hasdfil09g8h** + <note-number>

If a user password is specified then it is used to encrypt the note contents. The program uses AES/CBC/PKCS5 as the encryption algorithm. The decryption password is stored together with the encrypted text when the note is "unlocked". If the note is "locked" the stored decryption password is deleted. We also analysed the mandatory PIN protection mechanism and identified the hard coded debug PIN code **556711** using static analysis which displays a message in the following format:

```
debug-[prefHintColor]-[prefHintColor2]-[debugPinCodeInHex]-[SHA512OfDebugPin]
```

The fields *prefHintColor* and *prefHintColor2* are two random groups of six bytes extracted from the SHA512 hash of the user PIN code. This provides a high chance of hash collisions since we only need to calculate a SHA512 hash that contains these bytes. We created a script that can calculate a valid hash for the PIN code **123456** in less then a second. The application also enables the user to store their notes on the website *protectedtext.com* using a custom path. If the URL portion is known the notes can be downloaded using the following URL:

```
https://www.protectedtext.com/<custom-path>?action=getJSON
```

When the note is downloaded from the protectedtext website it is in a "locked" state. As a proof of concept (PoC) we wrote a multi-threaded application, which performs a dictionary attack on the encrypted note. Currently it can try approximately 87.500 passwords per second for a 20000 byte long note using all threads on an Intel i7 4790 processor running at 3.6 GHz. Performance can easily be improved, for example by utilizing the GPU.

4.2   Private Notepad

Using behavioural analysis we determined that the main database is located at */data/data/ ru.alexandermalikov.protectednotes/databases/notes.db*. It contains a SHA-1 hash of the user password, passcode and pattern lock. The key needed to decrypt the contents of a note is stored in the file */data/data/ ru.al exandermalikov.protectednotes/shared_prefs/protected_notes_preferences.xml* as the "encryption_key" variable.

The application uses AES/CBC/PKCS7 as the encryption algorithm with an empty initialization vector (IV). It first decrypts the key stored in *protected_notes_preferences.xml* using the Base64 encoded static value **4WJFtk-wwUJqTHd+dJNtAaw==** as the decryption key. The resulting value is then used to decrypt the contents of the user notes.

Private notepad uses a Google Firebase backend with Google remote procedure calls (gRPC) over the HTTP/2 protocol. Since our software for analysing network traffic did not support this protocol we used Frida to hook API calls and monitor the flow of data between the client and server. Through this method we observed that the notes are decrypted before being sent to Google Firebase. This means that the developer has the possibility to decrypt this information. Since the information is stored on servers from Google it might be possible to obtain it through a Mutual Legal Assistance Treaty (MLAT) request.

Any documents retrieved from the remote database were also stored unencrypted in a local cache database. In our case they were stored in the file */data/data/ru.alexandermalikov.protectednotes/databases/firestore. %5BDEFAULT%5D.private-notepad-bd4a4.%28default%29.*

4.3 Secure Notes

Secure Notes stored its notes in the folder */sdcard/.innorriorsnotes/* which is publicly accessible by the user and other installed applications (that target API level 29 or lower [23]). The file */data/data/com.inno.securenote/databases/secu renotepad* contains the password used for access control. If a pattern lock is enabled then it is stored in the file */data/data/ com.inno.securenote/files/pattern* as a byte array hashed with the SHA-1 algorithm.

The application uses the DES encryption algorithm although it advertises to use RSA. According to an article written by P. Zande in 2001 [26] for the SANS institute, the DES algorithm uses a 56-bits encryption key and is considered unsuitable for encrypting sensitive data. During the RSA Data Security Conference of 1999 it proved possible to break DES encryption within 28 h using distributed computing. This means that it should be feasible to decrypt any stored data without the need for knowing the password. However during the static analysis phase we discovered that the application uses the static password **kalandarkalandar** to decrypt any note stored on the file system.

When the user logs into the application any new or modified notes are sent to the URL "http://52.86.98.234/innorriors_securenotes/index.php" via a POST request, this URL is hard coded into the application. This even occurs without the user having enabled the synchronization feature of the application. The request contains the contents of the note and meta-data such as a timestamp, local filename and category. However it does not contain a user identifier, which means that any legitimate synchronisation features would be unable to function since the note is not associated with a user account. It is unclear if this is a bug or some form of malicious behaviour. At the time of writing it was not possible to create a working account for this application.

The login screen of the application includes a password recovery option. When activated the application sends the password and e-mail address to a script on the remote server. This scripts then sends an e-mail message containing the password to the specified e-mail address. If an investigator activates this feature he will be able to recover the password by acquiring network traffic since the connection is unencrypted. This also provides a method for a malicious user to send a legitimate looking phishing mail. The e-mail is sent from the mail address support@innorriors.com but the salutation and name of the app are supplied by the user. This enables an attacker to craft their own message originating from a legitimate address. The attacker can also specify the recipient of the message since it is part of the POST request to the server.

4.4 Memory Artifacts

Operations performed by an application, such as decryption or encryption of data, uses volatile memory to store results and intermediate values. If an investigator is able to capture this memory, he is able to acquire artifacts which are otherwise inaccessible. The following is a list of artifacts recovered from volatile memory during our experiments (Table 6):

Table 6. Recovered memory artifacts per application

	Safe notes	Private notepad	Secure notes
Decryption password	✓	✓	✓
Decrypted text	✓	✓	✓
Decrypted images	n/a	✓	n/a
Decrypted labels	n/a	✓	n/a
PIN code screen lock	✓	✓[a]	n/a
Pattern screen lock	n/a	✓	✓
Password screen lock	n/a	✓	✓
Cloud storage URLs	✓	✓	✓
Timestamps	✓	✓	✓
Filenames	✓	✓	✓
E-mail addresses	n/a	✓	✓
Account password	n/a	✓	n/a[a]
User ID	n/a	✓	n/a[b]

[a] The PIN code was was encountered multiple times since it was a 4 digit value. Therefore it is likely, but not conclusive, that one of these values was the actual code.
[b] Online features did not function.

We were able to recover all relevant artifacts from volatile memory. If a certain artifact is present in memory depends on user and application activity.

For example an image might only be loaded into memory if a certain note is viewed. Or a password is only present when a login activity is shown. Volatile memory eventually contains every bit of data used by the application, making it an invaluable source of information for the investigator, although it is currently very difficult to acquire.

5   Discussion

Application analysis proved to be a viable method for acquiring data. It should be used when other forensics solutions do not support acquiring data from a mobile device or when the software cannot decode/decrypt the application data. It is not an effective technique for acquiring a forensic image of a device or for trying to gain full control.

The main limitation of application analysis is that it is may be required to interact with the target application on the suspects device. This assumes that the investigator knows the access code of the suspect. However we have shown that our method can also be used to identify alternate storage locations such as cloud storage and determine how this information is most likely stored.

While we focused on the application as an attack vector, related research primarily looked at techniques that could be applied at the system level. For example by acquiring volatile memory or gaining executed privileges through exploitation of system components. These techniques are preferred over application analysis when system wide acquisition is the main goal of the investigation. They do however come with other prerequisites that cannot always be fulfilled.

Our methodology can be applied to a wide range of applications. By looking at our results, combined with the available literature, we expect other applications to exhibit the same behaviour. It also reinforces the idea that forensic investigators should not rely on commercial products alone. While these products are proven to be effective, their approach is still very traditional. Live data acquisition can yield interesting results and is worth the effort. We have proven that by analysing individual applications it is possible to acquire application data without the need for elevated privileges. While other methods can possibly acquire additional data, application analysis is relatively easy to employ and will work cross-platform.

Application analysis does not only provide a method for acquiring locally stored application data. By understanding how an application functions additional methods of acquisition can be identified. By applying our method to the Private Notepad application we identified Google Firebase as a secondary storage location.

6   Conclusion

Our research identified application analysis as a viable method for data acquisition. Although the Android operating system provides the developer with various methods for securely storing data, they are often not implemented. Developers rely on custom security mechanisms and obfuscation for securing stored data and do not seem to have an adequate understanding of security standards.

In our research we also observed that volatile memory is an important source of information. Encrypted data stored on non-volatile memory can often be detected in an unencrypted state in volatile memory. Currently, acquisition of volatile memory is not a realistic option for the majority of devices because of the required privileges. More research is needed to identify viable methods for volatile memory acquisition.

During our network analysis we discovered that interception tools such as *Burp Suite* and *mitmproxy* are currently unable to capture HTTP/2 traffic. We were therefore unable to capture Google remote procedure calls (gRPC) used for Firebase communication. Because of this we had to rely on the more complicated method of function hooking. Additional research could enable easier analysis of HTTP/2 traffic.

Finally our current solution is aimed at the Android operating system. Although the general approach can be applied to other mobile operating systems such as iOS, some aspects need to be modified. For example, our checklist only applies to Android APK files and cannot be used for Mach-O binaries used on iOS. Also the checklist could be expanded to encompass more interesting artifacts. It would also be interesting to provide metrics for our analysis results, similar to the Common Vulnerability Scoring System (CVSS) [5]. This would allow us to compare applications and to estimate the value of discovered artifacts. Since the current procedure is largely a manual task, it would be desirable to automate the process by creating an automated vulnerability analysis framework.

References

1. Aouad, L., Kechadi, T., Trentesaux, J., Le-Khac, N.-A.: An open framework for smartphone evidence acquisition. In: Peterson, G., Shenoi, S. (eds.) DigitalForensics 2012. IAICT, vol. 383, pp. 159–166. Springer, Heidelberg (2012). https://doi.org/10.1007/978-3-642-33962-2_11
2. Busstra, B., Kechadi, T., Le-Khac, N.-A.: Android and Wireless data-extraction using Wi-Fi. In: International Conference on the Innovative Computing Technology, pp. 170–175. IEEE (2014). https://doi.org/10.1109/INTECH.2014.6927769
3. Cerdeira, D., et al.: SoK: understanding the prevailing security vulnerabilities in TrustZone-assisted TEE systems. In: Proceedings of the IEEE Symposium on Security and Privacy (S&P), San Francisco, CA, USA, pp. 18–20 (2020)
4. Chelihi, M.A., et al.: An android cloud storage apps forensic taxonomy. In: Contemporary Digital Forensic Investigations of Cloud and Mobile Applications, pp. 285–305. Elsevier (2017)
5. Common Vulnerability Scoring System SIG, February 2018. https://www.first.org/cvss. Accessed 24 Aug 2020
6. Daryabar, F., et al.: Forensic investigation of OneDrive, Box, GoogleDrive and Dropbox applications on Android and iOS devices. Aust. J. Forensic Sci. **48**(6), 615–642 (2016)

7. Davi, L., Dmitrienko, A., Sadeghi, A.-R., Winandy, M.: Privilege escalation attacks on android. In: Burmester, M., Tsudik, G., Magliveras, S., Ilić, I. (eds.) ISC 2010. LNCS, vol. 6531, pp. 346–360. Springer, Heidelberg (2011). https://doi.org/10.1007/978-3-642-18178-8_30

8. Feng, H., Shin, K.G.: Understanding and defending the Binder attack surface in Android. In: Proceedings of the 32nd Annual Conference on Computer Security Applications, pp. 398–409 (2016)

9. Feng, P., et al.: Private data acquisition method based on system-level data migration and volatile memory forensics for android applications. IEEE Access **7**, 16695–16703 (2019)

10. Four Ways to Bypass Android SSL Verification and Certificate Pinning, January 2018. https://blog.netspi.com/four-ways-bypassandroid-ssl-verification-certificate-pinning. Accessed 10 Apr 2020

11. Frigo, P., et al.: TRRespass: exploiting the many sides of target row refresh. In: S&P, May 2020. https://download.vusec.net/papers/trrespass_sp20.pdf. https://www.vusec.net/projects/trrespassCode. https://github.com/vusec/trrespass

12. Götzfried, J., Müller, T.: Analysing android's full disk encryption feature. JoWUA **5**(1), 84–100 (2014)

13. Groß, T., Ahmadova, M., Müller, T.: Analyzing android's file-based encryption: information leakage through unencrypted metadata. In: Proceedings of the 14th International Conference on Availability, Reliability and Security, pp. 1–7 (2019)

14. Hayes, D., Cappa, F., Le-Khac, N.-A.: An effective approach to mobile device management: security and privacy issues associated with mobile applications. Digit. Bus. **1**(1), 100001 (2020)

15. HTTPS encryption on the web – Google Transparency Report, June 2020. https://transparencyreport.google.com/https/overview?hl=en_GB. Accessed 11 Jun 2020

16. Intel cuts Atom chips, basically giving up on the smartphone and tablet markets, April 2016. https://www.pcworld.com/article/3063508/intel-is-on-the-verge-of-exiting-the-smartphone-and-tablet-markets-aftercutting-atom-chips.html. Accessed 11 Jun 2020

17. Kocher, P., et al.: Spectre attacks: exploiting speculative execution. In: 40th IEEE Symposium on Security and Privacy (S&P 2019) (2019)

18. Liang, H., et al.: Witness: detecting vulnerabilities in android apps extensively and verifiably. In: 26th Asia-Pacific Software Engineering Conference (APSEC), pp. 434–441. IEEE (2019)

19. Loftus, R., et al.: Android 7 File Based Encryption and the Attacks Against It (2017)

20. Nilsson, A., Andersson, M., Axelsson, S.: Key-hiding on the ARM platform. Digit. Investig. **11**, S63–S67 (2014)

21. OWASP Mobile Top 10, June 2020. https://owasp.org/www-project-mobile-top-10. Accessed 13 Jun 2020

22. Security vulnerability search, April 2020. https://www.cvedetails.com/vulnerability-search.php?f=1&vendor=google&product=android&opgpriv=1. Accessed 15 Apr 2020

23. Storage updates in Android 11 j Android Developers, May 2021. https://developer.android.com/about/versions/11/privacy/storage. Accessed 8 Jun 2021

24. Thantilage, R., Le-Khac, N.-A.: Framework for the retrieval of social media and instant messaging evidence from volatile memory. In: 18th IEEE International Conference on Trust, Security and Privacy in Computing and Communications, pp. 476–482. IEEE (2019). https://doi.org/10.1109/TrustCom/BigDataSE.2019.00070

25. Tilo, M., Michael, S., Freiling, F.C.: Frost: forensic recovery of scrambled telephones. In: International Conference on Applied Cryptography and Network Security (2014)
26. Van De Zande, P.: The day DES died. In: SANS Institute (2001)
27. Van Der Veen, V., et al.: Drammer: deterministic rowhammer attacks on mobile platforms. In: Proceedings of the 2016 ACM SIGSAC Conference on Computer and Communications Security, pp. 1675–1689 (2016)
28. Wächter, P., Gruhn, M.: Practicability study of android volatile memory forensic research. In: IEEE International Workshop on Information Forensics and Security (WIFS), pp. 1–6. IEEE (2015)
29. Yang, S.J., et al.: Live acquisition of main memory data from Android smartphones and smartwatches. Digit. Investig. **23**, 50–62 (2017)
30. Zhang, X., et al.: Cryptographic key protection against FROST for mobile devices. Clust. Comput. **20**(3), 2393–2402 (2017). https://doi.org/10.1007/s10586-016-0721-3

Research on the Method of Selecting the Optimal Feature Subset in Big Data for Energy Analysis Attack

Xiaoyi Duan⑩, You Li⑩, Chengyuan Liu⑩, Xiuying Li$^{(\boxtimes)}$, Wenfeng Liu, and Guoqian Li

Beijing Electronic Science and Technology Institute, Beijing, China
lixiuying@besti.edu.cn

Abstract. At present, the application of machine learning in energy analysis attack is a research hot spot of energy analysis attack, and the selection of feature points is an important factor that affects the machine learning model, how to choose the optimal feature subset is a key factor related to the success or failure of energy analysis attack. AES algorithm emphasizes to increase the complexity of encrypted data by a large number of encryption rounds. It generally runs ten rounds of encryption operation, but the energy information studied by attackers is only a part of one round in ten rounds. Therefore, it is of great significance to effectively select the optimal feature subset with the least amount of data from a large number of data for energy analysis attacks. According to the characteristics of high-dimensional small features of energy data, this paper proposes a new optimal feature subset selection method-secondary feature selection method named F-RFECV. Firstly, the F-test is used to quickly eliminate a large number of irrelevant and redundant features to initially select candidate energy feature subsets, and then the redundant features are further eliminated by recursive feature elimination and cross validation, so as to obtain the optimal energy feature subset, which effectively realizes the problem of small feature recognition in high-dimensional features, thus improving the success rate of model attack in subsequent machine learning. Experiments show that the attack success rate can be increased by 17% by using the secondary feature selection method (F-RFECV).

Keywords: F-test · Recursive feature elimination · Selection of feature points · Energy analysis attack · Machine learning

1 Introduction

1.1 Relevant Work

In order to reduce the number of samples and the size of the template, some special points need to be selected as the feature points in the power trace. In the energy analysis attack, the common feature point selection principle is to select the point which contains the most information about the key-related operations as the feature point. In papers

P. Gladyshev et al. (Eds.): ICDF2C 2021, LNICST 441, pp. 109–126, 2022.
https://doi.org/10.1007/978-3-031-06365-7_7

[1–5], a generally accepted criterion is proposed for the feature point selection method of this principle, each clock cycle can only select one point as the feature point, because more points in the same clock cycle can not provide more information. If this generally accepted criterion is not followed, the classification performance of energy analysis attack will be poor. So far, many different methods of feature point selection have been introduced.

In 1996, Kocher et al. introduced the feature point selection method based on mutual information analysis [6] (MIA). This method is to evaluate the correlation between qualitative independent variables and qualitative dependent variables, and then select feature points; In 2001, Gandolfi et al. introduced the method based on Kolmogorov Smirnov Analysis [7] (KSA), which is a nonparametric test method. It quantifies the distance between the empirical cumulative distribution function (CDF) of two random variables to determine their similarity; In 2003, the method based on mean difference [8] (DOM) was introduced, because only the operation dependent component and data dependent component will affect the mean value. Therefore, the point where the mean value changes greatly is the key related operation point, that is, the feature point; In 2006, gierlichs et al. proposed a method based on the sum of squares of paired t-differences [4] (SOST). SOST is a statistic based on t-test, which is essentially the accumulation of t-values, that is, the accumulation of correlation degree; Archambeau et al. introduced the method based on principal component analysis [2] (PCA), the feature points are selected by projecting the data sets of multiple related features onto the coordinate system with fewer related features; In 2007, Mangard et al. introduced the method based on correlation power analysis (CPA) and the method based on signal-to-noise ratio (SNR) [9].

CPA is a method that uses Pearson correlation coefficient to help understand the relationship between features and response variables. This method measures the linear correlation between variables. SNR quantifies the amount of information leaked by a single point in the energy trace. The higher the SNR is, the easier it is to identify the available components from the noise, and the more information the point divulges. Therefore, high SNR points are selected as feature points; In 2008, Standaert et al. introduced the method based on Fisher linear discriminant analysis [10] (LDA). It is a supervised algorithm, similar to PCA, LDA also extracts a new coordinate axis, projects the original high-dimensional data to the low dimensional space, and directly optimizes the low dimensional space to obtain the best classification separability. In 2013, Mather et al. Proposed the variance based method [11] (VAR); Only the operation dependent component and the data dependent component will affect the difference. Therefore, the point with large variance is the key related operation point, that is, the feature point. In these methods, the point with the strongest signal strength estimation is selected as the feature point in each clock cycle. In 2014, Fan G proposed the method based on a select sample distribution similar to normal distribution points as the feature points of feature point selection method, the experimental results show that compared with the previous method, the template attack based on the feature points selected by this method has better classification performance [12]. In 2015, Roy proposed class-specific feature selection based on the same concept as LDA and MMC to maximize the distance between classes and minimize the distance between inner points of classes. The data were trained on the distributed platform Apache Spark, and the efficiency of the proposed method for the selection of high-dimensional data feature points was proved [13].

Research in 2017, He and others studied the feature selection of multivariate response coefficient models with a large number of covariates, aiming at the relatively limited data samples, it is difficult to estimate a large number of coefficient functions nonparametric, put forward a punishment least-squares framework, when only the relevant variables included in the model, the proposed method can uniformly identify relevant covariate, and the corresponding coefficient of convergence rate can be estimated with the same function [14]. In 2019, Ireneusz et al. used stack technology to improve the generalization ability of machine learning in processing feature point selection data in view of the imbalance of categories among data [15]. In 2020, Khosla et al. introduced topologically preserved distance scaling (TPDS) to enhance feature point selection, which aims to reproduce distance information in higher dimensions. In addition to providing better visualization than typical distance preservation methods, TPDS can also better classify data points in terms of narrowing feature points [16]. In addition, the paper [1] introduces that the energy analysis attack based on principal component analysis is inefficient due to its high computing requirements. The paper [11] introduces that the energy analysis attack based on principal component analysis may not improve the classification performance. The paper [17] introduce the rare condition that LDA based energy analysis attacks depend on equal covariance, which is not true for most encryption devices. Therefore, compared with PCA based energy analysis attack, it is not a better choice [17].

1.2 Our Contribution

At present, the existing feature selection methods are still facing difficulties in the field of high-dimensional small sample, and their full potential in energy analysis attack has not been fully utilized. In order to solve this problem, this paper proposes a new energy analysis attack feature point selection method. Compared with the previous methods, this method has a completely different basic principle. This paper proposes a feature point selection method (F-RFECV) based on F-test and recursive feature elimination + cross validation (RFECV), which combines the different advantages of filtering and wrappering feature selection methods to eliminate irrelevant and redundant features.

1. Firstly, F-test is used to evaluate correlation between feature points and class labels, quickly remove a lot of irrelevant and redundant features to initially select a subset of candidate energy features.
2. Then the recursive feature elimination + cross validation (RFECV) method is used to further eliminate redundant features and obtain the optimal subset of energy features, which effectively realizes the problem of small feature recognition in large data.

In addition, experiments show that our new feature point selection method has better classification performance than previous methods. Compared with the previous feature subset method, the proposed F-RFECV method can improve the attack success rate by 17%. Figure 1 compares the traditional feature point selection method with the F-RFECV feature point selection method proposed in this paper.

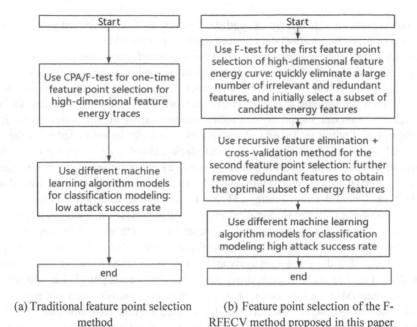

(a) Traditional feature point selection method

(b) Feature point selection of the F-RFECV method proposed in this paper

Fig. 1. Comparison of feature point selection methods

1.3 Structure of This Paper

The structure of this paper is as follows. In Sect. 2, the selection of attack point is introduced. In Sect. 3, this paper introduces the optimal feature subset selection methods in a large number of data, including feature point selection strategy, feature point selection based on F-test, recursive feature elimination + cross validation (RFECV) principle. In Sect. 4, this paper carries out experimental verification and discussion. In Sect. 5, this paper summarizes and looks forward to the future research.

2 Selection of Attack Points

In energy analysis attack, different attack points have different attack effects. Because the SBOX has the highest nonlinearity in various encryption algorithms, for energy analysis attacks, choosing SBOX as the attack point will get more information related to the algorithm. Therefore, in energy analysis attacks, SBOX output value is often selected as the attack point. When SBOX output is selected as the attack point, it can be divided into SBOX output Hamming weight model and SBOX output bit by bit model. Different attack models have different attack effects.

2.1 SBOX Output Hamming Weight Model

Hamming weight refers to the number of non-zero elements in a string. For the commonly used binary string, it is the number of 1 in the string. In energy analysis attacks,

Hamming weight model is generally used to represent the power consumption model of the operation data in the chip. Establish the label of energy trace and SBOX output Hamming weight, the key of cryptographic chip is further obtained by obtaining the Hamming weight of SBOX output. Taking AES algorithm as an example, for each byte of plaintext input, the output value of SBOX is in the interval of [0, 255], and they are not equal to each other. Hamming weight refers to the number of 1 in a binary value, so there are 9 kinds of Hamming weight output by SBOX.

2.2 SBOX Output Bit-by-Bit Attack Model

When the Hamming weight model is used to attack, it is necessary to first train a 9-classification model according to the Hamming weight label. Compared with the Hamming weight model, the Bit-by-bit model only needs binary classification per bit, and the number of classifications is less. Therefore, it is easier to classify by machine learning and can obtain better classification accuracy.

At the same time, when the Hamming weight model is used for the attack, the key cannot be obtained directly by obtaining the intermediate Hamming weight, so further analysis is needed to obtain the key. The common method is to carry out enumeration attack again, so it requires multiple energy traces to attack successfully. Compared with the Hamming weight model, the Bit-by-bit model needs only one energy trace to successfully attack, so the bit-by-bit model has higher efficiency and lower cost.

In conclusion, compared with the Hamming weight model, the Bit-by-bit model has better classification accuracy, higher efficiency and lower cost, so this paper chooses the Bit-by-bit model to attack. The comparison between the Hamming weight model and the bit-by-bit attack model is shown in Table 1.

Table 1. Comparison between Hamming weight model and bit-by-bit attack model

	The correct rate	The efficiency	The cost
Hamming weight model	Low	Low	High
Bit-by-bit attack model	High	High	Low

3   The Optimal Feature Subset Selection Method in Big Data

3.1   Feature Point Selection Strategy

Feature selection is a search optimization problem. For a data set of N features, the feature selection strategy is to find the optimal feature subset in 2N-1 non-empty feature subsets. The search strategy can be roughly divided into three categories:

(1) Exhaustive search. Exhaustive search refers to searching the feature subsets of all feature space sets. Its advantage is clear, that is, an optimal subset can be obtained, but this is limited to a data set with a small number of feature points; When the number of features of data sets is large, this method will bring disasters, that is, huge computing overhead and huge time cost.

(2) Heuristic search. Heuristic search avoids simple and brutal exhaustive search, but continuously adds or deletes features to the current feature subset according to a specific order in the search process, and finally obtains the best feature subset.

(3) Random search. Random search starts with a certain candidate feature subset generated randomly, and gradually approaches the global optimal solution according to certain heuristic information and rules.

The method of feature selection can be divided into three categories according to whether it is independent of the subsequent learning algorithm:

(1) Filter: The idea is to evaluate the pros and cons of each feature in the data set based on the data characteristics of the data set based on statistics, information theory and other disciplines, and finally sort the pros and cons of each feature, and select several better features to form the final feature subset. This paper can see that the filtering method relies on the data characteristics of the data set, rather than using specific learning algorithms to evaluate feature subsets.

(2) Wrapper: The idea of Wrapper method is to establish a machine learning model, and evaluate the pros and cons of this subset based on the prediction performance of the test feature subset in the machine learning model, and select or delete some features according to the pros and cons of the prediction performance. This method focuses on the pros and cons of the entire feature subset, and does not focus on the pros and cons of each feature in the feature subset. Therefore, the optimal subset obtained by this method does not mean that every feature in itself is optimal.

(3) Embedded: The idea of the embedded method is to first establish a machine learning model and train it, then obtain the weight coefficient of each feature and sort it, and finally select the feature point with a larger weight coefficient as the optimal subset.

This paper combines the different advantages of filtering and wrappering to eliminate irrelevant and redundant features, and proposes an energy feature selection method based on F-test and recursive feature elimination + cross validation method (F-RFECV). Firstly, the F-test is used to quickly eliminate a large number of irrelevant and redundant features to initially select candidate energy feature subsets, and then the redundant features are further eliminated by recursive feature elimination + cross validation (RFECV), so as to obtain the optimal energy feature subset, which effectively realizes the problem of small feature recognition in high-dimensional features.

3.2   First Feature Point Selection Based on F-test

The filtering method obtains the evaluation criteria of feature selection by using the intrinsic association of the data set itself, which is independent of the specific learning algorithm, and has good universality and low algorithm complexity. As a feature pre-filter, it is suitable for quickly eliminating a large number of irrelevant features from large-scale data sets. For big data, it is suitable for fast feature selection to select candidate feature points. In this paper, F-test based on filtering method is used to preliminarily select feature subset.

F-test, also known as joint hypothesis test, was proposed by Fisher, a British statistician, which is a test method to test whether the total variance of two normal random variables are equal. This paper uses the evaluation parameter F-score of F-test to select features. If two random variables $X = \{x_1, x_2, x_3, ..., x_n\}$ and $Y = \{y_1, y_2, y_3, ..., y_n\}$ obey normal distribution, the mean values of these two sequences can be obtained as follows:

$$\overline{X} = \frac{1}{n} \sum_{i=1}^{n} x_i \tag{1}$$

$$\overline{Y} = \frac{1}{n} \sum_{i=1}^{n} y_i \tag{2}$$

Therefore, it can be obtained the variances of the two sequences as follows:

$$S_x^2 = \frac{1}{n-1} \sum_{i=1}^{n} (x_i - \overline{X})^2 \tag{3}$$

$$S_y^2 = \frac{1}{m-1} \sum_{i=1}^{m} (y_i - \overline{Y})^2 \tag{4}$$

At last, it can be obtained the formula of $F(n-1, m-1)$ distribution as follows:

$$F = \frac{S_X^2}{S_Y^2} \tag{5}$$

For the data selected in the next section of this paper, each energy trace contains 435002 points, so it is suitable for fast feature point primary selection with F-test.

In this section, the feature points of the first bit and the second bit of SBOX output value are selected by F-test. The experimental results are shown in Fig. 2 and Fig. 3.

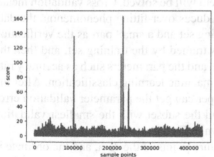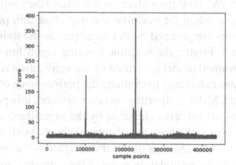

Fig. 2. F-test score of the first bit of Sbox output value in the first round

Fig. 3. F-test score of the second bit of Sbox output value in the first round

From Fig. 2 and Fig. 3, we can see that when the sampling point is performing key correlation calculation, there will be a spike at the sampling point. We select the sampling point as the feature point. We observe carefully and find that the feature points selected by the two bits are different, so we should select their corresponding features separately for each bit.

3.3 Second Feature Point Selection Based on Recursive Feature Elimination and Cross Validation

After the first feature point selection based on filtering, the feature subset can be initially selected. However, because the threshold value of the feature point method based on filtering is not easy to select, the feature points selected are still more, and it is not easy to effectively select the best feature points. Therefore, this article uses the characteristic advantages of the wrapping method mentioned above to perform the second feature selection on the basis of the selected feature subset, so as to achieve the purpose of selecting the optimal feature subset.

Recursive feature elimination (RFE) is a kind of wrapping feature selection algorithm. The principle of recursive feature elimination is to use machine learning algorithm to build a model and carry out multiple trainings. After each training, the features with smaller weights are eliminated by comparing the weight coefficients of each feature point. The above operations are performed on the new data set until all features are traversed, and the final subset is the final feature selection result.

In this paper, the classical SVM-RFE algorithm is used to select the best feature points, so this algorithm is used to describe the process of feature selection. First of all, in each round of training, all features N will be selected for training, so we get N classified hyperplanes $w * x + b = 0$, After the first training, the number of feature points with the smallest square value of the component in the weight w is deleted by using the SVM-RFE algorithm, then getting a data set with N-1 feature points; In the second training, the $N-1$ dimensional data set is input for training, and the algorithm will continue to remove the feature corresponding to the smallest square value of the middle component in the weight w. And so on, until the remaining feature numbers meet our requirements. The above optimal feature points seem to be perfect? Of course not. This paper realizes that before selecting RFE feature points, fixing the selected feature points is needed, but the best feature points are unknown. When this paper executes SVM-RFE through cross validation, the problem will be solved. Cross validation means that when the machine learning algorithm produces over-fitting phenomenon, the data sets are grouped, with a large part as the training set and a small part as the verification set. Firstly, the machine learning algorithm is trained by the training set, and then the trained model is verified by the verification set, and the parameters such as accuracy rate are calculated to evaluate the performance of machine learning classification. After the SVM-RFE algorithm is cross verified, this paper can get the parameter validation error of all subsets calculated by the algorithm, and the subset with the smallest validation error is the best classification subset. As shown in Fig. 4.

The abscissa of the above figure is the feature points of the data, and the ordinate is the cross validation score of the corresponding feature point subset. It can be seen from the figure that the best feature point selected by RFECV algorithm is 39.

4 Experimental Results and Analysis

The experimental data in this paper comes from the fourth stage of the international academic Contest of differential power analysis (DPA Contest V4, DPA_V4), which is collected from the AES-256 cryptography algorithm running on the ATmega163 chip,

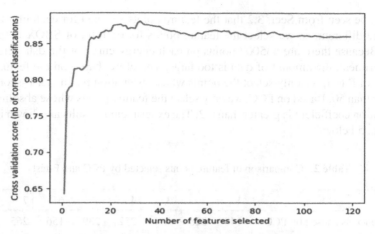

Fig. 4. Selection of feature points of RFECV

each trace contains 435002 points, In this paper, a total of 1000 energy traces in the data set are used for experiments. The experimental attack model is SBOX output Bit-by-bit model.

In order to verify the advantages of the proposed method, this paper compares the two feature point selection methods proposed with other methods. In this paper, Four machine learning algorithms, Support Vector Machine (SVC), Linear Discriminant Analysis (LDA), Decision Tree Classifier (DTC) and Logistic Regression Classifier (LRC) are used to build classification models on the candidate and optimal feature subsets, and the classification accuracy is used to evaluate the performance of different methods. The main experiments are as follows:

1) Filter method is used to select the first feature points to get the candidate feature subset. In order to verify the advantages of F-test based on filtering method, this paper compares it with Pearson correlation coefficient (PCC).
2) Secondly, on the basis of the candidate feature subset, this paper uses the wrappering method for the second feature point selection to get the optimal feature subset. In order to verify the advantages of recursive feature elimination and cross validation (RFECV) based on wrappering method, this paper compares it with Principal component analysis (PCA).
3) This paper compares the secondary feature selection method F-RFECV proposed in this paper with the primary feature selection method F-test.

4.1 Comparison of Feature Selection Between F-test and PCC Method

PCC and F-test are based on the mathematical features of data and label points, and both methods can distinguish target features from noise features. In this paper, the above two methods are used to select feature points, and four machine learning algorithms, SVC, LDA, DTC and LRC are used to classify and model the data after feature point selection, so as to observe which feature point selection method is more conducive to the energy analysis attack of the data set.

It can be seen from Sect. 3.2 that the feature points selected for each bit of SBOX output are different, so we select the feature points for each bit of SBOX output separately. Because there are 435002 points on each energy curve of the data selected in this experiment, the amount of data is too large. Therefore, based on the feature point selection of F-test, we only select the points whose evaluation parameter F-score value is greater than 50; Based on PCC, we only select the feature points whose absolute value of evaluation coefficient is greater than 0.2; The experimental results are shown in Table 2 and Fig. 5 below.

Table 2. Comparison of feature points selected by PCC and F-test

Bit	1	2	3	4	5	6	7	8
The dimensions chosen by PCC	148	228	154	252	239	156	265	278
The dimensions chosen by F-test	130	176	117	212	182	119	222	240

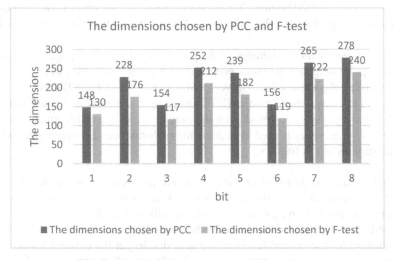

Fig. 5. The dimensions chosen by PCC and F-test

From Table 2 and Fig. 5, we can find that on the basis of distinguishing target features and noise features, the two feature point selection methods retain the mathematical characteristics of the data to the maximum extent, and the number of feature points has been greatly reduced. When F-test is used to select feature points, the feature points of each bit are smaller than those of PCC. However, does less feature points mean that it is a better feature subset? The answer is negative. Therefore, we further verified it.

In this paper, four machine learning algorithms, SVC, LDA, DTC and LRC, are used to classify and model the feature point selection results after PCC and F-test, and the classification accuracy is shown in the following Table 3 and Fig. 6:

From Table 3 and Fig. 6, we can see that although the feature points obtained by F-test feature point selection method are smaller than those obtained by PCC feature

Table 3. Classification of PCC and F-test feature points after selection

Number of bits	PCC				F-test			
	SVC	LDA	DTC	LRC	SVC	LDA	DTC	LRC
1	0.795	0.85	0.65	0.88	0.82	0.93	0.705	0.985
2	0.775	0.82	0.725	0.86	0.78	0.84	0.77	0.89
3	0.79	0.805	0.67	0.9	0.805	0.895	0.715	0.91
4	0.92	0.985	0.78	0.99	0.955	0.995	0.82	1
5	0.795	0.855	0.715	0.895	0.955	0.995	0.815	1
6	0.75	0.795	0.635	0.88	0.74	0.8	0.64	0.89
7	1	1	0.825	1	0.99	1	0.89	1
8	0.97	0.995	0.9	1	0.99	1	0.955	1

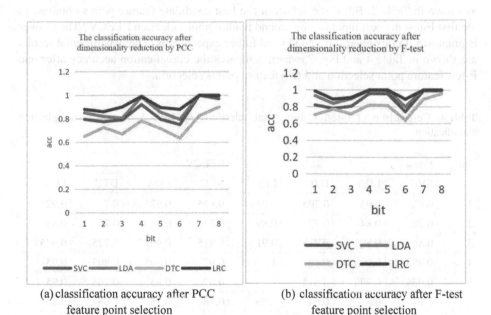

(a) classification accuracy after PCC feature point selection

(b) classification accuracy after F-test feature point selection

Fig. 6. Classification of PCC and F-test feature points after selection

point selection method, after selecting feature points by this method, the classification accuracy is still higher than PCC. Therefore, through the above experiments, this paper gets a conclusion: F-test feature point selection method is superior to PCC feature point selection method for single-bit preliminary feature point selection.

However, we further founds that a large number of irrelevant and redundant features were quickly eliminated by using F-test, and the feature-related points were initially selected. Although its feature point selection method is superior to PCC feature point selection method, its overall accuracy rate is not high. Therefore, this paper carries out the second feature point selection to further eliminate redundant features in order to obtain the optimal energy feature subset.

4.2 Comparison of Feature Selection Between Recursive Feature Elimination Plus Cross Validation (RFECV) and Principal Component Analysis (PCA)

After the first step of feature point selection, the classification result of the subset this paper obtained seems to be acceptable, but it cannot achieve the optimal classification result. Therefore, this paper introduces the second step of feature point selection, In this paper, the wrappering method is used for the second feature point selection to obtain the optimal feature subset. In order to verify the advantages of the RFECV based on the wrappering method proposed in this paper, this paper compares it with the PCA method.

In Sect. 4.1, on the basis of distinguishing the target features and noise features, through the F-test one-time feature point selection method, the mathematical features of the data are retained to the maximum extent, and an optimal feature subset is obtained, as shown in Table 2. But is the subset of the best candidate feature points obtained in the first F-test the best input for the second feature point selection RFECV? The answer is unknown. In this regard, we conducted futher experiments. The experimental results are shown in Table 4 and Fig. 7, which compares the classification accuracy after one F-test feature point selection and two feature points selection.

Table 4. Comparison of F-test feature point selection and RFECV feature point selection classification

Bit	F-test				RFECV			
	SVC	LDA	DTC	LRC	SVC	LDA	DTC	LRC
1	0.82	0.93	0.705	0.985	0.825	0.935	0.7	0.925
2	0.78	0.84	0.77	0.89	0.77	0.86	0.79	0.88
3	0.805	0.895	0.715	0.91	0.815	0.905	0.725	0.935
4	0.955	0.995	0.82	1	0.97	0.995	0.805	0.95
5	0.955	0.995	0.815	1	0.87	0.95	0.765	0.95
6	0.74	0.8	0.64	0.89	0.78	0.75	0.66	0.83
7	0.99	1	0.89	1	0.99	0.985	0.9	1
8	0.99	1	0.955	1	0.955	1	0.955	1

From Table 4 and Fig. 7, we find that after the first F-test feature point selection, the second feature point selection makes the classification accuracy of the machine learning algorithm seem to be lower. Then what went wrong? Obviously the first step of feature point selection is the problem. That is, for the second feature point selection method RFECV proposed in this paper, the best candidate feature point subset obtained by the first F-test feature point selection is not the best input for the second feature point selection.

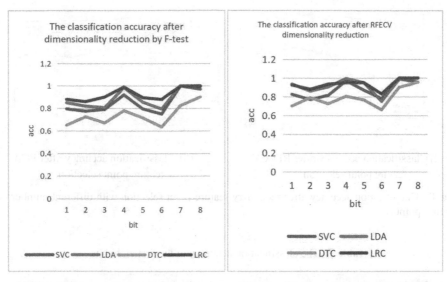

(a) Classification accuracy after feature
point selection by F-test

(b) Classification accuracy after feature
point selection of RFECV

Fig. 7. Comparison of classification accuracy after feature point selection by F-test and RFECV

In order to obtain the best input for the second feature point selection, we use F-test to obtain different feature subsets for experiments. As shown in Fig. 7, we find that the classification accuracy of the feature point selection of the 6th bit twice is the smallest. Therefore, we use F-test to obtain different feature subsets for the 6th bit, so as to obtain the best input for the second feature point selection. However, because the feature point selection based on RFECV takes too long, we only obtain the feature subset of 300, 600, 800, 1000, 1300, 1500 and 1700 feature points as the input of the second feature point selection. The PCA feature point selection method is compared with the work.

Four machine learning algorithm models of SVC, LDA, DTC and LRC are used for classification, and the experimental results are shown in Fig. 8. The classification accuracy of the second feature point selection using RFECV method is shown in Fig. 8(a). The classification accuracy of PCA method for the second feature point selection is shown in Fig. 8(b).

From Fig. 8, we can draw the following conclusions:

1) The different feature subsets obtained by the first F-test feature point selection have different effects on the secondary feature point selection.
2) Comparing with Fig. 8(a) and Fig. 8(b), we can see that when using DT, LDA and LRC machine learning algorithms, the classification effect of feature set based on RFECV is better than PCA, while for SVM classification, the classification effect of feature set based on RFECV feature point selection is slightly lower than that of PCA. Generally speaking, RFECV is superior to PCA in feature point selection.
3) According to Fig. 8(a), it can be seen that when the RFECV method is selected for the second feature point selection, with the increase of the number of features

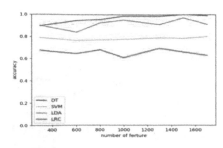

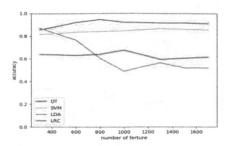

| (a) Classification accuracy after RFECV feature point selection | (b) Classification accuracy after PCA feature point selection |

Fig. 8. Classification accuracy after secondary feature point selection with different number of feature points

Table 5. The classification accuracy of the first eight bits

Bit	Feature points											
	1000				1300				1500			
	DT	SVM	LDA	LRC	DT	SVM	LDA	LRC	DT	SVM	LDA	LRC
1	0.735	0.82	0.985	1	0.715	0.88	1	1	0.745	0.855	1	0.99
2	0.74	0.81	0.99	0.995	0.755	0.81	0.99	0.98	0.73	0.83	0.995	0.99
3	0.715	0.8	0.795	0.945	0.71	0.84	0.97	0.995	0.725	0.865	0.99	0.98
4	0.735	0.885	0.985	1	0.795	0.985	1	1	0.83	0.995	1	0.99
5	0.825	0.975	1	1	0.77	0.88	1	1	0.715	0.89	0.975	1
6	0.645	0.77	0.95	0.985	0.66	0.79	0.91	0.985	0.67	0.785	0.97	1
7	0.935	1	1	1	0.865	1	1	1	0.9	1	0.995	0.98
8	0.97	1	1	1	0.99	1	1	1	0.985	1	1	1

selected in the first feature point selection, the classification accuracy after the two feature points selection also increases. Among them, when the number of feature points selected in the first time is 1500, the classification accuracy can reach 100% when using LRC method to classify the results after two feature points selection. In general, when the feature number of the input feature subset selected for the second feature point is maintained at 1000 to 1500, the classification result is optimal.

In order to obtain the optimal feature subset of all 8-bit in the first feature point selection by F-test, we carried out further experiments. At this time, we only carried out experiments when the feature points were maintained between 1000 and 1500. The experimental results are shown in Table 5 and Fig. 9. Table 5 and Fig. 9 list the classification accuracy of the feature subset of the first eight bits after two feature point selection by selecting different feature points in the first feature point selection.

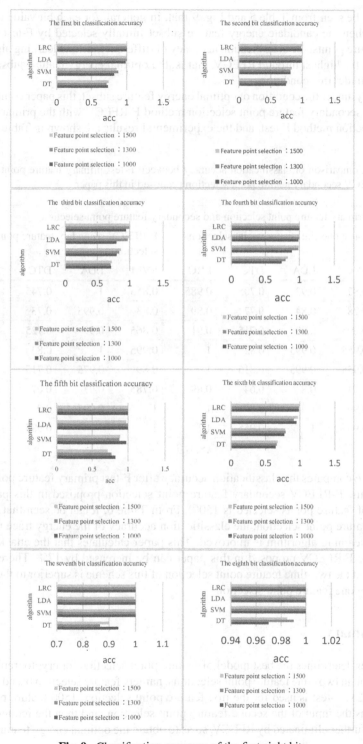

Fig. 9. Classification accuracy of the first eight bits

It can be seen from Table 5 and Fig. 9 that, in general, for each bit value of SBOX output, when the candidate energy feature subset initially selected by F-test contains 1500 feature points, the classification accuracy of different machine learning algorithms can reach the highest through RFECV, that is, the optimal energy feature subset can be obtained under this condition.

Finally, under the condition of optimal energy feature subset, this paper compares the proposed secondary feature point selection method F-RFECV with the primary feature point selection method F-test, and the experimental results are shown in Table 6.

Table 6. Comparison of classification accuracy between F-test primary feature point selection and F-RFECV secondary feature point selection proposed in this paper

Bit	Primary feature point selection and secondary feature point selection							
	F-test one-time feature point selection				F-RFECV secondary feature point selection			
	SVC	LDA	DTC	LRC	SVM	LDA	DTC	LRC
1	0.82	0.93	0.705	0.985	0.855	1	0.745	0.99
2	0.78	0.84	0.77	0.89	0.83	0.995	0.73	0.98
3	0.805	0.895	0.715	0.91	0.865	0.99	0.725	0.99
4	0.955	0.995	0.82	1	0.995	1	0.83	1
5	0.955	0.995	0.815	1	0.89	0.975	0.715	1
6	0.74	0.8	0.64	0.89	0.785	0.97	0.67	0.97
7	0.99	1	0.89	1	1	0.995	0.9	1
8	0.99	1	0.955	1	1	1	0.985	1

Table 6 compares the classification accuracy after F-test primary feature point selection and the F-RFECV secondary feature point selection proposed in this paper (the number of feature points selected is 1500). From Table 6, It can be seen that after the second feature point selection, the classification accuracy of the energy trace using the machine learning algorithm is improved. This paper calculates that the attack success rate of the F-RFECV proposed in this paper can be increased by 17%. Therefore, we believe that the two-time feature point selection of this scheme is superior to the scheme using only one feature point selection.

5   Summary

This paper determines the best model of feature point selection for cryptographic algorithm through two-time feature point selections, namely feature selection based on F-test and RFECV. F-test is used for the first feature point selection, 1500 feature points are selected as the input of the second feature point selection, and then the redundant features are further eliminated by RFECV, so as to obtain the optimal energy feature subset, which effectively realizes the problem of small feature recognition in high-dimensional features, thus improving the success rate of model attack in subsequent machine learning. Experiments show that the attack success rate can be increased by 17% by using the secondary feature selection method (F-RFECV).

Acknowledgments. This research was supported by the High-tech discipline construction funds of China (No. 20210032Z0401), the High-tech discipline construction funds of China (No. 20210033Z0402) and the open project of Key Laboratory of cryptography and information security in Guangxi, China (No. GCIS201912).

References

1. Rechberger, C., Oswald, E.: Practical template attacks. In: Lim, C.H., Yung, M. (eds.) WISA 2004. LNCS, vol. 3325, pp. 440–456. Springer, Heidelberg (2005). https://doi.org/10.1007/978-3-540-31815-6_35
2. Archambeau, C., Peeters, E., Standaert, F. -X., Quisquater, J. -J.: Template attacks in principal subspaces. In: Goubin, L., Matsui, M. (eds.) CHES 2006. LNCS, vol. 4249, pp. 1–14. Springer, Heidelberg (2006). https://doi.org/10.1007/11894063_1
3. B̈ar, M., Drexler, H., Pulkus, J.: Improved template attacks. In: COSADE2010 (2010)
4. Gierlichs, B., Lemke-Rust, K., Paar, C.: Templates vs. stochastic methods. In: Goubin, L., Matsui, M. (eds.) CHES 2006. LNCS, vol. 4249, pp. 15–29. Springer, Heidelberg (2006). https://doi.org/10.1007/11894063_2
5. Hanley, N., Tunstall, M., Marnane, W.P.: Unknown plaintext template attacks. In: Youm, H.Y., Yung, M. (eds.) WISA 2009. LNCS, vol. 5932, pp. 148–162. Springer, Heidelberg (2009). https://doi.org/10.1007/978-3-642-10838-9_12
6. Kocher, P.C.: Timing attacks on implementations of Diffie-Hellman, RSA, DSS, and other systems. In: Koblitz, N. (ed.) CRYPTO 1996. LNCS, vol. 1109, pp. 104–113. Springer, Heidelberg (1996). https://doi.org/10.1007/3-540-68697-5_9
7. Gandolfi, K., Mourtel, C., Olivier, F.: Electromagnetic analysis: concrete results. In: Koç, Ç.K., Naccache, D., Paar, C. (eds.) CHES 2001. LNCS, vol. 2162, pp. 251–261. Springer, Heidelberg (2001). https://doi.org/10.1007/3-540-44709-1_21
8. Chari, S., Rao, J.R., Rohatgi, P.: Template attacks. In: Kaliski, B.S., Koç, çK., Paar, C. (eds.) CHES 2002. LNCS, vol. 2523, pp. 13–28. Springer, Heidelberg (2003). https://doi.org/10.1007/3-540-36400-5_3
9. Mangard, S., Oswald, E., Popp, T.: Power Analysis Attacks: Revealing the Secrets of Smart Cards. Springer, Berlin (2007). https://doi.org/10.1007/978-0-387-38162-6
10. Standaert, F.-X., Archambeau, C.: Using subspace-based template attacks to compare and combine power and electromagnetic information leakages. In: Oswald, E., Rohatgi, P. (eds.) CHES 2008. LNCS, vol. 5154, pp. 411–425. Springer, Heidelberg (2008). https://doi.org/10.1007/978-3-540-85053-3_26
11. Montminy, D.P., Baldwin, R.O., Temple, M.A., Laspe, E.D.: Improving cross- device attacks using zero-mean unit-variance mormalization. J. Cryptographic Eng. **3**(2), 99–110 (2013)
12. Fan, G., Zhou, Y., Zhang, H., Feng, D.: How to choose interesting points for template attacks more effectively? In: Yung, M., Zhu, L., Yang, Y. (eds.) INTRUST 2014. LNCS, vol. 9473, pp. 168–183. Springer, Cham (2015). https://doi.org/10.1007/978-3-319-27998-5_11
13. Roy, A.: A classification algorithm for high-dimensional data. Procedia Comput. Sci. **53**, 345–355 (2015)

14. He, K., Lian, H., Ma, S.: Dimensionality reduction and variable selection in multivariate varying-coefficient models with a large number of covariates. J. Am. Statist. Assoc. **113**, 746, 754 (2017)
15. Ireneusz, C., Piotr, J., Thanh, N.N., Edward, S., Bogdan, T., Van Du, N.: Data reduction and stacking for imbalanced data classification. J. Intell. Fuzzy Syst. **37**(6), 7239 (2019)
16. Khosla, K., Jha, I.P., Kumar, A., Kumar, V.: Local-topology-based scaling for distance preserving dimension reduction method to improve classification of biomedical data-sets. Algorithms **13**(8), 192 (2020). https://doi.org/10.3390/a13080192
17. Choudary, O., Kuhn, M.G.: Efficient template attacks. In: Francillon, A., Rohatgi, P. (eds.) CARDIS 2013. LNCS, vol. 8419, pp. 253–270. Springer, Cham (2014). https://doi.org/10.1007/978-3-319-08302-5_17

Cheating Sensitive Security Quantum Bit Commitment with Security Distance Function

Weicong Huang[1](✉), Qisheng Guang[1], Dong Jiang[2], and Lijun Chen[1](✉)

[1] State Key Laboratory for Novel Software Technology, Nanjing University, Nanjing 210046, People's Republic of China
huangwc@smail.nju.edu.cn, chenlj@nju.edu.cn
[2] School of Internet, Anhui University, Hefei 230039, China

Abstract. Quantum bit commitment (QBC) aims to provide a secure commitment between two mutually suspicious parties. This paper presents a new quantum bit commitment protocol by introducing security distance function. Theoretical analysis shows that our protocol can guarantee the qubit commitment process is secure and has better performance than existing protocols in robustness. Since our protocol is simpler and more practical, it is feasible with current technologies.

Keywords: Quantum bit commitment · Security distance function · Cheat sensitive

1 Introduction

The rapid development of quantum computing poses a huge threat to classical cryptographic protocols which rely their security on computational complexity. This also facilitates the growth of quantum cryptography as its security is guaranteed by quantum mechanics, which provides unconditional security. Many classical cryptographic protocols have their quantum counterparts to promote security against both external eavesdropping and internal cheating. Bit commitment, which is first presented by Blum [1], is one of the most fundamental issues in modern cryptography. Since it is associated with many basic concepts in modern cryptography, including coin flipping [1,2], obvious transfer [3,4], and zero-knowledge proof [5–7], and is widely applied in real systems, such as business negotiation, electronic voting, and electronic currency, it has attracted intensive study. The process of bit commitment is generally divided into two phases, namely bit committing phase and unveiling phase. In first phase, the sender Alice chooses a bit c which she wants to commit to the receiver Bob;

W. Huang and Q. Guang—These authors contributed equally to this work.

© ICST Institute for Computer Sciences, Social Informatics and Telecommunications Engineering 2022
Published by Springer Nature Switzerland AG 2022. All Rights Reserved
P. Gladyshev et al. (Eds.): ICDF2C 2021, LNICST 441, pp. 127–138, 2022.
https://doi.org/10.1007/978-3-031-06365-7_8

then she encrypts this bit and sends it to Bob. In the second phase, Alice provides Bob with additional information for decoding, so that Bob gets all the information about c. A good bit commitment protocol should simultaneously satisfy the crucial property of concealing and binding. These two property are core principle of bit commitment protocols. The former means that Bob can't obtain any knowledge about the commit bit c before the unveiling phase. The later signifies that Alice can't modify c after the bit is committed to Bob.

Quantum bit commitment (QBC) protocol was first mentioned by Bennett and Brassard in 1984 [8], in the same article where they put forward the well-known BB84 quantum key distribution protocol. They did not realize their quantum tossing protocol implicated the idea of QBC. However, the protocol has a huge security loophole; that is, Alice can cheat Bob without being detected once she possesses quantum memory. Therefore, several QBC protocols [9,10] have been raised to address this problem. Unfortunately, Mayers *et al.* [11] and Lo and Chau *et al.* [12] respectively proved that unconditionally secure QBC does not exist in 1997. Later the same conclusion was also drawn by Kitaev *et al.* [13] and D'Arian *et al.* [14].

Although absolutely secure QBC does not exist in a general sense, studies over QBC are still favored by researchers. Two mainstream sub-fields have emerged from original QBC: relativistic QBC (RQBC) [15–18] and cheat sensitive QBC (CSQBC) [21–25]. RQBC protocols enhance security by introducing extra physical conditions, i.e., the theory of relativity, among which the most representative one was proposed by Kent in 1998 [15]. Afterwards, many other protocols based on the theory of relativity are discussed [16–18], following experimental demonstrations [19,20]. Though RQBC theoretically achieves unconditional security, it requires strict space-time factors, which are hardly satisfied in real systems, thus impeding the large-scale practical applications of RQBC.

Different from RQBC, CSQBC [21–25] offers a probability model of QBC. Specifically, the other can detect it with non-zero probability when one participant cheats, i.e., any cheating behavior risks will be discovered. Compared with RQBC, CSQBC does not require strict conditions, and consequently is highly practical. As a result, we mainly put our focus on CSQBC. In this paper we put forward a new CSQBC protocol which outperforms state-of-art protocols mainly in the following three aspects. First, the proposed protocol is very subtle, which can detect cheating through the raising of error rate. Second, our protocol is easily implemented by current optical devices, and can withstand certain system defects (there is no need for perfect single photon source, noiseless channel and quantum memory). Third, our protocol is more secure compared with existing CSQBC protocols [21–25]. As is shown in the security analysis, Alice's cheating would induce Bob's measurement error rate increasing by 12.5%, enabling Bob to judge Alice's cheating behavior effectively.

The rest of the paper is organized as follows. In Sect. 2, the definition and construction method of the security distance function is introduced. In Sect. 3, our proposed CSQBC protocol is given. In Sect. 4, the security of the protocol is analyzed. In Sect. 5, a detailed comparison and evaluation is provided. Finally, a brief conclusion is given.

2 Preliminaries

In order to guarantee the fairness of both parties involved in QBC process, we introduce the definition and construction method of security distance function, which is essential to our protocol.

2.1 Definition of Security Distance Function

Definition 1. *Security distance function.*
Function $f : \{0,1\}^n \to \{0,1\}^n$, $X, Y \in \{0,1\}^n$,

$$f(X) = Y. \tag{1}$$

If for any $X_1, X_2 \in \{0,1\}^n$ $(X_1 \neq X_2)$, and $f(X_1) = Y_1, f(X_2) = Y_2$, we have

$$d(X_1, X_2) + d(Y_1, Y_2) \geq m, \tag{2}$$

where $d(X, Y)$ represents the Hamming distance between two binary string X and Y[1], the function f is called as m-level security distance function(SDF).

The SDF is to guarantee a secure distance between different function inputs and outputs. However, in practical applications, due to channel noise, most of the optical pulses may be lost. Based on this, we extend the formal definition of the SDF, so that it can better conform to actual systems.

Definition 2. *Expanded security distance function.*
Function $g : \{0,1\}^n \times \{0,1\}^n \to \{0,1\}^n$, $X, Y \in \{0,1\}^n, l \in Z$,

$$g(X, Y) = l. \tag{3}$$

If for any $X_1, X_2 \in \{0,1\}^n$ $(X_1 \neq X_2)$, and $g(X_1, Y_1) = g(X_2, Y_2)$, we have

$$d(X_1, X_2) + d(Y_1, Y_2) \geq m. \tag{4}$$

The function g is called as m-level expanded security distance function (ESDF).

---

[1] Hamming distance between two binary string X and Y is the number of ones in $X \oplus Y$.

2.2   Construction of Security Distance Function

After defining SDF, the next issue is finding an approach to construct SDF. Herein, we introduce how to construct SDF by linear block code (n, k, d), which uses n-bits codeword to encode k-bits message, and the Hamming distance between any two codewords is d.

First, we introduce the construction process of the (n, k) linear block code [28]. Denoting the input message bits by $X = (x_1, x_2, ..., x_k)$, and the encoded block code (output of linear block code) by $Y = (y_1, y_2, ...y_n)$, the block-code bits y_i is calculated by the following equation:

$$y_i = g_{1i}x_1 + g_{2i}x_2 + \cdots + g_{ki}x_k, \tag{5}$$

where $g_{lm}(l = 1, 2, ..., k; m = 1, 2, ..., n)$ are binary coefficients. This definition can be put into a vector-matrix product:

$$Y = (y_1, y_2, ..., y_n) = (x_1, x_2, ..., x_k) \begin{pmatrix} g_{11} & g_{12} & \cdots & g_{1n} \\ g_{21} & g_{22} & \cdots & g_{2n} \\ \vdots & \vdots & \ddots & \vdots \\ g_{k1} & g_{k2} & \cdots & g_{kn} \end{pmatrix} = X\tilde{G}. \tag{6}$$

The matrix $\tilde{G}$ is called the generator matrix and

$$\tilde{G} = [I_k | P] = \begin{pmatrix} 1 & 0 & \cdots & 0 & p_{11} & p_{12} & \cdots & p_{1m} \\ 0 & 1 & \cdots & 0 & p_{21} & p_{22} & \cdots & p_{2m} \\ \vdots & \vdots & \ddots & \vdots & \vdots & \vdots & \ddots & \vdots \\ 0 & 0 & \cdots & 1 & p_{k1} & p_{k2} & \cdots & p_{km} \end{pmatrix}, \tag{7}$$

where I_k is the $k \times k$ identity matrix and P is the $k \times m$ matrix $(m = n - k)$. Defining Y_m as the last m-bit code of Y, i.e. $Y_m = (y_{k+1}, ..., y_n)$, we know

$$Y = (X | Y_m) = (XI_k | XP), \tag{8}$$

then we have $Y_m = XP$. Now we can construct a $(2n, n, n/2)$ linear block code according to the construction process of the above linear block code. Suppose the input message is $X = (x_1, x_2, ..., x_n)$, and the encoded block code (output of linear block code) is $Y = (y_1, y_2, ..., y_{2n})$, we can get $Y = X\tilde{G} = X(I_n | P_n) = (X | Y_n)$. According to definition of SDF, we define a SDF as

$$Y_n = XP_n, \tag{9}$$

where X is n-bit input, Y_n is n-bit output, and security distance would be $n/2$. A notable example is the Golay code, which is a $(23, 12, 7)$ linear block code with 12 information bits and 11 checking bits. We can extend its check bits to construct $(24, 12, 7)$, with $d \geq \frac{n}{2} = 6$, satisfying the requirement for subsequent security analysis.

3   Quantum Bit Commitment with Security Distance Function

In this section, we will describe the proposed QBC protocol in detail. SDF is employed in our protocol to generate sequence for verification. To improve the practicability of the protocol, we consider both ideal and defective cases.

3.1   QBC with SDF in Ideal Case

In ideal case, let's suppose that: a) Alice has perfect single photon source. b) Bob has infallible detecting devices. c) The transmission channel is noiseless.

The above ensures that any signal sent by Alice, including quantum signals and classic signals, can be accurately received and measured by Bob. Alice will choose a random basis sequence A, to encoded commit bit c, and generate checking string X according to basis sequence and SDF. The specific steps of our idea protocol are described as follows:

Phase 1: Committing Phase

(1) Alice and Bob determine the public security distance function f.
(2) Alice chooses her commit bit c, and selects a random basis string $A = \{a_1, a_2, ..., a_n\}$, which satisfies $c = a_1 \oplus a_2 \oplus ... \oplus a_n$, and $\oplus$ is the XOR operation.
(3) Alice calculates $X = f(A)$, where $X = \{x_1, x_2, ..., x_n\}$. Then she prepares photon sequence $|\phi_{a_i, x_i}\rangle$, where a_i and x_i respectively represent the bases and values of these photon sequence. The photons can be denoted as follows:

$$|\phi_{0,0}\rangle = |0\rangle, \qquad |\phi_{0,1}\rangle = |1\rangle,$$
$$|\phi_{1,0}\rangle = |-\rangle, \qquad |\phi_{1,1}\rangle = |+\rangle. \tag{10}$$

(4) Alice sends $|\phi_{a_i, x_i}\rangle$ to Bob. Bob measures the photons in $\{|0\rangle, |1\rangle\}$ or $\{|+\rangle, |-\rangle\}$ basis, and records measurement bases as A' and the results as X' (or Bob stores the photons if he has quantum memory).

Phase 2: Unveiling Phase

(5) Alice sends A, X and c to Bob.
(6) Bob compares A' and A. If the bases are the same, the value of X' in corresponding position is identical to X; otherwise, the probability that the value of X' in corresponding position is identical to X is 50%. Or Bob uses basis sequence to measured the photons stored in quantum memory and records the result as X'. Finally, Bob will check whether $c = a_1 \oplus a_2 \oplus ... \oplus a_n$ and $f(A) = X$.
(7) If Alice passes all tests, Bob accepts commitment bit c. Otherwise, Bob judges Alice as a cheater and rejects her.

3.2   QBC with SDF in Defective Case

In actual implementation, due to the imperfection of the single-photon source and the decoherence of the photon propagation by the channel noise, Bob usually does not receive all the light pulses sent by Alice. Therefore, Bob will inform Alice the positions of the light pulses he received by classical channel (synchronized by the clock, e.g., GPS). Then, Alice calculates the commit bit $c = r_1 \oplus r_2 \oplus ... \oplus r_n$ according to the value of the basis in the photon sequence received by Bob. The specific steps of our improved protocol are described as follows:

Phase 1: Committing Phase

(1) Alice and Bob determine the public extended security distance function g.
(2) Alice selects random basis strings $A = \{ a_1, a_2, ..., a_l \}$, and $X = \{x_1, x_2, ..., x_l\}$ $(l >> n)$.
(3) Alice prepares photons $|\phi_{a_i,x_i}\rangle$, and send $|\phi_{a_i,x_i}\rangle$ to Bob.
(4) When Bob receives sufficient photons, he informs Alice the positions of the light pulses he detected.
(5) Alice discards invalid information and part of the data to ensure that the number of information bits is n. Then Alice calculates $c = r_1 \oplus r_2 \oplus ... \oplus r_n$ and $l_a = g(R, X_R)$ and sends l_a to Bob, where $R = \{r_1, r_2, ..., r_n\}$ is the base sequence of remaining photons filtered by Alice and Bob, X_R is the value of remaining photons prepared by Alice.
(6) Bob measures the photons, and records measurement bases as R' and the result as X'_R (or Bob stores the photons if Bob has quantum memory).

Phase 2: Unveiling Phase

(7) Alice sends R, X_R and c to Bob.
(8) Bob compares R' and R. When the basis is same, the values of X in corresponding positions are same, otherwise the probability that X_R is the same is $1/2$, or Bob uses basis sequence to measured the photons stored in quantum memory, and records the results as X'_R. Bob will check that whether $c = r_1 \oplus r_2 \oplus ... \oplus r_n$ and $g(R, X_R) = l_a$.
(9) If Alice passes all tests, Bob accepts commitment bit c. Otherwise, Bob rejects Alice and judges Alice as a cheater.

4   Security Analysis

Generally speaking, Bob will always accept the committed bit c, as Bob's checking results are $f(R, X_R) = l_a$, and $X_R = X'_R$, when both Alice and Bob are honest. In fact, quantum bit commitment with SDF is a spacial case of QBC with ESDF. The difference between the two protocols is the method of creating connection between the checking sequence and bases sequence. In QBC with SDF, Alice can determine the checking sequence based on the basis sequence before sending her photons to Bob. But this checking sequence will be inaccurate when the signal is lost. QBC with ESDF solves this problem. Following we analyze the security of our protocols from two perspectives, concealing and binding.

4.1 Concealing

In concealing stage, we calculated the amount of information obtained by Bob before unveiling phase to analyze concealing of our protocol. For X_R, there is $\frac{1}{2}$ probability for the photon state to be the $|0\rangle$ or $|-\rangle$ if x_i is 0. The density matrix is

$$\rho_0 = \frac{1}{2}(|0\rangle\langle 0| + |-\rangle\langle -|) = \frac{1}{2}\begin{bmatrix} \frac{3}{2} & -\frac{1}{2} \\ -\frac{1}{2} & \frac{1}{2} \end{bmatrix}. \tag{11}$$

The state will be $|1\rangle$ or $|+\rangle$ with $\frac{1}{2}$ probability if x_i is 1. The density matrix is

$$\rho_1 = \frac{1}{2}(|1\rangle\langle 1| + |+\rangle\langle +|) = \frac{1}{2}\begin{bmatrix} \frac{1}{2} & \frac{1}{2} \\ \frac{1}{2} & \frac{3}{2} \end{bmatrix}. \tag{12}$$

Then,

$$\rho = \frac{1}{2}(\rho_0 + \rho_1) = \frac{1}{2}\begin{bmatrix} 1 & 0 \\ 0 & 1 \end{bmatrix}. \tag{13}$$

The Von Neumann entropy (VN entropy) is $S(\rho) = -\rho log_2(\rho) = 1$, and $S(\rho_0) = S(\rho_1) = 0.5983$. The mutual information is

$$H(X_R; X'_R) \leq S(\rho) - \sum_x p_x \rho_x = 0.4017. \tag{14}$$

Therefore, the Holevo bound is 0.4017 and the mutual information $H(X_R; X'_R)$ is bounded by it. Similarly, for R, the state will be $|0\rangle$ or $|1\rangle$ with $\frac{1}{2}$ probability if r_i is 0. The density matrix is

$$\rho_0 = \frac{1}{2}(|0\rangle\langle 0| + |1\rangle\langle 1|) = \frac{1}{2}\begin{bmatrix} 1 & 0 \\ 0 & 1 \end{bmatrix}. \tag{15}$$

The state will be $|+\rangle$ or $|-\rangle$ with $\frac{1}{2}$ probability if r_i is 1. The density matrix is

$$\rho_1 = \frac{1}{2}(|+\rangle\langle +| + |-\rangle\langle -|) = \frac{1}{2}\begin{bmatrix} 1 & 0 \\ 0 & 1 \end{bmatrix}. \tag{16}$$

Then,

$$\rho = \frac{1}{2}(\rho_0 + \rho_1) = \frac{1}{2}\begin{bmatrix} 1 & 0 \\ 0 & 1 \end{bmatrix}. \tag{17}$$

The Von Neumann entropy (VN entropy) is $S(\rho) = -\rho log_2(\rho) = 1$, and $S(\rho_0) = S(\rho_1) = 1$. The mutual information is

$$H(R; R') \leq S(\rho) - \sum_x p_x \rho_x = 0. \tag{18}$$

Bob can use positive-operator valued measurement (POVM) to get 40% information of X_R, and 0% for R. Now, we assume that Bob uses POVM to measure Alice's photons, and records measurement results as X_R'. Then he calculates $R' = g^{-1}(X_R', l_a)$. According to equation (3), for any $R \neq R'$, $g(R, X_R) = g(R', X_R')$. Due to definition of security distance function, we have

$$d(R, R') + d(X_R, X_R') \geq m. \tag{19}$$

If $X_R = X_R'$, then $d(X_R, X_R') = 0$ and $d(R, R') \geq m$; if $X_R \neq X_R'$, then the measurement basis chosen by Alice and Bob must be different, and R must not be equal to R'. Therefore, Bob cannot obtain more information about basis sequence R by using POVM.

4.2   Binding

In binding stage, we will calculate the probability of Alice's successful cheating. Theoretically, Bob cannot guess correct commit bit before unveiling phase in our protocol, but there also exists another question that is how to detect Alice's cheating behavior. Now, we assume that Alice is dishonest and Bob is honest, and analyze how our protocol detects dishonest Alice in a noisy channel.

Any of Alice's cheating methods will be seen as being implemented during the unveiling phase, as any action Alice does during the committing phase is considered a commitment process. We only need to ensure that Bob holds signal states $|\phi_{R,X_R}\rangle$ and connection parameter l_a when the committing phase is completed, where $R = \{r_1, r_2, ..., r_n\}$, $X_R = \{x_1, x_2, ..., x_n\}$ and $l_a = g(R, X_R)$.

Alice prepares $|\phi_{a_i,x_i}\rangle$ and sends to Bob, we assume that Alice's commit bit $c = a_1 \oplus a_2 \oplus ... \oplus a_n = 0$. Now Alice want to modify commit bit c to 1. In fact, Alice can achieve her purpose by modifying odd numbers of basis bits. We denote $k(0 \leq k \leq n)$ as number of basis bits that Alice wants to modify after committing phase. Alice prepares k entangled states as following.

$$|\phi_{AB}\rangle = \frac{1}{\sqrt{2}}(|0\rangle_A|0\rangle_B + |1\rangle_A|1\rangle_B) \tag{20}$$

The remaining $n - k$ photons are also single photon pulses. For the entangled states, if Alice and Bob choose the same measurement basis, then the results of the measurement are the same. Defining Alice's and Bob's final basis sequence as R and R', we have $c_0 = \oplus_{i=1}^{n} R_i = 0$, $c_1 = \oplus_{i=1}^{n} R_i' = 1$. Then, we have

$$d(R, R') \leq k. \tag{21}$$

According to definition of ESDF,

$$d(R, R') + d(X_R, X_R') \geq m, \tag{22}$$

$$d(X_R, X_R') \geq m - k. \tag{23}$$

When $k < \frac{m}{2}$, we have $d(X_R, X_R') \geq \frac{m}{2} > k$. Alice's control of k bits will introduce errors more than k bits. Therefore, the probability of Alice being discovered is 1. When $k \geq \frac{m}{2}$, we have

$$min\{d(X_R, X'_R)\} \leq \frac{m}{2}. \tag{24}$$

The probability of successful cheating is $P_A \leq \frac{1}{2^{\frac{m}{2}}}$. Also by calculating channel noisy error, we can get $P_A \leq \frac{1}{2^{\frac{m}{2}-ne_r}}$. Generally, we can set $m = \frac{n}{2}$, then we have $P_A \leq \frac{1}{2^{\frac{n}{4}-ne_r}}$.

4.3   Error Rate Introduced by Alice's Cheating

In the above, we have discussed the probability of Alice's successful cheating, but we did not consider the background noise of the channel. Channel noise can conceal some of Alice's cheating behavior, which is overlooked by some CSQBC protocols [15–18]. In our QBC protocol, Alice's cheating behavior will inevitably lead to an increase of the bit error rate. If the lower bound of Alice's bit error rate is greater than the upper bound of bit error rate induced by channel noise, any Alice's cheating behavior would be discovered. Therefore, we will calculate the lower bound of the bit error rate caused by Alice's cheating behavior.

We define N_x as the number of error bits in sequence X when Bob's measurement bases are equal to Alice's, N_r as the number of bits in sequence X when Bob's measurement bases are equal to Alice's, ans n as the number of information bits of the remaining photons. If Alice and Bob are honest, under the noiseless model, $\frac{N_x}{N_r} = 0$; under the noisy model, Er_{noisy} is defined as the upper bound of channel noise, $\frac{N_x}{N_r} \leq Er_{noisy}$. When Alice is dishonest, Alice prepares k entangled states to roughly cause $\frac{k}{2}$ error bits. When Bob performs the measurement, the probability that the bases same with Alice's is $\frac{1}{2}$. Therefore, the number of error bit N_x introduced by Alice is $\frac{k}{4}$. The number of bits N_r in sequence X is $\frac{n}{2}$. As the result, the error rate introduced by Alice is

$$Er_a = \frac{N_x}{N_r} = \frac{k/4}{n/2} = \frac{k}{2n}. \tag{25}$$

According to the conclusion in the above, the rate of successful cheating is the largest when $k = \frac{m}{2}$.

$$Er_a = \frac{k}{2n} \geq \frac{m}{4n} \tag{26}$$

When the parameter of ESDF is $m = \frac{n}{2}$, we have $Er_a \geq \frac{1}{8}$. Therefore, the error rate will increase by at least 12.5% when Alice cheats and this gives Bob sufficient conditions to judge Alice's legitimacy.

5   Comparison

Following we will compare our protocol with other CSQBC protocols [21–25] and show our protocol is superior to other CSQBC protocols.

The current CSQBC protocols have defects in theory or in practice. H.B et al.'s [21] protocol requires quantum memory and quantum computing to implement, while others CSQBC protocols [22–24] need prefect single photon source, which are both hardly realized with current technologies. Meanwhile, G. He *et al.* [27] demonstrated that in some CSQBC protocols [21–24], Bob can obtain sufficient information before unveiling phase, and deduce the commit bit. However, as discussed in Sect. 4.1, Bob cannot obtain any information about the commit bit before unveiling phase, and he can only speculate it randomly. The probability Bob can correctly guess the commit bit yields 50%. Thus, the security problem does not exist and our protocol is secure.

Li *et al.* [25] also proposed CSQBC based on single photon, in which Bob's successful cheating probability roughly equals the probability that Bob successfully speculates the commit bit, while Alice's successful cheating probability drops with negative exponent, approaching zero when signal length expands. Nevertheless, it needs perfect single photon source as well as noiseless channel. Our protocol reaches Li's security standard, that is when $m = \frac{n}{2}$, the probability of Alice successful cheating is $P_A = \frac{1}{2^{(\frac{1}{4}-e_r)n}}$, and the probability of Bob successful cheating is $P_B = \frac{1}{2}$. Besides, in the case of channel noise and signal loss, our protocol is compatible to most QKD protocols.

Meanwhile, Zhou *et al.* [26] proposed CSQBC based on Bell states. Here, we address some problems in its security analysis. The lower-bound of P_B should be $\frac{1}{2}$; Bob can randomly guess the commit bit with probability $\frac{1}{2}$ even if Bob does not cheat. However, the P_B defined in Zhou *et al.*'s seems unfair for other CSQBC protocols. Moreover, the probability of Alice's successful cheating should be $\frac{1}{2}$; Alice can cheat Bob by randomly modifying any b_i.

Table 1 shows the comparisons between our protocol and other protocols in different aspects. According to it, we can conclude that our protocol outperforms others in security, robustness, and practicability.

Table 1. Comparison between our protocol and other protocols in different aspects. P_A: the probability of Alice successful cheating; P_B: the probability of Bob successful cheating; Signal: S, single state; B, Bell state. PC, need of perfect channel; SP, need of single photon source: Y, yes; N, no. OTR: other technical requirements: QM, quantum memory; QC, quantum computing.

Protocol	P_A	P_B	Signal	PC	SP	OTR
H. B et al.	–	≥ 0.5	S	Y	N	QM, QC
other CSQBC	–	≥ 0.5	–	Y	Y	–
Li et al.	$\left(\frac{6+\sqrt{2}}{8}\right)^{\frac{n}{2}}$	≥ 0.5	S	–	Y	–
L. Zhou et al.	$\frac{1}{2^n}$	$\frac{1}{8^n}(\geq 0.5)$	B	Y	Y	–
Ours	$\frac{1}{2^{\frac{n}{4}-ne_r}}$	0.5	S	N	N	–

6   Conclusion

In this paper, we propose a quantum bit commitment protocol with security distance function, which is simpler and more secure than the existing quantum bit commitment protocols. Similar to the BB84 quantum key distribution protocol, our quantum bit commitment protocol utilizes the receiver's error rate to detect sender's cheating behavior. Theoretical analysis shows that our protocol can guarantee a secure quantum bit commitment process, and have better performance. Since our protocol has considered the ideal and the defective situations, it is robust and feasible with the current technologies.

Acknowledgments. This research is financially supported by the National Key Research and Development Program of China (Grant No. 2017YFA0303704), the Major Program of National Natural Science Foundation of China (Grants No. 11690030 and No. 11690032), the National Natural Science Foundation of China (Grant No. 61771236), the Natural Science Foundation of Jiangsu Province (Grant No. BK20190297) and Nanjing University Innovation Program for PhD candidate.

References

1. Blum, M.: Coin flipping by telephone a protocol for solving impossible problems. SIGACT News **15**(1), 23–27 (1983)
2. Kak, S.C.: A new method for coin flipping by telephone. Cryptologia **13**(1), 73–78 (1989)
3. Wei, C.Y., Cai, X.Q., Liu, B., Wang, T.Y., Gao, F.: A generic construction of quantum-oblivious-key-transfer-based private query with ideal database security and zero failure. IEEE Trans. Comput. **67**(1), 2–8 (2017)
4. Chou, Y.H., Zeng, G.J., Kuo, S.Y.: One-out-of-two quantum oblivious transfer based on nonorthogonal states. Sci. Rep. **8**(1), 15927 (2018)
5. Watrous, J.: Zero-knowledge against quantum attacks. SIAM J. Comput. **39**(1), 25–58 (2009)
6. Watrous, J.: Limits on the power of quantum statistical zero-knowledge. In: The 43rd Annual IEEE Symposium on Foundations of Computer Science, Proceedings, pp. 459–468. IEEE (2002)
7. Aharonov, D., Ta-Shma, A., Ta-Shma, A.: Adiabatic quantum state generation and statistical zero knowledge. In: Proceedings of the Thirty-Fifth Annual ACM Symposium on Theory of Computing, pp. 20–29. ACM (2003)
8. Bennett, C.H., Brassard, G.: Quantum cryptography: public key distribution and coin tossing. Theor. Comput. Sci. **560**(12), 7–11 (2014)
9. Brassard, G., et al.: A quantum bit commitment scheme provably unbreakable by both parties. In: Symposium on Foundations of Computer Science (1993)
10. Brassard, G., Crpeau, C.: Quantum bit commitment and coin tossing protocols. Lect. Notes Comput. Sci. **537**, 49–61 (1990)
11. Mayers, D.: Unconditionally secure quantum bit commitment is impossible. Phys. Rev. Lett. **78**(17), 3414 (1997)
12. Lo, H.K., Chau, H.F.: Is quantum bit commitment really possible? Phys. Rev. Lett. **78**(17), 3410 (1997)
13. Kitaev, A., Mayers, D., Preskill, J.: Superselection rules and quantum protocols. Phys. Rev. A **69**(5), 052326 (2004)

14. D'Ariano, G.M., et al.: Reexamination of quantum bit commitment: the possible and the impossible. Phys. Rev. A **76**(3), 032328 (2007)
15. Kent, A.: Unconditionally secure bit commitment. Phys. Rev. Lett. **83**(7), 1447 (1999)
16. Kent, A.: Unconditionally secure bit commitment by transmitting measurement outcomes. Phys. Rev. Lett. **109**(13), 130501 (2012)
17. Kent, A.: Unconditionally secure bit commitment with flying qudits. New J. Phys. **13**(11), 113015 (2011)
18. Kent, A.: Secure classical bit commitment using fixed capacity communication channels. J. Cryptol. **18**(4), 313–335 (2005)
19. Hardy, L., Kent, A.: Cheat sensitive quantum bit commitment. Phys. Rev. Lett. **92**(15), 157901 (2004)
20. Buhrman, H., et al.: Possibility, impossibility, and cheat sensitivity of quantum-bit string commitment. Phys. Rev. **78**(2), 022316 (2008)
21. Li, Y.-B., Wen, Q.-Y., Li, Z.-C., Qin, S.-J., Yang, Y.-T.: Cheat sensitive quantum bit commitment via pre- and post-selected quantum states. Quantum Inf. Process. **13**(1), 141–149 (2013)
22. Shimizu, K., et al.: Cheat-sensitive commitment of a classical bit coded in a block of m × n round-trip qubits. Phys. Rev. A **84**(2), 022308 (2011)
23. Li, Y.B., et al.: Quantum bit commitment with cheat sensitive binding and approximate sealing. J. Phys. A Math. Theor. **48**(13), 135302 (2015)
24. Lunghi, T., et al.: Experimental bit commitment based on quantum communication and special relativity. Phys. Rev. Lett. **111**(18), 180504 (2013)
25. Liu, Y., et al.: Experimental unconditionally secure bit commitment. Phys. Rev. Lett. **112**(1), 010504 (2014)
26. Desurvire, E.: Classical and Quantum Information Theory. Science Press (2013)
27. He, G.P.: Security bound of cheat sensitive quantum bit commitment. Sci. Rep. **5**, 9398 (2015)
28. Zhou, L., et al.: Game theoretic security of quantum bit commitment. Inf. Sci. **479**, 503–514, 135302 (2019)

Towards Mitigation of Data Exfiltration Techniques Using the MITRE ATT&CK Framework

Michael Mundt[1,2]($\boxtimes$) and Harald Baier[2]

[1] Esri Deutschland GmbH, Bonn, Germany
m.mundt@esri.de
[2] Research Institute CODE, Universität der Bundeswehr München,
Neubiberg, Germany
harald.baier@unibw.de
https://www.esri.de, https://www.unibw.de

Abstract. Network-based attacks and their mitigation are of increasing importance in our ever-connected world. Besides denial of service a major goal of today's attackers is to gain access to the victim's data (e.g. for espionage or blackmailing purposes). Hence the detection and prevention of data exfiltration is one of the major challenges of institutions connected to the Internet. The cyber security community provides different standards and best-practices on both high and fine-granular level to handle this problem. In this paper we propose a conclusive process, which links Cyber Threat Intelligence (CTI) and Information Security Management Systems (ISMS) in a dynamic manner to reduce the risk of unwanted data loss through data exfiltration. While both CTI and ISMS are widespread in modern cyber security strategies, most often they are implemented concurrently. Our process, however, is based on the hypothesis that the mitigation of data loss is improved if both CTI and ISMS interact with one another and complement each other conclusively. Our concept makes use of the MITRE ATT&CK framework in order to enable (partial) automatic execution of our process chain and to execute proactive simulations to measure the effectiveness of the implemented countermeasures and to identify any security gaps that may exist.

Keywords: Cyber Threat Intelligence · Data exfiltration · Information Security Management System

1 Introduction

The ubiquitous use of the Internet increases both the quantity and quality of network-based attacks and thus the need for protection against this class of risk.

Supported by organization Bundeswehr University Munich.

Widespread network-based attacks are attacks against the availability of services (e.g. denial of service attacks in their different variants) and attacks on the confidentiality of data, respectively. In this paper we address the second attack class, which is relevant for instance in the scope of espionage, blackmailing, or ransom. More precisely, while many research is published with respect to detection of a network breach, we focus on the detection and prevention of data exfiltration as a major challenge of contemporary network security.

A common category of concepts and measures to protect networks is Cyber Threat Intelligence (CTI). CTI is a way to improve cyber security by an improved assessing of the real existing threats. CTI provides information about the threats to business. CTI thus helps to understand and prioritize the relevance of known and yet unknown future cyber threats for one's own business. Therefore, it is an effective method to strengthen the security of business information systems [39, pp. 1–2].

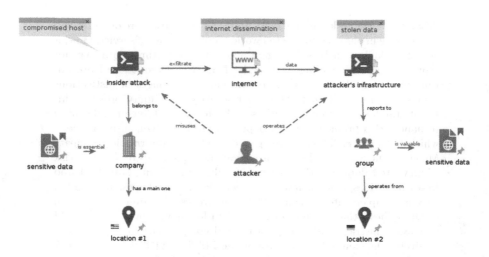

Fig. 1. Use case data exfiltration [33]

We use CTI as a base concept to specifically mitigate the dangers of data exfiltration for the respective business. Our use case and the relevant parties are illustrated in Fig. 1. As of today methods have been investigated to automatically derive the business context from the currently known vulnerabilities. Formatting and sharing technologies are increasingly used like the Structured Threat Intelligence eXpression (STIX) and the Trusted Automated eXchange of Indicator Information (TAXII) [39, p. 1]. Feeds, downloadable in JSON format, are increasingly being implemented to inform in a timely manner.

On the other hand institutions implement their cyber security strategy by releasing an Information Security Management Systems (ISMS). While often CTI and ISMS are implemented loosely coupled in a concurrent way, the goal of our paper is to introduce a concept to reduce the risk of unwanted data loss through data exfiltration in a dynamic manner by combining both CTI and ISMS. Furthermore, we use the MITRE ATT&CK framework to implement and later on automate CTI.

The main purpose of the paper at hand is to describe the connection between the CTI and ISMS processes and thus, building on two proven processes, to achieve added value in favor of reducing the risk of data theft. The Business Process Modulation and Notation is used for this and code examples are given for the implementation of this value-adding approach.

In more detail, our contributions are as follows: First, the essence of CTI [10] is examined in terms of how it can be procedural integrated into an organization and which parameters have to be supplied. Second the basic process for ensuring information safety and security [17,19] is checked to see whether suitable connecting points to CTI can be identified. After all, it is important to find the right controls [18] in order to effectively link the processes with one another. The ISO 27K series [19] is used as the framework for this work. Third the entire process is formally noted using [1] in order to provide companies with the necessary framework – a Business Process Management System (BPMS) [13] for the future as illustrated in Figs. 8 and 9. Finally we provide a sample use case based on the "SilverTerrier" group to show how our concept works.

The rest of the paper is organized as follows: in Sect. 2 we review and systemize the related work in our scope. Then Sect. 3 presents the concept of Cyber Threat Intelligence followed by Sect. 4, where we explain our proposal for usage of the MITRE ATT&CK framework to mitigate data exfiltration. Next we introduce Information Security Management Systems in Sect. 5. Our concept to jointly make use of Cyber Threat Intelligence and Information Security Management Systems is then presented in Sect. 6.1. We conclude our paper in Sect. 7 and point to future work.

2 Related Work

The work of this paper is going a first step towards bridging the gap between CTI and the current conditions of the enterprise IT-systems by combining CTI and ISMS using the MITRE ATT&CK framework. Respect is given to the current sensitive data on the assets of the enterprise. To the best of our knowledge, there is currently no existing research activity in this specific focus. In this section we present related work in the scope of data exfiltration, especially as part of an Advanced Persistent Threat (APT). Additionally related work with respect to the MITRE ATT&CK framework is discussed.

Scientific research regarding to adversary data exfiltration has a long history. Yet, 2014, the anatomy of typical attacks was examined. Referencing to an article of the Center for the Protection on National Infrastructure (CPNI) it was stated, that different advanced attackers were using different tactics. Different tactics are used to penetrate IT-systems of enterprises, institutions as well as Industry Control Systems (ICS) in order to identify sensitive, valuable data. Finally, identified sensitive data is exfiltrated by utilizing advanced data transfer hiding technologies [32, pp. 6–7]. The imperative of establishing effective security controls was distinguished [32, pp. 16–32].

Very early, the threat of unauthorized data exfiltration over various channels has been understood [38, pp. 8–12]. Therefore, the range is varying from the simple exploitation of websites, like YouTube (simply uploading Gigabytes of videos) or Tumblr, up to complex hex dumping of video frames [37, p. 4].

Until today, research has often been focused on examinations of specific methods. Single exfiltration channels have been investigated in order to figure out effective countermeasures, each. To name some of these data exfiltration methods: Structured Query Language (SQL) attacks against sensitive relational databases [12], cryptography signature based detection [22], detecting DNS over HTTPS [21], exploiting minification of web applications [34], stealthy data exfiltration from Industry Control Systems (ICS) by manipulating Programmable Logical Controllers (PLC) [11], bridging the air gap with audio signaling [30].

Accompanying the rising usage of encryption for storing and transferring data, appropriate techniques have been investigated to track data transmission in spite of encryption. The idea of deep packet inspection is one example for this [20]. The same intention is recognizable regarding the mushrooming implementations of steganography [40].

Multi layer approaches were exploited. In particular, Advanced Persistent Threats (APT) have learned to exploit multiple layers for achieving the diversion of sensitive data in a hidden manner. Interactively, detection capabilities have been researched with this trend [29].

Machine Learning was contemplated with confidence. Multi approaches have been evaluated and reviewed to utilize machine learning in order to reveal multi layer data exfiltration activities [3].

Innovation of information technology went hand in hand with more complex threats. Big data lakes have been born. The number of available data sources as well as the frequency of updating data by the Internet of Things (IoT) have grown significantly. Big data and real-time sensors were brought in. Corresponding, the necessity to examine misuse potential - among others data exfiltration - grew up and is culminating just today. Real time processing and streaming data processing will create new opportunities for big data analytics and will enable rapid threat prediction [25, pp. 58–59].

With the same speed in which the data exfiltration techniques are becoming more complex, defense approaches are enhancing. Geolocation-practice has been discovered today in order to filter valid participants for a data transmission and to prevent unauthorized data exfiltration [21]. Skills and training are advancing to foster the evolution of effective countermeasures; best practices lecture for the utilization of machine learning for cyber security purposes with python may be one example for this [15].

The Markov Belief Model figured out how to predict data exfiltration activities by APT. The model envisaged the likelihood in close correlation to the phase of the adversaries attack. Different phases of phases caused different operational figures. The Markov Belief Model transferred the prediction towards multiple phases of the attack. The likelihood of unauthorized data exfiltration is predicted with respect to each phase of the attack. The closer contemplation of the data exfiltration process itself was begun by Markov [14].

Different approaches have been reviewed. On the one hand, different levels are contemplated: strategic, operational, tactical level. Threat modeling is done at every level. On the other hand, Asset-Threat-Data-System concentric threat modeling approaches are pursued [23, pp. 3–4]. Information sharing becomes more important; MITRE provides for example the ATT&CK in the Structured Threat Information Expression (STIX) JSON format via Github [23, p. 14]. The future will bring further approaches in order to overcome the limits of today. So far, APT are not understood completely nor a bit detected in a timely manner. The future may require a more effective process. The process may have to consume the TTPs as well as historical and current data of attack vectors. Furthermore, current vulnerabilities in an enterprise IT have to be considered. With respect to the knowledge on current sensitive data of organizations assets, future trend processes will have to combine all the factors more holistically [23, pp. 14–15].

3   Cyber Threat Intelligence

Cyber security and forensics experts have to detect, analyze and defend against cyber threats in almost real-time. A timely response to cyber attacks is required. Without a deeper understanding of cyber attacks, effective countermeasures are hardly possible. The thought of limiting the threats makes threat intelligence gaining more importance. For this purpose, data mining techniques are being further developed in a targeted manner [10, p. 1]. A significant amount of data from security monitoring solutions and reports has to be transformed into knowledge. CTI is assigned this task.

The CTI model, which we use in our work, is depicted in Fig. 2. Indicators for the detection of cyber attacks are determined. The information about cyber attacks is systematically evaluated. Cyber criminals try to steal sensitive data. An attack follows a life cycle. It starts with spying on the target. Unfortunately, it often ends with criminal acts on the victim's IT system [10, p. 2].

Now it is particularly important to find the point of attack and uncover the vulnerabilities before cybercriminals exploit them. Points of attack are already extremely diverse today: non-traceable communication, 0day vulnerabilities, malicious PDF documents are just a few examples. The previous approaches show gaps. In addition, cybercriminals are increasingly using dangerous antiforensic and evasion disruptive measures. Other known disruptive measures require more modern approaches to forensic examination of exchanged and stored data. In the recent past, numerous countermeasures have been tried including artificial intelligence's machine learning [10, p. 3]. CTI is now focusing on the evaluation of cyber attack methods [10, p. 4].

The goals are improved detection and then improved responsiveness. A current awareness of the cyber threat situation is the basis. The companies have now reached a certain level of maturity. Data is recorded systematically. The exchange of data speeds up the process. Known threats are prioritized from the company's perspective. The implementation of security controls is being driven forward in a targeted manner. In order to collect high quality data, an ontology is required. This ontology must be as comprehensive as possible. A model serves this purpose. The model is the semantic representation of the cyber threats. It offers the possibility to standardize metrics. The model provides the basis for deriving quantitative metrics [24, pp. 1–2].

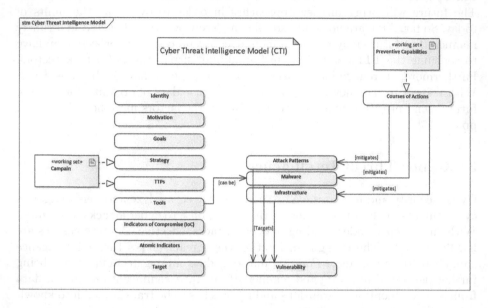

Fig. 2. Reference architecture: cyber threat intelligence model [24, p. 2]

Diverse taxonomies have already developed. Common Weakness Enumeration (CWE), Common Attack Pattern Enumeration and Characteristics (CAPEC) are two examples. The MITRE ATT&CK (Adversarial Tactics, Techniques and Common Knowledge) framework also offers usable insights into the entire life cycle of the attack, including the preparatory and follow-up phases. Finally STIX is the most used for sharing structured threat information.

The interrelationships as illustrated in Fig. 2 are fundamentally used as a model for CTI. In addition, the model is already being used today to build up knowledge bases, which in turn can then be systematically queried as required [24, p. 6]. In the case of the CTI model, the starting points for mitigating the threats are of particular interest here.

4 MITRE ATT&CK Framework

MITRE ATT&CK is a globally accessible knowledge base [27]. It provides a common taxonomy for CTI. It is about telemetry sensing and behavioral analytics. The ATT&CK model covers multiple technology domains: Enterprise, Mobile, Industry Control Systems (ICS). The model is a concrete instance and implementation of the abstract CTI model in Fig. 2. It provides a mitigation object structure, too.

Mitigations represent security concepts and technologies in the ATT&CK framework. These represented technologies help to prevent a technique or subtechnique being executed successfully. These mitigations are described vendoragnosticly. The ATT&CK Mitigation Model comprises the attributes Name, ID, Description, Version and Techniques addressed by mitigation.

The MITRE ATT&CK object model relationship is illustrated in Fig. 3. Its high-level components, like mitigation, are in relation one with the other. These are Adversary Groups, Technique/Sub-Technique, Software, Tactic and Mitigation. Each component is described with such an object structure, hence structures and relationships to describe adversaries' behavior are recorded in these object structures systematically. Figure 3 is showing the fundamental relationships of the objects [27] as well as an concrete sample of a manifestation of these objects regarding to a group named APT 39.

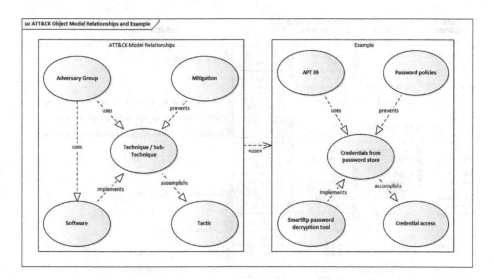

Fig. 3. ATT&CK object model relationships and example [27]

The ATT&CK Object Model implements the abstract layer of the Cyber Intelligence Model which is shown in Fig. 2. The TTPs were taken over directly, the Adversary Group entity of the MITRE ATT&CK framework corresponds to the identity of the CTI Model. The software component corresponds to the tools, etc. [27]. The data is continuously recorded within the MITRE ATT&CK framework on the basis of publicly accessible analysis reports of cyber analysts for current attacks. Therefore, current threat data is continuously managed within the MITRE ATT&CK framework.

In order to mitigate the risk of an attack, it is first of all necessary to understand possible techniques that can be used. The data now describes the known techniques and how they are used, along with aids for their detection and mitigation. The recommended measures relate to the attack technique currently under consideration [36, p. 1]. The standardization of the CTI is undertaken in order to be better informed about the cyber risks. The awareness of the situation becomes even better if this data is exchanged with other people at risk and affected. Effective cooperation arises. More analytics are now used to find hidden vulnerabilities and to make decisions about mitigating the threat posed by them [31, p. 310].

The MITRE ATT&CK Navigator offers a simple user interface to navigate through the MITRE CTI databases and to annotate facts [28]. We present a snapshot of it for the tactic 'Exfiltration' in Fig. 4. In its current version all domains are supported. These are Enterprise, Mobile, Industry Control Systems (ICS). In order to consider CTI for IT networks of organizations or companies, enterprise and possibly mobile are the right entry points.

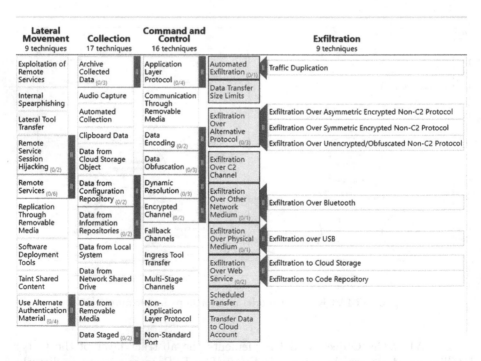

Fig. 4. ATT&CK navigator enterprise, tactic 'exfiltration' [28]

If an incident that has become known is evaluated, the applied techniques (including sub-techniques) are selected in the matrix of the MITRE ATT&CK Navigator and so the complete attack procedure is revealed. Conversely, the attack procedures of known groups can be selected from the CTI database in order to find out about their Tactics and Techniques [27]. One of the Tactics led is exfiltration.

In the course of CTI, conclusions can be drawn about the techniques and subtechniques used by known groups for exfiltration of sensitive information. If, in addition, the adversarial techniques used exploit weak points that also exist in your own company, then the focus can be identified in this way, at which the measures to mitigate the risk are currently to be located.

This process is then partially automated so that the necessary human interaction is concentrated on essential decisions. Therefore, the MITRE corporation maintains a GitHub repository [26]. Also Python libraries like [2,5] are applicable for transactional access to the data. The interfaces are standardized via STIX encoded in Java Script Object Notation (JSON) and the TAXII application protocol to transfer CTI via the Hypertext Transfer Protocol Secure (HTTPS) between participants [7]. The Python classes abstract the access to the interfaces and offer constructs for the direct evaluation of the data. The following Listing 1.1 shows the code block for loading of all currently available data sets regarding threats to enterprises into the processing memory. The loaded data can then be evaluated using differentiable filter methods so that, among other things, the mitigation measures with regard to current threats of data theft can be extracted.

```
import requests
from stix2 import MemoryStore

def get_data_from_branch(domain, branch="master"):
    """get the ATT&CK STIX data from MITRE/CTI. Domain
    should be 'enterprise-attack', 'mobile-attack' or '
    ics-attack'. Branch should typically be master."""
    stix_json = requests.get(f"https://raw.
    githubusercontent.com/mitre/cti/{branch}/{domain}/{
    domain}.json").json()
    return MemoryStore(stix_data=stix_json["objects"])

src = get_data_from_branch("enterprise-attack")
```

Listing 1.1. Access CTI via stix2 Python API [5]

Listing 1.2 is utilizing the Python "technique_mappings_to_csv.py" from the MITRE ATT&CK scripts [7] in order to extract mitigation measures against currently used exfiltration techniques. The results are written into a comma separated values file which is then easily visualized e.g. in a data mining application as shown exemplary in Fig. 5. This approach opens up the possibility of further automation. Above all, the open, documented interfaces enable efficient querying of the available CTI databases. Targeted queries allow an ever better focus on measures to mitigate the currently prevailing threats of data theft.

```
python3 technique_mappings_to_csv.py -d ''enterprise-
    attack'' -m mitigations -t exfiltration -s Current.
    csv
```

Listing 1.2. Querying and filtering MITRE CTI database

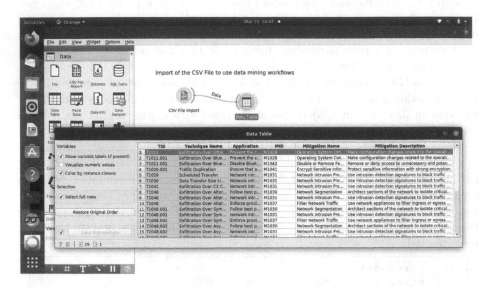

Fig. 5. Manual data mining with the results of CTI [16]

5   Information Security Management Systems

ISO/IEC 27000:2018 provides an overview of Information Security Management Systems (ISMS). Essential terms are defined. An attack is described with the attempt to destroy, uncover, change, disable, steal, gain unauthorized access to a value and use it without authorization [19, p. 7]. The relationship between stealing and data exfiltration is obvious. Furthermore, information is identified as a value that requires adequate protection of availability, confidentiality and integrity [19, p. 20]. Here it is the protection of confidentiality that is called into question by data exfiltration. It also states that appropriate measures are defined, implemented, monitored and, if necessary, improved so that the specific information security and business objectives of the organization are achieved. These measures can be seamlessly integrated into the business processes of the organization [22, p. 22].

Table 1. ISO actions for continuous improvement of the ISMS

ISO	Action
a)	Analyzing and evaluating the existing situation to identify areas
b)	Establishing the objectives
c)	Searching for possible solutions to achieve the objectives
d)	Evaluating these solutions and making a selection
e)	Implementing the selected solution
f)	Measuring, verifying, analyzing and evaluating results to determine that the objectives have been met
g)	Formalizing changes

It is precisely this question of the seamless integration of measures to mitigate the risk of data theft that must now be considered further. How can the measures to mitigate the risk of data theft be integrated into the ISMS? It must also be ensured that any risk assessment is carried out methodically and is suitable for producing comparable and reproducible results [19, p. 25]. All actions necessary to bring about an improvement are listed in sequential order as listed in Table 1. These mandatory actions for improvement, as these are listed in the ISO norm [19, p. 17], are repeated cyclically.

The nature of cyber security in practice is that it is not so obvious whether a decision may cause risk and damage [14, p. 1]. So, there is the need for a process. In order to run substantial business successfully, you have to get systematic about cyber security quickly. In today's networked systems, risks aggregate, cascade effects arise, inter-dependencies lead to accumulation of risks. It is essential to introduce systematic ways of identifying these risks [4, pp. 2–3]. Regular processes must be introduced or existing ones supplemented. In order to find the right entry point here, the basic processes of the company are first considered.

ISO 27001:2013 describes the requirements for an ISMS. Good planning is credited with preventing or at least reducing undesirable effects and achieving continuous improvement [17, p. 8]. It is written that it is imperative to determine the methods of monitoring, measurement, analysis and evaluation. In addition, the time and frequency of the inspection must be specified [17, p. 14]. These requirements will be carried over to mitigation measures. The objectives and corresponding procedures are listed in Table 2 and offer some interesting starting points for mitigating unwanted data exfiltration. The ISO 27002:2013 [18] then provides instructions for implementation of each procedure. The information from both documents is compiled here.

6   Concept and Example to Integrate CTI with ISMS

Looking at our hypothesis to link the two areas of CTI and ISMS using the MITRE ATT&CK framework to mitigate the threat of unwanted data exfiltration, all components have been introduced. In this section we turn to the details of the connection of CTI and ISMS. We first explain our concept in Sect. 6.1 and then apply it in Sect. 6.2 to a sample use case.

Table 2. Categories of measures [17, 18]

Identifier/Type	Description
A.8.1.1	**Inventory for values**
Procedure	Information and other values of the company are recorded, an inventory is drawn up and maintained
Measures	determine values, document importance, manage lifecycle (creation-processing-storage-transfer-deletion-destruction), designation of those responsible, compilation of an inventory list of values
A.8.2.1	**Classification of information**
Procedure	Information is classified based on legal requirements, its value, its criticality and its sensitivity to unauthorized disclosure
Measures	classify information considering confidentiality, use a uniform scheme relating to data exfiltration (safe-slightly-significant, short-term effects, serious impact on strategic goals)
A.12.6.1	**Handling of technical vulnerabilities**
Procedure	Information about technical weak points is obtained in good time. The hazard is assessed. Appropriate measures are taken to address the risk
Measures	Define tasks and responsibilities, identify data sources, define a time schedule for the reaction, assess risks, determine remedies, execute remedies, test patches, regular review and evaluation of the process, coordinate with incident response process, defining the actions in the situation without the possibility of mitigating the risk
A.14.3.1	**Protection of test data**
Procedure	Test data is carefully selected, protected and controlled
Measures	Avoid the use of Personally Identifiable Information (PII) or other sensitive test data, obtain authorization from the person in charge, delete test data, log, use of test data that is as similar as possible to the operating data
A.18.2.1	**Independent review of information security**
Procedure	The organization's approach to handling information security and its implementation are reviewed independently at regular intervals or whenever there are significant changes
Measures	Appoint an independent auditor, check at regular intervals or if there are significant changes, consider corrective action

6.1   Concept to Integrate CTI with ISMS

In this section we describe and show our concept to integrate CTI with ISMS. We make use of BPMN diagrams to explain our concept. BPMN diagrams in general offer a standardized form of notation in order to implement our proposed procedure across departments in the organization. The two diagrams showing our concept are depicted in Fig. 8 and Fig. 9, respectively.

First of all, Fig. 8 shows a Communication Diagram from the pool of BPMN template diagrams. The communication relationships between relevant actors of the CTI and the ISMS are shown. Leading actors as explained in Table 3 are involved on behalf of the areas of the organization. The cyber analyst is working on being aware of the current cyber threats. He pays special attention to the dangers of data theft. The CISO receives regulated knowledge of the current situation of threats to the organization. The cyber analyst reports to him. At the same time, the cyber analyst communicates the current threats to the information security officer. This information is used to target the activities of the ISMS. The Information Security Officer reports to the CISO on the current status of the ISMS. If necessary, possibilities for improvement are communicated with the CISO and suggested for implementation. CISO evaluates the status of CTI and ISMS and controls as required. After all, the CISO is responsible for the completeness and effectiveness of the ISMS vis-à-vis independent auditors. For this purpose, the relevant parameters are communicated and the results of the audit are received. The diagram shows these communication relationships and assigns the communication relationships to the actions in Table 1 and measures from Table 2. CTI and ISMS are linked to one another via the selected measures and found suitable actions of the ISO standard 27K. In this way, the ISO actions that are often already known and used can continue to be used with added value. The ISO standard is very often the basis for certification. If such a certification exists, it will not be affected by our solution and hence constitutes a decisive advantage of our proposed process.

Table 3. Leading actors

Actor	Description
CISO	Chief Information Security Officer. Control of the ISMS, here in particular the actions for continuous improvement
Indipendent auditor	Independent authority to review the existence and effectiveness of the ISMS processes
Cyber analyst	Selected and specially trained staff to develop current awareness of cyber threats
Information security officer	Employees to carry out the sub-processes and actions of the ISMS in the day-to-day operation of the company

In our second BPMN diagram shown in Fig. 9, the integration of CTI and ISMS is viewed from a further perspective. This time, an activity diagram is used. The activities of the actors are arranged in so-called swim lanes. In this way, the actions are assigned to the actors. Responsibilities and the process become visible. Figure 9 shows how the findings of the CTI are used specifically in the ISMS. In the event of a later automation, the identified, current threats to data theft or their mitigation measures are extracted and transferred as a configuration file. This configuration controls the need to select appropriate test data from the company. The rules, specified by the ISO for handling test data, are used here. The test data correspond as closely as possible to the sensitive data that is currently threatened. Permission to use these test data must be obtained in each case (ISO A.14.3.1). Finally, the configuration file of the CTI is used in turn to align the preventive protective measures. In line with the current threat situation, network protocols (e.g. DNS Query, HTTPS Replace Certificate, ICMP, BGP Open) and communication methods (e.g. DNS over TLS, Drop Box LSP) for simulating the attack are now being set appropriately. The simulation is now carried out focused on this configuration. Vulnerabilities to current threats become apparent. These vulnerabilities are quickly worked out into opportunities for improvement. The test data will then be deleted. Proposals for improvement that have been approved for implementation are formally incorporated into the documentation.

The entire process chain is repeated cyclically. The frequency is necessarily derived from the security ambitions of the organization. This concept of jointly making use of CTI and ISMS integrates resources gently into the organization and potentially quickly mitigates the risk of data theft. Through the preventive approach, the initiative against cyber attackers is regained. Through the use of organization-specific test data and the simulation on the IT system actually to be protected, concrete opportunities for improvement are highlighted that can be implemented immediately.

6.2   Example to Apply Our Concept

The international cyber reporting shows more and more references to the activities of the "SilverTerrier" group. The SilverTerrier group is attributed to Nigeria and is known to target high-tech companies [6]. The CTI of your institution is getting aware of the situation and is starting the procedure of our concept.

The MITRE ATT&CK framework is first exploited. The context shown in Fig. 3 is used to first determine which options are available to this group. The malware "Agent Tesla" is assigned to this adversary group. This malicious code is assigned the area of application via the ATT&CK framework to execute the "Exfiltration Over Alternative Protocol: Exfiltration Over Unencrypted/Obfuscated Non-C2 Protocol", Fig. 6, technique [8].

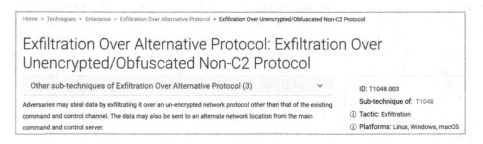

Fig. 6. MITRE ATT&CK framework identified technique [9]

This technique is described in the framework as follows: Sensitive data is encoded and compressed with publicy available algorithms and then exfiltrated using protocols like HTTP, FTP and DNS. The constant data traffic on these channels obscures the data exfiltration or at least makes it difficult to identify this adversary activity [9].

Mitigations		
ID	Mitigation	Description
M1037	Filter Network Traffic	Enforce proxies and use dedicated servers for services such as DNS and only allow those systems to communicate over respective ports/protocols, instead of all systems within a network.
M1031	Network Intrusion Prevention	Network intrusion detection and prevention systems that use network signatures to identify traffic for specific adversary command and control infrastructure and malware can be used to mitigate activity at the network level.
M1030	Network Segmentation	Follow best practices for network firewall configurations to allow only necessary ports and traffic to enter and exit the network.[27]

Fig. 7. MITRE ATT&CK framework mitigations [9]

The MITRE ATT&CK framework also shows mitigation measures in Fig. 7. By comparing these mitigation measures with the existing security measures of the ISMS, it can be determined immediately whether adequate measures are already being used to mitigate this risk. With reference to the communication diagram in Fig. 8, this is the first coordination between the cyber analyst and the information security officer. Both roles are described in Table 3.

The further course of action is now configured based on the identified threat situation. Appropriate test data from the organization is carefully selected in reference to the ISO security controls A.8.1.1, A.8.2.1 and A.14.3.1 in Table 2. The effectiveness of the countermeasures is specifically checked against this particular risk of data theft now. This is done by simulating this step for the domestic IT system as shown in Fig. 9. With reference to the current hazard, the protocols, e.g. HTTP, ICMP, DNS [9] are now deployed for the purpose of simulation. In this paper we propose our conclusive process, the data extraction methods have to be implemented and evaluated in a later phase of our work. If applicable, existing open source projects can help as the first code basis. The following list shows examples of some of the methods to do this:

– HTTP(S)
– ICMP
– DNS
– SMTP/IMAP
– Raw TCP

The simulation of the threat is executed as pointed out in Fig. 9. Technical vulnerabilities may become apparent in the process. Through the simulation, traffic data is reflected in the log files of the monitoring systems. In the extreme case, the simulated attack penetrates the protection of the organization. In any case, traces will remain which can later be evaluated and used to reinforce mitigation measures. Vulnerabilities are fed back into the regular ISMS and processed using the ISO 27002 A12.6.1 catalog of measures as referenced in Table 2. In addition, help is given by the MITRE ATT&CK framework on how the technique can be detected. Here are these suggestions for the example:

- Analyze network data for uncommon data flows (e.g., a client sending significantly more data than it receives from a server)
- Processes utilizing the network that do not normally have network communication or have never been seen before are suspicious
- Analyze packet contents to detect communications that do not follow the expected protocol behavior for the port that is being used.

Identified vulnerabilities and the recommendations to detect the specific risk are now included in the management of the vulnerabilities as input variables. They are evaluated in the context of the ISMS process for continuous improvement against the security goals of the organization and then implemented (Fig. 9). With this approach, the regular process for continuous improvement of the ISMS is proactively served with the results of the simulation. One anticipates the current danger and strengthens the protective measures before – here in this example – the group "SilverTerrier" [6] can successfully achieve the data theft.

Concretely, options to improve your own protective measures can be derived. For example, based on the results and logfiles of the simulation training data sets for machine learning or deterministic measures such as extended firewall rules can be created profitably. Because the results of the simulation are included in the ISMS process (Fig. 9), which is managed directly by the CISO (Fig. 8), the decision-making authority is given to make direct and immediate decisions for the organization. In this case, the mitigation measures against the current technique [9] are implemented or improved. In this way, the critical improvement can be introduced in a timely manner against the current threat of the APT [6].

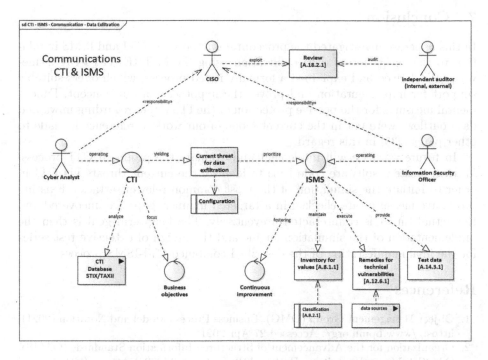

Fig. 8. BPMN - diagram communications for CTI & ISMS [38]

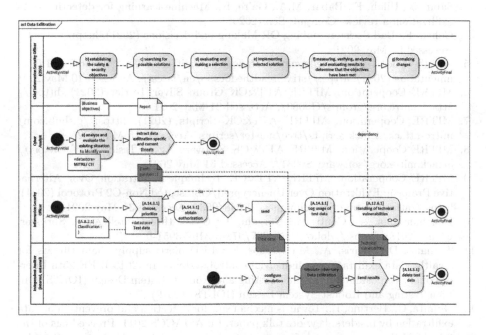

Fig. 9. BPMN - diagram activities for CTI & ISMS relating data exfiltration [38]

7 Conclusion

In this paper we investigated the procedural link between CTI and ISMS in relation to the mitigation of data exfiltration using the MITRE ATT&CK framework. We derived and explained a formally noted process, which offers suitable support for implementation and proves the hypothesis of our concept. Fundamental measures for the passive protection of the IT system regarding unwanted data outflows were not in the current scope of our work, a reference is made to other papers [35] in this regard.

In future work we will implement and evaluate the proposed CTI process. We will create a software code base to identify the current threats via CTI in order to initiate the simulation of the most common relevant attacks. Existing protective measures are checked in a targeted manner, gaps are uncovered and the actual threat is counteracted preventively. The long-term goal is then the implementation of the simulation engine and the design of extensive test series for the final manifestation of the described combined CTI-ISMS process.

References

1. Object Management Group (OMG). Business Process Model and Notation (2021). https://www.bpmn.org/. Accessed 27 Apr 2021
2. Organization for the Advancement of Structured Information Standards (OASIS). OASIS TC Open Repository: Python APIs for STIX 2 (2020). https://github.com/oasis-open/cti-python-stix2. Accessed 10 May 2021
3. Sabir, B., Ullah, F., Babar, M.A., Gaire, R.: Machine learning for detecting data exfiltration: a review. Comput. Sci. (2020)
4. Cohen, F.: Bad decision-making OR Making bad decisions (2021). http://all.net/. Accessed 05 May 2021
5. OASIS Cyber Threat Intelligence Technical Committee: STIX 2 Python API Documentation (2021). https://stix2.readthedocs.io/en/latest/. Accessed 10 May 2021
6. MITRE Cooperation: MITRE ATT&CK Group Silver Terrier (2021). https://attack.mitre.org/groups/G0083/. Accessed 31 May 2021
7. MITRE Cooperation: MITRE ATT&CK Scripts (2021). https://github.com/mitre-attack/attack-scripts/tree/master/scripts. Accessed 15 May 2021
8. MITRE Cooperation: MITRE ATT&CK Software Agent Tesla (2021). https://attack.mitre.org/software/S0331/. Accessed 31 May 2021
9. MITRE Cooperation: MITRE ATT&CK Technique Exfiltration Over Alternative Protocol: Exfiltration Over Unencrypted/Obfuscated Non-C2 Protocol (2021). https://attack.mitre.org/techniques/T1048/003/. Accessed 31 May 2021
10. Dehghantanha, A., Conti, M., Dargahi, T.: Cyber threat intelligence. Springer, Cham (2018). https://doi.org/10.1007/978-3-319-73951-9
11. Tychalas, D., Keliris, A., Maniatakos, M.: LED alert: supply chain threats for stealthy data exfiltration in industrial control systems. In: 2019 IEEE 25th International Symposium on On-Line Testing and Robust System Design (IOLTS) On-Line Testing and Robust System Design (IOLTS) (2019)
12. Ghinita, G., Bertino, E.: Towards mechanisms for detection and prevention of data exfiltration by insiders: keynote talk paper. In: ASIACCS 2011: Proceedings of the 6th ACM Symposium on Information, Computer and Communications Security (2011). https://doi.org/10.1145/1966913.1966916

13. Kühn, H., Bayer, F.: Prozessmanagement für Experten, Impulse für aktuelle und wiederkehrende Themen. Springer, Heidelberg (2013)
14. Louvieris, P., Ioannou, G., Powel, G.: A Markov multi-phase transferable belief model: an application for predicting data exfiltration APTs. In: Proceedings of the 16th International Conference on Information Fusion Information Fusion (FUSION) (2013)
15. Halder, S., Ozdemir, S.: Hands-On Machine Learning for Cybersecurity: Safeguard Your System by Making Your Machines Intelligent Using the Python Ecosystem. 9781788992282. 9781788990967. Packt Publishing, Birmingham (2018)
16. Anaconda Inc. Anaconda - Data Science technology for human sensemaking (2021). https://www.anaconda.com/. Accessed 01 Apr 2021
17. International Electronical Commission (IEC) International Standard Organization (ISO): Information Security Management (2013). https://www.iso.org/isoiec-27001-information-security.html. Accessed 30 Apr 2021
18. International Electronical Commission (IEC) International Standard Organization (ISO): Information technology—Security techniques—Code of practice for information security controls (2013). https://www.iso.org/isoiec-27001-information-security.html. Accessed 30 Apr 2021
19. International Electronical Commission (IEC) International Standard Organization (ISO): Information technology—Security techniques—Information security management systems—Overview and vocabulary (2018). https://standards.iso.org/ittf/PubliclyAvailableStandards/c073906_ISO_IEC_27000_2018_E.zip. Accessed 30 Apr 2021
20. Sherry, J., Lan, C., Popa, R.A., Ratnasamy, S.: Blind-box: deep packet inspection over encrypted traffic. In: SIGCOMM 2015: Proceedings of the 2015 ACM Conference on Special Interest Group on Data Communication (2015). https://dl.acm.org/doi/10.1145/2785956.2787502
21. Benton, K., Camp, L.J.: Firewalling scenic routes: preventing data exfiltration via political and geographic routing policies In: SafeConfig 2016: Proceedings of the 2016 ACM Workshop on Automated Decision Making for Active Cyber Defense (2016). https://doi.org/10.1145/2994475.2994477
22. Liu, Y., Corbett, C., Chiang, K., Archibald, R., Mukherjee, B., Ghosal, D.: Detecting sensitive data exfiltration by an insider attack. In: CSIIRW 2008: Proceedings of the 4th Annual Workshop on Cyber Security and Information Intelligence Research: Developing Strategies to Meet the Cyber Security and Information Intelligence Challenges Ahead (2008). https://doi.org/10.1145/1413140.1413159
23. Tatam, M., Shanmugam, B., Azam, S., Kannoorpatti, K.: A review of threat modelling approaches for APT-style attacks. In: Heliyon (2021). https://www.cell.com/heliyon/fulltext/S2405-8440(21)00074-8
24. Mavroeidis, V., Bromander, S.: Cyber Threat Intelligence Model: An Evaluation of Taxonomies, Sharing Standards, and Ontologies within Cyber Threat Intelligence (2021). https://www.duo.uio.no/bitstream/handle/10852/58492/CTI_Mavroeidis.pdf?sequence=4. Accessed 02 May 2021
25. Miloslavskaya, N.: Stream data analytics for network attacks prediction. Procedia Comput. Sci. **169**, 57–62 (2020). https://www.sciencedirect.com/science/article/pii/S1877050920302374
26. MITRE. ATT&CK Version 9.0. The Cyber Threat Intelligence Repository of MITRE ATTCK and CAPED catalogs expressed in STIX 2.0 JSON (2021). https://github.com/mitre/cti. Accessed 10 May 2021
27. MITRE. MITRE ATT&CK Framework (2021). https://attack.mitre.org/. Accessed 30 Mar 2021

28. MITRE: MITRE ATT&CK NAVIGATOR (2021). https://mitreattack.github.io/attack-navigator/. Accessed 30 Mar 2021
29. Allawi, M.A.A., Hadi, A., Awajan, A.: MLDED: multi-layer data exfiltration detection system. In: 2015 Fourth International Conference on Cyber Security, Cyber Warfare, and Digital Forensic (2015)
30. Guri, M., Solewicz, Y., Daidakulov, A., Elovici, Y.: Fansmitter: acoustic data exfiltration from (speakerless) air-gapped computers. Comput. Sci. (2016)
31. Haber, M.J., Hibbert, B.: Asset Attack Vectors: Building Effective Vulnerability Management Strategies to Protect Organizations. Apress, Berkeley (2018). ISBN 9781484236260
32. MWR InfoSecurity (Head Office). Detecting and Deterring Data Exfiltration - Guide for Implementers. In: Centre for the Protection of National Infrastructure (2014). https://www.researchgate.net/profile/Mohamed_Mourad_Lafifi/post/Any_good_ICS_Dataset_contains_exfiltration_data_leakages/attachment/5be5a43fcfe4a7645500ee64/AS%3A691074662141959%401541776447655/download/Detecting-Deterring-Data-Exfiltration-Guide-for-Implementers-.pdf
33. Maltego Organization: Website Maltego (2021). https://www.maltego.com/. Accessed 20 Apr 2021
34. Rajba, P., Mazurczyk, W.: Exploiting minification for data hiding purposes. In: ARES 2020: Proceedings of the 15th International Conference on Availability, Reliability and Security (2020). https://doi.org/10.1145/3407023.3409209
35. Ashley, T., Kwon, R., Sri, N.: Cyber threat dictionary using MITRE ATT&CK matrix and NIST cybersecurity framework mapping. In: 2020 Resilience Week (RWS) Resilience Week (RWS), pp. 106–112 (2020)
36. Ruef, M.: Monitoring-Detecting Attacks with MITRE ATT&CK. In: scip Labs, Zenodo (2019)
37. Antonatos, S., Braghin, S.: 4Kdump: exfiltrating files via hexdump and video capture. In: CS2 2019: Proceedings of the Sixth Workshop on Cryptography and Security in Computing Systems (2019). https://dl.acm.org/doi/10.1145/3304080.3304081
38. Sparx Systems. Website Sparx Systems - Enterprise Architect (2021). https://www.sparxsystems.de/. Accessed 21 Apr 2021
39. Xu, Y., Yang, Y., He, Y.: A representation of business oriented cyber threat intelligence and the objects assembly. In: IEEE 10th International Conference on Information Science and Technology (ICIST) Information Science and Technology (ICIST) (2020). https://ieeexplore.ieee.org/stamp/stamp.jsp?tp=&arnumber=7795373
40. Yoon, S.: Steganography in the modern attack landscape. In: Carbon Black (2019). https://www.carbonblack.com/blog/steganography-in-the-modern-attack-landscape/

PCWQ: A Framework for Evaluating Password Cracking Wordlist Quality

Aikaterini Kanta[1,2], Iwen Coisel[2], and Mark Scanlon[1]([⊠])

[1] Forensics and Security Research Group, School of Computer Science,
University College Dublin, Dublin, Ireland
`aikaterini.kanta@ucdconnect.ie, mark.scanlon@ucd.ie`
[2] European Commission Joint Research Centre (DG JRC),
Via Enrico Fermi 2749, 21027 Ispra, Italy
{`aikaterini.kanta,iwen.coisel`}`@ec.europa.eu`
`https://www.forensicsandsecurity.com/`

Abstract. The persistence of the single password as a method of authentication has driven both the efforts of system administrators to nudge users to choose stronger, safer passwords and elevated the sophistication of the password cracking methods chosen by their adversaries. In this constantly moving landscape, the use of wordlists to create smarter password cracking candidates begs the question of whether there is a way to assess which is better. In this paper, we present a novel modular framework to measure the quality of input wordlists according to several interconnecting metrics. Furthermore, we have conducted a preliminary analysis where we assess different input wordlists to showcase the framework's evaluation process.

Keywords: Password cracking · Wordlist · Dictionary · Contextual information

1 Introduction

Despite known security concerns, passwords still remain the most widely used and one of the easiest and most adopted methods of authentication. As password policies become more restrictive by enforcing the selection of stronger passwords, attacks also become more refined and sophisticated. Traditional password cracking methods have, in many cases, become less efficient due to the increase of the computational cost of the underlying algorithms and the strengthening of the passwords [3]. Salting the passwords[1] also drastically increases the complexity of the password cracking process when targeting several passwords as each salt must be consider independently.

In the case where a single password is considered, if the attacker is aware of information regarding the target, that information can be leveraged aiming at

---

[1] The salt is a random string (typically 3 to 5 random characters) that is concatenated to the password before hashing it. Identical passwords therefore have a different hash.

© ICST Institute for Computer Sciences, Social Informatics and Telecommunications Engineering 2022
Published by Springer Nature Switzerland AG 2022. All Rights Reserved
P. Gladyshev et al. (Eds.): ICDF2C 2021, LNICST 441, pp. 159–175, 2022.
https://doi.org/10.1007/978-3-031-06365-7_10

cracking the password in fewer attempts. An example of this type of situation would be a law enforcement officer wanting to access a password protected digital device of a suspect during the course of an investigation. In this case, time is of the essence in order to swiftly resolve the investigation or prevent further criminal acts.

Another particular case is when the targeted dataset can be associated to a particular context. An example would be a penetration testing campaign evaluating the strength of the passwords used by the user of a system. If such system is linked to a particular community - for example users of a video game service - the operator can use contextual information such as typical language used in this community, references from the topic, or any other type of contextual information to refine the password cracking process.

All the above information can be useful, to try to make more educated guesses about the password of a target or a community [10]. The ultimate goal is to recover the password faster than we would with current state-of-the-art approaches, by giving them a head start regarding the wordlist they use during the password cracking process. By creating a custom wordlist, that is tailored to the target and by checking first password candidates that are more likely to be chosen as the password by the target, we can have a more efficient password recovery process.

In this article, we have designed a modular framework to assess the quality of a wordlist to be used in password cracking processes. We have proposed several criteria that can be considered for such evaluation and explained why there cannot be a single and totally ordered metric to evaluate the wordlist. Our methodology relies on the Password Guessing Framework (PGF)[2], initially designed to evaluate and compare password guessing tools, that we have adapted and complemented for the need of this study. We are then discussing how this framework can and will be used to evaluate and improve wordlist generation processes depending on the conditions of particular scenarios.

2   Background and Related Work

2.1   Password Cracking Techniques

There is a vast array of password cracking techniques, that are used depending the situation, from the traditional, like an exhaustive search, to the recently developed, like machine and deep learning techniques, such as the ones based on Generative Adversarial Networks (GANs) [7]. A common approach is the dictionary attack in combination with mangling rules, which are grammar and slang substitutions and modifications that aim to imitate human tendencies during password selection. For example, using the number *3* instead of the letter *e*, adding a *!* at the end of the password, capitalising the first letter, etc. It is important to note that mangling rules widen the set of guesses significantly, because each new alteration has to be checked with all the password candidates. This is

---

[2] https://www.password-guessing.org/.

why a balance has to be achieved between the number of mangling rules that we want to test and the time we can afford for the recovery process. There are common mangling rules that are used by the community such as the Hashcat[3] Best64 rules.

Other common password cracking methods include rainbow tables [15], which are based on the idea of a time-memory trade-off where the hashes of plaintext passwords are pre-computed and stored for faster lookup. A common counter-measure to rainbow tables is the use of a `salt`, which is a random value concatenated to the plaintext password before it is hashed, rendering rainbow tables unpractical in all scenarios where salt is used.

There are many different password cracking algorithms, some of which have been around for years, like John the Ripper[4] and hashcat[5], and some which have emerged lately such as PassGan [7] which uses a Generative Adversarial Network (GAN) to learn password rules directly from leaked password lists, or the neural network based solution from Melicher et al. [14]. Along with those already mentioned, several other tools have been proposed and we cite few of them in what follows. OMEN [4] is using a Markov model to generate candidates in a decreasing order of probabilities. PCFG [25] which stands for Probabilistic Context-Free grammar, where the input dictionary is used to create a context-free grammar and assign probabilities to it. PRINCE[6] creates intelligent chains to all combinations of words from the input wordlist.

2.2 Analysis of Password Trends

Something else that has changed in recent years is that information about previous passwords is easily available on the internet. Every day we hear of new data breaches that expose passwords (plaintext or hashed) and sometimes accompanying information, such as emails, names, addresses, etc. For an attacker wanting to access a specific account belonging to an individual, the password cracking attack could be reduced to a simple lookup for a match in leaked lists. In fact, studies of password habits of users have shown that users tend to reuse passwords that they need to enter frequently [24] and they tend to underestimate the consequences of doing so.

Furthermore, even when passwords are not reused explicitly, there are password ties between older and newer passwords of the same user [19]. But, even in the good case where that particular user does not reuse the same password across different services, knowing their previous passwords or other information about them, can give great insight to the cracking process [9]. To this end, Tar-Guess, a framework that makes use of Personally Identifiable Information (PII) and cross-site information, has been proposed to make targeted guesses of users' passwords and it was shown to outperform current models for both the cases of non-savvy and security-savvy internet users [23].

---

[3] https://hashcat.net/.
[4] https://www.openwall.com/john/.
[5] https://www.hashcat.net.
[6] https://github.com/hashcat/princeprocessor.

But even if previous passwords of a user are not known, a case can be made that knowledge of passwords of other users can speedup the process [11]. In fact, studies have shown that there are common misconceptions people fall prey to when creating their password, such as thinking that by adding a symbol at the end of the password they make it more secure [6,18].

The password policy in place plays a role at the strength and guessability of a password. It has been shown that putting a password policy in place forces users to have more secure passwords, whereas users left to their own devices will generally choose weaker passwords [13]. But the stronger passwords required by password policies may lead users to either having trouble remembering and ending up writing down their passwords [12] or to use common techniques for bypassing the requirements without building a strong password [16]. For example, `Password1!` fulfills the requirement for uppercase, lowercase, symbols and numbers and is above eight characters, but would not be considered a strong password.

2.3   Password Strength Meter

Password strength meter is another field of study that is continuously evolving following the sophistication of password cracking attacks. The most basic strength meter is a simple 0/1 metric where basic rules must be respected by the password to accept it, and reject it otherwise, like the LUDS-8 from the NIST proposal back in 2004 [1]. There are nowadays several proposals relying on different approaches often aiming at giving a score instead of a yes/no. One of the most well-known meters is "zxcvbn" [26] in use in the Dropbox service and probably in many others as it is an open-source solution. Some meters rely on cracking techniques to assess the probability the password would be produced by such techniques, such as the OMEN-based solution [2] or the PCFG-based one [8,20]. Some meters are machine-learning based such as the neural network based meter of Melicher et al. [14] extended by Ur et al. [17], or the multi-modal approach of Galbally et al. [5]. While increasing the security of digital services by enforcing users to select strong and safe passwords, those meters also play a role in the analysis of password datasets to better understand human tendencies but also classifying passwords in classes of strength.

3   How Can Quality Be Measured?

The definition of a metric to measure and classify the quality of wordlist given as input to password cracking process is a difficult one. The expected features a wordlist should have, and be evaluated on, is likely to vary depending on the final cracking process and its context. The particular scenario of the attack, such as whether it is a targeted attack to a specific individual or a fishing attack that targets a group of people plays a role in the approach we take for creating a wordlist. Other factors, such as the language of the target(s), the type of service, etc., also have to be taken into account, since the approach will be different [22].

Therefore, creating a single metric for measuring the quality of dictionaries is not suggested. Instead, we are looking at a number of factors that can be taken into account, alone or combined, when deciding the type and makeup of a wordlist that is likely to make it the optimal candidate for a specific scenario. These factors are presented below.

3.1 Final Percentage of Passwords Cracked

This is the most straight-forward metric in password cracking, where a wordlist is evaluated based on the amount of passwords it has cracked from a target list. This metric is typically the most important one especially in the case where the concern is the volume of cracked passwords and the focus is not on a single target or a small number of targets.

Some password cracking processes have a fixed limit of candidates they can generate based on the size of the input wordlist. For example, a straight dictionary attack will generate as many candidates as there are in the wordlist, potentially multiplied by the number of mangling rules, if they are used. Some other processes can be considered as endless, such as for example Markov-based ones if they are not limited, and will continuously produce candidates like an unbounded exhaustive search would do. As a consequence, those endless processes would theoretically always retrieve 100% of the passwords if they are given enough time which in most cases is not practical. That is why it is necessary to set a limit to the number of candidates that a process is allowed to generate and test. Such limit can be adjusted depending on the complexity of the scenario we want to assess.

3.2 Number of Guesses Until Target

The previous metric alone is not enough to evaluate a wordlist as other factors can be relevant in some scenarios. For example, one wordlist may recover 75% of passwords while a second may get only 60%. But, it might be the case that the second one reached a score of 50% with less candidates generated than the first one. In some scenarios, the number of candidates that can be evaluated in a reasonable time is strongly limited because of hardware constraints or high complexity of the underlying function making the second wordlist more interesting for a particular scenario. Assessing the number of guesses needed to reach a targeted percentage of retrieved passwords can help to select a wordlist more suited to the conditions of some scenarios.

3.3 Progress over Time

Another metric that is strongly related to the amount of found passwords, is the pace in which the passwords are retrieved. During password cracking, an updated percentage of results at pre-established checkpoints, can give us insights into the performance of the dictionary over time. For example, at some point in the cracking progress, the amount of new passwords guessed at every checkpoint might start decreasing, which means that the new password candidates that are checked do not recover new passwords anymore. This is often another criterion to stop the process and also a hint, for dictionary lists that are ordered by count, that the size of the input wordlist can be decreased without a remarkable effect on performance. This criterion is the second derivative of the curve of found passwords over number of guesses and represents a process with an upper bound, compared to the metric outlined in Sect. 3.1.

3.4 Size of Wordlist

Closely related to the stop criterion of incremental progress over time, the size of the wordlist is another metric that can be taken into account. For example, when two wordlists, with a significant difference in size, produce similar numbers of cracked passwords, the smaller wordlist can be thought of as of better quality, as it needs less information to achieve the same results. From another point of view, when the foreseen process is machine learning based, a larger wordlist could be preferred to reinforce the training phase.

3.5 Better Performance with Stronger Passwords

Another metric that should be considered is the performance of a wordlist against difficult passwords. For example, if two wordlists are similar in the previous criteria, i.e. crack about the same number of passwords, do it at about the same amount of time and are of similar size, the one that cracks more difficult to recover passwords is stronger, and should be assigned a higher score. Often, in real world scenarios and if the hash function permits it, an exhaustive search is performed first for the weaker passwords. This means that a wordlist that performs well against passwords that cannot be recovered by a brute force attack, is more valuable.

3.6 Compound Metric

The above metrics, cannot accurately assess any individual wordlist. Focus on one, or more of the above is necessary, according to the target case. For example, when we are concerned with recovering as many passwords as possible, the percentage of success is what matters most. But, when we want the largest number of passwords in a specified amount of time, the trade off between success and time is important. When we focus on a single target, or a small number of targets, like during the course of an investigation, speed and possibly the performance against stronger passwords are important factors to consider. This criterion can be refined to look at the number of guesses needed to retrieve a given percentage of passwords of a certain strength class as defined later in Sect. 5.

Furthermore, it has been shown that large corpora of passwords obey Zipf's Law, meaning that the frequency of each popular password, would be inversely proportional to each rank, i.e. the second most popular password would appear approximately half as many times as the first [21]. According to this analysis, the level of fit of a particular dataset under this model, could be an indicator of strength of the dataset.

This brings forward the need for a compound metric, one that combines two or more of the above criteria, to get an evaluation tailored to a specific case.

4 Methodology

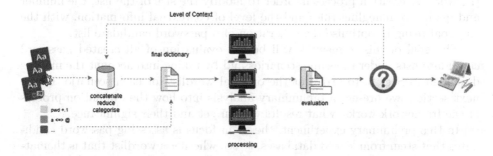

Fig. 1. Methodology

Based on the metrics analysed in Sect. 3, the evaluation of input wordlists, with the purpose of arriving at the optimal one, is a case by case scenario and is based on the individual needs, be it rate of success, time it takes to achieve a certain threshold or success at recovering one specific strong password.

Furthermore, the success of the input wordlist is not only based on the above factors, but also on the tools we use to do the password cracking. For example, PCFG works better and estimates more accurate probabilities when the input dictionary does not contain only unique entries, but repeated ones. However, such dataset with repetitions are rarely available to the research community. Therefore, in order to test wordlists, it is essential to have a few different tools to evaluate them with.

For this purpose, we have chosen to use four tools; John the Ripper, Omen, PCFG and Prince. The aim of this is not to compare these tools and find which is the better one, rather to make sure we have compared input dictionaries as thoroughly as possible. In order to perform this part of the process, we are using the Password Guessing Framework (PGF). This tool is an open source tool to automate the process of comparing different password guessers. As already mentioned, the reason we are using this tool is not to compare password guessers, rather to avail of its ability to automatise the setting up of the cracking process. Indeed, PGF allows the setting up of 'jobs' which will be processed sequentially, where you can define the parameters of the guessing tool, input dictionary, target list (hashed or plain), max number of guesses, etc. The results come in the form of *.txt and *.csv files containing an analysis of the number of found passwords, a list of those as well as data on cracking performance over time. All this information is then used by us for the evaluation of the input dictionaries.

As the methodology flowchart on Fig. 1 shows, the performance of the different input dictionaries is evaluated and presented or fed back to pre-processing. The pre-processing step, which is outside the scope of this paper and part of our future work, contains the creation of tailored input lists from existing or custom dictionaries, the tailoring of mangling rules to the specific scenario (keeping in mind whether the end goal is success ratio, time efficiency, recovery of a targeted password, etc.). The feedback from the evaluation process will re-trigger the wordlist creation process in order to modify the size of the list, the number and quality of mangling rules and the level of contextual information, with the end goal being to optimise the generation of a password candidate list.

The goal of this framework will be the evaluation of all created password candidate lists under the same scenarios and by taking into account the metrics discussed in Sect. 3, to arrive at the optimal wordlist for each scenario. In the next section, we present a preliminary analysis into how the evaluation process of the framework works, what results we can get and their significance.

In this preliminary experiment, the main focus is assessing password candidates that stem from leaked databases, to see whether a wordlist that is thematically similar to the list of passwords we want to crack can yield better results than a generic wordlist.

5   Preliminary Analysis

5.1   Dataset Selection and Creation

The datasets we used to conduct a preliminary experiment to gauge the role of context in password selection, can be summed up in Table 1. The dataset we have named Comb4 is a combination of four different leaked datasets from four categories, music, cars, videogames and manga. Our aim was to create a combination of datasets from different sources to cover a wide spectrum of user interests and ascertain whether the purpose of the forum for which the password is created for, plays a role during the creation process. Because of availability, the evaluation datasets are from only two of the above categories, manga and videogames. We have also used RockYou as a baseline to compare the other datasets with. The version of RockYou we used is the one with 14 million unique passwords but the full version of 32 million passwords was also tested with PCFG, but yielded to slightly better but similar results. All the datasets used in this experiment stem from an online database of leaked wordlists named *hashes.org*, the use of which has been reviewed and approved by the Office of Research Ethics of University College Dublin.

Table 1. Datasets in use

	Dataset	Size
Comb4	axemusic	252,752
	jeepforum	239.347
	minecraft	143,248
	mangatraders	618,237
Evaluation	boostbot	143,578
	mangafox	437,531
	RockYou	14,344,391

5.2   Example Use Case

In this example use case, the evaluation datasets, Boostbot and Mangafox, as well as RockYou are used without modification with all four password crackers and 10 billion candidates were generated and evaluated for each process. The results of the cracking progress over time for RockYou, Mangafox and Boostbot can be found in Figs. 2, 3 and 4 respectively. As can be seen on all three figures, PCFG performs better for all three datasets and especially in the case of RockYou the result is much more distinguished. Comb4 contains 1,253,531 passwords, of which 1,096,481 are unique. Of these, RockYou PCFG managed to crack more than 60% (768,341) or in case of unique passwords 617,016. This result is significantly more than the other three guessers, but also significantly more than Mangafox and Boostbot. In fact, RockYou performed better than both of those datasets with all four guessers.

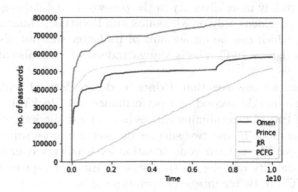

Fig. 2. Cracking progress over time with RockYou

This result is not a surprise because the first key difference between RockYou and Mangafox and Boostbot is their size, as seen in Table 1. RockYou is about 32 times larger than Mangafox and 100 times larger than Boostbot. This means

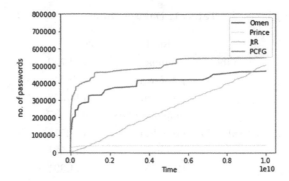

Fig. 3. Cracking progress over time with `Mangafox`

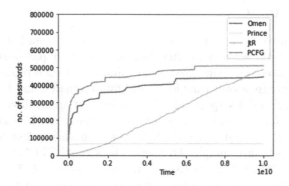

Fig. 4. Cracking progress over time with `Boostbot`

that there is certainly more diversity in the password candidates generated with rockyou. If then we focus only on Mangafox and Boostbot, Mangafox performed slightly better, which can be on account of its larger size but also on the fact that the largest dataset in Comb4 is Mangatraders, which is also another manga related leak.

Furthermore, we can see that Prince under performed with the smaller datasets, while it had the second best performance with RockYou. This is due to the principle of PRINCE combining entries of the input dictionary to create new candidates. The input in the two smaller dataset are more sophisticated than those in Rockyou. There, their concatenation leads to very complex candidates with a low probability of being in the targeted list. A pre-processing could be apply in PRINCE to better integrate such type of input wordlist.

JtR on the other hand, steadily improved throughout the cracking process, almost reaching PCFG towards the end for both Mangafox and Boostbot.

Table 2. Strength distribution in Comb4

	Comb 4	Axemusic	Jeepforum	Mangatraders	Minecraft
Class 0	46,645	4,143	34,832	6,471	1,199
Class 1	503,809	93,100	128,279	241,745	40,685
Class 2	395,202	87,158	58,189	205,218	44,637
Class 3	226,243	55,395	16,657	118,840	35,351
Class 4	81,624	12,898	1,388	45,962	21,376

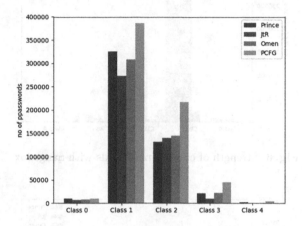

Fig. 5. Strength of cracked passwords with RockYou

Because the amount of cracked passwords, as mentioned in Sect. 3 cannot be the only metric to take into account - otherwise RockYou would have been the clear winner - we also looked at the strength classes of the cracked passwords by each dataset.

In order to evaluate that, we used zxcvbn, as referenced in Sect. 2. With zxcvbn passwords are divided into 5 classes, according to their strength, i.e. how well they would withstand a cracking attack, with class 0 being the least secure and class 4 being the most secure. This classification takes into account rules set by common password policies but also l33t speak, common passwords and patterns to make a determination. Table 2 shows the classification of Comb4 in these classes and Figs. 5, 6 and 7 show the cracked passwords per class for RockYou, Mangafox and Boostbot respectively, with all four password guessers.

As can be seen by the above figures for all three datasets, the distribution of found passwords follows the distribution amongst classes of the Comb4 dataset which can be seen in Table 2. For RockYou, we can see that PCFG as expected performed better on all classes (except class 0, where all four are on par) with an especially big difference for class 3 and 4 compared to the other guessers. When it comes to Mangafox, other than Prince, the performance was similar for the three other guessers. Interestingly, Mangafox and Boostbot were able to find about one third as many passwords in class 4 as RockYou with PCFG, especially considering the big difference in size. Even more remarkably, MangaFox and Boostbot outperformed RockYou in case of class 4 with both JtR and Omen.

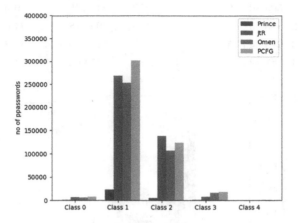

Fig. 6. Strength of cracked passwords with `mangafox`

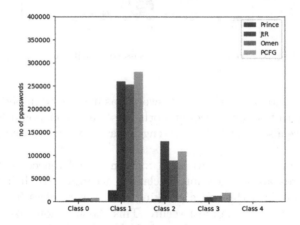

Fig. 7. Strength of cracked passwords with `boostbot`

Oftentimes, in real world scenarios, the way to go would not be to choose one password cracking guesser or input wordlist over the other but stack them. For this reason we wanted to see how using a big input dataset like RockYou could be complemented, rather than beat. Table 3 shows the number of unique passwords that were found only by Mangafox and Boostbot and not by RockYou, in total and also their distribution amongst the 5 classes of `zxcvbn`.

Table 3. Passwords found by Boostbot and Mangafox but not by RockYou

		JtR	Omen	Prince	PCFG
All	Boostbot	26,109	32,911	5,788	17,811
	Mangafox	26,694	37,977	3,608	22,121
Class 0	Boostbot	182	265	22	73
	Mangafox	210	227	35	109
Class 1	Boostbot	11,960	16,698	3,095	3,659
	Mangafox	12,005	14,603	1,664	5,393
Class 2	Boostbot	10,439	11,628	1,730	8,303
	Mangafox	12,192	16,702	1,476	11,303
Class 3	Boostbot	3,512	4,171	796	5,266
	Mangafox	2,285	6,325	373	4,868
Class 4	Boostbot	16	149	145	510
	Mangafox	2	120	60	448

As can be seen in Table 3, this is a substantial addition of found passwords. In fact, with PCFG, the addition of either the passwords recovered by Mangafox or Boostbot, brings a 14% increase to the total, which is an important addition, being that this is the class of passwords that is the least easy to recover. Even in the case of Prince that generally underperformed, 73% for Mangafox and 63% for Boostbot, of the passwords that were found with these two datasets, were not recovered by RockYou. The recovery of class 4 passwords with Omen was even more impressive because about twice as many passwords were recovered with Mangafox or Boostbot compared to RockYou. Finally, even in the case of JtR, with a meagre 2 passwords recovered from Mangafox and 16 from Boostbot, RockYou did not manage to find any of class 4.

5.3   Breakdown of Comb4

In order to assess the quality of the input wordlists even further, we decided to break down Comb4 into the four individual datasets it was generated from, axemusic, jeepforum, mangatraders and minecraft. The breakdown of these datasets to zxcvbn classes is shown in Table 2. Additionally, Table 4 shows the amount of passwords found of each dataset of Comb4, by each input wordlist for all four password guessers. The result that pops up is that in the case of Minecraft, and excluding the underperforming Prince, the amount of passwords found by RockYou, Mangafox and Boostbot are very similar. A possible explanation of these results is that the thematic proximity compensates for the difference in size. In fact, Boostbot is the smallest dataset (about 100 smaller than RockYou) but thematically is the one closest to Minecraft. And Mangatraders is still a lot more relevant to Minecraft than for example Jeepforum.

Still, we see that for the other three datasets, RockYou performs a lot better than Mangafox and Boostbot. Even in the case of Mangatraders, while the

Table 4. Breakdown of Comb4

		JtR	Omen	Prince	PCFG
Axemusic	RockYou	60,583	86,417	88,776	131,485
	Mangafox	57,923	67,934	6,456	93,843
	Boostbot	57,120	63,969	8,027	86,090
Jeepforum	RockYou	96,894	105,232	109,847	133,665
	Mangafox	93,250	74,535	7,461	92,265
	Boostbot	89,084	72,753	6,966	83,477
Mangatraders	RockYou	267,553	289,903	299,890	373,483
	Mangafox	260,126	234,834	18,067	255,964
	Boostbot	252,338	221,328	22,121	241,774
Minecraft	RockYou	39,050	42,630	36,335	55,226
	Mangafox	41,417	43,171	3,561	50,221
	Boostbot	40,624	39,345	5,741	43,953

results for JtR and Omen are close, RockYou's performance for PCFG is significantly better, since for PCFG the full RockYou list of 32 millions was used, so that PCFG can take advantage of repetitions of passwords to form better probabilities.

In this case, the size of the input wordlist makes the difference and this along with percentage of success is the one to watch. Still, as mentioned above, in real cases the goal is not to choose one wordlist over the other but to complement it. For this reason, we are looking again at another metric, performance for stronger passwords. In Table 5 we are looking at PCFG only, and focusing on the class 3 and class 4 passwords that were recovered by only Mangafox and Boostbot and not by RockYou. As can be seen, the percentage of passwords found by these two datasets and not RockYou was significantly higher for minecraft and mangatraders, the two datasets that were contextually closer to mangafox and boostbot.

Table 5. Breakdown by dataset for PCFG, Class 3 and Class 4

PCFG	Mangafox		Boostbot	
	Class 3	Class 4	Class 3	Class 4
axemusic	1.3%	0.4%	1.6%	0.5%
jeepforum	0.9%	0.6%	0.9%	0.4%
mangatraders	2.2%	0.7%	2.7%	0.9%
minecraft	4.1%	0.3%	3.4%	0.2%

6   Discussion

The question that arises from the preliminary results is, what do these two datasets have that RockYou does not? Both Mangafox and Boostbot stem from online leaks and there is no processing, augmentation or other customisation done to them. Furthermore, their size is small compared to the 14 million of RockYou passwords (32 million in the case of PCFG). The one advantage these datasets have, is that thematically they are closer to the target datasets.

Overall, the performances between the three wordlist are comparable when considering the JtR approach and close when considering with Omen, both of which are Markov based models. The results are really poor when it comes to Prince (for Mangafox and Boostbot) but a pre-processing on the wordlist to make a better usage of it could modify those results. PCFG works better than the other processes but with a clear advantage for RockYou. This is probably thanks to the difference of size, giving more chance to PCFG to infer and reuse the grammar. One way to possibly improve the results of PCFG with Mangafox and Boostbot could be to reuse the grammar trained from RockYou but feeding the special list with the content of the other dataset.

Both Mangafox and Boostbot have a better ratio of passwords found in Class 3 for Minecraft and in a less impressive manner on Class 4 for Mangatraders. The found passwords are significantly fewer for Axemusic and Jeepforum, probably due to a lesser proximity of the communities. Surprisingly, Mangafox performs better than Bootsbot on Minecraft and Boostbot better on Mangatraders than Mangafox, while we would have expect the results to be the other way around. Still, the communities of manga and videogames are more closely associated with each other than music and cars, so this close proximity might be the explanation. Finally, while Mangafox performs poorly on Class 3 of Jeepforum, it performs relatively well, even if the numbers are small, on Class 4.

7   Conclusion and Future Work

The developed framework provides a new methodology to assess and compare wordlists. It highlights that wordlists behave differently depending of the context of the target dataset and it can therefore be used to develop and assess wordlist generation processes in several scenarios. Focusing on the different classes of strength is also useful to evaluate the quality of wordlists to retrieve stronger passwords.

Our analysis highlighted also that the size and the composition of the wordlists have a strong impact on some processes, for example Prince and PCFG, while it is less visible for some other processes. Dedicated pre-processing shall be envisaged to better prepare the wordlists for those processes.

Therefore, it is clear that not one metric can stand alone, evaluate a wordlist thoroughly and assign a score that can predict how well that wordlist will do against a target. As was the case in this preliminary analysis, a compound metric will be needed for the evaluation, and even then, there should be room left for its parameterisation for each attack scenario.

Our future work will be twofold. On one hand it will focus on the design of a process to generate targeted wordlists which will be tailored to specific scenarios, with the aim to achieve better results for some targeted community or classes of strength. This process will involve the customisation of the wordlist based on contextual information known about the target, as well as by a constant feedback process with which the levels of contextualisation, the choice of mangling rules and the size of the input wordlist, will be optimised. Secondly, through the process mentioned above, further work will be conducted to assess and combine the metrics presented in this paper, and optimise them for the evaluation of wordlists.

References

1. Burr, W.E., Dodson, D.F., Polk, W.T.: NIST special publication 800–63 - electronic authentication guideline. Technical report, National Institute for Standards and Technology (2004)
2. Castelluccia, C., Dürmuth, M., Perito, D.: Adaptive password-strength meters from Markov models. In: NDSS (2012)
3. Du, X., et al.: SoK: exploring the state of the art and the future potential of artificial intelligence in digital forensic investigation. In: Proceedings of the 15th International Conference on Availability, Reliability and Security. Association of Computing Machinery (2020)
4. Dürmuth, M., Angelstorf, F., Castelluccia, C., Perito, D., Chaabane, A.: OMEN: faster password guessing using an ordered Markov enumerator. In: Piessens, F., Caballero, J., Bielova, N. (eds.) ESSoS 2015. LNCS, vol. 8978, pp. 119–132. Springer, Cham (2015). https://doi.org/10.1007/978-3-319-15618-7_10
5. Galbally, J., Coisel, I., Sanchez, I.: A new multimodal approach for password strength estimation-part I: theory and algorithms. IEEE Trans. Inf. Forensics Secur. 12(12), 2829–2844 (2017)
6. Haque, T., Wright, M., Scielzo, S.: Hierarchy of users' web passwords: perceptions, practices and susceptibilities. Int. J. Hum Comput Stud. 72(12), 860–874 (2014)
7. Hitaj, B., Gasti, P., Ateniese, G., Perez-Cruz, F.: PassGAN: a deep learning approach for password guessing. In: Deng, R.H., Gauthier-Umaña, V., Ochoa, M., Yung, M. (eds.) ACNS 2019. LNCS, vol. 11464, pp. 217–237. Springer, Cham (2019). https://doi.org/10.1007/978-3-030-21568-2_11
8. Houshmand, S., Aggarwal, S.: Building better passwords using probabilistic techniques. In: Proceedings of the 28th Annual Computer Security Applications Conference, ACSAC 2012, pp. 109–118. Association for Computing Machinery, New York (2012)
9. Kanta, A., Coisel, I., Scanlon, M.: A survey exploring open source intelligence for smarter password cracking. Forensic Sci. Int. Digit. Investig. 35, 301075 (2020)
10. Kanta, A., Coisel, I., Scanlon, M.: Smarter password guessing techniques leveraging contextual information and OSINT. In: 2020 International Conference on Cyber Security and Protection of Digital Services (Cyber Security), pp. 1–2. IEEE (2020)
11. Kanta, A., Coray, S., Coisel, I., Scanlon, M.: How Viable is Password Cracking in Digital Forensic Investigation? Analyzing the Guessability of over 3.9 Billion Real-World Accounts. Forensic Science International: Digital Investigation, July 2021

12. Kuo, C., Romanosky, S., Cranor, L.F.: Human selection of mnemonic phrase-based passwords. In: Proceedings of the Second Symposium on Usable Privacy and Security, SOUPS 2006, pp. 67–78. Association for Computing Machinery, New York (2006)
13. Liu, Z., Hong, Y., Pi, D.: A large-scale study of web password habits of Chinese network users. JSW **9**(2), 293–297 (2014)
14. Melicher, W., et al.: Fast, lean, and accurate: modeling password guessability using neural networks. In: Proceedings of the 25th USENIX Conference on Security Symposium, SEC 2016, pp. 175–191. USENIX Association, USA (2016)
15. Oechslin, P.: Making a faster cryptanalytic time-memory trade-off. In: Boneh, D. (ed.) CRYPTO 2003. LNCS, vol. 2729, pp. 617–630. Springer, Heidelberg (2003). https://doi.org/10.1007/978-3-540-45146-4_36
16. Shay, R., et al.: Designing password policies for strength and usability. ACM Trans. Inf. Syst. Secur. **18**(4), 1–34 (2016)
17. Ur, B., et al.: Design and evaluation of a data-driven password meter. In: Proceedings of the 2017 CHI Conference on Human Factors in Computing Systems, CHI 2017, pp. 3775–3786. Association for Computing Machinery, New York (2017)
18. Ur, B., et al.: "I added '!' at the end to make it secure": observing password creation in the lab. In: Eleventh Symposium on Usable Privacy and Security (SOUPS 2015), pp. 123–140 (2015)
19. von Zezschwitz, E., De Luca, A., Hussmann, H.: Survival of the shortest: a retrospective analysis of influencing factors on password composition. In: Kotzé, P., Marsden, G., Lindgaard, G., Wesson, J., Winckler, M. (eds.) INTERACT 2013. LNCS, vol. 8119, pp. 460–467. Springer, Heidelberg (2013). https://doi.org/10.1007/978-3-642-40477-1_28
20. Wang, D., He, D., Cheng, H., Wang, P.: FuzzyPSM: a new password strength meter using fuzzy probabilistic context-free grammars. In: 2016 46th Annual IEEE/IFIP International Conference on Dependable Systems and Networks (DSN), pp. 595–606 (2016)
21. Wang, D., Cheng, H., Wang, P., Huang, X., Jian, G.: Zipf's law in passwords. IEEE Trans. Inf. Forensics Secur. **12**(11), 2776–2791 (2017)
22. Wang, D., Wang, P., He, D., Tian, Y.: Birthday, name and bifacial-security: understanding passwords of Chinese web users. In: 28th USENIX Security Symposium (USENIX Security 2019), pp. 1537–1555. USENIX Association, Santa Clara, August 2019
23. Wang, D., Zhang, Z., Wang, P., Yan, J., Huang, X.: Targeted online password guessing: an underestimated threat. In: Proceedings of the 2016 ACM SIGSAC Conference on Computer and Communications Security, CCS 2016, pp. 1242–1254. Association for Computing Machinery, New York (2016)
24. Wash, R., Rader, E., Berman, R., Wellmer, Z.: Understanding password choices: how frequently entered passwords are re-used across websites. In: Twelfth Symposium on Usable Privacy and Security (SOUPS 2016), pp. 175–188. USENIX Association, Denver, June 2016
25. Weir, M., Aggarwal, S., De Medeiros, B., Glodek, B.: Password cracking using probabilistic context-free grammars. In: 2009 30th IEEE Symposium on Security and Privacy, pp. 391–405. IEEE (2009)
26. Wheeler, D.L.: zxcvbn: low-budget password strength estimation. In: 25th USENIX Security Symposium (USENIX Security 2016), pp. 157–173 (2016)

No Pie in the Sky: The Digital Currency Fraud Website Detection

Haoran Ou, Yongyan Guo, Chaoyi Huang, Zhiying Zhao, Wenbo Guo, Yong Fang, and Cheng Huang$^{(\boxtimes)}$

School of Cyber Science and Engineering, Sichuan University, Chengdu, China
opcodesec@gmail.com

Abstract. In recent years, digital currencies based on blockchain technology are growing rapidly. Therefore, many criminal cases related to digital currency also took place. One of the most common ways is to induce victims to invest. As a result criminals can obtain a large number of profits through fraud. Cybercriminals usually design the layout of digital currency fraud websites to be similar to normal digital currency websites. Use some words related to blockchain, digital currency, and project white papers to confuse victims to invest. Once the victims have invested a lot of money, they cannot use digital currency to cash out. Digital currency is also difficult to track due to its anonymity. In this paper, we classified and summarized the existing methods of identifying digital currency scams. At the same time, we collected 2,489 domain names of fraudulent websites in the digital currency ecosystem and conducted statistical analysis from the four aspects of website text, domain names, rankings, and digital currency transaction information. We proposed a method to detect the website based on domain name registration time, website ranking, digital currency exchange rate, and other characteristics. We use the random forest algorithm as a classifier. The experimental results show that the proposed detection system can achieve an accuracy of 0.97 and a recall rate of 0.95. Finally, the case study results show that the system gets better detection and accuracy than other security products.

Keywords: Blockchain · Digital currency fraud website · Ponzi scheme · Phishing

1 Introduction

Since the first Bitcoin emerged in 2009, with development of the blockchain technology and the digital economy ecosystem, digital currencies have seen explosive growth. In addition to Bitcoin, thousands of digital currencies appear from time to time. As of the end of 2018 [1], there are more than 2,000 different digital currencies. Their total market value of up to 100 billion US dollars, higher than the GDP of 127 countries (as of 2019) [2]. As an indispensable trading platform for the

P. Gladyshev et al. (Eds.): ICDF2C 2021, LNICST 441, pp. 176–193, 2022.
https://doi.org/10.1007/978-3-031-06365-7_11

ecosystem, hundreds of digital currency exchanges are emerging to facilitate transactions between digital assets and traditional legal tender or other digital assets.

However, various MLM currency scams under the guise of block-chain [3] are also increasing. These digital currency fraud websites use high rebates as a gimmick to attract everyone to participate and absorb membership dues to collect money. In the end, the scam was exposed due to the severance of the capital chain [4]. The general public lacks professional network security knowledge, and they are often deceived by the advanced technical guise of these websites and various lofty backgrounds to invest in and finally cause serious economic losses [5]. The existence of these coins seriously threatens the safety of people's property and hinders the normal ecological development of blockchain technology.

How to identify digital currency fraud sites and prevent fraud attacks is a hot spot [6]. The blockchain community has begun to pay attention to fraudulent websites in the digital currency ecosystem. Several open-source databases (such as Crypto Scam DB and Etherscam DB) have collected this type of malicious domain names and their related URLs. The scammers [7] take advantage of these domain names and addresses to defraud victims and raise funds to obtain economic benefits.

The current research in this area is mainly on the detection of Ponzi schemes based on digital currencies, and the scope of detection is often limited to Bitcoin. It is detected by analyzing the characteristics of the smart Ponzi scheme [8], extracting smart contracts [9], and analyzing the abnormal transaction behavior of Bitcoin [10]. On the other hand, there are also studies on phishing websites and phishing accounts related to Bitcoin [11]. However, at this stage, there is still a lack of research on the use of automated technology to identify and classify digital currency websites as to whether they are fraudulent.

In response to the above problems, this paper proposes a method for identifying digital currency fraud websites based on machine learning. we first need to screen out the effective features from the extracted website data. Then we use the classification model, to realize the automatic recognition of the website.

The contribution of this article as follows:

- We propose a detection method for digital currency fraud sites. The detection of digital currency fraud sites is still rare. We have analyzed and categorized the existing detection methods for fraudulent digital currencies. Most of the current research is about whether there are abnormal transactions in Bitcoin or other digital currencies or the detection of Ponzi schemes related to digital currencies.
- We extract effective features to improve the accuracy of website detection. After statistical analysis and related literature review, we extracted text, domain names, website rankings, and mainstream exchanges from digital currency fraud sites. Using random forest algorithms, we established a digital currency fraud site detection model and realized the detection of digital currency fraud sites and accurate classification of normal websites.

– Compared with the test results of Tencent website security center, our test results are more accurate. The experimental data set sources of this article are (https://cryptoscamdb.org/) and (https://www.badbitcoin.org/thebadlist/index). Based on this data set, the recall rate of the detection model is 0.95, and the accuracy is 0.97. At the same time, we conducted comparative experiments and feature importance analysis. Finally, there was a case study carried out to verify the accuracy of the classification results.

The rest of this article is structured as follows: Sect. 2 reviews the background and related literature on digital currency fraud sites. Section 3 discusses the data source and data extraction process used. Section 4 presents the classification results of machine learning algorithms and model performance evaluation. Section 5 ends with a discussion.

2 Background and Related Work

2.1 Digital Currency

Digital currency is a digital asset that uses cryptography to ensure its creation security and transaction security. The first and most famous digital currency, Bitcoin, was released in 2009 [12]. So far, there are more than 2500 different digital currencies. With the rise of digital currencies in 2017, people pay more and more attention to digital currency exchanges to obtain or trade digital currencies.

Digital currency exchange [9] is a market where users can buy and sell digital currency. Many of them only provide trading services between digital currencies, while a few provide fiat currencies (such as U.S. dollars or euros) for digital currency transactions. Similar to the stock market [13], people obtain benefits because of changes in digital currency prices. There are three types of digital currencies: centralized exchanges (CEX) managed by companies or organizations, decentralized exchanges (DEX) that provide automated processes for peer-to-peer transactions, and hybrid transactions that combine the two.

2.2 Ponzi Scheme

Ponzi scheme [14] refers to a means of investment fraud in the financial field. Many illegal pyramid schemes use Ponzi schemes to collect money. The essence of the Ponzi scheme is to pay the investors of the next round as proceeds to the investors of the previous round, and so on, involving more investors and funds. But investors and funds are limited. When investors and funds are unsustainable, the entire scam will immediately collapse.

Ponzi schemes [15] generally have common characteristics such as low risk, high return, and pyramid-like investor structure.

Bitcoin is currently used as the payment infrastructure for Ponzi schemes [16]. These are financial frauds disguised as high-profit investment projects: in fact, the Ponzi scheme only uses funds invested by new users who join the program to repay users, so when there are no longer new investments, it will collapse.

A large number of victims have realized that these websites are fraudulent and illegal in many countries, but Bitcoin-based Ponzi schemes are still spreading on the Internet [17]. A recent study investigated posts on bitcointalk.org (a popular Bitcoin discussion forum), and the results showed that there were more than 1,800 Ponzi schemes from June 2011 to November 2016. [18] Due to the lack of a data set of Bitcoin-related Ponzi addresses, it is very difficult to measure the economic impact of Bitcoin-based Ponzi schemes. Conservative estimates from September 2013 to September 2014, Bitcoin-based Ponzi schemes have raised more than 7 million U.S. dollars. [19]

The current research on digital currency fraud includes two categories, smart Ponzi schemes, and phishing.

2.3 Smart Ponzi Schemes Detection

Weili Chen et al. [14] obtained 200 smart Ponzi schemes by manually checking more than 3000 open-source smart contracts on the Etalum platform. Two characteristics are extracted from the transaction history and operation code of the smart contract. Finally, a classification model of the smart Ponzi scheme is proposed.

Marie Vasek et al. [8] studied the supply-demand relationship of Bitcoin-based Ponzi schemes. Daniel Liebau et al. [9] defined scams and used empirical data to evaluate the number of cases that met this definition to establish a digital currency world. Massimo Bartoletti et al. [1] conducted a comprehensive investigation on Ponzi scams and analyzed their behavior and impact from different perspectives.

Shen Meng et al. [20] took two types of abnormal trading behaviors, airdrop candy, and greedy capital injections, as typical representatives, and designed the two types of abnormal trading behavior judgment rules, and then abstracted the abnormal trading pattern diagram. On this basis, they use the subgraph matching technology to realize the recognition algorithm of Bitcoin's abnormal transaction behavior.

2.4 Phishing Scam Detection

Most of the existing methods of analyzing Bitcoin scams require the manual or semi-manual collection of websites related to digital currency scams on the Internet [21]. Then the researchers can use automated tools to analyze. Quantify the impact of the scam by examining the related transactions on the blockchain. Ross Phillips et al. [22] analyzed open-source blockchain-based website data. They applied DBSCAN clustering technology to the content of fraudulent websites. The result shows that the types of digital currency fraudulent websites are corresponding with prepaid and phishing fraud.

Xiongfeng Guo et al. [23] proposes a method of phishing account detection system based on blockchain transactions and uses Ethereum as an example to verify its effectiveness. Specifically, they propose a graph-based cascading feature extraction method based on transaction records and a GBM-based double-sampling set algorithm to establish a recognition model. A large number of experiments show that the algorithm can effectively identify phishing scams.

The existing detection methods (mentioned in Sect. 2.3 and Sect. 2.4) for information fraud websites do not detect digital currency fraud websites, but can only detect traditional phishing websites. Or it is only possible to classify the open-source digital currency fraud websites through the clustering algorithm. It cannot detect whether the website is a normal website or a digital currency fraud website.

Based on the research of open-source digital currency fraud websites, our paper designs a classification model of digital currency fraud websites based on machine learning algorithms by analyzing and extracting effective features such as text and domain names in the website. The model realize the two classifications of normal websites and digital currency fraud websites.

3   Methodology

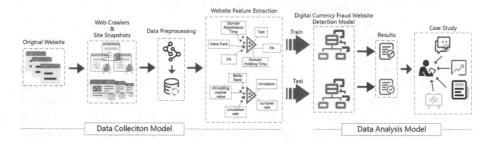

Fig. 1. The digital currency fraud website detection system

The framework of the digital currency fraud website detection system is shown in Fig. 1. Data sources include normal websites and digital currency fraud websites. For more information about it, see Sect. 3.1. We use web crawlers to collect the website's content, and for inaccessible websites, we use snapshots to collect related information. Next, we filter the website to remove unqualified websites and translate text. After data preprocessing operations, we obtain blacklist and whitelist data that meet the requirements. After analysis, we selected features such as text, search engines, website rankings (such as Alexa rankings), domain names, and mainstream exchanges to generate feature vectors as input to the detection model. Random forest (RF) is selected as the classifier, and support vector machine (SVM), naive Bayes (NB), and K-nearest neighbor algorithm (KNN) algorithms are comparative experiments. Use accuracy and precision indicators to evaluate the performance of the algorithm. Finally, for the detection results, we conduct a case study and verify the validity and accuracy of our detection results by consulting authoritative digital currency forums, exchange platforms, news media, and official announcements about the relevant comments and reports of this type of digital currency.

3.1 Data Collection and Preprocessing

Data Collection. It is divided into whitelist and blacklist data collection. The source of the whitelist data is the current mainstream digital currency websites and the Alexa's top 5000 websites. The blacklist includes digital currencies that are not on the mainstream trading platform and the publicly maintained blacklist list CryptoScamDB [24]. It is an open-source dataset website that stores more than 6,500 known fraud records on many chains such as Ethereum, Bitcoin, XRP, NEO, etc., which can be used to track malicious URLs and associate them with them Address. The entire website is open source, and all data sets and documents are available on GitHub. Among the collected websites are live websites and expired websites. We first traverse the secondary webpages belonging to the surviving website. After that, it needs to collect information such as pictures, text, DOM tree, homepage screenshots, and external URL links in the secondary webpages and the homepage. If we have no access to the webpage, we collect text and DOM tree information of these websites from screenshots.

Data Preprocessing. First of all, we translate the text of the collected websites. There is very little Chinese websites. According to the characteristics of the data set, we translate all other languages into English. As a result, the model can realize the detection of any language type website. Next, clean the text and delete all non-ASCII characters in the data. Finally, we obtain 3508 whitelisted websites with more than 12,000 pages and 2498 blacklisted websites with more than 12,000 pages.

3.2 Website Feature Extraction

Text Feature. Text information is an important part of the website and is widely used to identify phishing websites [25–27]. Among them, Adebowale et al. [25] proposed an intelligent phishing detection and protection scheme based on comprehensive features such as images, frames, and text. Digital currency scam website recognition also considers text features, while integrating other features for more accurate detection.

We use the Baidu translation interface to translate the source text information in the data set into English, delete punctuation marks and stop words, and perform word frequency statistics on the websites in the blacklist and whitelist. The top 300 words in the whitelisted word frequency statistics are removed from the top 300 words in the blacklisted word frequency statistics, which are used as the text features of the whitelisted website. Meanwhile, the words in the top

300 of the blacklisted word frequency statistics are removed from the top 300 of the whitelisted word frequency statistics and used as the text features of the blacklisted website.

Domain Feature. The domain is also one of the important features to effectively identify a digital currency scam website. Li Xiaodong et al. [28] proposed a multi-dimensional feature of the malicious website detection method. They incorporated the registration-level feature data into the study. Ross et al. [22] applied it to detect digital currency scam websites for the first time. The domain names selected in this paper have domain name registration time and domain name holding time.

Digital currency scam websites often have a relatively new registration time, and the domain name expires quickly, and the domain name is held for a short time. Statistics shows that 93% of normal website domain names were registered earlier than 2019, while only 45% of digital currency scam websites registered earlier than 2019. 41% of normal website domain names expire later than 2021, but only 18% of digital currency scam websites expire later than 2021. Finally, 71% of normal websites that hold domain names for more than 4 years, while only 18% of digital currency scam websites have more than 4 years.

Website Ranking Feature. The website ranking feature is a side reflection of the popularity and authority of the website [18]. We can collect evaluation data through the ranking and inclusion situation provided by well-known companies and research on phishing website identification. Hu et al. [29] used publicly available website ranking data to build a classifier based on the machine learning algorithm. The website ranking features selected in the model include Alexa rank (AR), Baidu index (BD), Domain Authority value (DV), and Page Authority value (PV).

Alexa website ranking analyzes website visits to determine the website's popularity and give the website's world ranking [30]. It is the current more authoritative website visits evaluation index; Baidu inclusion means that the website is crawled by Baidu search engine, which can be passed. The keywords are searched on Baidu. The more included, the higher the website weight and the more website traffic. Domain Authority value (DV) is an important index to measure the authority of a website. It has an effect on the authority of the whole site. Page Authority value (PV) can evaluate the authority of a page, and it affects the weight of a single page. According to statistics, 92.6% of digital currency scam websites are not in the previously collected Alexa top one million, and only 31% of normal websites are not in the previously collected Alexa top one million. Meanwhile, we counted the number of times that the domestic search engine Baidu included. 75% of digital currency scam websites that were not included by Baidu, and only 15% of normal websites were not included by Baidu.

Mainstream Exchange Feature. The characteristics of mainstream exchanges are unique to the identification of digital currency scam websites.

Digital currency scams use digital currency as a gimmick to lure victims. Regular digital currencies can inevitably be queried in mainstream exchanges, so we select the trading platform [31], circulation market value, circulation, circulation rate, and turnover rate as the characteristics of the digital currency listed on the market mainstream exchanges.

The trading platform on which coin is listed has not entered the comprehensive ranking of global exchanges and has not participated in the ranking; at the same time, the coin cannot inquire about the characteristics of the circulating market value, circulation, circulation rate, supply and turnover rate. The calculation formula for the feature is as follows:

$$Circulating\ market\ value = Circulation * Currencyprice \qquad (1)$$

$$Circulation\ rate\ (CR) = (\frac{Total\ circulation}{Maximum\ supply}) * 100\% \qquad (2)$$

The turnover rate is also called "turnover rate", which refers to the frequency of changing hands in the market within a certain period. It is an indicator reflecting the strength of liquidity. The 24H turnover rate calculation formula is as follows:

$$Turnover\ (TO) = \frac{24H\ Turnover}{Circulating\ market\ value} * 100\% \qquad (3)$$

3.3   Digital Currency Fraud Website Detection Model

The detection model of digital currency fraud websites proposed in this paper is implemented based on the random forest algorithm.

Random forest (RF) [32] is an ensemble learning algorithm, which is composed of a large number of decision trees aggregation, compared with a single decision tree, in order to reduce the variance of the experimental results. By aggregating the predictions of decision trees, a new prediction result is obtained. In the regression problem, the most direct and common process of random forest is to average the prediction results of a single decision tree, and use voting to determine the final prediction result, that is, the new prediction result of the T decision trees with the most classification The result is decided.

Now suppose that a fixed training data set D is composed of n observation results. a random forest algorithm model with T decision trees derives prediction rules based on the data set D. In an ideal situation, these prediction rules are estimated based on an independent test data set D_{test}, which consists of n_{test} test observations.

The true value of the i-th observation in the test data set $(i = 1, ..., n_{test})$ is represented by y_i. In regression, in the case of binary classification, it is represented as a value of 0 or 1. The predicted value $(t = 1, ..., T)$ output by the decision tree t is represented as $\hat{y}_{it}$, and $\hat{y}_i$ is used to represent the predicted value of the entire random forest output. In the case of regression, the calculation formula of $\hat{y}_i$ is as follows:

$$\hat{y}_i = \frac{1}{T}\sum_{t=1}^{T}\hat{y}_{it} \tag{4}$$

In the case of classification, the value of i is usually obtained by majority voting. For binary classification, it is equivalent to calculating the same average value as regression, and the calculation formula adopted is as follows:

$$\hat{p}_i = \frac{1}{T}\sum_{t=1}^{T}I(\hat{y}_{it} = 1) \tag{5}$$

Use i to represent the probability, and finally derive the calculation formula of i as:

$$\hat{y}_i = \begin{cases} 1, & \hat{p}_i > 0 \\ 0, & \text{others} \end{cases} \tag{6}$$

The random forest algorithm has the advantages of fast detection speed, high detection accuracy, good anti-noise ability, not easy to overfit, and few hyperparameters. At the same time, the random forest algorithm can get the feature importance ranking, can process discrete data, and does not need to normalize the data set. It can be well applied to the data set of our paper, and it can help analyze which feature has the greatest impact on the detection result. Based on the above reasons, we finally chose the random forest algorithm to apply to the digital currency fraud website detection model.

4   Experiment

4.1   Dataset

The experimental data set consists of two parts, the normal website (whitelist) and the digital currency fraud website (blacklist). Whitelist is composed of the current mainstream digital currency official website and the top 5000 websites in Alexa. Blacklist is composed of digital currency websites which are not included in the mainstream trading platform and a publicly maintained list of fraudulent websites. After screening, the data set used in the experiment has 3508 whitelist data and 2498 blacklist data. Each piece of data includes the website's text, domain name, search engine indexing, website ranking, mainstream exchanges, and other characteristics.

4.2   Experimental Environment and Evaluation Metrics

To evaluate the detection model, we conducted experiments using a Ubuntu server with a 4-core 3.2 GHz Intel Core i7-8700 processor, 6 GB GeForce GTX 1070 graphics processing unit (GPU), and 16 GB memory.

To evaluate the performance of the model, the following indicators are used:

True Positive (TP). The model correctly predicts that the digital currency fraud website is a digital currency fraud website.

True Negative (TN). The model correctly predicts a normal website as a normal website.

False Positive (FP). The model incorrectly predicts a normal website as a digital currency fraud website.

False Negative (FN). The model incorrectly predicted negative instances, that is, the model predicts that the digital currency fraud website is a normal website.

Accuracy (AC). The percentage of correctly classified records relative to the total records. If false positives and false negatives have similar costs, accuracy will be best:

$$AC = \frac{TP + TN}{TP + TN + FP + FN} \tag{7}$$

Precision (P). The percentage of predicted digital currency fraud sites to actual digital currency fraud sites:

$$P = \frac{TP}{TP + FP} \times 100\% \tag{8}$$

Recall rate (R). The ratio of the total number of correctly classified digital currency fraud websites to the total number of positive records. A high recall rate means that the class is correctly identified with a small amount of FN:

$$R = \frac{TP}{TP + FN} \times 100\% \tag{9}$$

F1-Score. This is the harmonic average (percentile) of precision and recall. It is a value near the smaller value of precision or recall. Provides a more realistic way to use precision and recall to evaluate the accuracy of the test. If the false positive and false negative values are very different, the F1 value works best:

$$F1 = \frac{2 \cdot P \cdot R}{P + R} \times 100\% \tag{10}$$

4.3   Experimental Settings

The ten-fold cross-validation method is used to test the performance of the model. Divide the data set into ten parts and take turns using 9 parts as training data and 1 part as test data for testing. Each test will get the corresponding accuracy and other indicators. The average value of indicators such as the accuracy of the results of 10 times is used as an evaluation of the performance of the model.

The experiment uses a random forest classification model based on scikit-learn, and the input of the model is a feature matrix containing 16 normalized features. In the stage of experimental preprocessing, use 90% data for training and 10% data for verification, and repeat the same experiment 10 times in total. In terms of parameter settings, follow the principles of availability. Set the number of decision trees in the random forest to 10, and set the maximum number of features allowed for a single decision tree to $\sqrt{N}$(where N is the total number of features). The maximum depth set to None, the minimum number of samples required for the subdivision of internal nodes set to 2, and whether to use sampling with replacement when building the decision tree set to True;

In terms of experimental evaluation, use sklearn.metrics to calculate evaluation indicators such as the accuracy, precision, recall, and F1 value of the experimental results. Three machine learning algorithms are used, Support Vector Machine (SVM), Naive Bayes (NB), and K-Nearest Neighbor Algorithm (KNN) as the as the comparative experiments.

4.4 Results and Discussion

Results Summary. For digital currency fraud websites, we take precision, recall, and F1 test model's performance. Then we analyze the website instances to prove the effectiveness of the model.

Table 1. Comparison of four algorithms evaluation

Method	Accuracy	Precision	Recall	F1
NB	0.46	0.45	0.99	0.62
SVM	0.90	0.95	0.83	0.88
KNN	0.94	0.93	0.96	0.95
RF	**0.97**	**0.98**	**0.95**	**0.96**

The experimental results are shown in Table 1. The random forest model used in this article has the highest accuracy and the most superior performance.Its accuracy is 0.97, precision is 0.98, recall is 0.95, F1-score is 0.96. Support vector machine and K-nearest neighbor algorithm can also achieve relatively good classification results, but the accuracy is lower than random forest. The accuracy of the support vector machine algorithm is 0.90, and the accuracy of the K-nearest neighbor algorithm is 0.92. The Naive Bayes algorithm has the worst performance. Its accuracy is only 0.46, precision is 0.45, recall is 0.99, and F1-score is 0.62.

ROC curve is shown in the Fig. 2. The horizontal axis represents the specificity of the false positive rate (FPR), which divides the proportion of all negative examples in the instance to all negative examples. The vertical axis represents the true positive rate (TPR), also recall rate. The different solid lines in the figure represent the ROC curves of different machine learning algorithms. Each point on the line corresponds to a threshold.

The larger the FPR, the more actual negative cases in the predicted positive cases.The larger the TPR, the more actual positive cases in the predicted positive

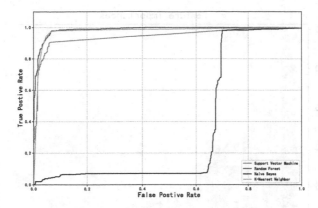

Fig. 2. ROC of four algorithms

cases. Ideal target: TPR = 1, FPR = 0, that is, the point (0,1) in the figure, so the closer the ROC curve is to the point (0,1), the more it deviates from the 45-degree diagonal, the better the algorithm performance.

Therefore, we can intuitively see from the figure that RF performance is the best, TPR is 0.96, and FPR is 0.06. SVM and KNN algorithms are second. The worst is NB, TPR is 0.99, FPR is 0.93.

Compared with Existing Detection Methods Tencent Security [33] is a leading brand in Internet security. Its URL Security Center can block malicious URLs and identify phishing websites within seconds. The website type detection that can be implemented by the website security center includes information fraud websites, such as fake investment and wealth management websites and fake brokerage websites. These two types of websites are similar to the digital currency fraud websites mentioned in this article. Therefore, we submit the blacklist and whitelist data sets used in this article to the Tencent Security Website Testing Center for testing and compare the statistical detection results with the detection model of this article.

The results of the comparative experiment are shown in Table 2. In the selected sample set, for this kind of fraudulent website based on digital currency, the Tencent Website Security Inspection Center's detection results of the website are divided into three categories, normal websites, risky websites, and unknown websites. We classify the detection results as normal websites and unknown websites as positive examples, and risk websites as negative examples to calculate the accuracy, precision, recall and F1 score of the detection results. The detection accuracy rate is 0.55, the precision rate is 0.55, the recall rate is 0.97, and the F1 score is 0.70. The experimental results show that the random forest algorithm and extracted website features used in this article can make the detection effect of digital currency fraud websites better.

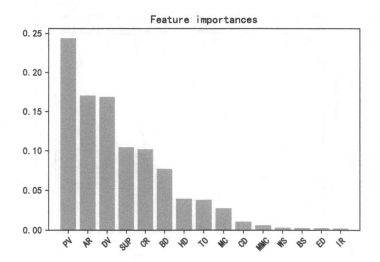

Fig. 3. Feature importance

Table 2. Compared with Tencent Security URL Security Center

Method	Accuracy	Precision	Recall	F1
Tencent	0.55	0.55	0.97	0.70
RF	**0.97**	**0.98**	**0.95**	**0.96**

Feature Importance. Figure 3 shows the input feature importance score of the digital currency fraud website detection model.

The idea of using the random forest [34] for feature importance evaluation is to observe the contribution of each feature on each tree in the random forest, and then take an average value, and finally compare these values.

We use the method of evaluating with the $Gini$ index here. [35] Variable importance measures are represented by VIM, and the $Gini$ index is represented by GI. Assuming there are m features $X_1, X_2, X_3..., X_m$, now we need to calculate the $Gini$ index score of each feature X_j, $VIM_j^{(Gini)}$, that is, the average change in the impurity of node splitting of the j-th feature in all decision trees in RF.

The formula for calculating the $Gini$ index is

$$GI_m = \sum_{k=1}^{|K|}\sum_{k'\neq k} p_{mk}p_{mk'} = 1 - \sum_{k=1}^{|K|} p_{mk}^2 \tag{11}$$

K indicates that there are K categories, and p_{mk} indicates the proportion of category k in node m. Intuitively, it is the probability that we randomly select two samples from node m, and their category labels are inconsistent.

The importance of feature X_j at node m, that is, the change in $Gini$ index before and after the branch of node m is as follows:

$$VIM_j^{(Gini)} = GI_m - GI_l - GI_r \tag{12}$$

Where GI_l and GI_r respectively represent the $Gini$ indices of the two new nodes after branching;

If the set of nodes that feature X_j appears in decision tree i is M, then the importance of X_j in the i-th tree is:

$$VIM_j^{(Gini)} = \sum_{i=1}^{n} VIM_{ij}^{(Gini)} \tag{13}$$

Finally, normalize all the obtained importance scores:

$$VIM_j = \frac{VIM_j}{\sum_{i=1}^{c} VIM_i} \tag{14}$$

The full name of the features are as follows:

1) *WhiteSet (WS).* Text data set of whitelist website.
2) *BlackSet (BS).* Text data set of blacklist website.
3) *Alexa Rank (AR).* Website's Alexa ranking.
4) *Baidu Index (BD).* Website being indexed by Baidu.
5) *Domain Authority Value (DV).* It is an important index to measure the authority of a website.
6) *Page Authority Value (PV).* It can evaluate the authority of a page, and it affects the weight of a single page.
7) *Supply (SUP).* Supply of digital currency.
8) *Circulation Rate (CR).* Circulation rate of digital currency.
9) *Turnover (TO).* It refers tothe frequency of changing hands in the market within a certainperiod.
10) *Mainstream Markets Count (MMC).* The number included by mainstream trading platforms.
11) *Markets Count (MC).* The number included by all of the trading platforms.
12) *Creation Date (CD).* Whether the domain name registration time is earlier than 2019, if yes, set it to 0, otherwise it is 1.
13) *Expiration Date (ED).* Whether the domain name expiration time is later than 2021, yes, set it to 0, otherwise it is 1.
14) *Handle Date (HD).* Whether the domain name has been held for more than 4 years, if yes, set it to 0, otherwise it is 1.

It can be found that the two features Page Authority Value(PV) and Alexa Rank(AR) have the greatest impact on the model classification results. Among them, the feature importance score of PV is 0.228, and AR is 0.213. BS has the least influence on the model, and the feature importance score is only 0.003.

4.5   Case Study

Our model identified a total of 2,498 digital currency fraud sites. We tested these sites in well-known secure URL detection center, Tencent [33]. It can detect phishing fraud, information fraud, false advertising, spam and other websites. We found that this detection center has difficulty determining the security of these digital currency fraud sites. According to the test results, more than 90% showed that no risk has been found or the safety is unknown.

To verify the accuracy of the identified websites, we conducted manual case analysis on 2,498 digital currency fraud websites detected by the model. By analyzing the website's text and image information, domain name features, website rankings, and token transaction information, we can make a relatively accurate judgment about whether the website is a digital currency fraud site. Take one of the digital currency fraud websites as an example, the specific analysis is as follows.

Taking the website (http://51-mdd.com/) as an example, we first checked the domain name information of the website. The registration time of the domain name is May 27, 2020, and the expiration time of the domain name is May 27, 2021. The domain name is only held for one year. It is in line with the late registration time and short holding time of our statistics on digital currency fraud websites. Next, query the ranking of the website. Check the Alexa rank of the website, not in the Alexa top one billion previously collected. The result can reflect that the number of page views and user coverage of the site is low. The website was not indexed by Baidu, while most of the websites can be inquired about the ranking and inclusion information on these professional website analysis agencies, such as Alexa and Baidu. Then we inquire about the transaction information of the digital currency on the major digital currency trading platforms. Basic transaction information such as the circulating market value, circulating quantity, circulation rate, and turnover rate of the digital currency cannot be queried at all.

Finally, analyze the content of the official website. The website provides two interfaces in Chinese and English. It is composed of the introduction, ecological construction, project functions, plans, and tokens. The website provides links to promotional videos and white papers, but they are not accessible at all. The content promoted by the website is camouflaged using blockchains, such as distributed operating systems, super security, cross-chain wallet, secure transaction, decentralization, open-source, and other words. The propaganda of the project used magnificent but very false words such as all-mankind, sustainability, the universe, and the world's top 500. Regarding the plan of the project, there is nothing to achieve. The content related to project profit is similar to the Ponzi scheme, low investment, high return, low risk, etc.

Based on the above characteristics, we can completely determine that the website is a digital currency fraud website. Similar analysis methods are used for the other websites, which have all or most of the above features. The case study confirms the validity of the features selected in this paper and the accuracy of the classification.

5   Conclusion

The purpose of this article is to analyze the characteristics of the website and realize the accurate classification of digital currency fraud websites and normal websites. In order to solve the above problems, we collected the top 5000 websites in Alexa and mainstream digital currency websites as whitelists. At the same time, we collected digital currency websites that were not disclosed on mainstream trading platforms and fraudulent websites that were publicly maintained as blacklists. The collected websites are filtered and the text is translated and cleaned, so the model can realize the classification of websites in any language type. After statistics and effectiveness analysis, we selected text, domain names, website rankings, etc. as features. Random forest algorithm is used as the website classification model, and the performance of the model is tested through ten-fold cross-validation. The accuracy rate is 0.97, and the recall rate is 0.95. This identification method helps to detect and classify digital currency fraud sites in a timely manner.

The classification of digital currency fraud websites based on website characteristics proposed in this article is a new insight. But there are still shortcomings. In future work, we will continue to research the following aspects: (1) Mainstream blockchain transaction methods (2) Mainstream blockchain traceability algorithm (3) Mainstream digital currency value tracking.

Acknowledgment. This research is funded by the National Natural Science Foundation of China (U20B2045, No. 61902265), Sichuan Science and Technology Program (No. 2020YFG0076).

References

1. Bartoletti, M., Carta, S., Cimoli, T., Saia, R.: Dissecting Ponzi schemes on Ethereum: identification, analysis, and impact. Fut. Gener. Comput. Syst. **102**, 259–277 (2020)
2. Tang, C., et al.: A large-scale empirical study on industrial fake apps. In: 2019 IEEE/ACM 41st International Conference on Software Engineering: Software Engineering in Practice (ICSE-SEIP), pp. 183–192. IEEE (2019)
3. Zhao, J.L., Fan, S., Yan, J.: Overview of business innovations and research opportunities in blockchain and introduction to the special issue. Financial Innovation **2**(1), 1–7 (2016). https://doi.org/10.1186/s40854-016-0049-2
4. Huang, D.Y., et al.: Tracking ransomware end-to-end. In: 2018 IEEE Symposium on Security and Privacy (SP). pp. 618–631. IEEE (2018)
5. Alrwais, S., Yuan, K., Alowaisheq, E., Li, Z., Wang, X.: Understanding the dark side of domain parking. In: 23rd USENIX Security Symposium (USENIX Security 14), pp. 207–222 (2014)
6. Agten, P., Joosen, W., Piessens, F., Nikiforakis, N.: Seven months' worth of mistakes: A longitudinal study of typosquatting abuse. In: Proceedings of the 22nd Network and Distributed System Security Symposium (NDSS 2015), Internet Society (2015)

7. McCorry, P., Möser, M., Ali, S.T.: Why preventing a cryptocurrency exchange heist isn't good enough. In: Matyáš, V., Švenda, P., Stajano, F., Christianson, B., Anderson, J. (eds.) Security Protocols 2018. LNCS, vol. 11286, pp. 225–233. Springer, Cham (2018). https://doi.org/10.1007/978-3-030-03251-7_27
8. Vasek, M., Moore, T.: Analyzing the bitcoin Ponzi scheme ecosystem. In: Zohar, A., et al. (eds.) FC 2018. LNCS, vol. 10958, pp. 101–112. Springer, Heidelberg (2019). https://doi.org/10.1007/978-3-662-58820-8_8
9. Liebau, D., Schueffel, P.: Cryptocurrencies & initial coin offerings: are they scams? An empirical study. J. Br. Blockchain Assoc. 2(1), 7749 (2019)
10. Kiffer, L., Levin, D., Mislove, A.: Analyzing ethereum's contract topology. In: Proceedings of the Internet Measurement Conference 2018, pp. 494–499 (2018)
11. Holub, A., O'Connor, J.: COINHOARDER: tracking a Ukrainian bitcoin phishing ring DNS style. In: 2018 APWG Symposium on Electronic Crime Research (eCrime), pp. 1–5. IEEE (2018)
12. Chen, W., Guo, X., Chen, Z., Zheng, Z., Lu, Y.: Phishing scam detection on ethereum: towards financial security for blockchain ecosystem. In: International Joint Conferences on Artificial Intelligence Organization, pp. 4506–4512
13. Dam, T., Klausner, L.D., Buhov, D., Schrittwieser, S.: Large-scale analysis of pop-up scam on typosquatting URLs. In: Proceedings of the 14th International Conference on Availability, Reliability and Security. pp. 1–9 (2019)
14. Chen, W., Zheng, Z., Ngai, E.C.H., Zheng, P., Zhou, Y.: Exploiting blockchain data to detect smart Ponzi schemes on Ethereum. IEEE Access 7, 37575–37586 (2019)
15. Bartoletti, M., Pes, B., Serusi, S.: Data mining for detecting bitcoin Ponzi schemes. In: 2018 Crypto Valley Conference on Blockchain Technology (CVCBT) (2018)
16. Chen, W., Zhang, T., Chen, Z., Zheng, Z., Lu, Y.: Traveling the token world: a graph analysis of Ethereum ERC20 token ecosystem. In: Proceedings of The Web Conference 2020, pp. 1411–1421 (2020)
17. Torres, C.F., Steichen, M., et al.: The art of the scam: demystifying honeypots in Ethereum smart contracts. In: 28th USENIX Security Symposium (USENIX Security 2019), pp. 1591–1607 (2019)
18. Bian, S., et al.: IcoRating: a deep-learning system for scam ICO identification. arXiv preprint arXiv:1803.03670 (2018)
19. Boshmaf, Y., Elvitigala, C., Al Jawaheri, H., Wijesekera, P., Al Sabah, M.: Investigating mmm Ponzi scheme on bitcoin. In: Proceedings of the 15th ACM Asia Conference on Computer and Communications Security, pp. 519–530 (2020)
20. Sang, S.M., An-Qi, Z.L.H., Sun Run-Geng, Z.C.: Abnormal transaction behavior recognition based on motivation analysis in blockchain. Digit. Curr. 44(01), 193–208 (2021)
21. Xu, J., Livshits, B.: The anatomy of a cryptocurrency pump-and-dump scheme. In: 28th USENIX Security Symposium (USENIX Security 19), pp. 1609–1625 (2019)
22. Phillips, R., Wilder, H.: Tracing cryptocurrency scams: clustering replicated advance-fee and phishing websites. In: 2020 IEEE International Conference on Blockchain and Cryptocurrency (ICBC), pp. 1–8. IEEE (2020)
23. Chen, W., Guo, X., Chen, Z., Zheng, Z., Lu, Y.: Phishing scam detection on Ethereum: towards financial security for blockchain ecosystem. In: Twenty-Ninth International Joint Conference on Artificial Intelligence and Seventeenth Pacific Rim International Conference on Artificial Intelligence IJCAI-PRICAI-20 (2020)
24. cryptoscamdb (2021). https://cryptoscamdb.org/

25. Adebowale, M.A., Lwin, K.T., Sanchez, E., Hossain, M.A.: Intelligent web-phishing detection and protection scheme using integrated features of images, frames and text. Exp. Syst. Appl. **115**, 300–313 (2019)
26. Ray, K.S., Kusshwaha, R.: Detection of malicious URLs using deep learning approach. In: Chakraborty, M., Singh, M., Balas, V.E., Mukhopadhyay, I. (eds.) The "Essence" of Network Security: An End-to-End Panorama. LNNS, vol. 163, pp. 189–212. Springer, Singapore (2021). https://doi.org/10.1007/978-981-15-9317-8_8
27. Verma, P., Goyal, A., Gigras, Y.: Email phishing: text classification using natural language processing. Comput. Sci. Inf. Technol. **1**(1), 1–12 (2020)
28. TIAN Shuang-Zhu, C.Y., YAN Zhi-Wei, L.X.D.: Illegitimate website detection based on multi-dimensional features. Computer Systems and Applications pp. 207–211 (2017)
29. Hu, Z., Chiong, R., Pranata, I., Susilo, W., Bao, Y.: Identifying malicious web domains using machine learning techniques with online credibility and performance data. In: 2016 IEEE Congress on Evolutionary Computation (CEC), pp. 5186–5194. IEEE (2016)
30. Vasek, M., Moore, T.: There's no free lunch, even using bitcoin: tracking the popularity and profits of virtual currency scams. In: Böhme, R., Okamoto, T. (eds.) FC 2015. LNCS, vol. 8975, pp. 44–61. Springer, Heidelberg (2015). https://doi.org/10.1007/978-3-662-47854-7_4
31. Xia, P., Wang, H., Zhang, B., Ji, R., Gao, B., Wu, L., Luo, X., Xu, G.: Characterizing cryptocurrency exchange scams. Comput. Secur. **98**, 101993 (2020)
32. Probst, P., Boulesteix, A.L.: To tune or not to tune the number of trees in random forest? J. Mach. Learn. Res. **18** (2017)
33. Tencent security URL security center (2021). https://urlsec.qq.com/index.html
34. Genuer, R., Poggi, J.M., Tuleau-Malot, C.: VSURF: variable selection using random forests. Pattern Recogn. Lett. **31**(14), 2225–2236 (2016)
35. Raschka, S.: Python Machine Learning. Packt Publishing Ltd., Birmingham (2015)

Understanding the Brains and Brawn
of Illicit Streaming App

Kong Huang[1], Ke Zhang[1], Jiongyi Chen[2], Menghan Sun[1], Wei Sun[1], Di Tang[1],
and Kehuan Zhang[1(✉)]

[1] The Chinese University of Hong Kong, Hong Kong, China
khzhang@ie.cuhk.edu.hk
[2] National University of Defense Technology, Changsha, China

Abstract. Content piracy has been the largest threat to the whole TV
and Media Industry around the world causing billions of dollars of economic loss. Copyright-protected contents, including movies, live soccer
matches, basketball games, dramas, etc., have been taken by "content
pirates" and redistributed through the Internet. In the last few years,
illegal IPTV providers in the form of an illicit streaming app running
on smartphones, smart TVs, and illicit streaming devices have become
extremely popular and take away significant subscription revenue from
legitimate pay-TV operators around the world. In this research, we study
the illicit streaming ecosystem from a new perspective by looking at the
illicit streaming apps: we build a semi-automated forensic tool to analyze the common codes, libraries, and network traffic of the apps that
facilitate illicit streaming services. As a result, we are able to investigate
their background and identify the technology providers behind them.
Our research provides insights into the proliferation of illicit streaming
services in app markets, as well as the overall illicit streaming ecosystem.

Keywords: Content piracy · Video streaming · Digital forensics

1 Introduction

Illicit streaming has been a new form of copyright infringement in the last decade.
The Intellectual Property Office of the UK government in [40] defines illicit
streaming as the watching of content without the copyright owner's permission
by any means, not just via hardware devices. This could be using a smart TV,
laptop, or mobile phone. Illicit streaming devices (ISD) are physical set-top boxes
or USB sticks connected to your TV. The hardware itself is not illicit, the crux of
the problem is the illicit streaming app (ISA) running on top. By definition, we
need to confirm with each copyright owner if the video contents on a streaming
app are unauthorized before they are officially called ISA.

ISA has become the most popular form of streaming piracy with 12 million
active users in the US [18]. Sandvine [44] has issued a report in 2017 about
the ISD piracy ecosystem, including unlawful device sellers and unlicensed video

P. Gladyshev et al. (Eds.): ICDF2C 2021, LNICST 441, pp. 194–214, 2022.
https://doi.org/10.1007/978-3-031-06365-7_12

providers and video hosts, which brought in revenue of an estimated 840 million a year in North America alone, at a cost of USD 4.2 billion to the entertainment industry. In a report from CNN Money in April 2018 [23], Southeast Asia has become the epicentre of the manufacturing and distribution of ISD which only cost as low as USD 150. In Singapore alone, the pay-TV subscribers have fallen 15% over the past 2 years because of piracy and it is predicted that it shall fall another 15% in the next 2 years.

From the above reports, it is not difficult to see that content piracy through illicit streaming is a huge problem affecting the content industry on a global scale. Law enforcers around the world face huge challenges because there are so many illegal streaming apps in the market [31]. After one ISA has been taken down, a new one just pops up with a different name within weeks if not instantly, which is also known as the so-called "whack-a-mole" phenomenon [24]. Thousands of streaming apps are available in app stores, some apps that have been removed due to their infringing contents but remain available as APKs to be downloaded from other Android app markets, which makes Android a more popular choice of ISA [1].

The intuition behind this study is that the proliferation of ISA, with over-lapping contents and non-trivial streaming technology and infrastructure, might have been fueled by the existence of technical enablers of some kind. ISAs that had been shut down would come back easily with another brand and app name. As such, our research aims to find out if ISAs are built with similar libraries, we can further identify the developers and their roles in the illegal streaming ecosystem. To this end, we collected data from two groups of Android streaming apps. The first group are the 1,360 live streaming apps collected from various Android app stores. The other group are the confirmed set with ISAs from different sources, which include ISAs taken down by some countries in the news, the ISAs verified with the content provider during our research, and the default apps found on known ISD in Hong Kong. We shall use the open-source code repository Github [7] or Google search engine to do a background check and identify the developers. We developed a tool to perform automatic software similarity analysis comparing methods, classes, and libraries in the installation package of the current application. The tool could also analyze network traffic and generate reports of selected ISAs during runtime.

Through our analysis of 21 confirmed ISAs and 10 legal streaming apps like YouTube, Netflix, etc., we found a set of third-party libraries that are potentially illicit streaming libraries. We checked the developers' background and investigate their involvement in the content piracy ecosystems. Many developers put their libraries in Github but our case studies show that these are just cover-ups of their larger and perhaps illegal roles behind. For instance, we found a company in Shanghai called Binstream.io which is the technology provider of a library "Tvbus" which are used by two of the confirmed ISAs. They operate an illegal streaming service called "Sopplus TV" and distribute over a hundred apparently unlicensed channels. We have reported to respective owners of the content and they acknowledged our findings. Using software similarity between 21 confirmed ISAs and 1360 apps from Android app stores, we can find another 23 apps that are similar with over 33% third-party libraries overlap. For instance, based on the ISA which is called UBLive, we can find V-Sat which is 94% and BR.TV which is 88% similar to that ISA. This demonstrates the use of software similarity to automatically identify potential ISAs among thousands of apps in the open app markets.

Contributions. Our work makes the following contributions:

- *New investigation.* We perform the first investigation into the illicit streaming ecosystem by analyzing illicit streaming apps at a large-scale. We developed an semi-automated tool which combines software similarity analysis and network analysis, helping us correlate different ISAs and identify technology developers.
- *New Discovery.* We demonstrated using our case studies of the ISA that common developer of multiple ISAs exist. We showed their involvement in the illicit streaming ecosystem through manual investigation, which may suggest a new choke point in fighting piracy. We shared the results with the Premier League [17] and Asia Video Industry Association (AVIA) [16], both organizations acknowledged our findings and shall take further investigations.

Roadmap. For the rest of the paper, we shall summarize the underlying operations and existing forensics of illicit streaming services as the background of the research in Sect. 2 and then propose our methodology in Sect. 3. In Sect. 4, we shall carry out a large scale study on the streaming app, and analyze the forensic findings using real cases. In Sect. 5, we shall list the related works, limitations, and future developments, and in Sect. 6 the conclusion.

2   Background

Free and Subscription Based Illicit Streaming Service. There have been two types of illicit streaming services. The ad-supported free illicit streaming service and the subscription-based illicit streaming service. The ad-supported service focus on drawing traffic and display digital advertisement to visitors. They can use cyberlockers, cloud storage, and BitTorrent as content distribution intermediaries. The subscription-based illicit streaming service collects money directly from the consumer, say for USD 300 per year with ISD, providing hundreds of high-quality live channels. Figure 1 illustrates the setup of ISA on mobile devices and TV set-top boxes (a.k.a. ISD). First, unlicensed contents are put on the CDN (Content Delivery Network) [25]. There are hundreds of stable and high-quality live channels, e.g. HBO, Disney, BBC, CNN, etc. The illegal service provider will use large Cloud and CDN providers for hosting and distributing content. At the client-side, ISA developed on smartphones or ISD will connect to the cloud server for control signals and stream content from the CDN. These illegal service provider may have their own illegal content sources or simply get from unlicensed content providers [1].

Current Measures to Combat ISA. International media companies and large pay TV operators will employ content protection solution providers (e.g. Friend MTS [38], OpSec [41], etc.) to investigate, monitor, and take-down illegal streaming services. Since there are thousands of ISA in the market, the content providers will select a handful of the most popular apps for monitoring. Network forensics will be performed to identify the underlying IP addresses of video streams for issuing blocking orders to internet service providers by the administration or court. The solution would cost as much as a hundred thousand US dollars per year. There are several inefficiencies in the current measures: (1) only a handful of most popular apps can be investigated in each cycle, (2) there is no simple way to find out which streaming apps are more likely to be illicit, (3) there is no knowledge base of confirmed ISA to assist the future investigation of new streaming apps.

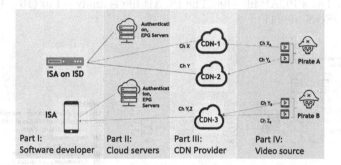

Fig. 1. Common ISA architecture

Ethical Discussion. To abide by an ethical framework throughout this study, when making ISD purchase, we limited to the top models in Hong Kong [27]. In total, we spent no more than USD 1,000 to minimize the amount of money flowing to the illegal services. We justify that by detailed analysis for various ISD (in fact it is the analysis of the default ISA running on top), which could not be performed without the purchase. We have sent our respective findings to the Premier League [17], AVIA [16], MoPub [9], AdColony [3], and Adincube [10]. It is also important to note that although this work may present information that could point to specific kinds of actions, including but not limited to take-down notices. It should not be used in any sort of legal proceedings as-is.

3   Our Methodology

ISA is one of the brains and brawn of the content piracy ecosystem. It made access to illegal content extremely easy to the mass audience. In this research, we aim to look at how the ISA are built and who are the developers behind them. We first leverage program analysis techniques to identify illicit streaming libraries from a known set of confirmed ISA. Then we perform large-scale analysis to identify other potential ISA that shares the same or similar illicit streaming libraries. This could provide some insights on how the potential ISA is similar to confirmed ISA by the illicit streaming libraries that they share.

In Fig. 2, we illustrated the overall workflow of our methodology. The first step is to crawl and download Android Application Package (APK) files of streaming apps from the common Android app store (1). Then manual upload confirmed ISAs and legal streaming apps to the system (2). The APK files will be decompiled into method objects (3). Each APK file will generate a method objects set and the set will be hashed using the MD5 function to build a feature vector for each APK file. When all APK feature vectors are completed, a feature matrix is generated in (4). Third-party libraries will be detected in (5) and the similarity between each pair of ISA is computed by Jaccard similarity in (6). Shortlisted APK (7) is connected to the internet via a VPN server. All IP traffics including requests (8) and responses (9) will go through the VPN server and be saved as a PCAP file [49]. The PCAP file is analyzed in (10). The overall result is a JSON file (11).

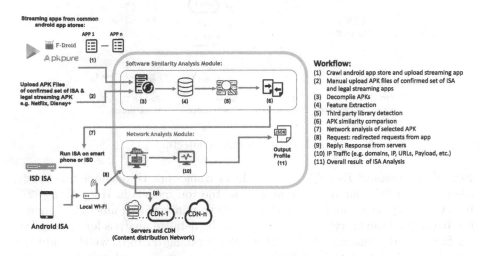

Fig. 2. Workflow of the ISA analysis

3.1 Detection of Illicit Streaming Libraries and Potential ISAs

In this subsection, we describe the automated techniques to find out illicit streaming libraries as well as potential ISA. However, the vastness of the ecosystem, the sheer volume of illegal streaming URLs, and the professionalization of pirate operations made it overwhelming to efficiently study ISA [22].

App Collection. To automate the search and crawling of apps from multiple app stores, we crawl .apk files from a list of popular Android app stores [2] [12] (the full list can be found in Sect. 4.1) using an open-source APK crawler [37].

Decompilation and Representation. The initial workflow of .apk files analysis consists of the following steps: 1) decompile each input APK adapting Androguard

[19] to get the Control Flow Graph (CFG) of each method and the methods list. 2) The opcodes in each CFG are hashed using MD5 [48] in depth-first order to bypass the potential name obfuscation and generate the signature of each method.

Feature Extraction. The process of feature extraction of Android APK in different level is inspired by LibD [34]. LibD focuses on clustering and identifying the third party libraries, while our target is to measure the similarity of a given pair of APK by observing the overlapped methods among Apps. Thus, we compare the similarity of APK pair in method level to retrieve as much as possible underlying similarity instead of merely library identification. The features can be extracted from the Control-Flow-Graph of each method by computing its MD5 hash code of the concatenation of opcodes. The full process is shown in Algorithm 1.

Algorithm 1: APK similarity comparison by method-level signature.

Data: A, ISA, OSA
Result: $simi\_scores$

1 **Function** SignatureExtraction(a):
2     $methods_a =$ GetMethods(Decompile(a))
3     $methods\_opcode\_str_a = \emptyset$ //Initialize an empty set
4   **for** $method$ in $methods_a$ **do**
5        $CFG_{method} =$ GetCFG($method$)
6        $opcode\_str_{method} =$ GetOpcodeStr(CFG_{method}))
7        $methods\_opcode\_str_a =$ cat($methods\_opcode\_str_a$, $opcode\_str_{method}$)
8   **end**
9     $sig_a =$ Hash($methods\_opcode\_str_a$)
10 **return** sig_a
11 **Function** SignatureOSA(OSA):
12     $sig_{OSA} = \emptyset$ //Initialize an empty set
13   **for** osa in OSA **do**
14        $sig_{OSA} = sig_{OSA} \cup$ SignatureExtraction(osa)
15   **end**
16 **return** sig_{OSA}
17 **Function** Similarity(A, ISA, OSA):
18     $sig_{OSA} =$ SignatureOSA(OSA)
19     $simi\_scores = \varnothing$ //Initialize an empty table
20   **for** a in A **do**
21   **for** isa in ISA **do**
22           $sig_{isa} =$ SignatureExtraction(isa)
23           $sig_a =$ SignatureExtraction(a)
24           $simi\_score_{<a,isa>} = \frac{|(sig_{isa} - sig_{OSA}) \cap sig_a|}{|sig_{isa}|}$
25           $simi\_scores[a][isa] = simi\_score_{<a,isa>}$
26   **end**
27   **end**
28 **return** $simi\_scores$

APK-Level Similarity Comparison. Each APK is represented by a set of method signatures that represent the features extracted from the above step. The reason for using the method-level signature instead of higher syntax structures is to retrieve the underlying overlapping as much as possible. The underlying methods used by the legal video applications will be excluded and the remaining methods set of the streaming app will be used to compare with the given APK, to identify potential ISAs. To eliminate the libraries that are also shared by legal streaming apps, we build a "standard streaming libraries" set of libraries used by well-known and most downloaded streaming apps in the US and China. The apk files of these official apps are collected from the app stores and analyzed using the same approach as the ISAs to get the full library list and methods-level signatures. The reason we included China streaming apps is that many ISAs in our confirmed set comes from ISD made in China and it helps to improve the accuracy of the illicit streaming libraries overall. The legal apps that we used in generating the standard streaming libraries are YouTube, Netflix, Disney +, Hulu, and HBO Max from the US. And iQiyi, Tencent video, TikTok, Youku, and Mango TV from China. The result set of unique libraries are the illicit streaming libraries.

Potential ISA Libraries Extraction. We extracted the library list of all apps in our dataset including the confirmed 21 ISAs by adapting LibD [34]. Most library names can be retrieved and in plain-text, while the rest part of libraries may be obfuscated during compilation to hide their names and shown as meaningless placeholders such as "a/b/c/". Though the library names obfuscated, the underlying methods level signature remains unchanged.

3.2   Network Traffic Analysis

Network Traffic Capture. For ISA that can run on ISD, we would not be able to use remote control APIs like the case in Roku or Amazon Fire TV [36], so we built a simple ISD control robot with an infra-red output signal of "channel up" after the ISA is launched manually. The robot will scan through all the channels available on the ISD with 15 s intervals in between. As to mobile ISA, due to different user interfaces, registration, and subscription required, we need to manually navigate the selected ISA. To perform a large scale network analysis of Mobile ISA, we need automatic Android app navigation. It is technically feasible and we shall discuss that in Sect. 5.3.

Table 1. Table of notation of Algorithm 1

Notation	Definition
A	The collected APK dataset
$a \in A$	The a is an input apk file in dataset A
isa, ISA	The set of confirmed ISA files
osa, OSA	The set of official (legal) streaming apps (OSA)
Decompile()	Decompile the input APK file a
$methods_a$	A set with all methods of APK a
GetMethods(a)	Generate methods of decompiled a
$method$	A method in $methods_a$
GetCFG($method$)	Generate the control-flow-graph of $method$
CFG_{method}	The control-flow-graph of $method$
GetOpcodeStr()	Generate the opcode string of the CFG of methods
$opcode\_str_{method}$	The opcode string list of $method$
$cat(str_1, str_2)$	Concatenate the string1, str_1, and string2, str_2
$methods\_opcode\_str_a$	The opcode string list of all methods of APK a
Hash()	MD5 hash function
sig_a, sig_A	The signature of a or A computed from hash function
$simi\_score_{<a,isa>}$	Similarity comparison between a and isa
$simi\_scores$	A key-value table for storing APK pairs and their similarity

Network Traffic Analysis. The network data collected during the startup of the apps and the content streaming. Our tool could create interaction diagrams and extract the IP addresses, domains, name of hosting companies, CDN, and their autonomous system network number automatically. We also look into the text strings from HTTP requests (e.g. Streaming URLs) and responses (payloads) and see if there is any match with the library or developer names we found in the software similarity module.

4 Findings

4.1 Data Collection

Streaming Apps from App Stores. We selected 34 common Android App stores, e.g. APKure, APKMirror, AppBrain, Aptoide, F-Droid, etc. We search these app stores with a combination of "live", "tv", "iptv" and "streaming". A total of 1,360 apps in Fig. 2 are uploaded for features extraction. Such automation ensures we could cover as many apps as we want to meet the challenge of the vast volume of streaming apps in app stores.

Confirmed Set of ISAs. First, we collected the default ISAs from ISD. In May 2018, the Customs and Excise Department of Hong Kong has seized four brands of ISDs (Boss V2, EVPad 3, Magic Plus, and UBox ProS) through a series of raid of retail outlets in Hong Kong [27]. Between April and July 2019, we purchased these four ISDs from the Hong Kong market plus another ISD recommended by the same store called the TurboTV S box. From them, we could download a total of 9 ISAs. Secondly, we searched the Internet and found from different sources about the shutdown of another 7 ISAs. And finally, we contacted a content owner's office in Singapore and they helped verified 5 more ISAs. Therefore a total of 21 ISAs has been included in our confirmed set of ISAs in Fig.2.

Software Analysis. We decompile 1,360 APK files and confirmed set with 21 ISAs using Androguard [19] to get the list of all methods and classes from all APK files. Meanwhile, the constant string variables found during decompilation are also extracted from the APK files for further online search analysis. Then, the control flow graph (CFG) of each method is built using the opcodes of smali code corresponding to each method to overcome the name obfuscation. This is inspired by the previous work of LibD [34]. After that, the CFG of all methods for each APK is hashed into a 16 bytes string as the signature of each method using MD5 [48] and consist of a feature vector. Note that here we only construct method-level features so the order of methods or elements in feature vectors are ignored. The similarity of a pair of feature vectors can be computed by Jaccard Similarity [46].

4.2 Key Findings on Illicit Streaming Libraries

There are total of 3,299 named libraries found from 1,360 APK, we stripe out standard libraries common between 10 legal streaming apps and focus on the use of illicit streaming libraries. Here are the key findings:

- **Online Advertising Platform.** The top matched library is MoPub used by 221 apps. MoPub is a mobile advertising platform owned by Twitter [9], which help the apps to monetize the traffic they gain from offering free illegal channels. This is the major business model for free illicit streaming services [1]. Not only MoPub, in the same category, there are also 83 apps using Adcolony [3], 19 using AppLovin [5], 10 using AdinCube [10], 7 using Vungle [14], 5 using Avocarrot [8] as shown in the Table 3.
  Implication: MoPub has established a policy for publishing partners and copyright infringement contents are prohibited. But in our results, they are inside one confirmed ISA "Terrarium TV". As for AdColony, they are awarded the Certified Against Fraud seal by the Trustworthy Accountability Group, but they are used by 4 ISA, "Terrarium TV, Tea TV, UKTV Now, LiveNet TV" [4]. The issue lies in the enforcement of the company policy and our tools

could help identify potential ISA using legitimate advertising platforms. Once the content owner confirms respective content infringement in the ISA, the advertising platform could immediately take action to stop serving ads and hence cut out the money chain to the ISA. It is a win-win situation for the content owner and advertising platform to ensure the later are not aiding and abetting ISA like TeaTV, UKTVNow and Terrarium TV [1].

- **Video Player.** Another major common library we found is the player or media framework. There are (1) "Vitamio" developed by Yixia.com from China [13] in 22 apps including 1 ISA "Supersport", (2) TVBus developed by Binstream.io from China in 4 apps including 2 ISA "SunshineTV, Supersport", and (3) NagasoftPlayer developed by Nagasoft from China in 3 apps including 2 ISA "SunshineTV, Supersport", (4) Forstwire from Forstwire Project in 2 ISA "MagicTV and ShowboxTV", and (5) Gemini from 2 ISA "SunshineTV, Supersport". Details are shown in Table 3.

  Implication: With the developer information, we can do a background check and see if the software companies have legitimate business registration and operations. Or if they are in fact part of the content piracy ecosystem fueling the development of multiple ISA. Which we shall discuss in detail in Sect. 4.5 Case Studies.

- **Data Provider.** There are also TV shows and movie data API provider called Trakt.tv, and the library uwetrottmann/trakt5 has been used by 4 apps including three ISAs (Terrarium TV, Magic TV, and TVZion). Trakt.tv API powers thousands of apps like media center plugins, mobile apps, watch apps, command-line utilities, and smart home integration.

  Implication: The free to use data API get quality data from legal services like Netflix, Hulu, and Disney+ and helps create many useful apps for good. However, it is also aiding and abetting many ISAs in the market.

4.3 Key Findings on Detection of Potential ISA

For each of the confirmed ISA, we shall strip off the common libraries from Android, Google, or other benign standard Java libraries, and check its similarity with all the 1,360 streaming app. We found 64 unique streaming apps that are similar to the one or many of the ISAs in the confirmed set. These 23 apps have over 33% similarity to one or more ISAs. We show the result in Table 2. Some of the similar apps to the confirmed set of ISAs are detailed below:

- **UBLive, UBVod and similar apps.** UBLive and UBVod are default ISAs found in ISD called UBox and are actually identical. V-Sat is 94% and BR.TV is 88% similar to them, which means these 2 apps are built nearly the same way as UBLive and UBVod. In one of the Android app store, V-SAT is described as "an app developed by Uldeck that brings together around 3,700 channels from all over the world, both general and specialized channels". From the description of BR.TV app in the app store, "With Brasil TV Live, you can watch all Brazilian TV live for free from your smartphone." Both are typical ISA type of promotions [15]. **Implication:** Using our software similarity comparison between APK, we are able to identify potential ISAs which are developed the same way as the known and confirmed set of ISAs. This helps the content providers to sort out the apps they want to take down first.

– **Tea TV and similar apps.** BN Live TV is 68%, USTV Hub is 56% similar to Tea TV. In one of the app store, BN Live TV has descriptions saying "Enjoy the most popular TV channels in Bangladesh" and USTV Hub has a website called USTVHub.com and describes its service as "Watch live tv channels/shows on your android phones or boxes free of charge", both are typical ISA types of promotions [15]. **Implication:** BN Live TV and USTV Hub may not belong to the same ISA family as Tea TV, but they are over 50% similar, an indication of similarity in functionalities, business models, and data sources. It allows content owners to make an informed decision among thousands of apps in the open market, which one to look into first.

4.4 Network Analysis Result

- Understanding the server IP and CDN provider of ISA. Both Supersport and SunShine TV uses CloudFlare (AS 13335). SuperSport app uses Ensu as CDN (ASN 18978) and SunShine TV uses OVH as CDN (ASN 16276). From our software analysis, we know the two ISA are 91% similar, yet they are using different CDN network providers because they are accessing a different list of contents.
  Implication: The software similarity analysis provides lower-level information that network-level analysis cannot provide.
- Call flow analysis. Our tool will automatically generate an interaction diagram for the ISA traffic captured. In Fig. 3, the Sunshine TV ISA will contact "weixingdianxitv.com" and in the HTTP request, it contains a phase called the "gemini-iptv" which are also resonant with the name of illicit streaming libraries that Sunshine TV used, e.g. com/gemini/application, com/gemini/-play, com/gemini/turbo, etc.
  Implication: The network analysis of apps runtime data may sometimes support the results of our static software analysis.

4.5 Case Studies

To further understand the effectiveness of our methodology in finding common infrastructures behind illicit streaming ecosystem, and developers supporting it, we analyze each case in-depth and share the results in the following.

TVBus and Binstream. Within the confirmed set with 21 ISAs, Sunshine TV and SuperSport contain the same library called "tvbus". We searched Github using the name "tvbus" and found that it is developed by a company called "binstream.io" (https://github.com/binstreamio/tvbus.android). This suggests that the two ISA share the common library "tvbus" developed by Binstream.io. Binstream.io is a P2P technology solution company in Shanghai city. On their website http://www.binstream.io, we learned that "tvbus.android" is a live streaming android SDK based on "P2P technology", and it's available on Android, Win32, macOS and Linux platform. We also found their media distribution solution called "SopPlus TV" using Binstream technology which matched the name of the content server in Github through tvbus protocol. We crawl and scrape the information from Binstream.com and got a channel list in JSON file including 108 channels distributed from the server of Sopplus TV, including HBO, CNN, BBC, and NHK which are unlikely to be licensed to a software company in China.

To relate our findings to the physical world, we extend our investigation manually, we contacted the company binstream.io and successfully got a demo APK named P2Player from them to evaluate their solution. The P2Player app comes with a dozen of live channels for testing purpose, connecting to a server also called "SopPlus TV".

From the above evidence, we could see that the company Binstream.io not only supplies its P2P-CDN hybrid technology solution in the form of a software development kit (i.e., TVBus library), they are involved in some sort of operation of an illegal streaming service called the "SopPlus TV", with unlicensed international live channels.

In summary, we found that Binstream.io is playing multiple roles in the illicit streaming ecosystem. Firstly as a technology provider supporting many ISA and ISD through "TvBus". Secondly, it operates an illegal streaming service in the name of "Sopplus TV". Thirdly, through our contact with them, they served as an illegal re-seller of over a hundred unlicensed live channels. We notice that the site binstream.io could not be accessed recently and for completeness sake, we include the site's image in Feb 2020 through web.archieve.org as reference [6].

Gemini IPTV. Sunshine TV and Supersport apps are default apps from Turbo TV S ISD. Besides "tvbus" they shared a set of libraries from "Gemini", called Gemini.custom, Gemini.play, Gemini.base64, Gemini.pay. While Sunshine TV has one more Gemini.Turbo library which Supersport did not. On the contrary, Supersport app has Gemini.ssport library which Sunshine TV did not. This suggests that both apps are more likely built with the same set of libraries. From the interaction diagram generate by network analysis of Sunshine TV Fig. 3, it contains a phase called the "gemini-iptv" in its content request, such result from network analysis resonant with the software analysis.

We further looked into the "Gemini" libraries using the Google search engine and found a relevant site called the geminiproject.tv. On this website, it is advertised that you can get over 22,000 channels from all over the world and they also offer a free trial and support multiple platforms. We tried to contact the service provider but the email is bounced and no response from their official Skype account. There is a Smart IPTV app available for download from the same website. We search further and find that the Smart IPTV service is hosted at the siptv.app website, while its subscription is sold on another website called IPTV.shop. From which one can subscribe 3-months illegal service at 30 Euros. Someone could also sign up to be a distributor of "Smart IPTV" services. In [42], Pandey et al. described "a middle-man third-party service, Omniverse, which offers most of the infrastructure and content required to operate a streaming media service". The distributors clearly stated the support from Omniverse in their websites and it was easy to establish the case of content infringement and took legal action. However, in our findings, the Sunshine ISA (and Supersport ISA) on TurboTV S ISD are operated as separate apps streaming from different CDN, which looks unrelated in their operations. Through the software analysis, we could associate different ISA in the market and identify more directions for further investigation.

5   Related Work and Discussions

In this section, we review prior researches about illicit streaming services and mobile app similarity and discuss about future works.

5.1   Illicit Streaming Services

There are some previous works on free illegal streaming services, their security, and user privacy issues. Rafique et al. [43] presented the first empirical study of free live streaming services, analyzed the deceptive advertising content within those free websites, and developed a classifier for potential dangerous web pages. Ibosiola el al. [29] studied the use of cyberlocker for online video piracy and identified a number of communities based on shared domains, shared hosting facilities, and high-level HTML similarity. Hsiao el al. [28] built a system to automatically detect new links to illegal live sport streaming sites and provided evidence that these sites seek to track and identify users extensively. In summary, previous researches utilized web crawling tools, HTML page similarity, and HTML features to automatically classify malicious web pages. In this paper, we look beyond websites and target a new and more popular form of content piracy using streaming apps on smartphones or streaming devices. The automated tools required to analyze web pages are different from the one we build to identify common libraries among ISA. To our best knowledge, this is the first study on software similarity of ISA.

There are a few researches on subscription-based illicit streaming services. Nikas et al. studied Kodi app and Kodi add-ons in [39]. Since the crackdown of Kodi by authorities around the world in 2018 [42], different Android ISA has gained more traction. In [42], Pandey et al. presented the first analysis of infringing subscription-based IPTV services and measured the network infrastructure, third party software providers, payment, and other intermediary services that are used by a subset of the infringing IPTV ecosystem. Inspired by the methodology in [42], we found that an important part of the ecosystem is missing, which is the client-side ISA and their developer. This is important as we have shown in our case study, technology solution provider or developer of ISA is not only taking the development role. In fact, some of them are performing like an "integrator" role, putting together pirated content sources, the platform, and the ISA for end users. They guarantee the ISA's service quality, time-to-market, stability, and scalability of the illicit streaming service.

In summary, previous works focused on network analysis, web crawling or URL link discoveries, which are limited by the pre-requisite to subscribe to different illegal services before they can analyze the service [42]. Our work help to fill in the void of studying the ISA itself and the developer ecosystem behind it. It provides a large-scale analysis and continuous screening to find potential ISA in Android app store, using the similarity to the illicit streaming libraries from known ISA. It is a simple and cost-effective method bypassing the complexity of service subscriptions and specific navigation of different apps.

5.2 Mobile Application Similarity

Our software similarity comparison approach mainly focuses on the syntax-based feature extraction of control flow graph in method level of Andriod APK, to find as many overlapping as possible. We use the Jaccard Similarity to measure the similarity among many ISA. Note that the features, e.g. values hashed from methods represented by Control Flow Graph (CFG), extracted by our approach are essentially from the program syntax. Syntactic features are straightforward representations of different program units of the target APK files. Similar methods have been widely used by many existing works for program similarity comparison and code clone detection [30,32] Besides syntax-based similarity method, there is also the semantic-based similarity method [30,33]. Ideally, they retrieve features by modeling the functionality of the program and usually reveal the underlying similarities of code snippets more accurately [26,35,45]. Similar to common syntax-based similarity methods, they are more suitable for general-purpose problems. We leave it as future works to integrate some suitable semantics-based methods to improve the accuracy of similarity between apps. We are also aware of the methods to prevent reverse engineering of Android applications, for example, dynamic code modification, dynamic loading, anti-debugging, etc. [50]. The challenge is well resolved by known techniques and tools like DexHunter [50], de-obfuscator [21] and Anti-ProGuard [20]. Our tool could also be integrated with these tools in the future. Last but not least, we focus on Java language because the Android APK is usually written in Java source code. We would consider supporting Kotlin [47] language as part of the future work.

5.3 Limitations and Future Developments

Firstly, our methodology could easily extend to Apple iOS applications using different software analysis tools. Secondly, we have focused on English based Android app stores and Github in this paper. In our research, we found that there are 21 apps using Vitamio including colombia-tv, live-tv-arabic-v11, live-tv-chile-chile2, live-tv-peru-per, live-tv-philippines, pak-india-live-tv, turkish-live-tv, and venezuela-ver-tv. It shows that ISAs could be developed for different countries and some of them may only be found in country-specific search engine and app stores around the world. By applying our analysis to more app stores, international ISA database could be built. Last but not least, spreading malware has been identified as one of the revenue streams for illicit streaming platforms [1]. Given the large library database we have accumulated, we could add the malware scoring system [11] to identify malicious apps.

6   Conclusion

In this research, we focus on specific digital forensic challenges of analysing Android streaming apps in content piracy ecosystem. We propose an additional software analysis before the more resource intensive network analysis and human investigation. We developed a tool to capture and analyze the APK of 1,360 apps and used that to explore the hypothesis of a common ISA developer supporting multiple illegal streaming services. The result is positive in that (1) it automates the software analysis of ISA to identify illicit streaming libraries and their usage in more streaming apps and (2) it helps identify more streaming apps in the Android markets that are similar to the ISA identified. In the case studies, we are able to identify common developer behind ISAs called the "Binstream.io" and "Gemini", and report that to content owners who acknowledged our findings. It proves that common ISA developers exist and act as an active part of the illicit streaming ecosystem. We also identify 23 similar apps using 21 confirmed ISAs. This demonstrates a new method in tackling content piracy through large-scale and automatic software similarity analysis in the identification of potential illicit streaming apps.

Acknowledgement. We thank anonymous reviewers for their insightful comments. This work was supported in part by National Key Research and Development Project (Grant No. 2019YFB1804400), and Hong Kong S.A.R. Research Grants Council (RGC) General Research Fund No. 14208019.

Appendix:

Table 2. List of streaming apps similar to confirmed set with 21 ISAs. Sample of the ISA APK files can be found at https://www.dropbox.com/sh/w6f7ecmbbl05snm/AACUlvuC0atGpJXBwB9Qwyhsa?dl=0.

ISA	No. of similar App	(App name, similarity to ISA)
LiveNet	2	('ustvhub', 0.508), ('bn-live-tv', 0.41309090909090906)
BeeTV	1	('fftv', 0.35528837776616135)
UKTVNow	3	('Embratoria', 0.49648924122310306), ('freeflix', 0.46266515666289165), ('fftv', 0.33620234050585124)
TeaTV	4	('bn-live-tv', 0.6805655403786245), ('ustvhub', 0.5563144021087947), ('Liveflix', 0.40750059908938413), ('Listas Wiseplay', 0.335849508746705)
MagicTV	2	('cinemaapk', 0.34298181818181817), ('BibhuTV', 0.3389090909090909)
Exodus	4	('PatoPlayer', 0.4994514536478332), ('Lots-Sports', 0.3959133296763577), ('Tvbox', 0.35161821173889196), ('live-br-tv', 0.33543609434997257)
UBLive and UBVod		('v-sat', 0.9411764705882353), ('BR.TV', 0.8823529411764706)
Mlive	6	('Mobizen Screen Recorder', 0.40213467273583425), ('PuraTV', 0.40087898289122587), ('jaz-live-tv', 0.3936587662847277), ('visionplus', 0.3738816512321457), ('HD_STREAMZ', 0.3690158530842882), ('Peladculas Online Gratis', 0.36634751216449535)
MBOX	3	('fftv', 0.4028169014084507), ('Embratoria', 0.35975855130784706), ('sportsangel', 0.32756539235412474)

Table 3. List of illicit streaming libraries and apps using them

No.	ISA Library	Developer	Confirmed set of ISA using the library	Streaming App List using the ibrary (Top 10 samples)
1	com/tvbus	binstream.io	SunshineTV, SuperSport	BoxStarFireLive, Sopplus
2	com/gemini		SunshineTV, SuperSport	Nil
3	io/vov/vitamio	Yixia.com	SunshineTV, SuperSport	colombia-tv com-tv-splivetv banana.six live-plus-tv live-sports-tv live-tv-arabic live-tv-chile-chile live-tv-free, live-tv-peru live-tv-philippines pak-india-live-tv playbox sport-live-tv turkish-live-tv venezuela-tv
4	com/nagasoft/ player	Nagasoft	SunshineTV, SuperSport	BoxStarFireLive
5	com/frostwire	Frostwire	MagicTV, ShowboxTV	Nil
6	com/mopub/ common	MoPub, Twitter	TerrariumTV	free-live-tv-for-india, jocker-iptv, listas-iptv-free, underground-iptv, usa-live-tv-channels-free, smart-iptv, nova-era-iptv, cobra-iptv, arabs-iptv, iptv-extreme
7	com/adcolony	AdColony	LiveNetTV, TeaTV, RedBoxTV, UKTVNow, TerrariumTV	Liveflix, TVEspaña, app673606, bn-live-tv, megatvplayer, elMubashir, Fftv, freeflix, tz-hd-live-tv
8	com/applovin	Applovin	BeeTV, LiveNetTV, TeaTV	GSE_SMART_IPTV, Listas_Wiseplay, Liveflix, Liveplanettv, TVTAP, USA Free Live TV, aostv, bn-live-tv, e-DoctorIPTV, freeflix
9	com/avocarrot	Glispa	LiveNetTV, UKTVNow, TerrariumTV	megatvplayer, splive_player
10	com/adincube	Ogury	TerrariumTV, TeaTV, UKTVNow	Listas Wiseplay, Liveflix, bn-live-tv, freeflix, ustvhub
11	com/vungle	Vungle	TerrariumTV, UKTVNow	Embratoria, USTV_Stable, tz-hd-live, uktv
12	com/uwetrottmann/ trakt5	Trakt.tv	MagicTV, TVZion, TerrariumTV	CinemaAPK

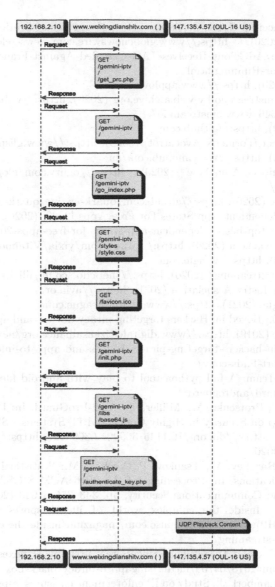

Fig. 3. Interaction diagram of Sunshine TV ISA.

References

1. Illegal IPTV in the European Union (2019). https://www.europol.europa.eu/sites/default/files/documents/tb0319764enn.en_.pdf
2. Ultimate Mobile App Stores List (2019). https://buildfire.com/mobile-app-stores-list/
3. Adcolony (2020). https://www.adcolony.com

4. AdColony receives TAG Certified against fraud recertification for third year running (2020). https://www.globenewswire.com/news-release/2020/03/12/1999716/0/en/AdColony-Receives-TAG-Certified-Against-Fraud-Recertification-for-Third-Year-Running.html

5. Applovin (2020). https://www.applovin.com

6. Archive for binstream.io by web.archive.org (2020). https://web.archive.org/web/20181214170646/www.binstream.io/

7. Github (2020). https://github.com

8. Glispa Connect (Formerly Avocarrot) (2020). https://www.glispa.com/connect/

9. Mopub (2020). https://www.mopub.com/en

10. Ogury acquires AdinCube (2020). https://ogury.com/blog/ogury-acquires-adincube-faq/

11. Quark-Engine (2020). https://github.com/quark-engine/quark-engine

12. Top Best Independent App Stores For Free Apps [2020] (2020). https://medium.com/codixlab/top-best-independent-app-stores-for-free-apps-2020-adf25bc55fd3

13. Vitamio by yixia.com (2020). https://github.com/yixia/VitamioBundle

14. Vungle (2020). https://vungle.com

15. What is illicit streaming? (2020). https://thepcdoc.co.uk/illicit-streaming/

16. Asia Video Industry Association (2021). https://avia.org/

17. Premier League (2021). https://www.premierleague.com/

18. Alliance, D.C.: Boxed in: Hackers targeting piracy devices and apps to infect users with malware (2019). https://www.digitalcitizensalliance.org/news/press-releases-2019/boxed-in-hackers-targeting-piracy-devices-and-apps-to-infect-users-with-malware-report-finds-copy/

19. Androguard_Team: A full python tool to play with android files. https://github.com/androguard/androguard

20. Baumann, R., Protsenko, M., Müller, T.: Anti-ProGuard. In: Proceedings of the 4th Workshop on Security in Highly Connected IT Systems - SHCIS 2017. ACM Press (2017). https://doi.org/10.1145/3099012.3099020, https://doi.org/10.1145/3099012.3099020

21. Bichsel, B., Raychev, V., Tsankov, P., Vechev, M.: Statistical deobfuscation of android applications. In: Proceedings of the 2016 ACM SIGSAC Conference on Computer and Communications Security, pp. 343–355. ACM (2016)

22. Bushnell, H.: Inside the complex world of illegal sports streaming. Muso Magazine (2019). https://www.muso.com/magazine/inside-the-complex-world-of-illegal-sports-streaming/

23. CNN: Why Fox and Disney hate Singapore's little black boxes (2018). https://money.cnn.com/2018/04/05/media/singapore-piracy-black-boxes/index.html

24. Mostert, F., Lambert, J.: Study on IP enforcement measures, especially anti-piracy measures in the digital environment (2019). https://www.wipo.int/edocs/mdocs/enforcement/en/wipo_ace_14/wipo__4_7-annex1.pdf

25. FACT: cracking down on digital piracy report (2017). https://www.fact-uk.org.uk/files/2017/09/Cracking-Down-on-Digital-Piracy-Report-Sept-2017.pdf

26. Hanna, S., Huang, L., Wu, E., Li, S., Chen, C., Song, D.: Juxtapp: a scalable system for detecting code reuse among android applications. In: Flegel, U., Markatos, E., Robertson, W. (eds.) DIMVA 2012. LNCS, vol. 7591, pp. 62–81. Springer, Heidelberg (2013). https://doi.org/10.1007/978-3-642-37300-8_4

27. Hawkes, R.: Eight arrests in HK content piracy crack down (2018). https://www.rapidtvnews.com/2018052952282/eight-arrests-in-hk-content-piracy-crack-down.html

28. Hsiao, L., Ayers, H.: The price of free illegal live streaming services (2019). https://doi.org/10.48550/arXiv.1901.00579

29. Ibosiola, D., Steer, B., García-Recuero, Á., Stringhini, G., Uhlig, S., Tyson, G.: Movie pirates of the caribbean: exploring illegal streaming cyberlockers. In: ICWSM (2018)

30. Jiang, L., Misherghi, G., Su, Z., Glondu, S.: DECKARD: scalable and accurate tree-based detection of code clones. In: 29th International Conference on Software Engineering (ICSE 2007). IEEE, May 2007. https://doi.org/10.1109/icse.2007.30, https://doi.org/10.1109/icse.2007.30

31. Johnson, R., Kiourtis, N., Stavrou, A., Sritapan, V.: Analysis of content copyright infringement in mobile application markets. In: 2015 APWG Symposium on Electronic Crime Research (eCrime). IEEE, May 2015. https://doi.org/10.1109/ecrime.2015.7120798, https://doi.org/10.1109/ecrime.2015.7120798

32. Kamiya, T., Kusumoto, S., Inoue, K.: CCFinder: a multilinguistic token-based code clone detection system for large scale source code. IEEE Trans. Softw. Eng. **28**(7), 654–670 (2002). https://doi.org/10.1109/tse.2002.1019480

33. Komondoor, R., Horwitz, S.: Using slicing to identify duplication in source code. In: Cousot, P. (ed.) SAS 2001. LNCS, vol. 2126, pp. 40–56. Springer, Heidelberg (2001). https://doi.org/10.1007/3-540-47764-0_3

34. Li, M., et al.: LIBD: scalable and precise third-party library detection in android markets. In: 2017 IEEE/ACM 39th International Conference on Software Engineering (ICSE), pp. 335–346. IEEE (2017)

35. Luo, L., Ming, J., Wu, D., Liu, P., Zhu, S.: Semantics-based obfuscation-resilient binary code similarity comparison with applications to software and algorithm plagiarism detection. IEEE Trans. Softw. Eng. **43**(12), 1157–1177 (2017). https://doi.org/10.1109/tse.2017.2655046

36. Moghaddam, H.M., et al.: Watching you watch. In: Proceedings of the 2019 ACM SIGSAC Conference on Computer and Communications Security - CCS 2019. ACM Press (2019). https://doi.org/10.1145/3319535.3354198, https://doi.org/10.1145/3319535.3354198

37. MSSUN: Android Apps Crawler (2014). https://github.com/mssun/android-apps-crawler

38. MTS, F.: Global monitoring platform (2019). https://www.friendmts.com/channel-protection/global-monitoring-platform/

39. Nikas, A., Alepis, E., Patsakis, C.: I know what you streamed last night: On the security and privacy of streaming. Digit. Invest. **25**, 78–89 (2018). https://doi.org/10.1016/j.diin.2018.03.004, https://doi.org/10.1016/j.diin.2018.03.004

40. UK Intellectual Property Office: Guidance about illicit streaming devices (2017). https://www.gov.uk/government/publications/illicit-streaming-devices/illicit-streaming-devices

41. OpSec: Antipiracy live streaming protection (2020). https://www.opsecsecurity.com/opsec-online/antipiracy-live-streaming-protection

42. Pandey, P., Aliapoulios, M., McCoy, D.: Iniquitous cord-cutting: An analysis of infringing IPTV services. In: 2019 IEEE European Symposium on Security and Privacy Workshops (EuroS&PW). IEEE (2019). https://doi.org/10.1109/eurospw.2019.00054

43. Rafique, M.Z., van Goethem, T., Joosen, W., Huygens, C., Nikiforakis, N.: It's free for a reason: exploring the ecosystem of free live streaming services. In: NDSS (2016)

44. Sandvine: 2017 Internet Phenomena - Subscription Television Piracy (2017). https://www.sandvine.com/hubfs/downloads/archive/2017-global-internet-phenomena-spotlight-subscription-television-piracy.pdf
45. Sounthiraraj, D., Sahs, J., Greenwood, G., Lin, Z., Khan, L.: SMV-hunter: large scale, automated detection of SSL/TLS man-in-the-middle vulnerabilities in android apps. In: In Proceedings of the 21st Annual Network and Distributed System Security Symposium (NDSS 2014). Citeseer (2014)
46. Wikipedia: Jaccard index (2020). https://en.wikipedia.org/wiki/Jaccard_index
47. Wikipedia: Kotlin (programming language) (2020). https://en.wikipedia.org/wiki/Kotlin_(programming_language)
48. Wikipedia: Md5 (2020). https://en.wikipedia.org/wiki/MD5
49. Wikipedia: pcap (2020). https://en.wikipedia.org/wiki/Pcap
50. Zhang, Y., Luo, X., Yin, H.: DexHunter: toward extracting hidden code from packed android applications. In: Computer Security - ESORICS 2015, pp. 293–311. Springer, Cham (2015). https://doi.org/10.1007/978-3-319-24177-7_15

Fine-Grained Obfuscation Scheme Recognition on Binary Code

Zhenzhou Tian[1,2($\boxtimes$)], Hengchao Mao[1,2], Yaqian Huang[1,2], Jie Tian[1,2], and Jinrui Li[1,2]

[1] School of Computer Science and Technology, Xi'an University of Posts and Telecommunications, Xi'an 710121, China
tianzhenzhou@xupt.edu.cn
[2] Shaanxi Key Laboratory of Network Data Analysis and Intelligent Processing, Xi'an, China

Abstract. Code obfuscation is to change program characteristics through code transformation, so as to avoid detection by virus scanners or prevent security analysts from performing reverse analysis. This paper proposes a new method of extracting from functions their reduced shortest paths (RSP), through path search and abstraction, to identify functions in a more fine-grained manner. The method of deep representation learning is utilized to identify whether the binary code is obfuscated and the specific obfuscation algorithms used. In order to evaluate the performance of the model, a data set of 60,000 obfuscation samples is constructed. The extensive experimental evaluation results show that the model can successfully identify the characteristics of code obfuscation. The accuracy for the task of identifying whether the code is obfuscated reaches 98.6%, while the accuracy for the task of identifying the specific obfuscation algorithm performed reaches 97.6%.

Keywords: Code obfuscation recognition · Binary code · Neural network

1 Introduction

Code obfuscation is a widely used software protection technique that can mitigates the risks caused by reverse engineering. It helps to protect software intellectual property by hiding the logic and sensitive data implied in the code. The

This work was supported in part by the Science and Technology of Xi'an (2019218114GXRC017CG018-GXYD17.16), the National Natural Science Foundation of China (61702414), the Natural Science Basic Research Program of Shaanxi (2018JQ6078, 2020GY-010, 2020JM-582), the International Science and Technology Cooperation Program of Shaanxi (2018KW-049, 2019KW-008), the Key Research and Development Program of Shaanxi (2019ZDLGY07-08), and the Special Funds for Construction of Key Disciplines in Universities in Shaanxi.

P. Gladyshev et al. (Eds.): ICDF2C 2021, LNICST 441, pp. 215–228, 2022.
https://doi.org/10.1007/978-3-031-06365-7_13

use of code obfuscation depends on the sensitivity of the application. Its applications are mainly on digital rights management, software licensing and white box encryption. Malicious code also makes extensive use of code obfuscation to hide its intentions, so as to evade detection and hinder analysis. Therefore, the problem of de-obfuscation has attracted widespread attention in the academic community, many researchers have attempted to recover the original code from obfuscated programs, while identifying the specific obfuscation algorithm [22] applied facilitates to a large extent the de-obfuscation process.

At present, most de-obfuscation techniques focus on the topic of automatically processing the obfuscated code to restore the original code. Generally, they only work on certain obfuscation algorithms. Some of existing approaches, including layout de-obfuscation [2], opaque predicate de-obfuscation [13], control leveling obfuscation [17] and virtualization de-obfuscation [4,15,20], all work under the premise of knowing the specific obfuscation algorithms used. In reality, researchers often face completely unknown malware in the form of executable code, which leads to two closely related problems. The first question, from the perspective of de-obfuscation, is whether the target program is obfuscated? For example, if the existing de-obfuscation techniques are used to analyze the target program that does not contain obfuscated code, not only the internal logic of the original program will be broken, it also causes the analysts to spend a lot of time doing useless work. The second question is, from the perspective of reverse engineering, what is the specific kind of obfuscation algorithm used to produce to target obfuscated program? Especially, it is worth mentioning that in recent years, new obfuscation algorithms have emerged one after another. Obviously, it is very necessary for analysts to understand the characteristics of each code obfuscation and quickly identify the obfuscation algorithms from the target program, which once can be identified in an automated way, will greatly reduce the difficulty of reverse analysis and time cost for security analysts.

In recent years, tremendous successes have been witnessed of applying deep learning models to diverse program analysis tasks, such as binary code clone detection [21], compiler provenance analysis [16] and vulnerability detection [19]. They generally leverage the many layers of non-linearities to automatically boost learning a latent vector representation with semantic richness. In this regard, this paper proposes to take each individual function within a binary program as the basic analysis subject. After processing a function into a set of reduced shortest paths, our method operates directly on the corresponding normalized assembly instructions to achieve fine grained obfuscation detection. Also, from the perspective of sequence analysis and structural analysis, we design a supervised learning model based on deep neural networks to achieve code obfuscation detection and obfuscation algorithm identification. Our main contributions are summarized as following:

– We propose a new form of function representation as a set of reduced shortest paths (RSP), through path search and abstraction on its control flow graph (CFG), to get the function represented in a more fine-grained and semantics-aware manner.

- We suggest to perform fine-grained binary code obfuscation recognition for each individual function by designing a lightweight function abstraction strategy and a deep representation learning model based on RNN and CNN. It reduces the impact of task complexity and human bias by handing over the important feature extraction and selection process of the function to less human intervened neural networks.
- We have implemented a prototype tool called OBDB (OBfuscation scheme Detector on Binary code), which integrates our proposed method. A dataset consisting of more than 60,000 samples is constructed by processing 11,000 programs collected from Google Code Jam (GCJ), with two of the most well-known code obfuscators including Tigress [1] and OLLVM [8]. The experimental evaluation results conducted on the dataset show that, the proposed method can effectively capture the significant features of specific code obfuscations. OBDB achieves rather good performance, with the accuracy of identifying whether the code is obfuscated reaches 98.6% and the accuracy of identifying the specific obfuscation algorithm reaches 97.6%.

2 Background

Code obfuscation is a technique that enforce control and data transformations on the program's source code or even its binary code while retaining the functionality of the original program, with the aim of making it more difficult to analyze and tamper with. Collberg et al. [3] makes a general taxonomy of obfuscating transformations. According to underlying basic schemes, obfuscation transformations can generally be divided into four categories: layout obfuscation, data obfuscation, control obfuscation and prevention obfuscation. So far, the research of code obfuscation algorithms has been relatively mature, various algorithms have emerged in recent years. Table 1 shows six typical code obfuscation algorithms supported in two widely used obfuscation tools, on the basis of which many other obfuscation algorithms have been derived.

Table 1. Six typical obfuscation algorithms

Tool	Obfuscation algorithm	Description
OLLVM	Instructions substitution (sub)	Replace binary operators including addition, subtraction and boolean operators
	Bogus Control Flow (bcf)	Add opaque predicates to make a conditional jump to the original basic block
	Control Flow Flattening (fla)	Break down the program's control flow
Tigress	Virtualize (vir)	Replace code with virtualized instructions and execute them by an interpreter
	AddOpaque (opa)	Add opaque predicates to split up the control flow of the code
	EncodeLiterals (lit)	Replace literal integers and strings with less obvious expressions

3   Overview of Our Approach

In this section, we will introduce the proposed method in detail. The overview of OBDB is shown in Fig. 1, which consists of the training and the detection phases. In the training phase, firstly a set of reduced shortest paths RSP are extracted and normalized to get each function expressed. To be specific, IDA-Pro [5] is used to analyze each function in the training set to obtain its control flow graph (CFG), on the basis of which all the shortest paths are extracted from the entry basic block to each other basic block in the CFG to obtain a path set SP. By checking the inclusion relationship between the paths in SP, a set of reduced shortest paths RSP can be generated. That is, for each path $p \in SP$, as long as it is not completely contained by all the other paths in SP, it will be considered as a reduced shortest path and added to the set RSP. With a light-weighted assembly instruction normalization scheme, each path in RSP is further abstracted to get rid of inessential details.

The collection of abstracted paths form the basic representation of a function, which are fed as the inputs to the neural network module to extract latent feature vectors that are indicative of the obfuscation algorithms. The whole model is finally trained by appending a dense and a softmax layer to process the latent vectors together with their ground truth labels as supervision. The detection phase is much simpler, which reads in an individual function, processes it with the function abstraction and utilizes the trained model to produce predictions.

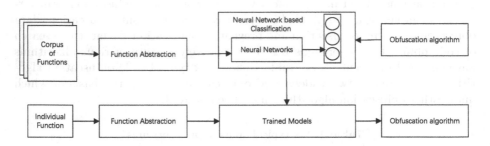

Fig. 1. The basic framework of the OBDB model

3.1   Function Abstraction

Reduced Shortest Path Extraction. A function must be expressed in a certain form such that it can be further analyzed. Typical methods include the use of raw byte sequences, assembly instruction sequences, or control flow graph to describe the function. As shown in many binary analysis tasks, adopting the original raw bytes has been proven to be an unwise choice [16]; while using the assembly code as a whole to describe the function, generally results in the loss of expressive structural information, which may be of significant importance to identify the features manifested in the obfuscated code by the obfuscation algorithms. To this end, we choose to use the CFG that implicitly encodes the possible execution paths as the basic representation form for each function. In particular, we retrieve and construct from each function's CFG all the reduced shortest paths, and use the assembly instructions that appear along these paths to get it represented. It ensures that, at the time of capturing instruction level obfuscation indicative features, the structural features can also be covered. Algorithm 1 gives the pseudo-code that converts the function into the assembly instruction sequences.

Algorithm 1. Reduced shortest path based function representation

---

Input:
    G: control flow graph of a function
    I_B: instruction set within each basic block
    T: the number of basic blocks
Output:
    RSP: the reduced shortest path representation of the input function
1: $SP \leftarrow \langle\ \rangle$
2: $path \leftarrow \langle\rangle$
3: $G_{acyclic} = \text{clear\_garph}(G_d)$ ▷ clear the loops in G to be a directed acyclic graph
4: $E = get_entry(G)$ ▷ get the entry node of the CFG
5: **for** each node B in $G_{acyclic}$ **do**
6:    **if** E is exactly B **then**
7:      continue
8:      $path = \text{Dijkstra}(G_{acyclic}, E, BB)$ ▷ using Dijkstra to find the shortest path
9:      $SP = SP \oplus path$ ▷ Add a new shortest path to the set
10:   **end if**
11: **end for**
12: **for** each p in SP **do**
13:   **if** containedBy(p, SP) **then**
14:     $RSP = RSP \oplus p$ ▷ Add p to the reduced shortest path set
15:   **end if**
16: **end for**

Instruction Normalization. After obtaining the instruction sequence of the function, the instruction consists of an opcode (i.e. the mnemonic) and a list of operands. It is usually unwise to process the original instructions directly. In our case, we want to capture the characteristics of the obfuscated algorithm, rather than the functionality of the function. In other words, we don't care whether the value 6 is assigned to the register eax or the value 10 is assigned to the register eax, but we are more concerned with the form and type of instructions chosen by the obfuscation algorithm. In this regard, by considering that these two instructions "mov eax, 6" and "mov eax, 10" are the same may be better choice to our problem. In addition, the memory addresses (such as the target address of the jmp instruction) are meaningless, they tend to be noises that distract the attention of successive neural network based training process. In addition, in order to avoid introducing too many human prejudices, we choose to use a lightweight abstraction strategy to process the original assembly instruction sequences in RSP. To be specific, we have formulated the following instruction abstraction rules:

- All the opcode of instructions remain unchanged.
- All registers in the operand remain unchanged.
- All base memory addresses in the operand are replaced with the symbol MEM.
- All immediate values in the operand are replaced with the symbol MEM.

For example, using the above normalization rules, the instruction "add eax, 6" will become "add eax, IMM", the instruction "mov ebx, add eax, 6" will become "mov ebx, MEM", and the instruction "mov ebx, [ebp−20]" will become "mov ebx,[ebp−IMM]".

3.2   Instruction Embedding

Before using the neural network based learning model to detect obfuscation algorithms, we must transform the normalized assembly instruction sequences into numerical vectors, such that they can be used as input to subsequent classifiers. As our designs choose to use advanced deep neural network to master the subtle features and patterns indicative of the applied obfuscation algorithms, we firstly utilize the widely adopted word embedding to assign a vector to each unique normalized instruction, based on which the whole instruction sequence can also be represented as a vector sequence.

There are several word embedding choices that can be leveraged for our application, of which the one-hot encoding has been widely deployed. It represents each unique word by a n-dimensional vector, with the ith dimension being set to 1 and all other dimensions being set to 0, where i is the index of the word in the vocabulary of size n. This technique is computationally intractable as the generated vectors are too sparse (the same dimension as the size of the whole vocabulary) and generally needs to do joint-learning with subsequent neural networks, making the learnt word semantics significantly task-specific. In this respect, OBDB leverages the popular skip-gram model [12] to learn more compact vector representations that carry instruction co-occurrence relationships and lexical semantics in an independent and unsupervised manner, so as to make the learnt vectors reusable in other binary analysis tasks. Specifically, we treat each basic block as a sentence and each abstracted instruction within the basic block as a word, and feed all the basic blocks from our binary collection to the skip-gram model to learn for each unique normalized instruction a d-dimensional vector, by minimizing the loss of observing an instruction's neighborhood (within a window w) conditioned on its current embedding. The objective function of skip-gram can be defined as [14]:

$$arg\min_{\Phi} \sum_{-w \leq j \leq w, i \neq j} -log\, p\left(e_{i+j}|\Phi(e_i)\right) \tag{1}$$

3.3   The BiGRU-CNN Model

Based on the instruction embedding learned with skip-gram, different schemes such as maximum pooling, average pooling or cascading can be exploited to aggregate the embeddings of each abstracted instruction sequence, and then feed it to any classification model for obfuscation algorithm identification. However, it still faces the following two limitations: (1) skip-gram assigns a static embedding vector to each instruction, and it does not know the context of the different sequences it interacts with; it may not be able to learn obfuscation-related features; (2) as instruction sequences are abstracted from functions, they may not only enjoy local instructions. In this regard, it needs sequence learning model to better capture representative obfuscation algorithm specific patterns and features from instruction sequences, so as to recognize the specific obfuscation algorithms applied. As advanced neural network structures, either RNN or CNN based models have ever been applied for representation learning sequences in NLP tasks. Therefore, in this work, OBDB attempts to combine RNN and CNN structures to learn the syntactic and structural information implied in the instruction sequences, so as to use both their advances to identify obfuscation algorithms. Figure 2 depicts the basic structure of our BiGRU-CNN based model.

Specifically, it firstly use a RNN-based layer to iteratively process each normalized reduced shortest path p_i in RSP into a numerical vector. RNN is chosen in our design for its ability of capturing long range dependencies between the normalized opcodes in a sequence, so as to capture the obfuscation indicative features. Yet, the naive RNN structure exposes the vanishing/exploding gradient issue in handling long sequences, while two improved structures LSTM and GRU have been proposed to alleviate the problem. Also, considering that GRU has a simpler structure and is generally believed to be more efficient than LSTM, we choose to use GRU in the current design.

The GRU unit reads in the input instruction sequence p_i through the hidden layer function $\mathcal{H}$ to generate a hidden vector state $\mathbf{h}_i$ at each timestep i. To improve the learning ability, OBDB further devises the bidirectional GRU (BiRGU) structure to jointly capture both the forward and backward sequential dependency and increase the amount of information available to the network. The hidden state vector h_i at timestep i can then concatenated as:

$$h_i = \left[\overrightarrow{h_i}; \overleftarrow{h_i}\right]. \tag{2}$$

After bidirectionally reading the entire input sequence, the hidden states $\mathbf{h}_t$ corresponding to the last timestep will act as the latent vector representation of the input sequence. After processing all the $p_i \in RSP$, all the encoded numerical vectors will be formed as a numerical matrix A, which is to be fed into a CNN based layer to further learn a latent vector representation.

The convolution layer can extract local contextual features with varying convolution kernels. In OBDB, k different filters with shape $n \times d$ are adopted for convolution operations on matrix A to obtain a new feature matrix $C \in \mathbb{R}^{(l-n+1) \times k}$, where n denotes the kernel size. To capture different aspects of features, we convolute A by varying kernels of size 2, 3 and 4 respectively. To reduce the dimensionality of learnt vectors and get OBDB focus on significant features, a pooling layer is applied that performs pooling operations on the produced convolutional features. There are usually two types, max-pooling and average-pooling, that are widely used. Maximum pooling is to select the maximum value in the vector after convolution operation as the local feature, while average pooling is to use the average value. In this paper, we choose maximum pooling. To prevent the neural networks from overfitting during the training phase, a dropout layer is also appended right after the CNN layer.

Finally, the output of the dropout layer is fed as inputs to subsequent dense and classification layers for predication. The classification layer is basically sigmod or softmax layer. Sigmoid is mainly used for binary classifications, and softmax can be used for multi-classifications. Specifically, we use the softmax function to achieve multi-classification. Simply put, the softmax function maps some output neurons to real numbers between 0 and 1, such that the sum of the probabilities of multi-classifications is exactly 1. The softmax function is defined as follows:

$$P_i = \frac{e^{V_i}}{\sum_{i-1}^{C} e^{V_i}} \tag{3}$$

where V_i is the output of the previous unit of the classifier, i denotes the class index, and the total number of classes is C.

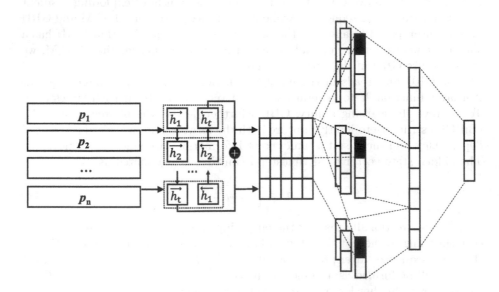

Fig. 2. BiGRU-CNN model structure diagram

4   Experiments and Evaluation

4.1   Dataset Construction

In the field of code analysis, publicly available labeled datasets for binary code are scarce, let alone datasets with obfuscation labels. In order to evaluate the performance of OBDB, we collected a large number of open source programs written in C programming language from the GCJ as a basis to build a data set. Specifically, we deal with these collected programs with the following steps:

(1) Firstly, we utilize the six typical obfuscation algorithms implemented in two widely use obfuscation tools to enforce obfuscation on the source code of each program. The specific obfuscation algorithms applied include the -bcf, -fla and -sub options in OLLVM, as well as the -AddOpaque, -Virtualize and -EncodeLiterals options in Tigress. For programs that are successfully obfuscated, the gcc compiler is then used to compile their obfuscated source code into binaries.

(2) Secondly, IDA Pro is used to identify and extract functions from each binary file. In addition, we removed some insignificant functions (functions that contain only several instructions, such as the stub functions), which are meaningless to analysis. In the current setting, we consider functions that contain less than 10 instructions to be trivial, which will not be considered by the dataset.

(3) Further, to prevent the neural network model from seeing in the training phase functions that are very similar to those in the testing phase, only distinct function are retained in the final dataset. Specifically, if a function has exactly the same normalized assembly instructions as any other function in the raw dataset, it will be considered as redundant. With these settings, we finally constructed a dataset consisting of 60,000 distinct and non-trivial obfuscated functions.

4.2   Implementation and Experimental Setup

We have implemented OBDB as a prototype tool. It uses ida pro to parse binary files to obtain functions and their original assembly instructions. The function abstraction module is implemented in Java programming language, while the neural network based representation learning and classification module is implemented with Python and the Tensorflow framework.

In the experimental settings, we randomly divide the entire dataset into training set, validation set and test set at a ratio of 80%, 10%, and 10%. The neural network model is trained using a Tesla V100 GPU with the Adam optimizer. The batch size is set to 128, and the initial learning rate is set to 0.001 (when the loss on the validation set stops improving for at least 5 epochs, the learning rate will be further divided by 10). In each epoch, the training samples are shuffled, the accuracy on the validation set is calculated. Besides, to avoid problems such as over-fitting and non-convergence, the early stopping mechanism is enforced to stop the training right after the epoch that the validation accuracy no longer improves. Finally, the model with the highest accuracy is considered as the finally trained obfuscation classifier, with which frequently used performance metrics including accuracy, precision, recall, and f1-score are evaluated and reported on the test set.

4.3   Experimental Results

In the following, we evaluate the performance of OBDB in identifying the existence of obfuscation and the specific obfuscation algorithms respectively. In addition, several other widely used deep neural network models have also been implemented and get compared with OBDB. Note that the precision, recall and f1-score in Table 2 all refer to the weighted average precision, recall and f1-score, respectively.

(1) Performance evaluation on identifying the existence of obfuscation
    In this experiment, we take the obfuscated/non-obfuscated label of each function as the ground-truth. That is, all the functions obfuscated with either of the six obfuscation algorithms are marked with the obfuscated label. Then, OBDB is trained and evaluated according to the experimental settings in Sect, 4.2. As shown in Table 2 the evaluation results, OBDB outperforms all the other comparison models with respect to the performance metrics, exhibiting a rather good accuracy of 98.6% and a high f1-score of 0.986.

Table 2. Detection results for the existence of obfuscation

Model	Accuracy	Precision	Recall	F1
CNN	95.78%	0.9576	0.9678	0.9598
BiLSTM	93.65%	0.9395	0.9368	0.9365
BiGRU	94.98%	0.9458	0.9378	0.9488
OBDB	**98.62%**	**0.9794**	**0.9889**	**0.9861**

(2) Performance evaluation on identifying the specific obfuscation algorithms
    In this experiment, the specific obfuscation algorithms applied on the functions are taken as the ground-truth labels to get OBDB trained and evaluated. That is, OBDB attempts to assign to each obfuscated function a certain label that indicates one of six obfuscation algorithms. According to the detection results, the total accuracy of OBDB reaches 97.6%, which is a bit lower than its accuracy reported on the task of identifying the existence of obfuscation. Besides, we compare it with Zhao's [23] method, which also designs a deep neural network based model to train classifiers for obfuscation scheme recognition. As reported in their work, the detection accuracy on recognizing the specific obfuscation algorithms reaches 89.4%, which is much lower than ours'. The about 9% performance gains achieved with OBDB than Zhao's

method may lie in that, OBDB adopts a more carefully designed function representation (a set of reduced shortest paths) that captures both syntactic and structural changes enforced by the obfuscation algorithms, while their method simply represent the function as a set of basic blocks. It indicates the superiority of our proposed novel function representation method in this task.

Figure 3 summarizes the true positive rates (TPRs) with respect to each obfuscation algorithm. As it shows, the TPRs vary across different obfuscation algorithms, indicating the different impacts enforced on the produced obfuscated code by different obfuscation algorithms. To be specific, the FPR for the -fla obfuscation in OLLVM reaches the highest, which is about 99.89%; while the FPRs for -lit and -sub obfuscations are the lowest, which are 94.63% and 94.65% respectively. As introduced in Table 1, the -fat option performs the control flow flattening obfuscation, which makes great changes to the control flow of the program. Our normalized reduced shortest path representation of functions that well captured the structural features just boosts the FPR on this obfuscation algorithm. Similarly, the reasons for the relatively lower FPRs of -lit and -sub lie in that, the changes introduced by these two kind obfuscation schemes which replace literals or strings are not that obvious as other obfuscation algorithms. In spite of that, the fairish FPRs indicate that OBDB still captures the subtle features indicative of these obfuscations. The TPRs for the other neural networks models are also evaluated and depicted in Fig. 4. As the data shows, OBDB still performs the best among all the models.

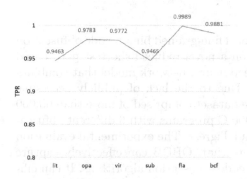 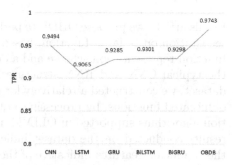

Fig. 3. TPRs in terms of differnt obfuscation algorithms

Fig. 4. TPRs in terms of different neural network models

5   Related Work

In recent years, the application of deep learning technology in the field of binary program analysis has achieved remarkable success [11,16]. Of the few works that implement obfuscation recognition, Zhao et al. [23] also adopts neural network based models. Different from their method that uses the set of basic blocks within a function to form the basic representation to be fed into subsequent neural networks, we propose to represent each function as a set of normalized reduced shortest paths extracted from its control flow graph, such that structural information can also be captured besides the syntactic information manifested by the assembly instructions appearing along the paths. It enables the subsequent neural network layers preferably capture subtle features that are indicative of the structural changes enforced by the obfuscation algorithms, so as to improve the whole detection performance.

In the literature, there are many code obfuscation detection approaches that focus on the scripting languages, such as JavaScript [10] and PowerShell [9], as well as on Android Apps [18], which also adopt machine learning and data mining based ways. JSObfusDetector detector [7] uses the SVM algorithm to get malicious JavaScript obfuscation scripts detected, after characterizing the number of string variables and the dynamic functions in JavaScript scripts. Wang et al. [18] extracts feature vectors from the Dalvik bytecode and uses it to identify the obfuscator provenance information within an App. On one hand, these methods works generally on the whole program level, and can not be easily adapted to the detection of obfuscation provenance on binary code, due to the missing of certain features that present in the source code but get lost during the compilation phase. Besides, rather than extracting and selecting features with manually defined templates, OBDB resorts to the powerful learning ability of neural network models and the largest number of training data to improve the accuracy and efficiency of the detection methods.

6   Conclusion

In this article, we propose OBDB to perform fine-grained binary code obfuscation recognition on isolated function, based on a novel reduced shortest path based function representation scheme and a deep neural network model that combines the typical CNN and RNN structures. Due to the lack of publicly accessible dataset, we constructed a relatively large dataset comprised of more than 60,000 obfuscated functions, by processing 11,000 C programs with 6 different obfuscation algorithms supported in OLLVM and Tigress. The experimental evaluation results conducted on the dataset indicate that, OBDB can effectively capture the significant features indicative of the code obfuscation algorithms. It can efficiently identify the existence of obfuscation with an accuracy of 98.6%, the accuracy of identifying the specific obfuscation algorithm also reaches a high score of 97.6%. Future work includes enriching the dataset with more samples and more kind obfuscation algorithms, as well as designing other neural representation learning models, such as the graph neural network (GNN), to comprehensively consider the CFG Node attributes and structural characteristics.

References

1. The tigress diversifying c virtualizer (2021). https://tigress.wtf/
2. Bichsel, B., Raychev, V., Tsankov, P., Vechev, M.T.: Statistical deobfuscation of android applications. In: Proceedings of the 2016 ACM SIGSAC Conference on Computer and Communications Security (2016)
3. Collberg, C., Thomborson, C., Low, D.: A taxonomy of obfuscating transformations (1997)
4. Coogan, K., Lu, G., Debray, S.: Deobfuscation of virtualization-obfuscated software: a semantics-based approach. In: CCS 2011 (2011)
5. Ferguson, J.: Reverse Engineering Code with IDA Pro. O'Reilly Media, San Francisco (2008)
6. Hindle, A., Barr, E.T., Su, Z., Gabel, M., Devanbu, P.T.: On the naturalness of software. In: ICSE 2012 (2012)
7. Jodavi, M., Abadi, M., Parhizkar, E.: JSObfusdetector: a binary PSO-based one-class classifier ensemble to detect obfuscated javascript code. In: 2015 The International Symposium on Artificial Intelligence and Signal Processing (AISP), pp. 322–327 (2015)
8. Junod, P., Rinaldini, J., Wehrli, J., Michielin, J.: Obfuscator-LLVM - software protection for the masses. In: 2015 IEEE/ACM 1st International Workshop on Software Protection, pp. 3–9 (2015)
9. Li, Z., Chen, Q., Xiong, C., Chen, Y., Zhu, T., Yang, H.: Effective and light-weight deobfuscation and semantic-aware attack detection for PowerShell scripts. In: Proceedings of the 2019 ACM SIGSAC Conference on Computer and Communications Security (2019)
10. Likarish, P., Jung, E., Jo, I.: Obfuscated malicious javascript detection using classification techniques. In: 2009 4th International Conference on Malicious and Unwanted Software (MALWARE), pp. 47–54 (2009)
11. Massarelli, L., Luna, G.A.D., Petroni, F., Querzoni, L., Baldoni, R.: Investigating Graph Embedding Neural Networks with Unsupervised Features Extraction for Binary Analysis. Internet Society (2019)
12. Mikolov, T., Chen, K., Corrado, G., Dean, J.: Efficient estimation of word representations in vector space. In: ICLR (2013)
13. Ming, J., Xu, D., Wang, L., Wu, D.: Loop: Logic-oriented opaque predicate detection in obfuscated binary code. In: Proceedings of the 22nd ACM SIGSAC Conference on Computer and Communications Security (2015)
14. Perozzi, B., Al-Rfou, R., Skiena, S.: DeepWalk: online learning of social representations. In: Proceedings of the 20th ACM SIGKDD International Conference on Knowledge Discovery and Data Mining (2014)
15. Salwan, J., Bardin, S., Potet, M.: Symbolic deobfuscation: from virtualized code back to the original. In: DIMVA (2018)
16. Tian, Z., Huang, Y., Xie, B., Chen, Y., Chen, L., Wu, D.: Fine-grained compiler identification with sequence-oriented neural modeling. IEEE Access 9, 49160–49175 (2021). https://doi.org/10.1109/ACCESS.2021.3069227
17. Udupa, S.K., Debray, S., Madou, M.: Deobfuscation: reverse engineering obfuscated code. In: 12th Working Conference on Reverse Engineering (WCRE'2005), pp. 10–54 (2005)
18. Wang, Y., Rountev, A.: Who changed you? Obfuscator identification for android. In: The 4th International Conference on Mobile Software Engineering and Systems (MOBILESoft), pp. 154–164 (2017)

19. Wang, Y., Wu, Z., Wei, Q., Wang, Q.: NeuFuzz: efficient fuzzing with deep neural network. IEEE Access **7**, 36340–36352 (2019)
20. Xu, D., Ming, J., Fu, Y., Wu, D.: VMHunt: a verifiable approach to partially-virtualized binary code simplification. In: Proceedings of the 2018 ACM SIGSAC Conference on Computer and Communications Security (2018)
21. Xue, H., Venkataramani, G., Lan, T.: Clone-slicer: detecting domain specific binary code clones through program slicing. In: Proceedings of the 2018 Workshop on Forming an Ecosystem Around Software Transformation (2018)
22. Yadegari, B., Johannesmeyer, B., Whitely, B., Debray, S.: A generic approach to automatic deobfuscation of executable code. In: 2015 IEEE Symposium on Security and Privacy, pp. 674–691 (2015)
23. Zhao, Y., Tang, Z., Ye, G., Peng, D., Fang, D., Chen, X., Wang, Z.: Semantics-aware obfuscation scheme prediction for binary. Comput. Secur. **99**, 102072 (2020)

Backdoor Investigation and Incident Response: From Zero to Profit

Anthony Cheuk Tung Lai[1,2](✉), Ken Wai Kin Wong[1,2], Johnny Tsz Wun Wong[2], Austin Tsz Wai Lau[2], Alan Po Lun Ho[2], Shuai Wang[1], and Jogesh Muppala[1]

[1] Hong Kong University of Science and Technology, Hong Kong, China
{lct,wkwongal}@connect.ust.hk
[2] VX Security Research Group (VXRL), Hong Kong, China

Abstract. We have investigated an incident in an online gaming company about an unauthorized access to the transactional database, the attacker modifies the gaming transaction to win the game. The attacker compromises the database occasionally without explicit footprints, basically this company has just engaged enterprise-grade firewall and anti-virus software but its anti-virus control failed to detect the existence of a backdoor file. After 4-month of investigation, with additional layered defense and monitoring, we have discovered the backdoor and carried out an incident response successfully. In view of this incident, OilRig attack [1] and Solarwinds Supply Chain Hack [2], we can foresee this type of incident will continue. Therefore, in this paper, we propose an incident response methodology matrix called BackDoor Incident Response Model (BDIRM) to handle incidents with backdoor effectively, thereby accelerating to eradicate the risk and impact of backdoor against organizations.

Keywords: Incident response · Backdoor · Malware · Targeted attack · APT

1 Background

Backdoor is a trigger-based malware, which generates traffic and its communication over authorized protocols (e.g., HTTP and DNS). Backdoor malware typically looks legitimate, which are usually ignored by network and system administrators.

We have carried out a security monitoring and incident response for an online gaming company. During our monitoring over the database system, we have found the modified transactions are executed by malicious stored procedures (see Fig. 1a and Fig. 1b). We have attempted to apply various industry popular incident response frameworks [3, 3]. The high-level methodology of incident response is comprehensive, and we can successfully identify and implement the incident response at the database server. However, it failed to detect and identify highly stealthy malware backdoor and attack origin with existing frameworks (Fig. 2). As a result, attackers keep getting into the system from time to time to make unauthorized transactions, even servers have been patched with up-to-date vulnerability and anti-virus definitions.

P. Gladyshev et al. (Eds.): ICDF2C 2021, LNICST 441, pp. 229–247, 2022.
https://doi.org/10.1007/978-3-031-06365-7_14

The online company has a basic infrastructure diagram for us to reference and change control of configuration and deployment details are inadequate.

We have found that a backdoor was installed to a Microsoft Web server for at least four months until we have established and implemented an incident response matrix to uncover this backdoor, which hits our checkpoints.

The revealed backdoor comprises functions to access a database and modify table entries of a transaction. The backdoor allows an attacker to interact with it to execute various built-in SQL query commands against the application and database and database system administrator (SA) process take-over statement (Fig. 1a) and create unauthenticated and authorized sensitive transaction records (Fig. 1b).

```
rdata:000000018005AB40 ; CHAR aAlterServerRol[]
rdata:000000018005AB40 aAlterServerRol db 'ALTER SERVER ROLE [processadmin] ADD MEMBER [%s]',0
rdata:000000018005AB40                              ; DATA XREF: AlterServerProcessAdmin+42↑o
rdata:000000018005AB71                    align 8
rdata:000000018005AB78 ; CHAR aAlterServerRol_0[]
rdata:000000018005AB78 aAlterServerRol_0 db 'ALTER SERVER ROLE [processadmin] DROP MEMBER [%s]',0
rdata:000000018005AB78                              ; DATA XREF: sub 180025540+42↑o
rdata:000000018005ABAA                    align 10h
rdata:000000018005ABB0 aSetNocountOnDe_2 db 'SET NOCOUNT ON;',0Dh,0Ah
rdata:000000018005ABB0                              ; DATA XREF: sub 180025A60+77↑o
rdata:000000018005ABB0          db 'declare sa_clear_cur cursor for',0Dh,0Ah
rdata:000000018005ABB0          db 'select spid from sys.sysprocesses where loginame = ',27h,'sa',27h
rdata:000000018005ABB0          db ' and hostname != ',27h,27h,0Dh,0Ah
rdata:000000018005ABB0          db 'open sa_clear_cur',0Dh,0Ah
rdata:000000018005ABB0          db 'declare @sa_spid int, @top1SQL varchar(max)',0Dh,0Ah
rdata:000000018005ABB0          db 'fetch next from sa_clear_cur into @sa_spid',0Dh,0Ah
rdata:000000018005ABB0          db 'while @@FETCH_STATUS = 0',0Dh,0Ah
rdata:000000018005ABB0          db 'begin',0Dh,0Ah
rdata:000000018005ABB0          db 9,'set @top1SQL = ',27h,'KILL ',27h,' + RTRIM(@sa_spid)',0Dh,0Ah
rdata:000000018005ABB0          db 9,'exec(@top1SQL)',0Dh,0Ah
rdata:000000018005ABB0          db 9,'fetch next from sa_clear_cur into @sa_spid',0Dh,0Ah
rdata:000000018005ABB0          db 'end',0Dh,0Ah
rdata:000000018005ABB0          db 'close sa_clear_cur',0Dh,0Ah
rdata:000000018005ABB0          db 'deallocate sa_clear_cur',0Dh,0Ah,0
rdata:000000018005AD57                    align 8
rdata:000000018005AD58 ; const CHAR byte 18005AD58
```

Fig. 1a. Backdoor attempts to alter the privileges of the system and take over system process privilege.

```
.rdata:000000018005A19B                    align 20h
.rdata:000000018005A1A0 ; CHAR aSetNocountOnIf[]
.rdata:000000018005A1A0 aSetNocountOnIf db 9,9,'SET NOCOUNT ON',9,9,'if (object_id(',27h,'tempdb..#dynupper',27h
.rdata:000000018005A1A0                              ; DATA XREF: sub 180022B50+B6↑o
.rdata:000000018005A1A0          db ') is null)',9,9,9,'begin',9,9,9,'return;',9,'end',9,9,'declare @U'
.rdata:000000018005A1A0          db 'sername varchar(MAX) = ',27h,'%s',27h,9,9,'declare @MTime int'
.rdata:000000018005A1A0          db ' = %d',9,9,'declare @tmpCSAgent table(csid int)',9,9,'declare @tm'
.rdata:000000018005A1A0          db 'pTmpID int = -1',9,9,'declare @MAXFOR int = 0',9,9,'set @tmpTmpID'
.rdata:000000018005A1A0          db ' = (select top 1 ParentCSID from Account where Username = @Userna'
.rdata:000000018005A1A0          db 'me)',9,9,'insert into @tmpCSAgent values(@tmpTmpID)',9,9,'REPER:',9
.rdata:000000018005A1A0          db 'set @tmpTmpID = (select top 1 Parent from CSAccount where ID = @t'
.rdata:000000018005A1A0          db 'mpTmpID)',9,9,'if @tmpTmpID != -1 and @MAXFOR < 1',9,9,9,'begin',9
.rdata:000000018005A1A0          db 9,9,'insert into @tmpCSAgent(csid) values(@tmpTmpID)',9,9,9,'set @'
.rdata:000000018005A1A0          db 'MAXFOR = @MAXFOR + 1',9,9,9,'goto REPER',9,9,9,'end',9,9,'else',9
.rdata:000000018005A1A0          db 9,9,'begin',9,9,9,'if exists(select * from CSAccount where ID in(s'
.rdata:000000018005A1A0          db 'elect csid from @tmpCSAgent) and DATEDIFF (mi, CSAccount.LastLogi'
.rdata:000000018005A1A0          db 'n, GETDATE()) <= @MTime)',9,9,9,'begin',9,9,9,9,'update #dynu'
.rdata:000000018005A1A0          db 'pper set st = 1 where un = @Username',9,9,9,9,'end',9,9,9,'else',9
.rdata:000000018005A1A0          db 9,9,9,'begin',9,9,9,9,'update #dynupper set st = 0 where un = @Us'
.rdata:000000018005A1A0          db 'ername',9,9,9,9,'end',9,9,9,'end',9,9,9,9,'select * from #dynu'
.rdata:000000018005A1A0          db 'pper where un = @Username',0
.rdata:000000018005A552                    align 4
.rdata:000000018005A554 aSt_0        db 'st',0        ; DATA XREF: sub 180022B50+164↑o
.rdata:000000018005A557                    align 20h
.rdata:000000018005A560 ; CHAR aSetNocountOnDe[]
.rdata:000000018005A560 aSetNocountOnDe db 9,'SET NOCOUNT ON',9,'declare @Username varchar(MAX) = ',27h,'%s',27h
.rdata:000000018005A560                              ; DATA XREF: sub 1800236F0+B6↑o
.rdata:000000018005A560          db ';',9,'declare @MAXFOR int = 0',9,'declare @tmpCSAgent table(csid '
.rdata:000000018005A560          db 'int)',9,'declare @tmpTmpID int = -1',9,'set @tmpTmpID = (select t'
.rdata:000000018005A560          db 'op 1 ParentCSID from Account where Username = @Username)',9,'inse'
.rdata:000000018005A560          db 'rt into @tmpCSAgent values (@tmpTmpID)',9,'REPER:',9,'set @tmpTmp'
.rdata:000000018005A560          db 'ID = (select top 1 Parent from CSAccount where ID = @tmpTmpID)',9
.rdata:000000018005A560          db 'if @tmpTmpID != -1',9,'begin',9,9,'insert into @tmpCSAgent (csid)'
.rdata:000000018005A560          db ' values (@tmpTmpID)',9,9,'set @MAXFOR = @MAXFOR + 1; if @MAXFOR <'
.rdata:000000018005A560          db ' 100 begin goto REPER end',9,'end',9,'select ID, CreateDate, User'
.rdata:000000018005A560          db 'name, Name, LastLogin, LastLoginIP from CSAccount where ID  in (s'
.rdata:000000018005A560          db 'elect csid from @tmpCSAgent);',9,9,0
.rdata:000000018005A7CA                    align 10h
```

Fig. 1b. Partial SQL queries to show Backdoor malware attempts to create fake transactions in temporary database table.

Incident Response Steps

NIST	SANS
1) Preparation	1) Preparation
2) Detection and Analysis	2) Identification
3) Containment, Eradication, & Recovery	3) Containment
	4) Eradication
	5) Recovery
4) Post-Incident Activity	6) Lessons Learned

Fig. 2. Incident Response Steps from NIST [3] and SANS [4].

In a typical Web application system architecture, we engage three-tier design, and the data access layer is always deployed as a data access layer between a business logic layer in the Web application server and database [5]. It is not common to deploy a Web Server layer (before the presentation layer). In certain scenarios, a native extended module is developed to have database tables or logs backup, temporary transaction table clean up and different database maintenance tasks.

We have uploaded the backdoor malware named as Transtatic.dll to VirusTotal [6] which is a popular online malware scanner, it is found that all existing Anti-Virus software including Windows Defender, Symantec Antivirus and Firewall cannot detect the backdoor (Fig. 3a and 3b).

Fig. 3a. We have uploaded the backdoor DLL file with file name Transtatic.dll (SHA-256: 124fd83e874b36dafbc87903037e4c014d81e699b523339ce46e93d4dab772da) to VirusTotal and none of the anti-virus software can detect it.

Fig. 3b. We have uploaded another published backdoor DLL file (SHA-256: 497f6aaf90f901e7dfe5bc9dbf805403e5b18fe9009bd70c9cf4dfcb84d8c5e7) from OilRig APT campaign to VirusTotal and there is one out of seventy-two anti-virus software can detect it.

In most of the target attacks, known as Advanced Persistent Threat (APT), which targets a specific type of industry and/or an organization, aiming for espionage, financial interest and service disruption. A Target Attack is well organized by a group of determined, well-focused and coordinated attackers [7] and deliver the attack in various stages including reconnaissance (also known as information gathering), attack vector delivery, exploit and compromise the target and maintain a persistent connection with the infected systems [8], backdoor serves the purpose of revisiting of the compromised system.

In view of the stealthy characteristic in the binary of and network traffic generated from backdoor, we hope to propose a novel incident response matrix specifically for Backdoor, which not only include binary executable backdoor but also html or php-based backdoor and Webshell.

2   Challenge in Analyzing Backdoor and Incident Response

2.1   Limitation of Behavioral Analysis

Most malware samples can be analyzed via behavioral (as known as dynamic) analysis, which means that we execute the malware and study the behavioral indicators. While it is applicable well to common malware samples, it is not applicable for our scenario. Overall, for the Web server backdoor, we need a particular setup of a server to load the native module, and once it is launched, there will be no active footprints made by the backdoor as it waits for the command from the attacker. Malware analysts should reverse engineer the backdoor before carrying out any interaction with the backdoor. Depending on the complexity of the backdoor sample, reverse engineering can be very resource-intensive and impractical to facilitate real-world incident response and detection.

2.2 Emerging Backdoor Threat

Our observation shows that an attacker inclines to believe that if a backdoor to the web server is installed, it becomes impossible for the security administrator to discover, given the web server traffic is usually high. The context of request headers can be varied a lot, and it is challenging to identify malicious requests. There are research works using machine learning or deep learning models to detect Malware threat in this context. However, we argue that in realistic enterprise environments, the application of machine learning and deep learning will notably delay the transactions and cause performance bottlenecks.

Even in the best case, the security administrator can identify the attack requests, due to web server log limitations, it only captures simple GET requests in URI. As backdoor attacks are always communicating via HTTP POST request instead of GET request, it is impossible to have a full diagnosis of the malicious activity. Moreover, there is a large target attack campaign named OilRig [1], so called "Advanced Persistent Threat (APT)" that has engaged the IIS native module as their backdoor to access victims' servers.

2.3 Lack of Practical Backdoor-Specific Incident Response Methodology

There are different industry-recognized incident response frameworks and methodologies. For example, NIST [3] and SANS [4] have suggested similar high-level methodology in conducting incident response as follows:

1. Preparation
2. Detection and Analysis
3. Containment, Eradication and Recovery
4. Post-Incident Activity

To analyze Malware, FIRST [9] suggests performing media and surface analysis, reverse engineering, dynamic analysis, and comparative analysis. MITRE Att&ck [10] proposes a more detailed breakdown to identify Command and Control communication. However, those are still falling to conceptual checkpoints.

We hope to extend the methodology in practical and experimented backdoor incident response areas with our real-life experience, which provides shortcuts to detect and identify backdoor efficiently and effectively.

3 Incident Response Model

We are now proposing a BackDoor Incident Response Model (BDIRM) with an algorithm to identify compromised hosts and detect and analyze backdoor with the matrix.

Illustrated in the following network graph (Fig. 4), We define the graph G as $G = (V,E)$ where V denotes a set of servers, computers or accounts $(v_1,v_2,v_3,...,v_N)$, named as *nodes*. E is a relationship set of connections $(e_1,e_2,e_3,...,e_N)$, between pairs of nodes, named as *edges*. We label the blue line as the connection between two trusted systems/parties deemed by the organization. We label the connection as red line when there is a connection between a trusted system and another untrusted system or between two untrusted systems. We have defined the number of authenticated systems connected to the node v_i as $Ns(v_i)$ and number of different user accounts used to authenticate to different systems as $Nua(Ns(v_i))$. To differing the different configuration c_i with a legitimate one in a node, we define it as $Di[c_1,c_2,...,c_N]$.

Attackers attempt to take over each connection or trusted parties to become their stepping-stone to reach out the final target, in this case is the database, blue and green nodes are trusted from the organization perspective. With this algorithm, we have detected and identified the backdoor incident effectively:

Algorithm 1. BackDoor Incident Response Detection Algorithm (BDIRDA)

For every node (v_i): start with the least number of trusted connections to the target node:

a. Examine user authentication and Delete-Create-Execute-Delete-Create operations or activities over the files/stored procedures/scripts/user account in the event or/and activity logs in different systems or/and application of the potential compromised host.

b. Examine the number of authenticated systems connected to the examined node $(Ns(v_i))$ AND examine the number of different user accounts used to authenticate to different systems $(Nua(Ns(v_i)))$.
If the ratio $Nua(Ns(v_i))/Ns(v_i) > 1$, it is suspicious where a single node (v_i) is authenticated to many different systems with multiple different user accounts that are not in normal business practice.

c. Differ configuration files of any service available to untrusted parties with the intended and legitimate configuration $Di[c_1,c_2,...,c_N]$.

d. Label the node(v_i) and edge (e_i) connected to and from any node (v_N) as red if any item from 1 to 3 is positive and suspicious.

If any red node (v_i) satisfies any of above checkpoints from a) to d):

Run check in Backdoor Incident Response Matrix for node(v_i).

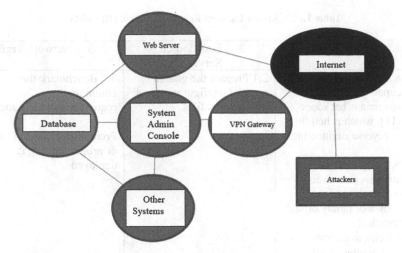

Fig. 4. High level graph of node deployment in online gaming company.

For the matrix, it covers backdoor, backdoored server and network traffic illustrated with the following table. We have demonstrated the following methodology in our real-world backdoor detection in an online gaming company. We have added several analyses which may not be applicable in our incident, however, it will be useful in other types of backdoor incidents for generic analysis purposes (Table 1).

3.1 Static Analysis of Backdoor

We have investigated into the backdoor sample Transtatic.dll (SHA256: 124fd83e874b36dafbc87903037e4c014d81e699b523339ce46e93d4dab772da) from an online gaming company, successfully identified the following characteristics:

1. They support upload, download, and command execution functions. The Backdoor manipulates a stealthier approach by taking Content-Type in HTTP header [20] with "IMAGE/type" as png, jpg, and gif, so as to upload data to, download data from, and executing a command against the victim IIS Web server (Fig. 5a).
2. Response data is sent with the Content Type "Text/Plain".
3. When both Malware upload the data, they will detect the end of upload completion if an error or failure message is found after a while loop of data transfer (Fig. 5b). The backdoor will use GetTickCount function to count the time when uploading the data, which is also aligned with the Malware writer's preference in calculating the time (Fig. 5c).
4. Keywords and API used in both Backdoor samples include *RegisterModule, CHttpModule,* "*Server Error*", "*Failed*", etc.

In view of the above findings, we have considered these IIS native module backdoor indicators and developed a scanner, thereby giving different indicators to server administrator for reference, whether he/she can carry out further investigation over suspicious Microsoft Web Server IIS native modules.

Table 1. BackDoor Incident Response Matrix (BDIRM)

1. Backdoor	2. Backdoored Server	3. Network Traffic
1.1 a. Identify the function capability of the suspicious backdoor [11], which is helpful to reverse engineering. b. Carry out static analysis and reverse engineering of the backdoor binary or/and webshell. It helps to update search rules in 3.3. c. Emulate the binary in emulation framework [12] for dynamic analysis. d. Write Yara rules [13] with artifacts found from items a – c. It will be useful to scan and discover any backdoors in other nodes of machines or systems.	2.1 Prepare the golden copy of configuration and deployment files.	3.1 Benchmark the common request/response header. Prerequisite: SIEM [14] or proper logging is deployed.
1.2 Carry out similarity check with published backdoor whether they share similar code instruction structure and commands with binary differing [15] and TLSH[16]. It helps to update search rules in 3.3.	2.2 Compare the golden copy of configuration and deployment files with those with the potentially hacked server.	3.2 Monitor high volume of HTTP request/response. Monitor unpopular incoming and outgoing IP addresses.. Prerequisite: SIEM or proper logging is deployed

(*continued*)

Table 1. (*continued*)

1.3 Scan all DLLs to detect any abnormally high number of encoded base64 strings, obfuscated SQL and Powershell scripts and possible system command(s) and file upload/download/delete command(s).	2.3 Examine activity and error logs of the hacked server to detect any successful or failed loading of suspicious external programs or/and modules.	3.3 Write search rules to detect and alert unpopular user agent and cookie values from the logs. Write search rules to detect and alert suspicious requests based on findings in 1.1, 1.2, 1.3 and 2.4.
1.4 Apply Shannon entropy detection over the binary to detect obfuscated, compressed and/or encrypted code distribution [17].	2.4 Export and dump the volatile memory of the backdoored server. Repeat 1.3, scan and detect any abnormally high number of encoded base64 strings, obfuscated SQL and Powershell scripts and possible system command(s) and file upload/download/delete command(s). [18]	3.4 Network traffic deobfuscation: Detect encrypted and encoded traffic. [19]

```
v9 = *(_BYTE **)(v7 + 8);
if ( *v9 != 'I' || v9[1] != 'M' || v9[2] != 'A' || v9[3] != 'G' || v9[4] != 'E' || v9[5] != '/' )
  return 0i64;
v10 = v9[6];
if ( v10 == 'j' )
{
  if ( v9[7] == 'p' && v9[8] == 'g' )
  {
    sub_180002360(v9, (unsigned int)v8, &v34);
RFI 34·
```

Fig. 5a. Stealthy approach of data upload, data download and command execution in Transtatic.dll. It takes in IMAGE/jpg as part of Backdoor command to download victim data from backdoored Microsoft IIS Web server.

```
v3,
500i64,
"Server Error",
0i64,
```

Fig. 5b. Provide "Server Error" message when data is downloaded in Transactic.dll.

```
(_QWORD      )&XMMWORD_1800/0B9C = XMMWORD_1800/0B9C     0;
LABEL_47:
    if ( v19 != v20 )
    {
        v23 = v19 + 8;
        do
        {
            if ( GetTickCount() - *(_DWORD *)(*(_QWORD *)v19 + 80i64) < 0xEA60 )
            {
```

Fig. 5c. Use of GetTickCount in upload function. Attacker enters IMAGE/png as command to upload the data to the backdoored IIS Web server.

We realize there is research about detecting trigger-based Malware based on network traffic and machine learning approaches; the assumption is we can identify the backdoor traffic and have samples for supervised learning. However, the samples in the IIS native module are missing, and it will cause a high degree of false positives and negatives.

3.2 Similarity Comparison with published Backdoor

According to our matrix, we carry out a binary similarity comparison between the OilRig and our revealed backdoor and see whether they come from the same APT campaign or family. To this end, we use a popular binary code diffing tool named BinDiff [21]. We report the overall similarity score is 0.18 (Fig. 6a) and for the function responsible for uploading and downloading data, the similarity score is 0.27 (Fig. 6b). The similarity is useful and applied to identify variants (Fig. 6c) instead of a completely different purpose IIS native module backdoor.

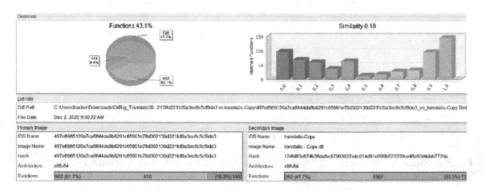

Fig. 6a. Binary similarity between OilRig and online transtatic backdoors.

Similarity ▼	Confidence	Address	Primary Name	Type	Address	Secondary Name
0.27	0.51	0000...	sub_180002580	Normal	0000...	sub_180003620
0.26	0.27	0000...	sub_180001FA0	Normal	0000...	sub_180003020
0.26	0.27	0000	fflush	Library	0000	sort_lpp

Fig. 6b. Function similarity. It indicates the upload/download function similarity as 0.27 between OilRig and transtatic backdoors.

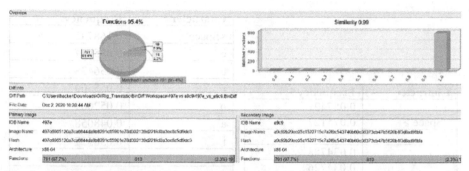

Fig. 6c. Variant similarity. It exhibits similarity value as 0.99 for OilRig backdoor variants. There are 19 functions that are modified.

3.3 Scanning Potential Backdoors

The scanner has the following functions for string-based detection and assembly instruction-based detection based on our investigation and correlation of our findings:

String-Based Detection
Other than the keyword and string pattern matching, we have attempted to identify whether the SQL strings and Powershell scripts are obfuscated through cosine similarity comparison between vectors of collected strings from SQL/Powershell script repositories and the target native module DLL file. The Cosine similarity is used in detecting obfuscated code in viruses [22] to detect virus variants more effectively. The more obfuscated strings of SQL and Powershell scripts are found, the higher the probability it is a backdoor Malware. Here is our methodology:

1. Build the frequency table of characters over files. By using the tool, we generate two standard Top 30 Character Frequency tables (Fig. 7a and Fig. 7b) and attached full tables in Appendix, one for SQL files and the other one for powershell files. The legitimate SQL and Powershell scripts files are collected from Microsoft's [23] and Azure's [24] GitHub repositories, respectively.

2. Extract the strings from a target file by using "Strings". It will scan a file for Unicode or Ascii strings of a default length of 3 or more characters.
3. Classify the strings by finding the language keywords. If the string contains SQL language keywords, it will be classified as SQL language. If it also contains PowerShell language keywords, it will also be classified as PowerShell language.
4. Build the frequency table of the classified strings.
5. Calculate the cosine similarity of the frequency table of the classified strings and the frequency table of the standard language files (Fig. 7c).
6. Find all base64 encoded strings.
7. Find the specific keywords, such as *"DownloadString", "upload", "download", "chttpmodule", "encode", "decode"*.

Character	Frequency
0	0.087421
\<Space \>	0.075127
e	0.047623
a	0.034788
3	0.034726
6	0.034533
C	0.033376
4	0.033155
,	0.032057
9	0.032014
t	0.031492
1	0.025061
i	0.024927
r	0.022208
o	0.021458
n	0.021324
5	0.019975
'	0.019325
c	0.019143
d	0.017487
D	0.017420
7	0.016492
2	0.016190
F	0.015992
E	0.013884
8	0.013748
m	0.012664
l	0.010761
T	0.010660
S	0.010444

Character	Frequency
\<Space\>	0.168742
e	0.085947
t	0.056438
r	0.055300
o	0.052609
a	0.048058
i	0.038527
s	0.036009
n	0.035964
c	0.030310
-	0.025493
u	0.025067
m	0.020010
p	0.019976
l	0.019949
$	0.018316
d	0.016633
g	0.013452
"	0.012247
N	0.011838
S	0.010192
A	0.010040
h	0.009941
.	0.008611
y	0.007967
b	0.007843
f	0.007659
I	0.007238
P	0.006948
R	0.006778

Fig. 7a. Top-30 Character Frequency table for SQL file.

Fig. 7b. Top-30 Character Frequency table for Powershell files.

Experiments

We have scanned our current backdoor samples and legitimate Microsoft IIS native module DLL files under the Microsoft Web Server IIS system folder (Fig. 7c).

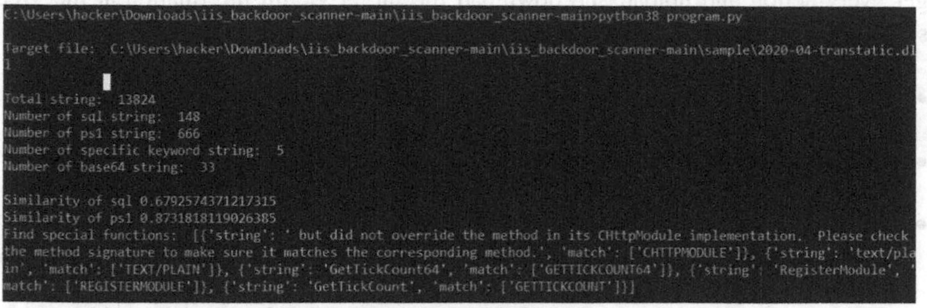

```
C:\Users\hacker\Downloads\iis_backdoor_scanner-main\iis_backdoor_scanner-main>python38 program.py

Target file:  C:\Users\hacker\Downloads\iis_backdoor_scanner-main\iis_backdoor_scanner-main\sample\2020-04-transtatic.dll
1
Total string:  13824
Number of sql string:  148
Number of ps1 string:  666
Number of specific keyword string:  5
Number of base64 string:  33

Similarity of sql 0.6792574371217315
Similarity of ps1 0.8731818119026385
Find special functions: [[{'string': ' but did not override the method in its CHttpModule implementation.  Please check
the method signature to make sure it matches the corresponding method.', 'match': ['CHTTPMODULE']}, {'string': 'text/pla
in', 'match': ['TEXT/PLAIN']}, {'string': 'GetTickCount64', 'match': ['GETTICKCOUNT64']}, {'string': 'RegisterModule', '
match': ['REGISTERMODULE']}, {'string': 'GetTickCount', 'match': ['GETTICKCOUNT']}]]
```

Fig. 7c. Scanning Statistics of Backdoor.

From Table 2, we can find both backdoor malwares hit a high number of keyword and API indicators, SQL strings and Powershell script strings. The obfuscation index on both SQL and Powershell scripts do not exhibit significant deviation between malware backdoor and the legitimate native module. However, standard Microsoft native modules, CustomError and HTTPCache, have been found to have indicators similar to backdoor behaviors. This requires further investigation over binary signatures and hash to determine whether an existing library is backdoored or not.

Table 2. String-based Backdoor Indicators.

Native module filename	No. of SQL strings	No. of ps1 strings	No. of interesting strings/keywords and API	No. of Base64 encoded strings	Obfuscation index SQL	Obfuscation index ps1
Backdoor: Transtatic.dll from Online Gaming incident (SHA256 124fd83e874b36dafbc87903037e4c014d81e699b523339ce46e93d4dab772da)	148	666	5	33	0.679	0.873
OilRig (Backdoor) (SHA256 497e6965120a7ca6644da9b8291c65901e78d302139d221fcf0a3ec6c5cf9de3)	82	161	32	12	0.627	0.938
AnonymousAuthenticationModule	5	19	3	0	0.649	0.931
CustomErrorModule	2	52	3	4	0.625	0.597
DefaultDocumentModule	5	9	3	1	0.625	0.789
DirectoryListingModule	4	13	3	2	0.620	0.730
HTTP Cache Module	5	48	3	2	0.627	0.599
HTTPLoggingModule	4	34	3	2	0.645	0.805
ProtocolSupportModule	4	11	3	1	0.624	0.804
RequesteFilteringModule	21	26	4	0	0.650	0.863
StaticCompressionModule	2	26	3	5	0.624	0.730
StaticFileModule	8	29	3	4	0.628	0.749

Assembly Instruction-Based Detection

Previously, we have observed the outbound data is exported via "text/plain" with command strings only. In our scanner, we suggested the following instruction-based detection methodology to provide a backdoor indicator, as the backdoor needs a command to trigger every action and upload and download the target victim information at the Web server:

- Search "text/plain" and other content-type values in the target IIS native module DLL file.
- Locate the function that contains the reference to the "text/plain" or other content-type values string.
- Identify all *cmp* instructions and *strstr* instructions that are used for comparison with operands with ASCII character code only. For Windows binaries, we will identify invocations of *CompareStringA* function.
- If high numbers of *cmp*, *strstr* and *CompareStringA* are found under a data export function, we deem this as an indicator of a backdoor.

Table 3. Instruction-based backdoor indicators.

Native module filename	No. of CMP	No. of StrStr	No. of calling CompareStringA	Identified character sequence and command
Transtatic.dll (Backdoor)	25	0	0	Yes
OilRig (Backdoor)	32	4	0	Yes
IIS RAID (Backdoor)	0	0	4	Yes
AnonymousAuthenticationModule	0	0	0	No
CustomErrorModule	0	0	0	No
DefaultDocumentModule	0	0	0	No
DirectoryListingModule	0	0	0	No
HTTPCacheModule	0	0	0	No
HTTPLoggingModule	0	0	0	No
ProtocolSupportModule	0	0	0	No
RequestFilteringModule	0	0	0	No
StaticCompressionModule	0	0	0	No
StaticFileModule	0	0	0	No

We have included a summary table of indicators (Table 3) for both malicious and legitimate native modules. We have found that numbers for malicious backdoor with higher numbers in *CMP*, *StrStr* and *CompareStringA* compared with other legitimate native modules, and it satisfies our assumption: a typical native module to extend Web server capability will not engage command execution and SQL queries into business data in a database.

3.4 Deobfuscation of Binary and Network Traffic Content

Capturing network traffic of a potential compromised host is crucial for further analysis. Attackers prefer to use various encoding including ROT-13 encoding, URL encoding, simple XOR encryption techniques and string obfuscation techniques to hide their commands and activities [25].

In the incident response scenario, the database and Web server transaction, we propose the following algorithm to capture and analyze the traffic on incremental time snapshot basis, which is practically reduce the performance overheads caused by network traffic capture:

Algorithm 2. Detection of obfuscated data in captured network traffic on incremental

For every suspicious node (v_i) (with which the server connects to untrusted parties):
    a.   Identify all timestamps (T_i) of compromised transactions and change of files.
    b.   For each previous incident timestamp T_i, we start monitoring at T_i +/- j where j= 1, 5,10,15,30, 45 and 60 minutes at node (v_i):
              Capture the network traffic (N_{ij}).

For every captured network traffic (N_{ij}):
    a.   Apply XOR string detection.
    b.   Apply URLencode and ROT-13 encoding detection.
    c.   Apply obfuscated string detection.
    Detect if any of (a - c) is satisfied.

3.5 Backdoor Entropy Analysis

Attackers need to pack the binaries or/and any files which are helpful to their attack in a stealthy manner, including software packing, compression and encryption. In our mentioned incident, all the artifacts are presented in clear text, the string-based and pattern matching techniques are good enough to identify. However, the scope of examination is incomplete. Here is the algorithm to detect any suspicious backdoor or obfuscated/encrypted/compressed files in the node with Shannon Entropy [17].

Algorithm 3. Detection of obfuscated files in node with Shannon Entropy

---

Entropy ← Array[][]

For every node v_i:
  For each server configuration c_j:
    Entropy[i][j] = Shannon entropy(v_i, c_j)

For every Entropy[i][j] of calculated Shannon entropy:
  a. Compare with the freshly built configuration file(s) and system file(s).
  b. Identify all discrepancy of entropy value and carry out further examination of the suspicious file(s).
  c. Identify all high entropy values and carry out further examination of the suspicious file(s).

---

4 Related Work

In backdoor detection-related research areas, there are no similar publications to innovate an incident response model for Backdoor investigation, however, there are still individual research approaches to Backdoor analysis researchers suggest detecting interactive network traffic streams in non-standard service port [26]. There is research about detecting malware via threshold random walk model in port scanning, however, this approach can be evaded if an attacker has ability to create high-quality hit lists with well-designed active intervals [27].

Attack graph [28] is a representation for all possible paths of attack towards a network or system. It's a widely used technique on identifying the most critical regions of a system toward attack scenarios. For example in [29] the author has used Minimum Cost SAT solver (MCSS) and iteratively distilled critical attack graph surface from a full attack graph. In their paper, they suggested that the attacker will pick the attacking route with minimum effort. Hence, MCSS can be used to locate the minimum-cost attacking route in a network. In [30] the author proposed an approach to measure the likelihood of lateral movement happening on a selected node by considering the reachability of it from any arbitrary nodes in the attack graph. A graph-based system called Latte [31] to identify malicious lateral movement path and the network connection graph is established with Kerberos service ticket requests and another research reveals lateral movement using authentication logs [32], which symbolises the criticality of authentication logs management.

Log2vec [33] is a deep learning approach that aims at detecting APT attacks or user's malicious behavior through capturing and representing rich relationships among user's operations. However, this approach assumed victim user's account will perform various activities that prepare for lateral movement, which may not be the case in a lot of APT attack.

5 Discussion

Backdoor investigation is a challenging task because of its stealthy and trigger-based nature. Once we have identified the incident and the impacted server, we are required to trace and figure out how the attacker gets into the system. Network and systems logs may not be adequate for investigation especially when parameters used by attackers to deliver the payload and commands are not logged.

We have suggested a Backdoor IR matrix, there are limitations in different scenarios. In binary emulation, the emulation can be successfully done if we can develop all necessary API calls in the framework, otherwise, the emulation will stop because of missing several API libraries. Suspicious backdoor binaries and modules must be loaded and emulated in another server with the same version and patch level for further analysis instead of taking a binary emulation approach.

Outsourcing to operating system product vendors for investigation and forensic analysis is challenging. The vendor has requested the online gaming customer to access the production database remotely for forensic study, which is not in compliance with enterprise cybersecurity policy. The vendor has provided forensic tools and requested the customer to install and execute, however, the memory image dump causes the performance and file system memory overhead, which are not feasible in our incident response.

As an incident handler, business owners are always concerned about whether there is no more malware installed in other systems, other than figuring out the impacted systems and compromised servers along with the attack path, we still need to scan and find out any other backdoor and malware deployed by attackers. In consideration of business impact, the business owner is reluctant to take down the system and prefer live incident response.

6 Conclusion

In this paper, we propose a BackDoor Incident Response Model (BDIRM) to investigate backdoor incidents, analyze backdoor, backdoored server and network traffic with application. The proposed model has been successfully implemented with our online gaming customer, identified and eradicated the incident. On top of the existing industry incident response guidelines, we contribute this systematic and practical model to the incident response community to identify and detect highly stealthy backdoor malware.

Acknowledgement. I would like to express my very great appreciation to my supervisor, Dr. Jogesh Muppala, who gives detailed guidance to my research and valuable advice and review from Dr. Shuai Wang. Moreover, I am very thankful to my co-authors including Ken Wong, Austin Lau and Johnny Wong who have contributed to the model design, carried out experiments and tools development and Alan Ho as we carry out deep reverse engineering over the backdoor. I appreciate Dr. Zetta Ke and Dr. Dongsun Kim to review my paper and Halvar Flake and Christian Blichmann to share and discuss deep and modern Malware and Backdoor detection related research with me. Finally, I thank anonymous reviewers for their valuable feedback. This work was supported in part by a Bridge Gap Fund of TTC/HKUST (Project ID: BGF.003.2021).

References

1. Falcone, R.: OilRig uses RGDoor IIS Backdoor on Targets in the Middle East (2018). https://unit42.paloaltonetworks.com/unit42-oilrig-uses-rgdoor-iis-backdoor-targets-middle-east/. Accessed 7 December 2020
2. Baker, P.: The SolarWinds hack timeline: Who knew what, and when? (2021). https://www.cso online.com/article/3613571/the-solarwinds-hack-timeline-who-knew-what-and-when.html
3. Cichonski, P., Millar, T., Grance, T., Scarfone, K.: Computer Security Incident Handling Guide. CSRC (2012). https://csrc.nist.gov/publications/detail/sp/800-61/rev-2/final
4. Incident Response SANS: The 6 Steps in Depth. Cynet. (n.d.). https://www.cynet.com/inc ident-response/incident-response-sans-the-6-steps-in-depth/
5. Liu, K., Tang, S., Wan, J., Ding, S., Qin, X.: Improved layed architecture for developing semantic web application. In: 2010 2nd International Conference on Future Computer and Communication, vol. 3, pp. V3–769. IEEE (2010
6. VirusTotal, Virustotal.com (2020). https://www.virustotal.com/gui/
7. Li, F., Lai, A., Ddl, D.: Evidence of advanced persistent threat a case study of malware for political espionage. In: 2011 6th International Conference on Malicious and Unwanted Software, pp. 102–109. IEEE (2011)
8. Hardy, S., et al.: Targeted threat index Characterizing and quantifying politically-motivated targeted malware. In: 23rd {USENIX} Security Symposium ({USENIX} Security 14, pp. 527–541 (2014)
9. CSIRT Services Framework Version 2.1. FIRST (2019). https://www.first.org/standards/fra meworks/csirts/csirt_services_framework_v2.1
10. Command and Control. Command and Control, Tactic TA0011 - Enterprise | MITRE ATT&CK® (2018). https://attack.mitre.org/tactics/TA0011/
11. Fireeye. fireeye/capa. GitHub (2020). https://github.com/fireeye/capa
12. Qilingframework. qilingframework/qiling. GitHub (2020). https://github.com/qilingframew ork/qiling
13. VirusTotal. VirusTotal/yara. GitHub (2013). https://github.com/VirusTotal/yara
14. Detken, K., Rix, T., Kleiner, C., Hellmann, B., Renners, L.: SIEM approach for a higher level of IT security in enterprise networks. In: 2015 IEEE 8th International Conference on Intelligent Data Acquisition and Advanced Computing Systems: Technology and Applications (IDAACS), pp. 322–327 (2015). https://doi.org/10.1109/IDAACS.2015.7340752
15. Haq, I.U., Caballero, J.: A survey of binary code similarity. ACM Comput. Surv. 54, 3, Article 51, 38 (2021). https://doi.org/10.1145/3446371
16. Trendmicro. trendmicro/tlsh. GitHub (2015). https://github.com/trendmicro/tlsh
17. Lyda, R., Hamrock, J.: Using entropy analysis to find encrypted and packed malware. IEEE Secur. Privacy Magaz. 5(2), 40–45 (2007). https://doi.org/10.1109/msp.2007.48
18. https://www.fireeye.com/blog/threat-research/2016/06/automatically-extracting-obfuscated-strings.html
19. https://resources.infosecinstitute.com/topic/network-traffic-analysis-for-ir-content-deobfu scation/
20. MIME types (IANA media types) (2019). https://developer.mozilla.org/en-US/docs/Web/HTTP/Basics_of_HTTP/MIME_types. Accessed 7 December 2020
21. zynamics.com - BinDiff (2020). https://www.zynamics.com/bindiff.html. Accessed 7 December 2020
22. Karnik, A., Goswami, S., Guha, R.: Detecting obfuscated viruses using cosine similarity analysis. In: First Asia International Conference on Modelling and Simulation (AMS 2007), pp. 165–170. IEEE (2007

23. microsoft/sql-server-samples   (2020).   https://github.com/microsoft/sql-server-samples.
    Accessed 7 December 2020
24. Azure/azure-docs-powershell-samples (2020). https://github.com/Azure/azure-docs-powers
    hell-samples. Accessed 7 December 2020
25. Cannell, J., and ABOUT THE AUTHOR Joshua Cannell Malware Intelligence Analyst..
    Obfuscation: Malware's best friend. Malwarebytes Labs (2016). https://blog.malwarebytes.
    com/threat-analysis/2013/03/obfuscation-malwares-best-friend/
26. Zhang, Y., Paxson, V.: Detecting backdoors. In Proceedings of the 9th conference on USENIX
    Security Symposium - Volume 9 (SSYM 2000), vol. 12. USENIX Association, USA (2000).
27. Jung, J.: Real-Time detection of malicious network activity using stochastic models. Ph.D.
    thesis, Massachusetts Institute of Technology (2006)
28. Jha, S., Sheyner, O., Wing, J.: Two formal analyses of attack graphs. In: Proceedings of the
    2002 Computer Security Foundations Workshop, pp. 45–59, Nova Scotia (2002)
29. Huang, H., Zhang, S., Ou, X., Prakash, A., Sakallah, K.: Distilling critical attack graph surface
    iteratively through minimum-cost sat solving. In: Proceedings of the 27th Annual Computer
    Security Applications Conference. ACM, pp. 31–40 (2011)
30. Johnson, J.R., Hogan, E.A.: A graph analytic metric for mitigating advanced persistent threat.
    In: 2013 IEEE International Conference on Intelligence and Security Informatics (ISI). IEEE,
    pp. 129–133 (2013)
31. Liu, Q., et al.: Latte: Large-Scale Lateral Movement Detection. MILCOM 2018 - 2018 IEEE
    Military Communications Conference (MILCOM), pp. 1–6 (2018) https://doi.org/10.1109/
    MILCOM.2018.8599748
32. Bian, H., Bai, T., Salahuddin, M.A., Limam, N., Daya, A.A., Boutaba, R.: Uncovering lateral
    movement using authentication logs. IEEE Trans. Netw. Serv. Manage. 18(1), 1049–1063
    (2021). https://doi.org/10.1109/TNSM.2021.3054356
33. Liu,, F., Wen, Y., Zhang, D., Jiang, X., Xing, X., Meng, D.: Log2vec: a heterogeneous graph
    embedding based approach for detecting cyber threats within enterprise. In: Proceedings
    of the 26th ACM SIGSAC Conference on Computer and Communications Security (CCS),
    pp. 1777–1794 (2019)

Automated Software Vulnerability Detection via Pre-trained Context Encoder and Self Attention

Na Li, Haoyu Zhang, Zhihui Hu, Guang Kou, and Huadong Dai(⊠)

Artificial Intelligence Research Center, Defense Innovation Institute, Beijing, China
zhanghaoyu10@nudt.edu.cn, hddai@vip.163.com

Abstract. With the increasing size and complexity of modern software projects, it is almost impossible to discover all software vulnerabilities in time by manual analysis. Most existing vulnerability detection methods rely on manual designed vulnerability features, which is costly and leads to high false positive rates. Pre-trained models for programming language have been used to gain dramatic improvements to code-related tasks, which considers syntactic-level structure of code further. Thus, we propose an automated vulnerability detection method based on pre-trained context encoder as well as self-attention mechanism. Instead of current static analysis approaches, we treat the program source code as natural language and introduce the pre-trained contextualized language model to capture the program local dependencies and learn a better contextualized representation. The extracted source code feature vectors are then fed into a designed Self Attention Networks (SAN) module. We develop the SAN module based on Long-Short Term Memory (LSTM) model and self attention, which learns the long-range dependencies of program vulnerable points more efficiently. We conduct experiments on two source code level C program benchmark datasets, where four different evaluation metrics are applied for comparing the vulnerability detection performances of different systems. Extensive experimental results demonstrate that our proposed model outperforms previous state-of-the-art automated vulnerability detection method by around 7.2% in F1-measure and 2.6% in precision.

Keywords: Automated vulnerability detection · Self attention · Pre-trained language model · Transfer learning

1 Introduction

Software vulnerabilities usually refer to the internal defects of software, and these defects may be used to damage the software systems. To improve the security of software systems, a series of software development security principles have been proposed. With the development of computer technology, the demand and scale

© ICST Institute for Computer Sciences, Social Informatics and Telecommunications Engineering 2022
Published by Springer Nature Switzerland AG 2022. All Rights Reserved
P. Gladyshev et al. (Eds.): ICDF2C 2021, LNICST 441, pp. 248–264, 2022.
https://doi.org/10.1007/978-3-031-06365-7_15

of software are expanding rapidly. Meanwhile, the number and complexity of codes are increasing exponentially. Due to the increasing complexity of modern programs and the wide application of software, the number of malicious software attacks also continues to rise. Thousands of software vulnerabilities are reported by the Common Vulnerabilities and Exposures [1] and National Vulnerability Database [5] each year. Many can propagate quickly owing to the prevalence of code cloning and open-source software. These vulnerabilities pose a serious threat that potentially allows attackers to compromise systems and applications.

Traditional vulnerability detection techniques include static and dynamic analysis of programs [8]. The static analysis which analyzes source code without running the program has high coverage, and the dynamic analysis which discovers the nature of programs by running the software has a low false positive rate. Most of the static or dynamic systems and studies for vulnerability detection are based on pre-defined rules [2,4,6] and code similarity metrics [12], which rely on experts experiences to define features. These existing tools for static or dynamic analysis techniques generated by human experts typically only detect a limited subset of possible errors. And, it is subjective to define the features of software vulnerabilities accurately for experts, which sometimes leads to an error-prone task. In other words, vulnerability detection rules are very difficult to be defined accurately and completely. Therefore, more intelligent and automatic research for vulnerability detection instead of human experts to manually define has been the future trend. As deep learning in natural language processing (NLP) develops rapidly, researchers used neural networks based vulnerability detection technology to achieve vulnerability features automatically. The large amount of open-source code make it possible to learn the patterns of software vulnerabilities intelligently and recent work shows great potential in this field [14,16,24,27]. However, capturing effective and high-quality vulnerability features from the program source code is still a difficult and unsolved problem.

To solve the problem of difficulty in capturing vulnerability features and automatic vulnerability detection, in this paper we propose a novel model that consists of a pre-trained context encoder based vulnerability representation module and a self-attention enhanced Long-Short Term Memory (LSTM) module. Different from traditional static word embeddings, our approach learns word level vulnerability representations by designing a transfer learning framework based on Bidirectional Encoder Representation from Transformers (BERT) model [10,23], where the pre-trained model is first fine-tuned on the vulnerability source code. BERT is a successful pre-trained context language model in NLP, and it can effectively capture syntactic and semantic vulnerability information with the fine-tuning process. Then, for further improving the accuracy of vulnerability detection, LSTM with self attention mechanism is selected for vulnerability classification learning. LSTM model is an extension of Recurrent Neural Network (RNN) [18]. In the SAN module, attention layer is added between the LSTM layer and the output layer for adjusting the weight of each sequence. The LSTM-attention model can extract key information points in vulnerability source code. Compared with state-of-the-art intelligent methods, it can be seen that our method outperforms them by a large margin in four metrics: false positive rate, false negative rate, precision, and F1-measure.

The rest of this paper is organized as follows: Sect. 2 reviews the related work about detecting software vulnerability automatically. Section 3 presents our method for automatic vulnerability detection on source code. Section 4 describes details of experiment evaluation metrics, corresponding results, and analysis. Finally, Sect. 5 concludes the paper.

Our Contributions. First, we propose the design and implementation of the pre-trained context encoder-based vulnerability representation on source code. We leverage transfer learning that allows us to obtains high-quality deep context-dependent representations through fine-tuning the pre-trained model, which encodes the symbolic form into the real vector value. The experiments show that compared with the different language representation models, our method has given rise to overall task performance. Second, since there are long-range dependencies of program vulnerable points, we present the SAN module for learning the dependency of vulnerability information. Finally, we conduct experiments to confirm the effectiveness of our approach. Meanwhile, through a series of sub-experiments, the method that we proposed can achieve the desired goals.

2 Related Work

To detect vulnerability automatically, the techniques learning patterns in source code that may be related to software vulnerabilities have been proposed by researchers. In [12,15], both methods detect software vulnerabilities based on identifying similar code. Different than machine learning techniques trying to learn patterns from large amounts of vulnerability features, they are limited to vulnerable code clones. In [21], the authors present a vulnerability detection technique based on combining N-gram analysis and feature selection algorithms, which could reduce the feature and search space by machine learning-based feature selection algorithms. In [25], this paper aims at extracting search patterns for taint-style vulnerabilities in C source code, and the programs are represented as code property graphs which are traversed as features for vulnerability classification based on k-means clustering algorithm. Traditional machine learning techniques focus on inferring the features from the pre-classified vulnerabilities.

Deep learning based recent development techniques is capable of learning vulnerability features automatically. In [17], this paper proposes a vulnerability detection system named VulDeePecker. The VulDeePecker obtains vector representation from code gadgets which are small pieces of relevant code sliced by a commercial code analysis product Checkmarx. To acquire vector representation, VulDeePecker uses word2vec [7] to vectorize the code gadgets, then applies the vectors to the Bi-LSTM network to classify vulnerabilities. In this paper, it can be shown that the application of deep learning to vulnerability detection is feasible, however, there are still some defects. With word2vec to vectorize the source code, VulDeePecker may lose important semantic information in context about the vulnerabilities, which affects the effectiveness of the vulnerability detection model. In [16], to improve VulDeePecker, the researchers propose a framework called SySeVR, which aims at achieving program representations for syntax and semantic information associated with vulnerabilities. In addition, it also adds different types of machine learning models to cover more types of vulnerabilities. In [26], the paper proposes the Devign model based on a graph neural network, which includes a novel Conv module to find features in a graph's heterogeneous node features for graph-level classification. Additionally, Devign also could craft with automatically property graphs to learn vulnerable patterns through using graph neural networks.

3   The Methodology

Figure 1 shows an overview of our proposed method, which aims to automatically detect vulnerabilities in the source code level. It first transforms code gadgets into symbolic representation when the input data flows through the Pre-Processing stage. In the Fine-tuning stage, it fine-turns the released BERT-Base pre-trained model by using the symbolic code gadgets extracted randomly from the training code gadgets. The output of the Fine-tuning stage is used as the model for representation learning in the next two stages. It transforms the symbolic form of source code into a real vector value in the Embedding stage. Finally, in the Classifier training stage, the detection model is trained and will be applied to predict whether test samples are vulnerable or not.

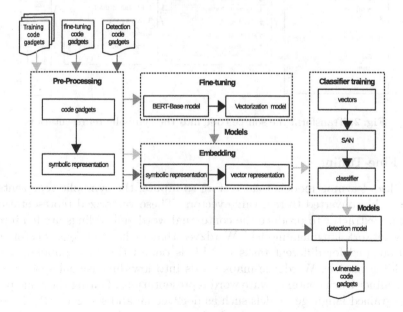

Fig. 1. Overview of the proposed automatic software vulnerability detection method.

3.1   Pre-processing

Instead of taking an entire code file as input, a code gadget is a small code snippet acquired by using the program slicing technique, and it performs slicing based on the risk library/API function calls which are closely related to the vulnerabilities. By encoding code gadgets in symbolic representation, user-defined variables and functions in code gadgets are mapped to the uniform symbolic form. In this step, it can not only retain semantic information [28] but also improve the efficiency of training and reduce unnecessary time and space cost of embeddings.

As shown in Fig. 2, the sample in the form of the source code is transformed into the symbolic representation in the Pre-Processing stage. First, it extracts library/API function calls and assembles slices which are generated from the arguments of the library/API function into code gadgets. Second, it transforms variables into symbolic names (e.g., "V1", "V2") and user-defined functions into symbolic names (e.g., "F1", "F2"). As risk library/API function calls may cause different types of vulnerabilities, multiple functions mapped to the uniform symbolic name can increase the generalization ability of classifier training.

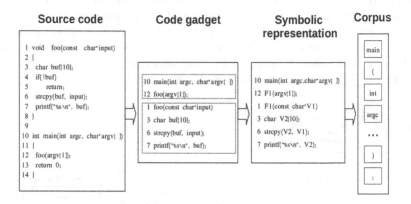

Fig. 2. Transform the source code into the symbolic representation.

3.2   Fine-Tuning

Since deep learning models take vectors as inputs, the symbolic representation needs to be converted to real value vectors. These vectorized representation as a feature extractor to produce the contextual word embeddings are fed into the neural network language models. Word2vec that makes the dense vector representation used for different tasks in NLP is one of the most popular in these embedding models. Word2vec maps words into low-dimensional space vectors, but it cannot learn context-aware word representations. During the same period, coarse-grained language models such as doc2vec [3] and sent2vec [21], have also received some attention. These methods try to encode paragraph, sentence or document into a fixed-dimensional vector representation, but the generalization performance of these sentence embedding models is too poor. Some sentence embedding models are also proposed at the same time, such as doc2vec [3] and sent2vec [21]. However, these sentence embedding models try to learn a fixed-length feature representation, rather than the contextual representation for each token. Different from traditional word embeddings which only allow a single context-independent representation for each word, BERT language representation [10,23] uses the masked language model for pre-training a deep bidirectional transformer that can fuse the left and the right context. BERT model is the first fine-tuning based representation model that has shown effective performance on a large suite of sentence-level and token-level tasks. BERT which stands for deep bidirectional transformers can not only obtain learn context-aware word representations but also be a context encoder. And, it is also the meaning of the pre-trained context encoder in the title.

In the Fine-tuning stage, the released BERT-Base pre-trained model (Uncased: 12-layer, 768-hidden, 12-heads, 110M parameters) is leveraged to obtain the fine-tuning model named Vectorization. As illustrated in Fig. 3, both pre-training and Vectorization model have the same architectures. The model is first initialized with the same pre-trained parameters, then the symbolized source codes extracted randomly are used to fine-tune BERT. As different layers of the neural network can capture different syntax and semantic information, it requires us to select appropriate outputs used as a reference for fine-tuning. Considering the over-fitting problem, the value of the last layer is too close to the target. Therefore, the outputs of the penultimate layer are taken. During fine-tuning, all parameters are fine-tuned in Vectorization model end-to-end.

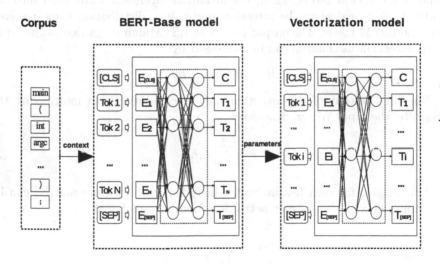

Fig. 3. In the Fine-tuning stage, obtain the fine-tuning model named Vectorization.

3.3 Embedding

Vectorization model is applied to obtain the vector representation of context. Vectorization model takes symbolized source codes as input, then outputs the vector representation after extracting text features. BERT input embeddings are the sum of the token embeddings, the segmentation embeddings, and the position embeddings. These inputs are tokenized before being sent to token embeddings, then two special tokens used to divide sentences are inserted at the beginning ([CLS]) and the end ([SEP]) of the tokenization. In the Embedding stage, each word is transformed into a fixed-dimensional vector representation.

3.4 Classifier Training

Recurrent Neural Network (RNN) [18] is a typical neural network used to process sequence data. RNN is more suitable to deal with long-distance dependence problem, but the problem of gradient disappearance exists in the process of RNN modeling. To solve this problem, many variants of RNN have been proposed, such as LSTM and Gated Recurrent Unit (GRU) [9,11].

The neural network based on attention mechanism [19] can extract important features in the text by training word vector representation. In the SAN module, "key points" in vulnerabilities can be detected through the role of attention mechanism, and they are often important information for vulnerability classification. A typical network structure of the SAN module is shown in Fig. 4. The inputs in the Fig. 4 are the vectors after embeddings, and these inputs will pass through the LSTM layers. Then, the attention layers are introduced into the hidden layer to calculate the attention probability distribution value received from the LSTM layers. The output matrix of LSTM units regarded as the input of the attention mechanism can be expressed by:

$$H = (h_1, h_2, ..., h_T) \tag{1}$$

The final output of the attention unit is computed with multiplying the weight by the input vector, denoted as:

$$v = \sum_i^t \alpha_i h_i \tag{2}$$

The weight, for each feature vector included in the feature matrix, can be accomplished with the softmax activation function as follows:

$$\alpha_t = \frac{e^{q^T h_t}}{\sum_i^T e^{q^T h_i}} \tag{3}$$

Finally, the softmax function is responsible for representing and formatting the classification result, which provides feedback for updating the neural network parameters in the training phase. The output is the SAN module with fine-tuned model parameters, and the output of the detection phase is the classification results.

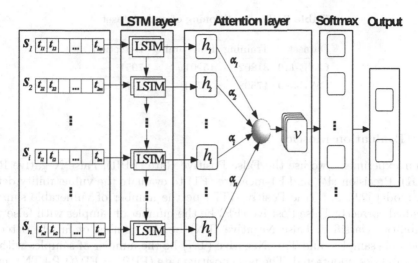

LSTM layer   Attention layer   Softmax Output

Fig. 4. A typical network structure of the SAN module.

4 Experiment and Results

4.1 Datasets

The datasets used in this paper come from Code Gadget Database (CGD) [17], which include two datasets as the samples: the buffer overflow vulnerabilities (CWE-119) and resource management error vulnerabilities (CWE-399). Each sample in the datasets is small pieces of the C source code with above known vulnerabilities in software products. The number of samples is shown in each dataset as follows in Table 1. Each dataset is divided into two parts by 4:1, where the larger part is used for training and the other one is for detection. Besides, half of each training set is randomly selected from the training set for fine-tuning. Table 2 summarizes the partitioning of each dataset, where the second column represents the number of samples for training, the third column represents the number of samples for fine-tuning and the fourth column represents the number of samples for detection.

Table 1. The datasets in code gadget database (CGD).

Dataset	Samples	Vulnerable	Not vulnerable
CWE-119	39753	10440	29313
CWE-399	21885	7285	14600

Table 2. The partitioning of each dataset.

Dataset	Training	Fine-tuning	Detection
CWE-119	31802	15901	7951
CWE-399	17508	8754	4377

4.2 Evaluation Metrics

In our experiment, we use the False Positive Rate (FPR), False Negative Rate (FNR), Precision (P), and F1-measure (F1) to evaluate the vulnerability detection model [22]. Let True Positive (TP) be the number of vulnerable samples classified correctly, False Positive (FP) be the number of samples with false vulnerabilities classified, False Negative (FN) be the number of falsely detected vulnerable samples, and True Negative (TN) be the number of samples with no vulnerabilities undetected. The false positive rate (FPR) = FP/(FP+TN), measures the proportion of falsely classified positive vulnerabilities in all samples that are not vulnerable. False Negative Rate (FNR) = FN/(FN+TP), measures the proportion of falsely classified negative vulnerabilities in all samples that are vulnerable. Precision (P) = TP/(TP+FP), represents the proportion of correctly classified vulnerable samples in all classified vulnerabilities. F1-Measure(F1) = $2 \cdot P \cdot R/(P + R)$, is the harmonic average of accuracy and recall. The values of the above four indicators range between [0, 1]. In this study, we prefer to achieving FPR and FNR, whose values are closer to 0. For other indicators, the closer their values are to 1, the better the model will achieve.

4.3 Implementation Details

BERT is trained on the common corpus. However, the models trained by this common corpus cannot fully extract the intrinsic meaning of vulnerability source code, so model fine-tuning is required. We focus on fine-tuning the pre-trained BERT model and applying it to vulnerability vector representation. In this work, we choose the BERT-Base (Uncased: 12-layer, 768-hidden, 12-heads, 110M parameters) pre-trained model rather than the BERT-Large, because, in our experiment, the BERT-Base is already sufficient to the dataset. The hyperparameters remain as the default settings and the maximum length of the inputs is 128. After the pre-processing, variable names and function names are converted into symbolic representation, which reduces the number of different tokens and improves the efficiency of fine-tuning. In order to avoid overfitting and improve the generalization ability of the model, the output information of the penultimate hidden layer of the Vectorization model is selected by using embeddings. The vector dimension of Vectorization is 128×768, where the vector dimension of one word is 768 and the number of words to represent a sample is 128.

In this paper, the hyper-parameters tuned for SAN learning are shown in Table 3. The neural networks are implemented in Python using Keras and the distributed embeddings are implemented from Vectorization by fine-tuning BERT. Our experiments were run on a machine with TITAN V GPU.

Table 3. The parameters for SAN learning.

Parameter	Value
Batch size	128
Hidden layers	5
Learning rate	0.001
Sample length	128

4.4 Results Analysis

Select Neural Networks. Our experiments are carried out on two different types of vulnerability datasets: CWE-399 and CWE-119. Two datasets are performed with the same hyper-parameters and experimental procedures. Through the comparison between SAN and LSTM on the results of vulnerability source codes, it is illustrated that attention mechanism makes a positive impact on vulnerability detection. In order to select the best model for classification learning, we compare SAN and Gated Recurrent Unit with self attention (GRU-attention). Then, we apply the traditional machine learning methods naive Bayes (NB) on the same dataset and compare the classification effects with the previous deep learning models to illustrate the advantages of adopting SAN. The comparison results are shown in Table 4.

It's shown that the SAN module proposed in this paper is superior to the other three classification models. By comparing the table from top to bottom, it can be seen that the vulnerability detection effect of deep learning is significantly better than that of traditional machine learning method. FPR and F1-measure of SAN are better than that of LSTM. Both models use LSTM neural network layer to extract key information of vulnerability source codes. But, the difference between the two models is that one is added the attention layer on the basis of the LSTM layer. The comparison between the both shows that the attention layer highlights important information to improve the performance.

The experimental results of SAN are better than that of the GRU-attention. Both of the two experimental models have the attention layer and the main functions of the attention layer are basically the same, in addition, the model structure is basically the same. The difference is that the first layer of the model is LSTM layer, and the other is GRU layer. Through analysis of the evaluation indexes in this experiment, it can be seen that LSTM performs better than GRU in extracting key information of vulnerability characteristics. Among the above four classifiers, it can be concluded that SAN is better than GRU-attention in the dataset. The attention layer optimizes performance by highlighting key information. Therefore, SAN has a more balanced performance.

Table 4. Comparison of different classification models.

Model	CWE-399				CWE-119			
	FPR(%)	FNR(%)	P(%)	F1(%)	FPR(%)	FNR(%)	P(%)	F1(%)
LSTM	22.2	3.6	90.8	93.5	3.7	8.2	85.1	88.3
GRU-attention	2.4	5.2	93.8	94.3	2.7	7.1	88.8	90.9
NB	5.9	18.4	86.7	84.0	7.3	18.1	72.1	76.7
SAN	**1.1**	**4.4**	**95.2**	**95.4**	**1.3**	**6.7**	**94.3**	**93.8**

Table 5. Comparative experimental results of different embedding tools.

Embedding tool	CWE-399				CWE-119			
	FPR(%)	FNR(%)	P(%)	F1(%)	FPR(%)	FNR(%)	P(%)	F1(%)
word2vec	2.8	4.7	94.6	95.0	2.9	18.0	91.7	86.6
doc2vec	3.8	9.7	91.9	91.1	3.9	16.9	88.1	85.5
Vectorization	**1.1**	**4.4**	**95.2**	**95.4**	**1.3**	**6.7**	**94.3**	**93.8**

Effectiveness of Fine-Tuning. In order to verify the effectiveness of Fine-tuning, we conduct comparative experiments with word2vec and doc2vec. Vectorization is the representation model that is obtained from the fine-tuning stage. It can be seen from Table 5 that our method outperforms word2vec and doc2vec for the same dataset. The doc2vec model is an improvement on the basis of the word2vec model. Both of them are the static approach and cannot be dynamically optimized for specific tasks. It can be also observed that the neural network trained from the CWE-399 datasets outperforms the neural network trained from the CWE-119 datasets in terms of all four metrics. This can be explained by the fact that the number of CWE-399 datasets is far smaller than the number of CWE-119 datasets. What is more, CWE-119 which are the buffer overflow vulnerabilities have more complex forms than CWE-399 which are the datasets of resource management error vulnerabilities.

Table 6. Comparative with other pattern-based vulnerability detection systems.

System	FPR(%)	FNR(%)	P(%)	F1(%)
Flawfinder	47.0	66.2	21.8	26.5
VUDDY	4.1	91.0	45.9	15.0
Vuldeepecker	2.9	18.0	91.7	86.6
Our method	**1.3**	**6.7**	**94.3**	**93.8**

Comparison of Different Vulnerability Detection Systems. For examining the effectiveness of our method, we also perform a comparative experiment with other pattern-based vulnerability detection systems. Open source tool Flawfinder [4] is the traditional vulnerability detection method based on static analysis. VUDDY [12] is elected because it represents the approach based on code similarity. Vuldeepecker and ours are the deep learning-based system for vulnerability detection. Table 6 summarizes the comparison.

Our method outperforms the other pattern-based vulnerability detection systems on the same dataset. Flawfinder has high FNR (47%) and FPR (66.2%), because vulnerability detection method applies the static vulnerability analysis, which leads to high false positive rate and over-reliance on detection rules. VUDDY incurs low FPR (4.1%) but high FNR (91%), which is the result at a very low value for F1-measure (15.1%). It can be interpreted as VUDDY to detect vulnerabilities by code similarity. However, if it is used for vulnerabilities that are not caused by code cloning, a high false negative rate will occur. Compared with Vuldeepecker, our method performs better on all four metrics. Instead of fine-tuning representation model stage, Vuldeepecker directly applies word2vec model for embeddings. Our method improved by 1.6% in FPR, 11.3% in FNR, 2.6% in P, 7.2% in F1-measure, which are respectively better than their counterparts in Vuldeepecker. It indicates that transfer learning and fine-tuning models for representation can effectively improve the effect of vulnerability detection.

To the best of our knowledge, we are the first to use the fine-tune BERT model for vulnerability representation. The above experimental results show that our method can not only learn semantic meanings of vulnerability source codes but also learn higher-level concepts within the vulnerability source codes such as syntactic structures and semantic roles. In this way, it has the ability to capture the features of vulnerabilities from context and improve vulnerability detection.

The Hyper-parameter Values. In the experiment, there are many hyper-parameters that need to be set and adjusted according to the accuracy and loss rate of the experiment after each iteration. Then, we adopt a 10-fold cross validation to learn the classification model, then select the best hyper-parameters values for vulnerability detection. Figure 5 shows the value of Precision of SAN

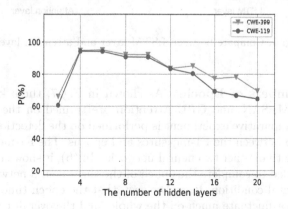

Fig. 5. Precision of SAN for 2 datasets with the different number of hidden layers.

with respect to the 2 datasets affected by the different number of hidden layers. It can be observed that the Precision of both SAN reaches the maximum at the 4 or 5 layers, and the Precision of both SAN declines with the number of layers greater than 7. Note that the other hyper-parameters of SAN can be adjusted in a similar way

The Output of Attention Layer. With the same lines of source code as input, we visualize the output values of the LSTM layer and the attention layer. In the same picture, the depth of color represents the difference of attention. It can be observed in Fig. 6 that the color distribution of LSTM layer is relatively uniform, and that means the difference between output values of LSTM layer is not obvious. The other picture, the difference of color in the attention layer is obvious, which can be considered that more obvious the color difference is, the greater the fluctuation of attention. And it intuitively illustrates that the attention layer can allocate the corresponding weight to highlight the key features of the vulnerability source codes.

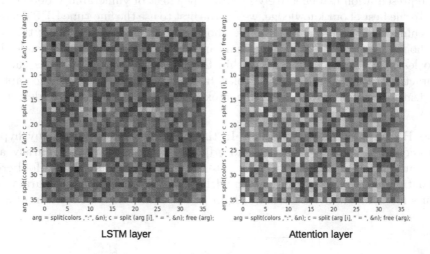

Fig. 6. Compare between LSTM layer and attention layer.

Different Numbers of Epochs. As shown in Fig. 7, three kinds of neural networks: LSTM, SAN, and GRU-Attention are trained on the same training set. In (a), a comparative experiment is performed on the detection set to obtain the relationship between the F1-measures and epochs. The F1-measures of SAN is always higher than other two neural networks. In (b), it shows the trend curve of the time needed to complete the epoch of the three neural networks under the same experimental condition. It can be seen that the epoch time of each neural network does not fluctuate much on the whole, and the overall time tends to be stable. Generally, after the minimum epoch time is passed, the training time will no longer fluctuate greatly during the retraining. It can be seen that the curves of SAN and GRU-attention model are relatively close, but SAN takes less time to complete an iterative training and its training speed is relatively fast.

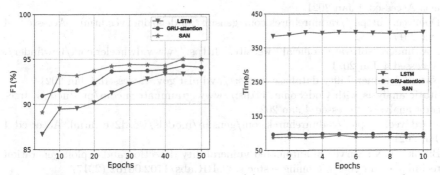

(a) F1-measures of three neural networks (b) Epoch time of three neural networks. with the different number of epochs.

Fig. 7. Iterative experiments across three kinds of neural networks

5   Conclusion

This paper introduces a novel approach for detecting vulnerability from source code and shows effective improvements when learning vulnerable programming patterns automatically. Through fine-tuning the pre-trained model and applying it to embeddings, our proposed method extracts syntactic and semantic information of vulnerabilities in source code context. It alleviates the difficulty in describing the features of software vulnerabilities accurately and provides precise information for vulnerability detection. By transfer learning, we obtain the vulnerability representation model from the pre-trained BERT on large-corpus task. And it is also confirmed that the effectiveness of transfer learning has improved in methodology through experimental results.

The SAN module is used for learning and training vulnerability samples to get the detection model in our methods. Different from general LSTM without attention layer, SAN can capture key points of vulnerabilities and perform better on the precision, where these experimental conclusions aim to provide some guidelines for researchers to choose neural networks in future vulnerability detection studies. And it is shown that our method has been superior to the state-of-the-art methods.

Acknowledgment. This paper is supported by the Major Research Project of National Natural Science Foundation of China (No. 91948303).

References

1. Common vulnerabilities and exposures. https://cve.mitre.org. Accessed 4 Jan 2021
2. Cppcheck: a tool for static C/C++ code analysis. https://cppcheck.sourceforge.net. Accessed 4 Jan 2021
3. Doc2vec. https://radimrehurek.com/gensim/models/doc2vec.html. Accessed 4 Oct 2017
4. Flawfinder software official website. https://www.dwheeler.com/flawfinder/. Accessed 4 Jan 2021
5. National vulnerability database. https://nvd.nist.gov. Accessed 4 Jan 2021
6. Static analysis with CodeSonar. https://www.grammatech.com/products/source-code-analysis. Accessed 4 Jan 2021
7. Word2vec. https://radimrehurek.com/gensim/models/word2vec.html. Accessed 4 Jan 2021
8. Brooks, T.N.: Survey of automated vulnerability detection and exploit generation techniques in cyber reasoning systems. CoRR abs/1702.06162 (2017)
9. Cho, K., van Merrienboer, B., Bahdanau, D., Bengio, Y.: On the properties of neural machine translation: encoder-decoder approaches. In: Wu, D., Carpuat, M., Carreras, X., Vecchi, E.M. (eds.) Proceedings of SSST@EMNLP 2014, Eighth Workshop on Syntax, Semantics and Structure in Statistical Translation, Doha, Qatar, 25 October 2014, pp. 103–111. Association for Computational Linguistics (2014). https://doi.org/10.3115/v1/W14-4012
10. Devlin, J., Chang, M., Lee, K., Toutanova, K.: BERT: pre-training of deep bidirectional transformers for language understanding. In: Burstein, J., Doran, C., Solorio, T. (eds.) Proceedings of the 2019 Conference of the North American Chapter of the Association for Computational Linguistics: Human Language Technologies, NAACL-HLT 2019, Minneapolis, MN, USA, June 2–7 2019, Volume 1 (Long and Short Papers), pp. 4171–4186. Association for Computational Linguistics (2019). https://doi.org/10.18653/v1/n19-1423
11. Hochreiter, S., Schmidhuber, J.: Long short-term memory. Neural Comput. **9**(8), 1735–1780 (1997). https://doi.org/10.1162/neco.1997.9.8.1735
12. Kim, S., Woo, S., Lee, H., Oh, H.: VUDDY: a scalable approach for vulnerable code clone discovery. In: 2017 IEEE Symposium on Security and Privacy (SP), pp. 595–614 (2017). https://doi.org/10.1109/SP.2017.62
13. Le, Q.V., Mikolov, T.: Distributed representations of sentences and documents. In: Proceedings of the 31th International Conference on Machine Learning, ICML 2014, Beijing, China, 21–26 June 2014. JMLR Workshop and Conference Proceedings, vol. 32, pp. 1188–1196. JMLR.org (2014)
14. Li, Z., Zou, D., Tang, J., Zhang, Z., Sun, M., Jin, H.: A comparative study of deep learning-based vulnerability detection system. IEEE Access **7**, 103184–103197 (2019). https://doi.org/10.1109/ACCESS.2019.2930578
15. Li, Z., Zou, D., Xu, S., Jin, H., Qi, H., Hu, J.: VulPecker: an automated vulnerability detection system based on code similarity analysis. In: Proceedings of the 32nd Annual Conference on Computer Security Applications, ACSAC 2016, pp. 201–213. Association for Computing Machinery, New York (2016). https://doi.org/10.1145/2991079.2991102

16. Li, Z., et al.: SySeVR: a framework for using deep learning to detect software vulnerabilities. CoRR abs/1807.06756 (2018)
17. Li, Z., et al.: VulDeePecker: a deep learning-based system for vulnerability detection. In: 25th Annual Network and Distributed System Security Symposium, NDSS 2018, San Diego, California, USA, 18–21 February 2018. The Internet Society (2018)
18. Mikolov, T., Sutskever, I., Chen, K., Corrado, G.S., Dean, J.: Distributed representations of words and phrases and their compositionality. In: Burges, C.J.C., Bottou, L., Ghahramani, Z., Weinberger, K.Q. (eds.) Advances in Neural Information Processing Systems 26: 27th Annualsplncs0 Conference on Neural Information Processing Systems 2013. Proceedings of a Meeting Held 5–8 December 2013, Lake Tahoe, Nevada, United States, pp. 3111–3119 (2013)
19. Mnih, V., Heess, N., Graves, A., Kavukcuoglu, K.: Recurrent models of visual attention. In: Ghahramani, Z., Welling, M., Cortes, C., Lawrence, N.D., Weinberger, K.Q. (eds.) Advances in Neural Information Processing Systems 27: Annual Conference on Neural Information Processing Systems 2014, 8–13 December 2014, Montreal, Quebec, Canada, pp. 2204–2212 (2014)
20. Pagliardini, M., Gupta, P., Jaggi, M.: Unsupervised learning of sentence embeddings using compositional n-gram features. In: Walker, M.A., Ji, H., Stent, A. (eds.) Proceedings of the 2018 Conference of the North American Chapter of the Association for Computational Linguistics: Human Language Technologies, NAACL-HLT 2018, New Orleans, Louisiana, USA, 1–6 June 2018, Volume 1 (Long Papers), pp. 528–540. Association for Computational Linguistics (2018). https://doi.org/10.18653/v1/n18-1049
21. Pang, Y., Xue, X., Namin, A.S.: Predicting vulnerable software components through N-gram analysis and statistical feature selection. In: Li, T., et al. (eds.) 14th IEEE International Conference on Machine Learning and Applications, ICMLA 2015, Miami, FL, USA, 9–11 December 2015, pp. 543–548. IEEE (2015). https://doi.org/10.1109/ICMLA.2015.99
22. Pendleton, M., Garcia-Lebron, R., Cho, J., Xu, S.: A survey on systems security metrics. ACM Comput. Surv. 49(4), 62:1–62:35 (2017). https://doi.org/10.1145/3005714
23. Qiu, X., Sun, T., Xu, Y., Shao, Y., Dai, N., Huang, X.: Pre-trained models for natural language processing: a survey. CoRR abs/2003.08271 (2020)
24. Russell, R.L., et al.: Automated vulnerability detection in source code using deep representation learning. In: Wani, M.A., Kantardzic, M.M., Mouchaweh, M.S., Gama, J., Lughofer, E. (eds.) 17th IEEE International Conference on Machine Learning and Applications, ICMLA 2018, Orlando, FL, USA, 17–20 December 2018, pp. 757–762. IEEE (2018). https://doi.org/10.1109/ICMLA.2018.00120
25. Yamaguchi, F., Maier, A., Gascon, H., Rieck, K.: Automatic inference of search patterns for taint-style vulnerabilities. In: 2015 IEEE Symposium on Security and Privacy, SP 2015, San Jose, CA, USA, 17–21 May 2015, pp. 797–812. IEEE Computer Society (2015). https://doi.org/10.1109/SP.2015.54
26. Zhou, Y., Liu, S., Siow, J.K., Du, X., Liu, Y.: Devign: effective vulnerability identification by learning comprehensive program semantics via graph neural networks. In: Wallach, H.M., Larochelle, H., Beygelzimer, A., d'Alché-Buc, F., Fox, E.B., Garnett, R. (eds.) Advances in Neural Information Processing Systems 32: Annual Conference on Neural Information Processing Systems 2019, NeurIPS 2019, 8–14 December 2019, Vancouver, BC, Canada, pp. 10197–10207 (2019)

27. Zou, D., Wang, S., Xu, S., Li, Z., Jin, H.: μvuldeepecker: a deep learning-based system for multiclass vulnerability detection. IEEE Trans. Dependable Secure Comput., 1 (2019). https://doi.org/10.1109/TDSC.2019.2942930
28. Zhang, H., Cai, J., Xu, J., Wang, J.: Complex question decomposition for semantic parsing. In: Proceedings of the 57th Annual Meeting of the Association for Computational Linguistics, pp. 4477–4486. Association for Computational Linguistics, Florence. Italy, July 2019. https://aclanthology.org/P19-1440. https://doi.org/10.18653/v1/P19-1440

A CNN-Based HEVC Video Steganalysis Against DCT/DST-Based Steganography

Zhenzhen Zhang[1], Henan Shi[2], Xinghao Jiang[2(✉)], Zhaohong Li[3], and Jindou Liu[3]

[1] School of Information Engineering, Beijing Institute of Graphic Communication, Beijing 102600, China
[2] School of Electronic Information and Electrical Engineering, Shanghai Jiao Tong University, Shanghai 200240, China
xhjiang@sjtu.edu.cn
[3] School of Electronic and Information Engineering, Beijing JiaoTong University, Beijing 100044, China

Abstract. The development of video steganography has sparked ever-increasing concerns over video steganalysis. In this paper, a novel steganalysis approach against Discrete Cosine/Sine Transform (DCT/DST) based steganography for High Efficiency Video Coding (HEVC) video is proposed. The distortion of DCT/DST-based HEVC steganography and the impact on pixel value of HEVC videos is firstly analyzed. Based on the analysis, a convolutional neural network (CNN) is designed. The proposed CNN is mainly composed of three parts, i.e. residual convolution layer, feature extraction and binary classification. In the feature extraction part, a steganalysis residual block module and a squeeze-and-excitation (SE) block are designed to improve the network's representation ability. In comparison to the existing steganalysis methods, experimental results show that the proposed network performs better to detect DCT/DST-based HEVC steganography.

Keywords: Video steganalysis · Steganography · DCT/DST · HEVC · CNN

1 Introduction

Steganography is an art and science of covert communication. It conveys secret information without arousing any suspicion, and has been widely used by military institutions, government departments, financial institutions, and so on. However, the abuse of steganography may bring potential hazards to the safe of society. Steganalysis, the counter measure to steganography, solves the problem and detects the presence of secret information in the cover, which can prevent the leakage of confidential information, reveal illegal information, and is becoming a hot topic in the area of information security.

With the rapid development of Internet and advanced video compression technique, digital video has becoming one of the most popular media in peoples' lives, which makes video steganalysis drawing more and more attention of researchers. In the existing video steganalysis technology, most steganalysis algorithms [1–4] use handcrafted

P. Gladyshev et al. (Eds.): ICDF2C 2021, LNICST 441, pp. 265–276, 2022.
https://doi.org/10.1007/978-3-031-06365-7_16

classification features, i.e. the extraction of classification features in these methods rely solely on the experience of relevant researchers. Sheng et al. [1] utilized the change rate of Prediction Unit (PU) partition types before and after re-compression to detect intra-prediction mode based HEVC video steganography. Zarmehi et al. [2] estimated the cover frames and computed features both from video frames and residual matrix. Huang et al. [3] designed Combination-based Group Proportion and Difference (CGPD) classification features. Zhai et al. [4] analyzed the common statistical characteristics of the motion vector consistency (MVC) and constructed an effective universal feature set for steganographic methods.

Deep learning technology has been widely used in computer vision and other fields in recent years. Compared with traditional handcrafted features, convolutional neural network (CNN) can extract multi-dimensional abstract features by self-learning and do not depend on the experience of experts, which makes deep learning show stronger advantages. However, the majority of steganalysis methods based on deep learning are proposed for digital image steganography, fewer are focus on digital video steganography. Liu et al. [5] designed the first CNN, named Noise Residual Convolutional Neural Network (NR-CNN) for H.264 steganography. Then Huang et al. [6] constructed a novel feature extraction neural network model, which can estimate the embedding rate of steganography. Furthermore, HEVC, as the new and promising video coding standard, owns much fewer steganalysis methods than its corresponding steganography. Therefore, in this paper, we will focus on HEVC videos, and design new CNN-based steganalysis method.

Video steganography usually hide data in the compression process. According to the hiding location of secret data, video steganography can classified into 5 categories, i.e. DCT/DST based [7, 8], motion vector based [9, 10], intra prediction mode based [11, 12], inter-block partition type based [13, 14], and bitstream based [15, 16] steganography. DCT/DST based steganography is a common category, which makes its corresponding steganalysis method a research topic. However, compared with other steganalysis, there are limited number of DCT/DST domain HEVC video steganalysis, especially motion vector and inter-block partition type HEVC steganalysis. Shi et al. [17] developed a combination feature of Special Frames Extraction (SFE) and a temporal to spatial transformation to detect DCT/DST based HEVC steganography. On one hand, the classification features used in [17] are handcrafted. On the other hand, the classification accuracy can be further improved. Thus in this paper, we will analyze DCT/DST HEVC steganography and develop a novel and effective steganalysis method based on CNN.

The rest paper is organized as follows. Section 2 analyzes the distortion of DCT/DST-based HEVC steganography and its impact on pixel value of HEVC videos. Section 3 describes the designed CNN, and the experiment results and analysis are given in Sect. 4. Finally, the paper is concluded in Sect. 5.

2 Analysis of Pixel Change in DCT/DST-Based HEVC Steganographic Video

2.1 Analysis on Intra-frame Distortion of DCT/DST-Based HEVC Steganography

As a new generation video coding standard, HEVC brings in various new techniques to improve compression efficiency. One of the innovations is the flexible partition of blocks. In HEVC, Coding Tree Unit (CTU) is the basic processing unit, and each coding picture is firstly divided into non-overlapping CTUs. Then each CTU is further sub-divided into coding units (CU) following the quadtree structure. When coding each CU, flexible prediction unit (PU) and transform unit (TU) is adopted to get the optimal rate distortion. PU and TU decide the prediction mode and transform size of the CU, respectively.

Figure 1 shows DCT/DST-based steganography in HEVC coding process, and the red block denotes the position of DCT/DST-based steganography. DCT/DST-based steganography often modifies the quantized transform coefficients, and thus closely tied to TUs. HEVC supports four TU sizes: 4×4, 8×8, 16×16, and 32×32. For 4×4 sized TU, DST is adopted to implement transformation, and DCT is adopted for other sized TUs. For simplicity, 4×4 sized TU is taken as an example to analyze the distortion of steganography in this paper.

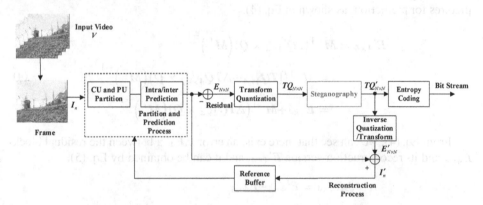

Fig. 1. DCT/DST-based steganography in HEVC coding process.

For a given video V, it can be considered as a frame sequence I_n, $(n = 1, 2, \cdots, T)$ with the length of T frames. For each frame I_n, partition and prediction process is performed successively, and then multiple residual block $E_{N \times N}$ can be obtained, where $N \times N$ means the size of the PU block. Take 4×4 residual block $E_{4 \times 4}$ as example, after prediction, DST transform and quantization is following. Let $TQ_{4 \times 4}$ denotes the quantized DST of $E_{4 \times 4}$, it is calculated as Eq. (1), where Q means the quantization step determined by the Quantization Parameter (QP), M is shown in Eq. (2), and M^T is the transpose matrix of M.

$$TQ_{4 \times 4} = \left(ME_{4 \times 4} M^T \right) \times \frac{1}{Q} \tag{1}$$

$$M = \begin{bmatrix} P & Q & R & S \\ R & R & 0 & -R \\ S & -P & -R & Q \\ Q & -S & R & -P \end{bmatrix} \qquad (2)$$

In DCT/DST-based steganography, $TQ_{4\times4}$ will be modified. Directly modifying $TQ_{4\times4}$ would cause error propagation, so measures must be taken to avoid error propagation in DCT/DST-based steganography. Equation (3) shows the hiding rule of reference [18], where m denotes the secret information to be hided, and $TQ'_{4\times4}$ means the quantized DST coefficients after modification.

$$\Delta TQ_{4\times4} = TQ'_{4\times4} - TQ_{4\times4}$$
$$= \begin{bmatrix} m & 0 & -m & m \\ 0 & 0 & 0 & 0 \\ 0 & 0 & 0 & 0 \\ 0 & 0 & 0 & 0 \end{bmatrix} \qquad (3)$$

After steganography module, $TQ'_{4\times4}$ will be inverse quantized and inverse transformed to get reconstructed residual block $E'_{4\times4}$ which will be used to obtain reference pictures for prediction, as shown in Eq. (4).

$$E'_{4\times4} = M^{-1}\left(TQ'_{4\times4} \times Q\right)\left(M^T\right)^{-1}$$
$$= M^{-1}\left((TQ_{4\times4} + \Delta TQ_{4\times4}) \times Q\right)\left(M^T\right)^{-1} \qquad (4)$$
$$= E_{4\times4} + M^{-1}\left(\Delta TQ_{4\times4} \times Q\right)\left(M^T\right)^{-1}$$

From Eq. (4), we can see that there exist an error $\Delta E_{4\times4}$ between the residual block $E_{4\times4}$ and its reconstruction version $E'_{4\times4}$, and it can be obtained by Eq. (5).

$$\Delta E_{4\times4} = E'_{4\times4} - E_{4\times4}$$
$$= M^{-1}\left(\Delta TQ_{4\times4} \times Q\right)\left(M^T\right)^{-1} \qquad (5)$$
$$= Q \times m \times \begin{bmatrix} 0 & 0 & 3PR & 0 \\ 0 & 0 & 3QR & 0 \\ 0 & 0 & 3R^2 & 0 \\ 0 & 0 & 3RS & 0 \end{bmatrix}$$

$\Delta E_{4\times4}$ is caused by the modification introduced by the steganography. We can see that the error is tiny, but it will still cause distortion in pixel domain, because the error will be further integrated to the reference frame and have an impact on the following coding pictures. In the next subsection, we will test the effect of DCT/DST-based steganography on pixel values.

2.2 Analysis of Pixel Value Changes in DCT/DST-Based Steganography

In order to test the effect of DCT/DST-based steganography on video pixel values, reference [19] which modifies quantized DST to hide information was used as the test steganography. In the experiment, four YUV videos with different resolution and scenes were used as test samples. The videos were compressed with and without steganography, respectively, and the pixel value change ratio between these two video versions was calculated. Please note that only the luminance component was tested in the experiment. As shown in Eq. (6), $P(x, y)$ and $P'(x, y)$ represent the luminance value at row x and column y in one picture with and without steganography, respectively. $F(x, y)$ means the pixel value change ratio caused by the steganography. The larger the $F(x, y)$, the greater the influence of steganographic algorithm on the video pixel value is.

$$F(x, y) = \frac{|P(x, y) - P'(x, y)|}{255} \times 100\% \tag{6}$$

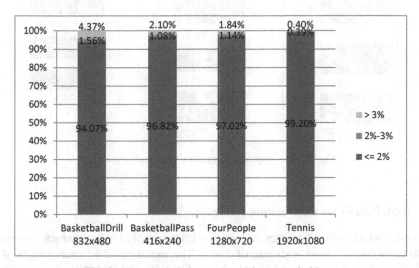

Fig. 2. The pixel change ratios of four tested videos.

To intuitively display the results, the percentages of pixels with change rate $F(x, y)$ below 2%, between 2% and 3%, and greater than 3% in each tested video were calculated and shown in Fig. 2. We can get that the percentages of pixels with change rate below 2%, between 2% and 3%, and greater than 3% are 96.78%, 1.04%, 2.18% at average, respectively. The result indicates that the change rate of nearly 97% pixels is below 2%, and the pixel change is tiny after steganography. However, the tiny change inspired us to explore CNN to learn more abstract features to distinguish DCT/DST-based steganography.

3 Proposed Steganalysis Network

The steganalysis network proposed in this paper is shown in Fig. 3. Single channel of gray images with size of 128×128 are taken as input of the network. According to the shape of input, the shape of each layer is also marked in Fig. 3. The proposed network is mainly composed of three parts, i.e. high pass filter convolution layer, feature extraction and binary classification, and the three parts are marked by black dotted bordered box in Fig. 3. The high pass filter convolution layer is marked in yellow in Fig. 3, and is used to remove the influence of image content to the training network. The feature extraction part consists of five convolution layers, three pooling layers, an integration of steganalysis residual block module and a squeeze-and-excitation (SE) block. The binary classification part includes a full connection layer and softmax layer.

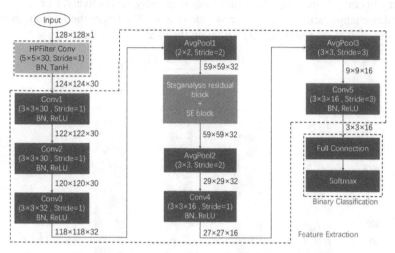

Fig. 3. The proposed steganalysis network structure.

3.1 High Pass Filter Convolution Layer

The yellow block in Fig. 3 denotes the high pass filter convolution layer which is consisted of 30 convolution kernel with size of 5×5. The initial value of each weight of the convolution kernel is set according to high pass filter core in SRM [20] which is suitable for pixel-based steganalysis. The introduction of the 30 high pass filters makes the proposed network focus on the noise caused by the steganography, rather than the content of the image itself, and thus set a good starting point for the training process of the proposed network.

In addition, it is a crucial work to select an appropriate activation function since it introduces nonlinear factors into the neural network, and thus makes the network can approximate various nonlinear models. In this paper, TanH is adopted as activation function of the high pass filter convolution layer. Compared with common used Relu activation function, it won't set the negative value of samples as zero and lead to information loss, and much more suitable for capturing features for tiny changes caused by the steganography.

3.2 Steganalysis Residual Block

The green block in Fig. 3 is the integration of steganalysis residual block and SE block. Steganalysis residual block adopts the ResNet structure. For convolutional neural network, generally speaking, the deeper the network is, the better the classification accuracy is. But deepening the network always results in problems such as gradient disappearance, and causes performance degradation of the network. Therefore, ResNet is designed to solve the problem, and we introduce it to the proposed network, and the structure is shown in Fig. 4. Furthermore, the steganalysis residual block has another function. It is used to further remove the video content and makes its output closer to the secret information.

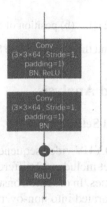

Fig. 4. The structure of the steganalysis residual block.

3.3 Squeeze-and-Excitation (SE) Block

Traditional CNNs are trained to capture spatial correlations between features, while Hu et al. [21] devised a new CNN unit from a different aspect and termed as SE block. SE block can explicitly model the interdependencies between each channel of convolutional features, and efficiently improve the representation quality of CNN with slight computational burden. Thus we adopt the SE block to our CNN to improve the network's representation quality. The structure of SE block and the position of the SE block in our CNN are displayed in Fig. 5. Please note that according to the illustration of SE block's application in ResNet in reference [21], the SE block should be integrated to the steganalysis residual block, rather than independent from it.

In conclusion, for a 128 × 128-sized gray image, it is firstly sent into the high pass filter layer which including 30 convolution kernel, and 128 × 128 × 30 feature maps can be obtained as the output of the high pass filter layer. Then the 128 × 128 × 30 feature maps are taken into the feature extraction part. According to the flow shown in Fig. 3, after experiencing a series of convolution layer, pooling layer, especially the steganalysis residual block module and SE block, 3 × 3 × 16 feature maps can be obtained as the output of feature extraction part. Then 3 × 3 × 16 feature maps are put into binary classification part, and the decision whether it is DCT/DST-based steganography is given as the output of the network.

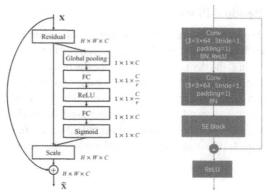

(a) SE block (from reference [21])   (b) position of SE block in the proposed CNN

Fig. 5. Structure of SE block and the position of the SE block in the proposed CNN.

4   Experiment Results and Analysis

4.1   Data Set and Experimental Setup

In our experimental part, 110 4:2:0 YUV video sequences with resolution of 1920×1080 are used as video set. The video set includes 22 different kinds of scenes, and the length of each video sequence is 100 frames. In order to construct a video set that is suitable for CNN, each YUV sequence is separated into non-overlapped subsequences with size of 128×128. Then the subsequences are used to construct no-steganography set and stenography set for CNN. For both no-steganography set and stenography set, X265(version 2.8) and HM16.7 are adopted to compress and de-compress each subsequence. The GOP structure is "IPPP", and the adopted QP is 22.

The steganography method we adopted is reference [19] since it is an efficient and classic method in DCT/DST based HEVC steganography. The steganography set and no-steganography set are used as positive samples and negative samples of CNN, respectively. Please note that because reference [19] focuses on the DST coefficients of I picture, only I pictures of each subsequence are selected as positive samples and negative samples in the experiments.

Before inputting samples into the proposed CNN, each sample is required to be decoded into portable graymap file format (PGM) gray image. In addition, in order to maximize the difference between the sample content, not all the 128×128 subsequences are used as samples. Since each 1920×1080 YUV picture can be divided into 120 128 $\times$ 128 blocks, the first 20 128 $\times$ 128 blocks of the first I picture are selected, and the next 20 128 $\times$ 128 blocks of the second I picture are selected, and the selecting process is repeated until the 120 128 $\times$ 128 blocks are selected. Then the selecting process is implemented on each I picture. Finally 55,000 positive samples and 55,000 negative samples can be obtained, among which 49000 are used for training and 6000 for testing.

In this paper, deep learning platform PyTorch is selected to construct the proposed CNN. Except for ResConv in Fig. 3, the weights and offsets of other convolution layers are initialized with Kaiming uniform distribution. Optimizer AdaDelta with rho 0.95, weight decay 5×10^{-4}, eps 1×10^{-8}, and initial learning rate 0.1 is employed. Cross entropy loss function is adopted as the cost function, and batch size and epoch is set as 32, and 200, respectively.

4.2 Experimental Results

In this section, the performance of the proposed CNN is illustrated, and the efficiency of the steganalysis residual block and SE block is described. For convenience of description, the CNN without steganalysis residual block and SE block is abbreviated as no-SRB-SE, and the CNN with SE block but without steganalysis residual block is abbreviated as SE-no-SRB. The no-SRB-SE and SE-no-SRB CNN structures are described in Fig. 6.

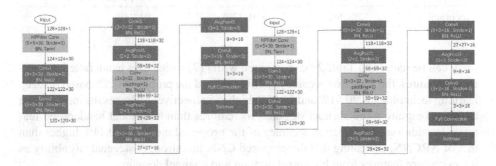

(a) no-SRB-SE CNN structure   (b) SE-no-SRB CNN structure

Fig. 6. no-SRB-SE and SE-no-SRB CNN structure.

The numbers of parameters and detection accuracy of each CNN structure are listed in Table 1. We can see that the no-SRB-SE CNN owns the lowest detection accuracy 91.22%. After adding the SE block to no-SRB-SE CNN, the detection accuracy is increased by 0.38%, and reaches 91.6%. The reason is that SE block can integrate the correlations between each channel of convolutional features to spatial correlations between features, and increase the representation ability of the CNN. Furthermore, by using the steganalysis residual block, the detection accuracy can be further improved by 0.21%, and achieves 91.81%. The result shows the efficiency of the steganalysis residual block.

Table 1. The numbers of parameters and detection accuracy of each CNN structure.

CNN structure	no-SRB-SE	SE-no-SRB CNN	Proposed CNN
Parameters	43406	43534	52846
Accuracy	91.22%	91.60%	91.81%

4.3 Comparative Analysis

To evaluate the performance of the proposed CNN, two steganalysis methods to detect DCT/DST based steganography methods are selected for comparison. The first one, called SFE-AU [17], is the latest work to detect DCT/DST based steganography and uses handcrafted classification features. The second one, called NRCNN [5], is the first video steganalysis CNN and is an universal steganalysis method. Table 2 describes the comparative results of the three methods.

Table 2. The detection accuracy of the three methods.

Method	SFE-AU	NRCNN	Proposed CNN
Accuracy	70.76%	91.37%	91.81%

It can be seen from Table 2 that compared with [17] which uses handcrafted classification features, the detection accuracy of NRCNN and the proposed CNN based on deep learning technology is 20.61% and 21.05% higher, respectively. The results indicate that CNN can capture more abstract steganalysis features than traditional handcrafted features. In addition, the detection accuracy of the proposed method is 0.44% higher than that of NRCNN, indicating that the proposed CNN has stronger steganalysis ability as it can capture features from both pixel domain and channel domain.

5   Conclusion

In this paper, targeting on detecting DCT/DST based HEVC steganography, a novel steganalysis algorithm is proposed by introducing the CNN. In the proposed CNN, high pass filter convolution layer consisting of thirty convolution kernels is firstly adopted to reduce the impact of image content on the network. Then steganalysis residual block and SE block are introduced to improve the network's representation ability and get better classification accuracy. In the experimental parts, the latest traditional steganalysis method which uses handcrafted features, and one universal steganalysis method based on CNN are used as comparison methods to evaluate the performance of the proposed method. The comparative results show that the proposed steganalysis performs better than other two existing methods. In our future work, we will further modify the structure of the proposed CNN and improve its detection accuracy.

Acknowledgement. This work is funded by the National Key R&D Program of China (2018YFC0831405), Joint Funding Project of Beijing Municipal Commission of Education and Beijing Natural Science Fund Committee (KZ201710015010), The Scientific Research Common Program of Beijing Municipal Commission of Education (No. KM202110015004, No. KM202010015001, No. KM202010015009), and Initial funding for the Doctoral Program of BIGC (27170120003/037, 27170120003/020).

References

1. Sheng, Q., Wang, R., Huang, M., et al.: A prediction mode steganalysis detection algorithm for HEVC. J. Optoelectron. Laser **28**(4), 433–440 (2017)
2. Zarmehi, N., Akhaee, M.: Digital video steganalysis toward spread spectrum data hiding. IET Image Proc. **10**(1), 1–8 (2016)
3. Huang, K., Sun, T., Jiang, X., Dong, Y., Fang, Q.: Combined features for steganalysis against PU partition mode-based steganography in HEVC. Multimedia Tools Appl. **79**(41–42), 31147–31164 (2020). https://doi.org/10.1007/s11042-020-09435-y
4. Zhai, L., Wang, L., Ren, Y.: Universal detection of video steganography in multiple domains based on the consistency of motion vectors. IEEE Trans. Inf. Forensics Secur. **15**, 1762–1777 (2019)
5. Liu, P., Li, S.: Steganalysis of intra prediction mode and motion vector-based steganography by noise residual convolutional neural network. In: IOP Conference series: Materials Science and Engineering, vol. 719, issue 1, p. 012068. IOP Publishing (2020)
6. Huang, X., Hu, Y., Wang, Y.: Deep neural network detection method for motion-vector-based video steganography. J. South China Univ. Technol. (Nat. Sci. Ed.) **48**(8), 1–9 (2020)
7. Li, H., Wang, H., Wu, H.: Multi-classification information hiding algorithm for H.264/AVC video with high capacity in QDCT domain. J. Optoelectron.·Laser **28**(4), 404–410 (2017)
8. Nguyen, D., Nguyen, T., Hsu, F., et al.: A novel steganography scheme for video H. 264/AVC without distortion drift. Multimedia Tools Appl. **78**(12), 16033–16052 (2019)
9. Rana, S., Kamra, R., Sur, A.: Motion vector based video steganography using homogeneous block selection. Multimedia Tools Appl. **79**(9–10), 5881–5896 (2019). https://doi.org/10.1007/s11042-019-08525-w
10. Yang, J., Li, S.: An efficient information hiding method based on motion vector space encoding for hevc. Multimedia Tools Appl. **77**(10), 11979–12001 (2018)
11. Dong, Y., Sun, T., Jiang, X.: A high capacity hevc steganographic algorithm using intra prediction modes in multi-sized prediction blocks. In: Yoo, C.D., Shi, Y.-Q., Kim, H.J., Piva, A., Kim, G. (eds.) IWDW 2018. LNCS, vol. 11378, pp. 233–247. Springer, Cham (2019). https://doi.org/10.1007/978-3-030-11389-6_18
12. Wang, J., Wang, R., Xu, D., Li, W.: An information hiding algorithm for HEVC based on angle differences of intra prediction mode. JSW **10**(2), 213–221 (2015)
13. Yang, Y., Li, Z., Xie, W., Zhang, Z.: High capacity and multilevel information hiding algorithm based on pu partition modes for HEVC videos. Multimedia Tools Appl. **78**(7), 8423–8446 (2019)
14. Tew, Y., Wong, K.: Information hiding in HEVC standard using adaptive coding block size decision. In: IEEE International Conference on Image Processing, pp. 5502–5506. IEEE (2014)
15. Xu, D., Wang, R., Shi, Y.: Data hiding in encrypted H.264/AVC video streams by codeword substitution. IEEE Trans. Inf. Forensics Secur. **9**(4), 596–606 (2014)
16. Zhang, H., Cao, Y., Zhao, X., Haibo, Y., Liu, C.: Data hiding in H.264/AVC video files using the coded block pattern. In: Shi, Y.Q., Kim, H.J., Perez-Gonzalez, F., Liu, F. (eds.) IWDW 2016. LNCS, vol. 10082, pp. 588–600. Springer, Cham (2017). https://doi.org/10.1007/978-3-319-53465-7_44
17. Shi, H., Sun, T., Jiang, X., Dong, Y., Xu, K.: A HEVC video steganalysis against DCT/DST-based steganography. Int. J. Dig. Crime Forensics **13**(3), 19–33 (2021)
18. Chang, P., Chung, K., Chen, J., Lin, C., Lin, T.: A DCT/DST-based error propagation-free data hiding algorithm for HEVC intra-coded frames. J. Vis. Commun. Image Represent. **25**(2), 239–253 (2014)

19. Liu, Y., Liu, S., Zhao, H., Liu, S.: A new data hiding method for H.265/HEVC video streams without intra frame distortion drift. Multimedia Tools Appl. **78**(6), 6459–6486 (2018)
20. Ye, J., Ni, J., Yi, Y.: Deep learning hierarchical representations for image steganalysis. IEEE Trans. Inf. Forensics Secur. **12**(11), 2545–2557 (2017)
21. Hu, J., Li, S., Sun, G.: Squeeze-and-excitation networks. In: Proceedings of the IEEE Conference on Computer Vision and Pattern Recognition (CVPR), pp. 7132–7141. IEEE (2018)

Do Dark Web and Cryptocurrencies Empower Cybercriminals?

Milad Taleby Ahvanooey[1](✉), Mark Xuefang Zhu[1](✉), Wojciech Mazurczyk[2],
Max Kilger[3], and Kim-Kwang Raymond Choo[3]

[1] School of Information Management, Nanjing University (NJU),
PO.Box 210023, Nanjing, People's Republic of China
M.taleby@ieee.org, xzhu@nju.edu.cn
[2] Institute of Computer Science, Faculty of Electronics and Information Technology,
Warsaw University of Technology (WUT), Warsaw, Poland
wojciech.mazurczyk@pw.edu.pl
[3] Department of Information Systems and Cyber Security, University of Texas at
San Antonio (UTSA), San Antonio, TX 78249-0631, USA
Max.Kilger@utsa.edu, raymond.choo@fulbrightmail.org

Abstract. The dark web is often associated with criminal activities such
as the sale of exploit kits using cryptocurrencies as payment. However,
the difficulty in determining the identities of dark website owners and
the tracing of the associated transactions compounds the challenges of
investigating dark web activities. In this study, we explore how cryptocurrencies have been involved in cybercriminal activities on the dark
web and the factors that drive cryptocurrency investments. Then, we
present several recommendations and guidelines for prospective investors
to help identify determinant factors for assessing investment risks in the
cryptocurrency marketplace. We also present several potential research
opportunities in cryptocurrency.

Keywords: Cryptocurrency · Dark web · Cybercrime · Crypto
market · Trustworthiness analysis

1 Introduction

The dark web has been, and continues, to be exploited by numerous malicious
threat actors such as organized crime groups, terrorists, cybercriminals, and
state-sponsored actors. Such marketplaces allow malicious threat actors to monetize their illicit services (e.g., exploits, hacking tools, and/or stolen information
such as credit card and other sensitive information). Cryptocurrencies are one
of the widely used payment methods on dark web marketplaces since they facilitate anonymous transactions [1], and the availability of hard-to-trace payment
platforms compounds the challenge of law enforcement agencies in investigating
malicious cyber activities on dark web.

There have been a small number of success stories, where law enforcement
agencies have had reportedly taken down several illicit online marketplaces [2].
For example, according to Europol's January 2021 report [1],

© ICST Institute for Computer Sciences, Social Informatics and Telecommunications Engineering 2022
Published by Springer Nature Switzerland AG 2022. All Rights Reserved
P. Gladyshev et al. (Eds.): ICDF2C 2021, LNICST 441, pp. 277–293, 2022.
https://doi.org/10.1007/978-3-031-06365-7_17

DarkMarket.onion was the largest online drug market on the dark web that has been shut down to date by law enforcement agencies. The vendors in this illicit marketplace had profited €140 million by trading all kinds of drugs as well as selling anonymous SIM cards, stolen or forged credit card details, counterfeit money, and ransomware/malware kits [3].

There are, however, hundreds to thousands of active dark markets that are still active. Not surprisingly, there are ongoing efforts in studying dark web and the associated illicit services [1]. For example, researchers have designed tools and technologies can be used by law enforcement agencies to track illicit activities on the dark web (e.g., cryptocurrency forensics [4–7]).

In this study, we study the risks associated with dark web activities, including payment systems (e.g., cryptocurrencies). We also study the factors that underpin investments in cryptocurrencies, with the aim of identifying criteria that online investors can use to inform their decision-making in cryptocurrency investments.

The rest of the article is organized as follows. The next section presents the relevant background materials. Next, the third section focuses on recently active dark markets and their services. We also present three related factors that underpin cryptocurrency investments. Then in the fourth section, we seek to determine the trustworthiness of the cryptocurrency market, by analyzing data from trustworthy resources. In the fifth section, we discuss the associated risks of the cryptocurrency market and present mitigating solutions. Finally, the last section concludes this paper.

2   Background: Dark Web and Cryptocurrencies

Darknet can be broadly defined to be a secret, encrypted, and/or covert (or anonymized) communication system. Such a hidden communication channel is generally not accessible or visible to ordinary Internet users. Dark web or The Onion Router (Tor) networks are two concepts that are associated with darknet, whose design is to ensure the anonymity of users' activities. For example, the Tor browser supports "hidden websites" utilizing an addressing strategy that depends upon randomly generated secret keys and defined by an address extension with ".onion" (e.g., http://ax555xx.onion). TOR can also be employed to provide anonymous access to existing online sites [8]. The hidden nature of the .onion websites on the Tor network can be abused to facilitate various illicit services (e.g., Silk Road marketplace), where anonymous payment systems (e.g., cryptocurrencies) are generally used in such cybercriminal activities [9,10].

Now, we will briefly summarize the various malicious cyber activities that are known to be conducted on dark web and facilitated using cryptocurrencies.

- **Ransom and ransomware:** Ransomware is one type of malicious software (also referred to as malware), where the attacker threatens victims by blocking access to their sensitive information unless a ransom is paid (typically using some cryptocurrency) [11,12]. Cryptocurrency has also been used as a form of payment in physical, real-world kidnapping [13]. As depicted in Fig. 1, according to the global cyber security annual report in [14] July 2021, there have been discovered a total of 304 million ransomware cyberattacks worldwide in 2020, which was a 62% rise compared to 2019, and the second highest rate since 2016.

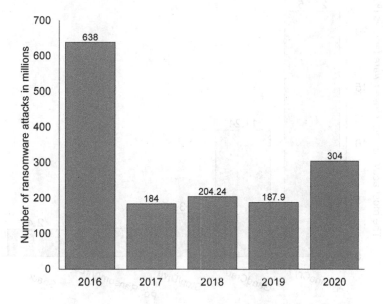

Fig. 1. Number of ransomware attacks per year 2016–2020

Moreover, according to the latest crypto-ransomware family analysis reported by the Kaspersky Lab in [15] April 2021, the number of specific users that confronted ransomware on their devices was "1,091,454" a decrease compared to "1,537,465" in 2019. Among these numbers, to date of the Kaspersky's report, WannaCry holds 21.85% of the share (see Fig. 2), which is the highest infection rate in the history, with damage in overall at least $4 billion across 150 countries.

– **Money laundering:** Money laundering is the process of hiding the origins of illicit proceeds (e.g., proceeds of crime), usually via a complex sequence of transactions (including those involving cryptocurrency).
– **Firearms trafficking:** It has been known that the dark web has been abused to facilitate the trading of illegal firearms or weapons, and cryptocurrencies are used as payments [16]. For example, according to a study conducted on the international firearms trade by RAND Europe in 2017 [17], the dark web services have reportedly increased the accessibility of weapons for the same prices compared to the black market on the street.

– *Child pornography/abuse/exploitation):* It has been known that cryptocurrencies have been used to pay for commercial child pornography, abuse,
exploitation materials and/or services (e.g., over a webcam) [18].

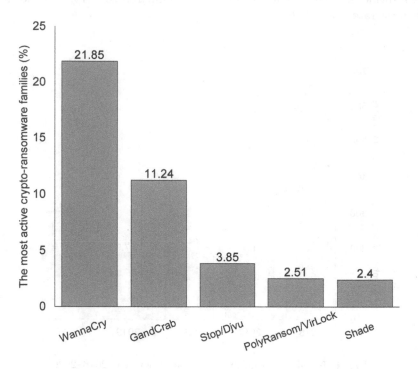

Fig. 2. Five most active crypto-ransomware families in 2020 discovered by
Kaspersky [15].

– *Contract Killers:* There exist many dark websites that allow one to hire a
hitman to murder another person [9]. For example, a White-hat hacker named
"bRpsd" reportedly helped the FBI to arrest several hitmen in May 2016 by
hacking into the "Besa Mafia" site on the dark web, and leaking contract
information such as user accounts, client messages and other information.
This hidden website provided a link between hitmen and clients, and the
price of a murder service reportedly ranged between 5, 000$ and 200, 000$.
In addition, it was reported that one could also employ a contractor to mug
(instead of murdering the victim by paying 500$ or to set a target car on fire
for 1, 000$ [19].
– *Human trafficking:* This is an online black marketplace where criminals
utilize hidden websites to sell human trafficking services, for example in organ
trade or sex trafficking [20]. According to the U.S. State Department [21],
there were 118,932 victims of human trafficking in 2019. However, only 11,841
traffickers were prosecuted with only 9,568 successful convictions. It has been

also observed that most of the traffickers utilize tools such as encryption and constantly switch between profiles and sites on the darknet to avoid being tracked by law enforcement agencies.

- **Drug trafficking:** Like the other criminal activities, the dark web provides an anonymous marketplace for drug dealers (suppliers) and addicts (consumers) to sell or purchase drugs using cryptocurrencies such as Ethereum, Bitcoin, Monero, and Ripple [16,20]. According to Europol's January 2021 report [1], "DarkMarket.onion" was the largest online drug black market that has been shut down by law enforcement agencies in a collaborative operation involving the United Kingdom (the National Crime Agency), the U.S. (DEA, FBI, and IRS), Germany, Denmark, Moldova, Australia, and Ukraine. In addition, it was revealed that "DarkMarket" had +500,000 users, 24,000 dealers, and 320,000 transactions. Among these transactions, more than 4,650 Bitcoins and 12,800 Monero tokens were paid.

- **Hacking community services:** There exist a number of hacking forums or communities throughout the dark web that provide underground marketplaces for trading different tools or services, as well as stolen/leaked information – see also Table 1 [22,23].

3   Cryptocurrency: A New Stage for Economic Globalization

Over the last decade, the globalization of online markets, and the use of cryptocurrencies as untraceable payment systems have increased their international popularity and changed the face of the digital economy and black market trade by developers who are involved in controlling various types of criminal cartels [20]. As a result, the popularity of cryptocoins and their international availability have led to the very dynamic increase in value, that rise in pressure on them from global regulatory bodies and governments.

However, law enforcement agencies and regulatory organizations have sometimes taken quite severe and differing countermeasures to limit or ban trading with cryptocurrencies in various economic unions and countries such as the EU, China, the USA, and more. But these efforts have technically failed as the number of cryptocurrency trades and their market values have exponentially increased and have had a revolutionary global impact over the last two years [24]. These regulatory agencies are expected to ponder whether their actions and multinational policies have made any impact or demonstrate benefits to the world digital markets. These agencies and governmental bodies are attempting to carefully balance the problems of digital economy control and the perceived downsides of crypto market such as money laundering as a strategy to support terrorism or cybercrimes [25].

Below, we discuss three key, important economic characteristics or determinant factors and none of them can be wholly satisfied by the untraceable cryptocurrencies such as Bitcoin, Ethereum, or Monero. These characteristics

Table 1. Examples of dark web-based forums/markets and their associated services [22, 23]

Name	Examples of services provided	Membership information
Nulled	This is a dark market to trade through sale or purchase hacked or leaked information by cybercriminals. To transact payment operations, this site utilizes cryptocoins such as Litecoin, Bitcoin, and Ethereum	Created: 2015 Members: +3,900,000 Language: English Current status: active
Dread	This is a Tor-based Reddit-style forum where members can post, share, and comment among different groups. While the main aim of Dread is to provide a censorship free forum, it also affords several other services such as pentesting or ethical hacking and selling stolen information	Created: 2018 Members: +15,000 Language: English Current status: active
CrackingKing	This is a tutorial platform that provides tools and educational materials for learning hacking strategies. Also, members can find leaked or stolen information as well as get access to their linked available markets	Created: 2002 Members: +394,000 Language: English Current status: active
CryptBB	This is a private hacking community in which a rigorous application policy is deployed for accepting members who can pass an interview. Also, they recently added a new hidden market on their website named "newbies" for trading drugs using cryptocoins such as Bitcoin and Monero	Created: 2017 Members: +356,000 Language: English Current status: active
FreeHacks	This is a Russian community platform that gathers cybercriminals and hackers to solidify and expand their information in the field	Created: 2011 Members: +200,000 Language: Russian Current status: active
RaidForums	This is an online marketplace for trading cyber attack tools and hacked databases to commit credential stuffing attacks	Created: 2015 Members: +445,000 Language: English Current status: active
XSS.is	This is a Russian forum that provides knowledge on illicit topics related to hacking, malware applications, and financial fraud. Some of such services and tools which are anonymous could only be unlocked by paying for a premium account	Created: 2018 Members: +200,000 Language: Russian Current status: active

can impact the investors' decision-making when they are choosing a target cryptoasset to invest in by highlighting the potential risks.

If we consider cryptocoins as a new type of alternative investment asset, we can define the following three economic factors that can impact the decision-making of investors: *legitimacy of investment source*, *price explosiveness*, and *correlation of price changes with other assets* such as miners, trading rules and others. Most significantly, the diversifying and hedging capability of these cyptocurrencies cannot be underestimated [12].

In the following points, we briefly explain the determinant factors on the decision-making of investors considering the risk as a multidimensional phenomenon [26]. Technically, we believe that the risk of investments in cryptocurrencies involves key influential factors that can be measured as a function of probabilities and consequences. In other words, we need to discover the factual evidence from the digital currency systems which can be characterized by the following factors.

- *Legitimacy of investment source:* This factor involves identifying the trustworthiness of a cryptocurrency system by analyzing the existence of a support agency or a branch that provides online or offline services for investors. In some cases, an investor needs to receive some systematic support where there is a problem with the online wallet-login or transactions such as the case where an online wallet is locked out. It is essential to provide these types of support services to address the possible risks and protect the rights of investors in such systems. For example in Bitcoin, if an investor forgets their wallet password, he or she has no way to reset it or access the owned Bitcoins. In other words, the investor loses all the funds due to forgetting the wallet password [27]. To measure this factor, we assign a binary value (0 or 1) according to the existence of support services for each cryptocurrency.
- *Price explosiveness or explosivity:* This factor represents an asset's exponential price increase which involves evaluating the existence of bubbles in cryptocurrency prices by considering its price in several periods. That is, an asset bubble refers to an extreme price acceleration that could not be expressed by the typical primary economic variables [28,29]. The Generalised Supremum Augmented Dickey-Fuller (GSADF) test is used to identify the explosiveness periods which can be expressed as follows:

$$\Delta_t = \mu + \beta\Delta_{t-1} \sum_{i=1}^{p} \delta_{r_w}\beta\Delta_{t-i} + \epsilon_t. \tag{1}$$

where Δ_t is the price of cryptocoin in time t, and μ, β, δ are parameters predicted utilizing Ordinary least squares (OLS) regression, as well as, p is the number of lags set according to BIC, $r_w = r_2 - r_1$ is a rolling interval window that begins and ends respectively with a fraction r_1 and a fraction r_2 [28]. The $H_0 : \beta = 1$ represents the null hypothesis against $H_1 : \beta > 1$ which indicates explosive bubbles.
- *Correlation of price changes with other external factors:* This factor involves measuring effective dependencies such as volume of trades, nature of untraceable trades, and crypto-mining, which can impact the price changes in the crypto market. Since such dependencies involve unique strategies which each cryptocoin utilizes to provide trading services or to attract

investors/traders, the process of measuring the price impact is a very complicated task. Herein, let us assume that the price impact is a behaviorally-based measure which is partially justified according to the Kyle model [30], and relies on two linear economic variables: *traded volume* and *permanent in time* [31]. In the Kyle model, an insider investor and noise investors request orders that are convinced by a Market Maker (MM) in each time step Δt. Therefore, the price adjustment rules Δp of the MM can be considered as a linear impact in the whole signed volume, as follows:

$$\Delta p = \lambda \epsilon v. \tag{2}$$

where λ is an impact measure and is thoroughly proportional to the liquidity of the crypto market. In other words, the price adjustment is somewhat permanent, which is, the price change among time $t = 0$ and $t = T = N\Delta t$.

$$p_T = p_0 + \sum_{n=1}^{N-1} \Delta p_n = p_0 + \lambda \sum_{n=1}^{N-1} \epsilon_n v_n. \tag{3}$$

In this equation, it is assumed that the impact $\lambda \epsilon_n v_n$ of trades within the nth time interval continues unabated up to some specified time. According to price manipulation by the [32], the adjustment of linear price in the Kyle model is the only condition that does not permit price manipulation; hence, the *provided impact is constant (permanent)*. This impact stays permanent as the sign of the trades should not be serially correlated if the price is to track an unpredictable (random) path. We refer the interested reader to [31] for checking details of the mathematical proof for the above-mentioned equation. In the Kyle model, the schedule of trading by an insider is exactly such that the ϵ_n is not correlated [30]. However, the real data from markets (e.g., cryptocurrency) shows the sign of correlations of the traded volume during various timescales [31]. According to the theory of modern portfolio introduced by Markowitz [33], the risks of exposure to a specific asset can be decreased by maintaining a varied portfolio of assets; the more independent or less correlated assets, the lower systematic risk, and as a result, the superiority of the diversified portfolio. From a practical perspective, a conventional way to vary the portfolio is through international diversification by maintaining global stocks [34]. Considering the above provable factors, the risks of investments in cryptocurrencies can be assessed more efficiently.

4   Cryptocurrency Trustworthiness Analysis

In this section, we conduct an empirical analysis of the top five most reputed cryptocurrencies (cryptoassets) by considering the determinant factors on the decision-making of investors that we have summarized in Sect. 3.

4.1   Legitimacy Analysis of Cryptoasset Source

To analyze this determinant factor, we have investigated the trustworthiness of each cryptoasset considering the available information related to their transparency and physical location of their company or organization by checking their official websites and law enforcement agency reports such as through the US Attorney's office and the U.S. Securities and Exchange Commission. Table 2 lists the detailed results of our investigation. During our study, we considered five conventional cryptoassets that are currently receiving a very large volume of trades from investors so far. Among such assets, three of them, including Bitcoin, Ethereum, and Ripple provide untraceable transactions by keeping the identity of users anonymous. They do not offer any tracking or monitoring services for law enforcement agencies in case of emergencies to find criminals who have used such payment systems for covering their crimes [35,36].

On the other hand, two cryptoassets including Tether and Ripple give some transparent services to law enforcement agencies when they present official warrants and prove their legal claim to the information. However, according to the NY Attorney General's report, Tether and Bitfinex deceived investors and the crypto market by exaggerating reserves, concealing roughly $850 million in losses around the world, and NY Attorney General Letitia James subsequently banned all trading activity using such cryptoassets in the state of New York [37,38].

4.2 Price Explosiveness Analysis

To identify price explosivity as a determinant factor, we investigated the price explosiveness of selected cryptoassets (see Table 3), considering economic measures such as the volume of trade, bubbles in the price of assets, and the volatility of price changes during a month period from April 19th, 2021 to May 19th, 2021. To collect real-world data from trustworthy resources, we obtained the volume of trade and price changes by following the same sources as the other references [28,43].

However, the existing price explosiveness analysis measures consider the volume of trade and the real price for calculating the bubbles of financial assets using the Eq. 1, but we believe that the source of an asset is authentic; thus, we can rely upon such measures. Otherwise, because the three evaluated cryptoassets (e.g., BTC, ETH, and XMR) do not offer any regulatory support and financial standards, the use of such measures is technically useless. To prove this assumption, as depicted in Table 3, it can be observed that the price of the evaluated cryptoassets has been changing roughly, i.e., a BTC's price decreased by $17,893 and ETH's price gained $614 during a month.

If we calculate all trade activities over the aforementioned period, the number of financial losses that BTC holders face will be over $100 Million which has been caused by the price manipulation in the meantime. Technically, the blockchain-based cryptoassets (e.g., BTC, ETH, and XMR) can perform a hard fork function [44] to invalidate transactions, since there is no regulatory support for such assets, they can even manipulate the wallet of clients [35–40]. Therefore, the lack of regulatory support and standards opens a lot of concerns regarding their legitimacy and transparency. It has been reported that approximately $400 million of investments in Initial Coin Offerings (ICOs) utilizing Ethereum platform have been stolen by attackers in 2017 [45,46].

Table 2. Legitimacy analysis of conventional cryptoassets' source considering the existence of physical company and their regulatory support.

Name	Description on cryptoasset source/company	Legitimacy analysis
Bitcoin (BTC) [35]	BTC is an open-source P2P Electronic Cash System invented by an unknown individual or a group of anonymous individuals who go by the name of Satoshi Nakamoto. There is no available/known company that physically is affiliated with this system	Release date: January 2009 Transactions: untraceable Current status: active Legitimacy: (×)
Ethereum (ETH) [56]	ETH or Ether is an open-source cryptocurrency platform introduced by a programmer named Vitalik Buterin. In theory, he claimed that Ether enables Distributed Applications (DApps) and Smart Contracts to be designed and executed without any interference, downtime, control, or fraud from a third party. In 2016, an attacker employed a security backdoor/flaw in the DAO project and stole $50 millions of Ether. Later, the ETH community voted to hard fork the blockchain to invalidate the stolen $50 M of Ether	Release date: July 2015 Transactions: untraceable Current status: active Legitimacy: (×)
Ripple (XRP) [39,40]	XRP is a real-time digital-currency-exchange open-source platform designed by Ripple Labs Inc., which is a US-based technology company. The U.S. Securities and Exchange Commission regulated the Ripple Labs Inc. and incorporated it in the state of Delaware by issuing a license number "SEC-CIK #0001685012" in October 2016	Release date: December 2012 Transactions: transparent Current status: active Legitimacy: (✓)
Monero (XMR) [36]	XMR is a privacy-focused cryptoasset which works based on an open-source mining protocol called RandomX. There is no available known company that is physically affiliated with this cryptoasset. However, there is untrustworthy research which suggests the founder of Bitcoin is also the designer of Monero	Release date: April 2014 Transactions: untraceable Current status: active Legitimacy: (×)
Tether (USDT) [37,41]	USDT is a token-backed cryptoasset issued by Tether Ltd. The USDT was originally named "realcoin" and its website states that it is incorporated in Hong Kong with offices in the USA and Switzerland but without giving details. Basically, Tether aims at maintaining the digital currency valuations stable, i.e., a "stablecoin" which was initially supposed to always be worth $1.00. However, according to the New York Attorney General, "Tether's claims that its virtual currency was fully backed by U.S. dollars at all times was a lie" [38]	Release date: July 2014 Transactions: transparent Current status: active Legitimacy: (✓)

Table 3. Price explosiveness analysis of selected cryptoassets considering a month of volatility [42].

Cryptoasset	Price: April 19th, 2021 at 12:00:00 AM	Price: May 19th, 2021 at 11:00:00 PM	Growth (↑)/Loss (↓) rate	
			1 month (%)	1 month (%)
Bitcoin BTC	$55,384	$37,491	↑ +0.00%	↓ −32.3%
Ethereum ETH	$2,158	$2,772	↑ +28.4%	↓ −0.00%
Ripple XRP	$1.330	$1.215	↑ +0.00%	↓ −9.05%
Monero XMR	$318.98	$240	↑ +0.00%	↓ −32.9%
Tether USDT	$0.9998	$1.002	↑ +0.003%	↓ −0.00%

4.3 Correlation of Price Changes with Other External Factors

Technically, there are external influential factors such as the open-source structure of the platform (e.g., BTC, ETH, XRP, XMR), crypto-miners (e.g., BTC, XMR) and so their correlation with price changes is questionable. Below, we describe the correlation of the aforementioned external factors on price changes in detail.

- *Open-source-based cryptoassets:* In general, open-source software is a type of program in which source code is openly published under a license so that the main designer - whether it is a company, a person, or a copyright holder - will allow other end-users the rights to study, change, use and share it for any purposes. Since most cryptoassets have been developed based on open-source protocols such as BTC, ETH, XRP, and XMR, they are susceptible to reverse engineering attacks. In other words, attackers can easily find the source code of cryptoassets systems and study their security flaws to implement the *hard fork* or crack wallet passwords [10]. Due to the emergence of open-source crypto-projects, greedy strategists are developing similar ideas and try to attract more investments for these platforms every day. This feature is the main reason for the appearance of +700 cryptoassets and their often rapidly changing valuations. On the other hand, the anonymity of such cryptoassets keeps their owners identities invisible and protects them from being caught by law enforcement agencies in the case where any kind of fraud or abuse happens [47].
- *Crypto-miners* are machines (e.g., Bitwats [BT, DBT, CBT]) or software (e.g., Kryptex, BitMine, ECOs) which help clients to mine cryptocurrency to make a small amount of crypto-coin per hour without spending any money for it. In other words, miners make profits by completing "blocks" of verified transactions that are newly added to the blockchain. In practice, the designers of cryptocurrencies utilize such miners to cover the traceability of transactions. There exist two mechanisms for mining: *i)* solo-mining (or mining alone), *ii)* joining a pool. Utilizing a mining pool instead of solo-mining mechanisms has several privileges: it raises the possibility of receiving payments for mining and decreases the necessity of a specific mining machine.

However, the use of a mining pool is not always beneficial since it depends on several variable characteristics such as the computational power needed for mining complexity as well as the current hash rate of the pool. The high number of clients in pools are to be expected to mine a block rapidly, but the amount of mined reward is lower than solo-mining. Recently, due to the profitability, convenience, and pseudonymity of cryptoassets, they are becoming ideal targets for cybercriminals such as ransomware operators. Moreover, the increasing popularity of crypto-coins and the development of malware can result in the infection of their infrastructures or devices by turning them into a covert form of mining machines [47,48].

According to the Micro Trend report in 2017, 4,894 Bitcoin miners were discovered, which generated more than 460,259 Bitcoins by undercover mining activities. Moreover, the report mentioned that over 20% of such miners were related to a network or web-based cyberattack [47]. Similarly, according to the latest Avira Protection Labs report on 25 January 2021 [48], they registered a 53% increase in cryptomining malware-based cyberattacks in Q4-2020 compared to Q3-2020. They believe that while several Bitcoin holders are struggling to access their wallets [27], the price of one Bitcoin was valued about +$36,000. Later, its price reached +$63,000 on 15 April 2021, which is the highest growth rate in this cryptocurrency's history [42]. Unsurprisingly, the Avira team speculated that there exists a connection between the number of crypto-mining malware activities and Bitcoin's fast price rise.

5   Discussion and Future Suggestions

Currently, the dark web and cryptoassets are one of the main sources of anonymous activities and the Tor browser is freely available for downloading on the Internet. Consequently, due to such hidden services, the public is becoming intensively concerned about how they can protect their information and investment funds in the digital world. However, law enforcement agencies such as the FBI, Europol, and Interpol have expended a significant level of effort to reduce the risks on both global economic systems as well as reduce the humanitarian costs these systems generate. However, there are still a number of opportunities in the dark market and cryptoasset ecosystems (see Table 1, and Table 2) which could allow cybercriminals to take advantage of such services and further violate human rights without being apprehended by law enforcement agencies. Below, we discuss various open challenges and suggest possible countermeasures to reduce the risks of the dark web and cryptoassets.

– *Regulatory limitations and Internet governance:* Governments or regulatory organizations must introduce strategies for regulating user activities on the dark web. As we mentioned in Sect. 2, the number of dark markets is increasing dramatically as well as an increase in the various types of crimes taking place through such hidden web services without being adequately monitored. Therefore, they must be suppressed by newly developed cyber forensics tools so that the privacy of innocent users is protected and both traditional as well as cybercriminals are caught as quickly as possible. For example, the FBI utilizes a Computer and Internet Protocol Address Verifier (CIPAV) tool for identifying the location of users who have disguised their identity by employing Tor network services or proxy servers [20]. The abilities and resources of law enforcement agencies such as China's Ministry of Public Security (MPS), the FBI, Europol, and Interpol among others can be merged and coordinated efficiently to deploy their defensive policies or cyber-forensics tools for monitoring such services [1,49]. Moreover, it is important that many governments around the world must cooperate with the aforementioned law enforcement agencies to mitigate the risks of dark web services.

- **Cryptocrimes and ransomware attacks:** The crypto market has faced an unbelievable growth in terms of the total volume of trade in 2020 due to the increasing thousands of investors who are turning to crypto-coins every day as a method through which to store market place assets of value during the COVID-19 crisis. Nevertheless, the rise of money through digital exchanges provides a potential target or opportunity for both traditional as well as cybercriminals looking to execute scams, frauds, and asset theft. Statistics have shown that fraud was one of the leading cybercrimes in 2020, followed by theft and ransomware attacks [50,51]. According to statistical data reported by CipherTrace's annual Crypto Anti-Money Laundering and Crime Report in 2021 [50], $1.9 Billion was stolen by the crypto criminals in 2020, which had decreased compared to $4.5 Billion in 2019. Similarly, such crimes reached a value of $1.7 Billion through the facilities of the crypto market in 2018, and this amount increased approximately 165% in 2019 [51]. Note that such statistical data implies that there exists an urgent necessity for "heavy-handed" tools to be utilized by law enforcement agencies for suppressing such crypto crimes by blocking dark web-based hacking forums and websites (see Table 1). In general, most of the hacking service providers do not communicate via common messaging applications about selling their ransomware or malware products. They employ encrypted messaging platforms such as Telegram to have covert conversations with their clients that are beyond the reach of law enforcement agencies. Technically, often these new generations of malware have no generic patterns or abnormal activities since they are customized according to the requirements of the buyer and thus gain the advantage of being difficult to detect. Moreover, hacking service providers present various means to compose convincing content for phishing cyberattacks utilizing legitimate documentation and authentic invoices [3,20]. To defeat these kinds of phishing attacks, we strongly recommend law enforcement agencies establish special task forces for tracking and blocking various methods of payment through legitimate and pseudo-legitimate payment systems which are being used by phishing attacks for money laundering through the crypto market. While law enforcement agencies have taken a number of mitigation actions to reduce such cyberattacks, the aforementioned statistics provide sufficient evidence that they have failed to significantly reduce or eliminate these threats so far.

- *Increasing awareness of investors:* During our investigation, we found that most investors do not have sufficient knowledge regarding the legitimacy of cryptocurrencies and their associated risks in large part due to a large magnitude of advertisements which highlight only the fast growth and the potential profits without sufficiently outlining the risks involved. Moreover, they are not aware that some anonymous cryptoassets are used by criminal organizations for payment services as well as investment instruments and are likely to increase the number of traditional and cybercrimes crimes committed every day. It is apparent that a small group of such cryptocurrency clients do not even care about the source of their investments and they are simply looking to profit from such assets as a *"safe heaven"* [12]. Let us ask a key question of investors who would like to invest in anonymous cryptocoins such as Bitcoin, Ethereum, Monero, etc. [1]. If they know that a financial asset supports underground criminal organizations in covering hacking services, money laundering, contract killers, drug-dealers, and other illicit and investing their money in these ecosystems? Also, there are other risks of losing their money through online facing insecure wallet policies such as no password reset strategy or legitimate support services such as offering assurances that they can shut down their system overnight or invalidate transactions using a *hard fork* such as ICOs did in 2017 [45,46]. The risks of cryptocoin loss have become the primary concern of cryptocurrency holders as well as the research community. To reduce the amount of investment in ambiguous cryptoassets with high risk, investigators must utilize provable determinant factors (see Sect. 3) and introduce risk assessment models such as AI-based fuzzy expert systems for providing efficient multiple criteria decision-making which can convince new investors to make reasonable decisions when they are investing in cryptoassets. Moreover, governments must take proper actions by facilitating an increasing awareness of people for creating a stable and reasonable balance between the trustworthiness of these systems as well as considering new proactive procedures and regulations in investment policies and restrictions regarding the use of the crypto market in the near future.
- *Cryptocoins as a threat to humanity:* Cryptoassets technically rely upon the integrity of the blockchain for exchanging transactions between clients' wallets. According to a recent technical report by Akamai security intelligence & threat research team on February 2021 [52], cybersecurity experts have discovered a botnet with a new defense mechanism against takedowns that employs the blockchain Ledger. In general, to disable a botnet, security experts take over the server which controls it remotely, and the botnet is disabled when there is no command to execute. However, botnet developers have come up with novel mechanisms to make such countermeasures more difficult to succeed. Since the new generations of botnets operate based on the blockchain ledger, they are globally accessible and difficult to take down. Such botnets seem to be secure against counterattacks. Technically, blockchains are a kind of "distributed ledger technology" in which a record of all transactions must be saved in all blocks since the initiation as well as each transaction requires access to or its available copy. Let us ask a question

here, what if one records a malicious code (or material) into the blockchains?, that is, "poisoning the blockchain". In this case, every Bitcoin holder receives a copy of the malicious code and the security of blockchain fails [46,53]. Nevertheless, China's MPS, the USA's FBI, Europol, and other law enforcement agencies could suppress the cryptocoins into oblivion [1]. But unfortunately, the actions of the aforementioned law enforcement agencies did not stop or significantly reduce the number of trades using untrustworthy cryptocurrencies so far [42], and new cryptoassets are increasing (e.g., +700) every day and opening uncountable dark market spaces for cybercriminals without being controlled. If proper actions against such online crypto market are not taken, criminals can run any kind of illicit operations freely and will damage the legitimate economies of nation-states and negatively affect human lives now and in the future.

6 Concluding Remarks

Thousands of newcomers are reportedly seeking to invest in cryptocurrencies every day. However, many (prospective) investors may not be aware that cryptocurrencies have been used to facilitate a broad range of malicious cyber activities (e.g., ransomware, human trafficking, trading of exploit kits and zero-day vulnerabilities). Hence, in this empirical investigation, we studied the factors that motivate cryptocurrency investment, as well as summarizing the various cybercriminal activities that are facilitated by cryptocurrencies. We hope that this study will contribute towards a better understanding of the risks associated with cryptocurrencies and cryptocurrency investments.

Acknowledgment. This work was supported in part by the National Natural Science Fund of China (NSFC) research fund for International Young Scientists (Reference No. 6211101164).

References

1. Darkmarket: World's largest illegal dark web marketplace taken down (2021). https://www.europol.europa.eu/
2. Cascavilla, G., Tamburri, D.A., Van Den Heuvel, W.-J.: Cybercrime threat intelligence: a systematic multi-vocal literature review. Comput. Secur. **105**, 102258 (2021)
3. Dargahi, T., et al.: A cyber-kill-chain based taxonomy of crypto-ransomware features. J. Comput. Virol. Hacking Tech. **15**(4), 277–305 (2019). https://doi.org/10.1007/s11416-019-00338-7
4. Fröwis, M., et al.: Safeguarding the evidential value of forensic cryptocurrency investigations. Forensic Sci. Int. Digit. Invest. **33**, 200902 (2020)
5. Vesely, V., Zadnk, M.: How to detect cryptocurrency miners? By traffic forensics! Digit. Invest. **31**, 100884 (2019)
6. Tziakouris, G.: Cryptocurrencies-a forensic challenge or opportunity for law enforcement? An interpol perspective. IEEE Secur. Priv. **16**(4), 92–94 (2018)

7. Volety, T., et al.: Cracking bitcoin wallets: I want what you have in the wallets. Future Gener. Comput. Syst. **91**, 136–143 (2019)
8. Dalins, J., Wilson, C., Carman, M.: Criminal motivation on the dark web: a categorisation model for law enforcement. Digit. Invest. **24**, 62–71 (2018)
9. Zhou, G., et al.: A market in dream: the rapid development of anonymous cybercrime. Mob. Netw. Appl. **25**(1), 259–270 (2020). https://doi.org/10.1007/s11036-019-01440-2
10. Conti, M., et al.: A survey on security and privacy issues of bitcoin. IEEE Commun. Surv. Tutor. **20**(4), 3416–3452 (2018)
11. The State of Ransomware (2021). https://secure2.sophos.com/
12. Feng, W., Wang, Y., Zhang, Z.: Can cryptocurrencies be a safe haven: a tail risk perspective analysis. Appl. Econ. **50**(44), 4745–4762 (2018)
13. Crypto-Ransomware Attacks: The New Form of Kidnapping (2015). https://blog.trendmicro.com/crypto-ransomware-attacks-the-new-form-of-kidnapping/
14. Annual number of ransomware attacks worldwide from 2016 to 2020 (2021). https://www.statista.com/statistics/494947/ransomware-attacks-per-year-worldwide/
15. The most active crypto-ransomware families (2021). https://securelist.com/ransomware-by-the-numbers-reassessing-the-threats-global-impact/101965/
16. ElBahrawy, A., et al.: Collective dynamics of dark web marketplaces. Sci. Rep. **10**(1), 1–8 (2020)
17. International Fire arms trade on the dark web (2021). https://www.rand.org/randeurope/research/projects/international-arms-trade-on-the-hidden-web.html
18. da Cunha, B.R., et al.: Assessing police topological efficiency in a major sting operation on the dark web. Sci. Rep. **10**(1), 1–10 (2020)
19. How a bitcoin whitehat hacker helped the FBI catch a murderer (2021). https://bitcoinmagazine.com/
20. Kaur, S., Randhawa, S.: Dark web: a web of crimes. Wireless Pers. Commun. **112**(4), 2131–2158 (2020). https://doi.org/10.1007/s11277-020-07143-2
21. Beating Human Trafficking on the Dark Web (2021). https://cobwebs.com/beating-human-trafficking-on-the-dark%20web/
22. Online Trade NULLED (2020). https://allwpworld.com/
23. The Top 5 Dark Web Forums (2021). https://webhose.io/blog/dark%20web/the-top-5-dark%20web-forums/
24. Yen, K.-C., Cheng, H.-P.: Economic policy uncertainty and cryptocurrency volatility. Finance Res. Lett. **38**, 101428 (2021)
25. Morton, D.T.: The future of cryptocurrency: an unregulated instrument in an increasingly regulated global economy. Loy. U. Chi. Int'l L. Rev. **16**, 129 (2020)
26. Olsen, R.A.: Investment risk: the experts' perspective. Financ. Anal. J. **53**(2), 62–66 (1997)
27. Lost Passwords Lock Millionaires Out of Their Bitcoin Fortune (2021). https://www.nytimes.com/2021/01/12/technology/
28. Gronwald, M.: How explosive are cryptocurrency prices? Finance Res. Lett. **38**, 101603 (2021)
29. Liu, Y., Tsyvinski, A., Wu, X.: Common risk factors in cryptocurrency. Technical report, National Bureau of Economic Research (2019)
30. Kyle, A.S.: Continuous auctions and insider trading. Econometrica J. Econometric Soc. **53**(6), 1315–1335 (1985)
31. Bouchaud, J.P.: Price Impact. Encyclopedia of Quantitative Finance (2010)
32. Huberman, G., Stanzl, W.: Price manipulation and quasi-arbitrage. Econometrica **72**(4), 1247–1275 (2004)

33. Rubinstein, M.: Markowitz's "portfolio selection": a fifty-year retrospective. J. Finance **57**(3), 1041–1045 (2002)
34. Heston, S.L., Rouwenhorst, K.G.: Does industrial structure explain the benefits of international diversification? J. Financ. Econ. **36**(1), 3–27 (1994)
35. Bitcoin Inc.: Information (2021). https://bitcoin.inc/
36. Monero Inc.: Information (2021). https://www.getmonero.org/
37. Tether Limited. Information (2021). https://tether.to/
38. Attorney General James Ends Virtual Currency Trading Platform Bitfinex's Illegal Activities in New York (Bitfinex and Tether) (2021). https://ag.ny.gov/
39. Ripple Labs Inc.: Information (2021). https://ripple.com/
40. U.S. S.E.C. or EDGAR System (2021). https://sec.report/CIK/0001685012
41. Tether LTD legal supports (2021). https://tether.to/legal/
42. The global crypto market cap, a trustworthy platform for showing the price updates of cryptoassets (2021). https://coinmarketcap.com/
43. Omane-Adjepong, M., Alagidede, I.P.: Multiresolution analysis and spillovers of major cryptocurrency markets. Res. Int. Bus. Finance **49**, 191–206 (2019)
44. Ethereum Inc.: Information (2021). https://ethereum.org/en/about/
45. U.S. Department of Justice, Attorney General's report (2020). https://www.justice.gov/archives/ag/page/file/1326061/download
46. Hackers Have Stolen $400 Million From ICOs (2017). https://fortune.com/2018/01/22/ico-2018-coin-bitcoin-hack/
47. Security 101: The Impact of Cryptocurrency-Mining Malware (2017). https://www.trendmicro.com/
48. Coinminers target vulnerable users as Bitcoin hits all-time high (2021). https://www.avira.com/en/
49. Helping police worldwide understand and investigate digital crimes, Interpol Police (2021). https://www.interpol.int/en/How-we-work/Innovation/Darknet-and-Cryptocurrencies
50. Cryptocurrency Crime and Anti-Money Laundering Report (2021). https://ciphertrace.com/
51. crypto-criminals stole $1.9B (2020). https://www.finaria.it/
52. Bitcoins, Blockchains, and Botnets (2021). https://blogs.akamai.com/
53. Systematic Approach to Analyzing Security and Vulnerabilities of Blockchain Systems, MIT Working Paper (2021). https://web.mit.edu/smadnick/www/wp/2019-05.pdf

Lightweight On-Demand Honeypot Deployment for Cyber Deception

Jaime C. Acosta[1]([✉]), Anjon Basak[2], Christopher Kiekintveld[2], and Charles Kamhoua[1]

[1] DEVCOM Army Research Laboratory, Adelphi, USA
jaime.c.acosta.civ@army.mil
[2] Department of Computer Science, University of Texas at El Paso, El Paso, USA
cdkiekintveld@utep.edu

Abstract. Honeypots that are capable of deceiving attackers are an effective tool because they not only help protect networks and devices, but also because they collect information that can lead to the understanding of an attacker's strategy and intent. Several trade-offs must be considered when employing honeypots. Systems and services in a honeypot must be relevant and attractive to an adversary and the computing and manpower costs must fit within the function and budget constraints of the system.

It is infeasible to instigate a single, static configuration to accommodate every type of system or target every possible adversary. The work we describe in this paper demonstrates a novel approach, introducing new capabilities to the Cyber Deception Experimentation System (CDES) to realize selective and on-demand honeypot instantiation. This allows honeypot resources to be introduced dynamically in response to detected adversarial actions. These honeypots consist of kernel namespaces and virtual machines that are invoked from an "at-rest" state. We provide a case study and analyze the performance of CDES when placed inline on a network. We also use CDES to start and subsequently redirect traffic to different honeynets dynamically. We show that these mechanisms can be used to swap with no noticeable delay. Additionally, we show that Nmap host-specific scans can be thwarted *during a real scan*, so that probes are sent to a honey node instead of to the legitimate node.

Keywords: Cybersecurity · Network security · Dynamic honeypots · Experimentation · Testbed

1 Introduction

Honeypots for the most part are static and do not change even as unusual or adversarial behavior is detected. The research in this field is growing rapidly as novel technologies allow for more adaptability. These honeypots vary in scope; some focus on breadth while others focus on depth. OWASP Python-Honeypot

© ICST Institute for Computer Sciences, Social Informatics and Telecommunications Engineering 2022
Published by Springer Nature Switzerland AG 2022. All Rights Reserved
P. Gladyshev et al. (Eds.): ICDF2C 2021, LNICST 441, pp. 294–312, 2022.
https://doi.org/10.1007/978-3-031-06365-7_18

[11], KFSensor [6] and many others ([9,14] contains a substantial list) are capable of mimicking several nodes and services simultaneously, using a software backend. Others, such as HADES [7], provide high-fidelity, full-system mirroring.

Still lacking are comprehensive, easily configurable and deployable honeynet infrastructures that are capable of running on the types of small-scale devices that are seeing broad and expanded usage in the commercial and military sectors. This includes the Internet of Things (IoT), Internet of Battlefield Things (IoBT), vehicular systems, and many more. We foresee these devices in the future each hosting and deploying a minimal, yet carefully selected set of honeynets when malicious behavior is suspected. Honeynet inclusion and deployment must be flexible, allowing the use of small-scale, low-to-medium fidelity, as well as large-scale (for which traffic may have to be redirect off-machine) real-system mirroring. We also foresee the use of small-scale, possibly battery-powered, special purpose devices placed on networks, between existing nodes, to monitor and automatically deploy these defense mechanisms on-the-fly; all leveraging technologies such as kernel network namespaces, container technologies, virtualization, and software defined networking. Novel research in computational decision theory, game theory, and machine learning will be used to coordinate and optimize the deployment of specific resources based on observations of the network and the costs and constraints on implementing and deploying specific network modifications.

Before this vision can be used in real operating environments, a substantial amount of analysis studies must demonstrate the feasibility of these approaches as well as limitations and expectations in live networks. Real data is also necessary to estimate the costs and effectiveness of different strategies for use in decision-making modules. Towards this goal we provide the following contributions in this paper:

- A novel implementation and source code for the cybersecurity deception experimentation system (CDES) that uses Open vSwitch for traffic redirection. This novel implementation is scalable and applicable on real networks, unlike its predecessor.
- A case study used to analyze performance in terms of packet round-trip time delay when using CDES inline on a network.
- Empirical evidence for a realistic use case showing that CDES has the ability to dynamically thwart network probes using a standard network scanning tool.

The rest of the paper includes a description of relevant work in this domain, followed by a description of the improvements made to CDES. Next, we define our case study, which focuses on a simple scenario in which traffic is dynamically redirected to honeynets. Finally, we report on the experimental results and discuss directions for future work.

2 Related Work

There are several free and open-source honeypot projects available to the public [9] that mostly provide different capabilities. For example, the growing trend of Web Application Attacks has given rise to associated honeypots. The django-admin-honeypot [3] hosts false login pages to note any malicious attempts, Node-pot [13] is a NodeJS honeypot, and StrutsHoneypot [12] specifically targets attackers looking to exploit the Apache Struts service. Others aim to attract adversaries looking to target physical devices; for example, ADBHoney [4] emulates an Android running an Android Debug Bridge, AMT Honeypot [16] reflects a vulnerable Intel Firmware. Conpot [5] and GasPot [17] look like industrial control systems, which are common in critical infrastructure networks.

Others are more broad in the capabilities they provide. Honeyd [10] was released in 2003 and with much acclaim. Many people have developed additions to the original code base and extended the functionality, which includes being able to mimic various services and nodes. Released more recently, KFSensor [6] is a low-to-medium fidelity honeypot for Windows that provides multiple services running on multiple ports and even on various IP Addresses. SIREN works similarly for Linux systems, including ARM systems, and is available as open source.

HADES [7], developed by Sandia National Laboratories, is a large-scale honeynet platform capable of mimiking large networks and systems, including the ability to mirror entire networks and switchover on-the-fly. When an attacker is detected in the operational network, it is migrated into a deception network where the configurations and monitoring capabilities can be changed dynamically.

Still lacking are honeypot systems that are lightweight, able to run on small-scale systems, and still able to provide multiple levels of fidelity. Additionally, such a system need to be extensible, open source, and easy to configure and deploy. Performance analysis is also critical to real deployment and largely lacking in the literature. This is especially important when incorporating decision algorithms to strategically (using RL or Game theoretic algorithms) deceive attackers [1,2] with minimal latency and system load, especially when deployed on constrained systems. We believe that on-demand instantiation is a solution that will allow intelligent, adaptive use of these systems suitable to resource-constrained environments.

3 Implementation

The Cybersecurity Deception Experimentation System (CDES) [1] is a standalone, emulation-based platform that is aimed at running small-to medium scale network scenarios. It is built using a modular architecture to encourage adaptation and extension, and it is open source. CDES runs in parallel to the Common Open Research Emulator, which provides many of the fundamental emulation functions including network creation and execution mechanics as well as a graphical interface. CDES is based on a three-stage pipeline that comprises the Monitor, Trigger, and Swapper components. These are shown in Fig. 1.

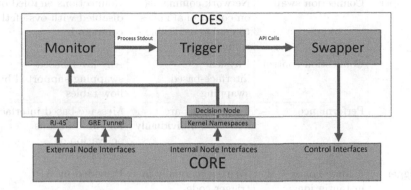

Fig. 1. CDES and the interfaces with CORE

The Monitor observes the output of a particular system process; for example, previous versions of CDES have used the Suricata Intrusion Detection System along with other tools to observe the network. This output is passed to the Trigger, which contains logic (as editable Python code) to determine how to consolidate and process the inputs. The Swapper provides an API that allows a user to execute connection redirection. This component communicates with the CORE backend through various interfaces to achieve this behavior. More information on the internals of CDES along with several samples are available in [1].

The original version of CDES was developed for testing primarily within emulated scenarios, where all nodes reside on a single machine. We have made several modifications to CDES in order to make it more usable on a real network, and to improve the general performance and usability of the system. These changes are backward compatible with the original version, so previous scenarios will work with CORE version 6 and below. Scenarios developed with the CDES updates have been tested on CORE version 6.2.0–7.4 (the latest version as of the writing of this paper). We describe these enhancements below.

3.1   Including Real Networks

CDES previously relied on three different node types to work, two of which we modified. The *decision node* is where the three-stage pipeline is executed, the *conditional nodes* are connected to the decision node, but only if enabled by the Swapper. The third node type, the *conditional connection gateway* was not modified.

Originally, the Swapper would enable or inhibit communication with a node by running an interface command (specifically ifconfig or ip) on the conditional

Table 1. High-level CDES improvements and upgrades

Source	Type	Prior state	Modification
Swapper	Connection swap	Network commands on conditional nodes to enable or disable connections	Connections enabled or disabled with ovs-ofctl commands
	Connection control	Physical interface-based swapping	Any layer-based swapping supported by flow tables
	Performance	Connections are activated individually	Message-based interface for simultaneous activation or deactivation
Trigger	Ad-hoc honey VM instantiation	Written manually in trigger code	Provided by API
Dec. node	Decision node implementation	Layer-2 switch node services	Layer-3 node running Open vSwitch

node. This meant that the conditional node had to exist within the emulation scenario; in other words, this could not be an external node, such as a physical node or a virtual machine. To alleviate this issue, we developed a subclass for the Swapper that instead is based on Open vSwitch that controls the direction of the traffic directly on the decision node. The conditional node can now be a device external to CORE (e.g., incorporated into a scenario using the RJ-45 adapter) (Table 1).

Therefore, the decision nodes now execute ovs processes. Every interface on these nodes is added to a default ovs bridge and flow entries are added and removed depending on which connections are designated as enabled or disabled, through calls to the Swapper. To improve performance, the Swapper now executes all system call operations in a single function call, allowing a user to specify active and inactive connections within a single function parameter. Feedback from users of the system indicated that the previous way of specifying conditional connection nodes (using an integer value) was difficult, because the ordering was not always consistent. To remediate this, we created a messaging system, where different message types use different formats to indicate actions and nodes. This is also how we maintained backward compatibility with previously developed scenarios. Using Open vSwitch also comes with many additional benefits, including the ability to specify swapping at various layers in the network stack, including Ethernet-based, IP Address based, etc.

3.2   Ad-Hoc Virtual Machine Instantiation

To faciliate the task of dynamically instantiating external virtual nodes, we added functions to the backend Trigger API for pausing, saving, resuming, and starting virtual machines. A user can specify whether the virtualization system is local (running VirtualBox on the host) or remote (in which case an SSH session is instantiated and run as a specified user). Instead of VBoxManage, a user may also specify to use pyvbox; which would require that the VirtualBox SDK be installed on the host running VirtualBox.

3.3 Decision Node Configuration

In addition to incorporating Open vSwitch processes on the decision node, the base type had to change. Recent versions of CORE have evolved and added new features; at the same time, some interfaces have also changed. Layer 2 switch nodes are no longer able to be assigned services. To adapt for these changes, the decision node is now a layer 3 node that behaves like a switch (using ovs). A benefit of this change is that now processes can be spawned on decision nodes during a running emulation. This also better fits the logical design and usage of CORE. However, adding and using this type of node in the CORE GUI may cause some confusion, since by default the node is treated as a router node instead of a switch node, e.g., IP addresses are generated and then auto-assigned when connected to another node.

One of the fundamental objectives of CDES is to leverage CORE without requiring any modifications to CORE. We have kept this model, but we also provide users with the option to alleviate some of the confusion presented by the issue mentioned in the previous paragraph. We modified 3 source files (linkcfg.tcl, ip4.tcp and ip6.tcl) that will provide a switch behavior for decision nodes when used in the graphical interface. These are optional and the system will still run correctly without including these changes.

These modifications also made it possible to incorporate CDES into CORE scenarios with mobile wireless nodes. In the first case, we tested this functionality by designating a wireless node as a decision node. The Swapper can switch between the different wireless networks, which in the real world are synonymous with different wireless network interfaces connected to different SSIDs. This also works with what we call base station nodes (with one wired connection and at least one wireless connection).

The code base now include several new samples, including the changes described above as well as several which use SDN components (Open vSwitch, Ryu, etc.) in CORE.

4 Case Study

We envision CDES being used inline on a network, on a limited resource device that will have minimal impact on network throughput. To demonstrate this we developed two separate experimentation setups.

In the first, CDES runs on a recent laptop with considerable memory and a decent processor. In this setup, which we call *In-VM*, CORE is used within a virtual machine. This facilitates deployment, modification, and maintenance.

This setup makes it easy to install CORE, configure the trigger rules, and apply updates to CDES and then transfer the latest version as an importable virtual machine. Other VMs are easily added and their network configurations are preserved. No changes are required to execute the setup across different machines, even those with different host operating systems. For this setup, we used a Laptop with 64 GB RAM and the Intel Xeon E3-1505M v6 3.0 GHz processor. The host operating system is 64-bit Windows 10 and CORE is installed on a virtual machine running Ubuntu 20 64-bit LTS.

The second setup, which we call *Native*, runs CDES installed on an older, less capable laptop. Virtualization is used only to host the honeynet VMs. This laptop had 16 GB of RAM and a 2.6 GHz Intel Core i7-4720HQ. Ubuntu 20 64-bit LTS was the host operating system.

In both cases, the CDES laptop was placed on an isolated network between two communicating nodes (see Fig. 2). On the left side is the scanning machine. This is where traffic originates and where we measure round-trip time for packets. This laptop was the same model as the host used for the In-VM set up; all specs were the same, except that is was running Ubuntu 20 64-bit LTS instead of Windows.

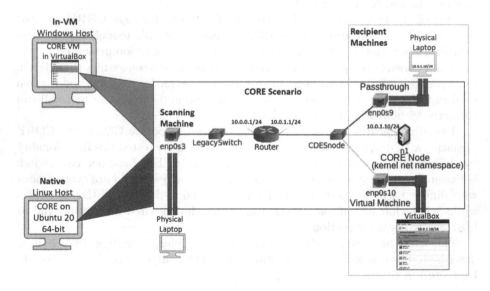

Fig. 2. Case study scenario, developed in CORE

The CDES laptop is connected to the network using two physical interfaces. The left interface (through enp0s3 in Fig. 2) is connected to the scanning machine using a USB 3.0, 1 Gbps dongle, and on the right is the native, hardwired network interface card included with the laptop. It is worth noting that there were no differences in results when we reversed the ordering of these interfaces. When using the In-VM setup, VirtualBox was used to run the CDES node with three virtual network interfaces. The first was bound to the Ethernet dongle in bridged mode. The second was an internal network shared with two *honey* virtual machines, a minimal Linux TinyCORE VM, allocated with 2 processors and 128 MB RAM and an Ubuntu 20 64-bit LTS VM, allocated with 2 processors and 2 GB of RAM. Finally, the third adapter is bound to the laptop's internal 1 Gbps network interface card, which is used as the passthrough.

This right-most interface on the CDES laptop connects to a 1 Gbps Ethernet switch, which is also connected to the passthrough machine. This machine the same laptop model as that used for the In-VM CDES node, running Ubuntu 20 64-bit LTS so that it mirrors one of the honey VMs.

The honey VMs (connected through the virtual interface enp0s10) and the passthrough machine (connected through enp0s9) are all configured to use the same IP Address and the same MAC address. This is so the honey virtual machines closely mimic the passthrough node from a networking perspective. It also eliminates the need for additional address resolution traffic when redirection occurs, which would otherwise cause intermittent delays.

The primary objectives of this case study are as follows:

1. Determine the impact on total throughput that a CDES node will introduce on the network
2. Understand the delays that are introduced with the additional processing required for CDES to work; specifically when switching between a passthrough network, a local kernel network namespace (also known as a native CORE node) and two types of virtual machines connected to a CORE scenario using a CORE RJ-45 node.
3. Demonstrate the capabilities of CDES for thwarting adversarial behavior, specifically network service probes.

We used delays in ICMP echos and requests to measure performance impacts on the network. In each setup, the scanning machine sent requests at a rate of 10 per second. For network probes, the scanning machine used Nmap with different timing templates. This is explained further in the following sections.

5   System-in-the-Middle Overhead Analysis

We measure overhead first with static connections (no CDES or swapping) and then with dynamic connections (using CDES with different instantiation and swapping configurations) in order to characterize delays associated with the different setups.

5.1   Static Connections

To establish a baseline with respect to network delays and the additional load introduced by the CDES node and accompanying software, we measured the ICMP echo-response delays without any intermediate nodes during a 1000-s test. We temporarily removed the CDES node and connected the scanning machine to

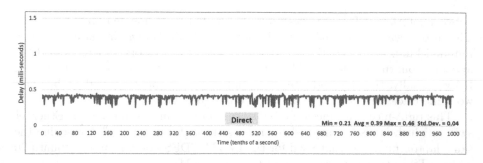

Fig. 3. Ping delays when scanning machine is directly connected to passthrough machine

the passthrough machine through the network switch. The delays are very stable, as expected in such as small and simple networking configuration. Figure 3 shows the delays with statistics exhibited during the duration of the test.

Next, we measured the delays associated with adding an intermediate node. In the case of the native setup, these delays encompass processing done by the hardware and the kernel. In the case of the In-VM setup, results are shown in Fig. 4.

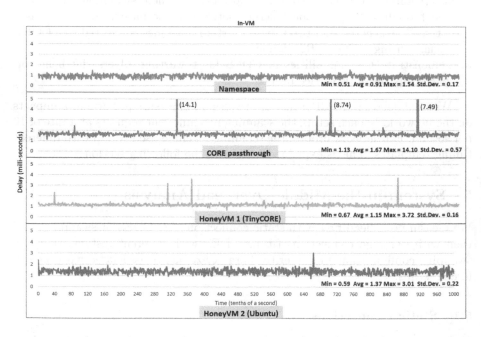

Fig. 4. Ping delays when scanning machine traffic flows through within-VM CORE

Additional delays are caused by the processing required for the VirtualBox bridged adapter and the virtual machine hosting CORE; no other user processes were instantiated. In general, the namespace node responds the quickest. This is because the incoming packets are not redirected to external systems; packets arrive and are processed by a specific kernel network namespace. The CORE passthrough, which is the case when packets are redirected through the second physical network interface is the slowest. In this case, packets are pushed through the network switch to the recipient laptop and processed by that second physical device and its OS kernel.

Additionally, there are several sporadic delays throughout, sometimes rising to 0.14 s with the passthrough. To test whether this behavior was consistent, we repeated the experiment with different combinations of hardware, Operating System (Linux), and virtualization platform (VMWare). The same behavior persisted. This is likely due to the internal switching mechanisms used by the virtualization software. However, it is also worth noting that even though these additional and sporadic delays exist, the delays are still relatively short, on average within 1 ms–2 ms compared to 0.5 ms–1.01 ms for the native setup. The standard deviations are all below 0.6 ms during the 100-s runs.

The results associated with the native setup are shown in Fig. 5. Delays when using the CORE node as the recipient (kernel network namespace) are on average only 0.12 ms higher. Adding the additional node, as seen with CORE passthrough, adds 0.62 ms to the average delay time. The min and max delays in this setup are all within 1.02 ms, demonstrating connection stability even with the additional processing.

When comparing the two setups, it is clear that In-VM introduces more delay across all tests, but they are similar. Depending on the needs of the administrator (e.g., fidelity versus ease of use) both setups are viable, especially in the case where a namespace is used.

5.2 Dynamic Connections Using CDES

We used CDES to swap between the different possible recipient nodes (passthrough, namespace, honey1 VM and honey2 VM). Both of the honey VMs were connected to the CORE scenario using the RJ-45 node and only one was active at any given time. For this reason, even though all of these recipient nodes were configured to use the same addresses there were no conflicts. We tested three different sets of configurations. In the *no_inst* configuration, the honey VM is instantiated before the scenario starts and it is never stopped. The *pause_resume* configuration starts with all VMs in a suspended state, with memory allocated beforehand, but machines are activated only when resumed. The machines are again suspended when they are no longer in use. It is important to note that the ordering of execution has an important role. A VM is instantiated on a thread, and the CDES swapping logic waits until this operation is complete until swapping to use the associated connection. When a VM is toggled for suspension, the swapping does not occur until the machine the operation is complete. This

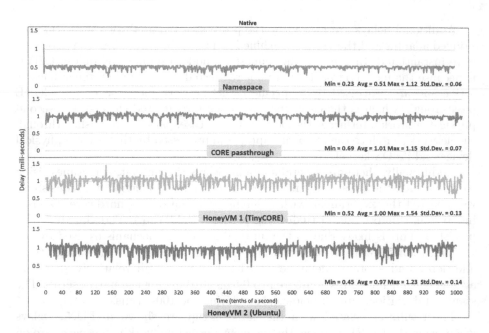

Fig. 5. Ping delays when scanning machine traffic flows through native-installed CORE

model we used in the case study favors possible delays instead of possible duplicate packets. This eliminates the case where, if two connections were to be active at the same time, both recipient nodes could respond to the ICMP echo request. The scanning machine would see these as duplicate packets.

Lastly, in the save_state case, the VMs are offloaded, but their state is saved to disk and restored when they are instantiated. We used the same mechanics and logical execution as the *pause_resume* configuration. In the In-VM setup, the VMs are halted and started as needed using an ssh connection to the host machine and subsequently running the VBoxManage binary to control the VM. In the native setup, we simple called the VBoxManage binary directly.

To measure the delays associated with the various CDES redirections, the redirection would occur every 30 s for a total of 7 times (210 s), and in the following order: passthrough, namespace, passthrough, honey1 VM, passthrough, honey2 VM, passthrough. This behavior was implemented in the CDES Trigger script using the CORE graphical interface, and required only 12 additional lines of Python code.

We started with the no_inst configuration (shown in Fig. 6 and we noticed immediately that in both setups, there was no noticeable delay when the swaps occurred and zero packets were lost. However, as expected from previous results, the delays associated with the namespace were noticeably lower (shown in the upper graphs). We added an intentional delay of 400 ms to the link connecting the CDES node to the namespace node. This decreased the standard deviations from 0.19 ms to 0.09 ms in the Native setup and 0.63 ms to 0.51 ms in the In-VM setup, as shown in the lower graphs.

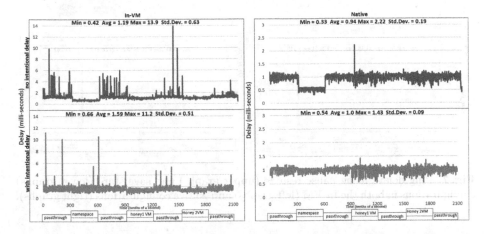

Fig. 6. Ping delays using CDES without (upper graphs) and with (lower graphs) intentional delay in both the In-VM (left graphs) and Native configurations (right graphs).

Also coinciding with the results presented in the previous subsection, the In-VM setup exhibits more sporadic behavior than the Native. However, these results are in the range of milliseconds. In more complex and congested networks, the sporadic behavior may be harder to notice.

The delays associated with the pause_resume and save_state configurations using intentional delay are shown in Fig. 7. In both configurations, there were no dropped packets. In the case of the pause_resume, there is very little noticeable difference in delays when compared to the no_inst configuration. The minimum increase was below 0.08 ms, the average increase was 0.4 ms and the max increase was within 0.15 ms. The standard deviation changed only by 0.01 ms. The resume VM operation completed within 1 s in both the In-VM and Native case. Since the switchover doesn't occur until the VMs are instantiated, this reduces (and in this case virtually eliminates) additional CDES-incurred delay.

The save_state configuration did not perform as well, especifically when instantiating the Honey2 VM (Ubuntu). Originally, we thought that these results would closely mimic those in the pause_resume configuration due to ordering of the the the swapping logic, but we noticed that this was not the case; there were additional delays, up to slightly over 2 full seconds. Closer observation revealed that when a VM is started from a saved state, there is a response gap between the time that the VM is fully functional and interactive to when its network devices become active. In the case of the Ubuntu VM this was 2 s. However, it seems that the packets are queued by the virtualization software, since eventually there were responses and no packets were lost. This was the case in both setups, in which the total varied by at most 11 ms. Memory and CPU did not seem to

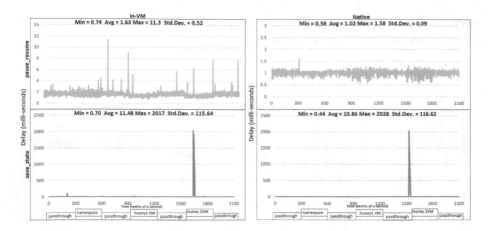

Fig. 7. Ping delays using pause_resume (upper graphs) and save_state (lower graphs) configurations in both the In-VM (left graphs) and Native configurations (right graphs).

play a role in this behavior, as they were both below maximum utilization. We discuss these results in the next section.

6   CDES System Utilization

We analyzed the performance in terms of both CPU and memory utilization in the native setup for the three configurations. CPU usage was recorded using the mpstat tool, which is part of the sysstat package. The load of the system was recorded once per second. The results are shown in Fig. 8.

In both the no_inst and pause_resume configurations, the memory is constant at 25%, which is roughly 4 GB of memory, throughout the scenario. Utilization varies much more during save_state, when the VMs are instantiated and shutdown dynamically. There is only a small increase of roughly 2–3% when the TinyCORE VM (honey1 VM in the chart) is instantiated, but the increase is roughly 10% when instantiating the Ubuntu VM (or honey2 VM). The memory usage is not instantaneous. As we show in the graphs, this is gradual and occurs over 3–5 s.

CPU performance is show in the graphs on the right side of the figure, including statistics for the executions. Since all of the configurations start at 100% utilization (due to CDES instantiation) the maximum statistic is based on the data after 1 s. CPU utilization is much more stable in the configurations where VMs are not instantiated from a saved state, as observed in the average being 2.8%–2.98% and standard deviation between 6.81% and 6.79%. Still, even when using the less capable laptop, the usage remained below 25% throughout.

In summary, the usage of CDES should depend on the availability of resources. When used on a device with limited memory, and when the inherent delays (presented in Sect. 5, are acceptable, the save_state configuration is

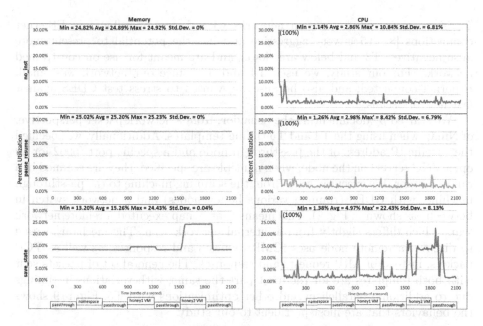

Fig. 8. CPU and memory utilization during the execution of the three configurations.

best. When CPU utilization must remain constant and when delays are a critical factor, then the pause_resume configuration is better suited as it behaves very similar no_inst configuration. The no_inst configuration has no benefits in the case study that we present here. However, there may be situations when honey systems must be configured and tuned dynamically. In this case, a hybrid system would work best. As an example, some honey nodes would be instantiated at th start, but as information becomes available, they could be modified (by starting services or changing IP Addresses/MAC Addresses) through scripting, or stopped all together while another set of honey nodes are instantiated.

7   CDES Performance Against Network Probes

According to [18], reconnaissance is the first step in the Cyber Kill Chain and includes target identification and profiling. We wanted to determine the feasibility of using CDES to directly mitigate this stage in the kill chain by redirecting the traffic of a scanning device during a scan. We ran several tests using the Nmap software on the scanning machine against a recipient node.

Nmap [8] is a well-known tool used to discover nodes on networks as well as the services they are hosting. Nmap accepts a wide range of flags that determine it's behavior, ranging from specifying nodes to specifying network ports, and timing. There are five timing templates included by default in Nmap. These allow a user to indicate general behavior related to how fast and how stealthily a scan should be executed. In general, the highest templates (T4 and T5) favor speed;

T4 is recommended for use on networks with decent broadband or Ethernet connections [8]. T5 is very aggressive and has the potential to present more false negatives. T3 and below are slower and are meant for use on constrained networks. For our study, we used T4 and T5, since our network was small, Ethernet-connected, and also because we wanted to stress test CDES against fast network scans.

We started by documenting the behavior, from a network packet perspective, of Nmap when using the T4 and T5 timing templates. Additionally, we specified the specific IP address of the passthrough node and a specific port (5902 for an open VNC server) on the node; when multiple are specified, they are scanned in a random order. We executed scans from the scanning machine to the passthrough machine, with CDES (running various honey nodes) and a network switch in between (as shown in Fig. 2). This means that Nmap executed a remote network scan, which differs slightly from a internal network scan. The mechanism used to discover a remote node uses ICMP requests and responses, as well as TCP packets, instead of ARP requests and responses. The general set of packets sent with both templates are for the most part the same, with variations in timings due to additional parallelism and other optimizations with T5. Figure 9 shows the behaviors that are most pertinent to our study.

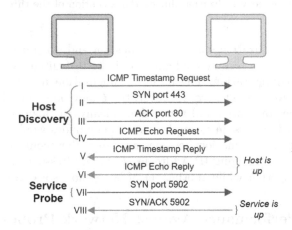

Fig. 9. Network exchanges during Nmap timing templates T4 and T5.

The Nmap behavior occurs in two phases: Host Discovery and Service Probe. Nmap starts by sending a sequence of ICMP and TCP packets (I–IV) to determine if a host is running and responding. The ordering of the packets during the I–VI are not always the same. If the host replies (V and VI), then port probing starts; the scanning machine sends TCP handshake packets (VII) and services that are running will respond (VIII). The TCP packets in the Host Discovery phase do not influence the results of the entirety of the scan. That is, if port 443 was specified as the scan port, an additional TCP SYN packet to port 443 will be sent again during the service probe phase.

We tested whether CDES could swap a connection between the two phases. Specifically, if the swap is fast enough to occur between the time an ICMP Echo Request is observed (IV) to the time that Nmap begins probing for services (VII). This way, even if a real host is discovered, the service probes will be directed to a honey node.

First, we ran Nmap with T4 and T5 five times and recorded timing information. Generally, the total time for the scans, when specifying a port (5902 in our case), were between 0.45 s and 0.54 s for T4; T5 took between 0.44 s and 0.46 s. With both templates, the time between I–IV from Fig. 9 was less then .01 ms. The time from the last packet in Host Discovery (IV) to the first packet in Service probe (VII) occurred within 0.3 s. Therefore, for CDES to achieve our desired effect, it had to respond within 0.3 s.

The CDES Monitor was configured to run a custom network packet sniffer developed using PyPacker [15]. Anytime an ICMP Echo Request packet was encountered, an indicator would print to stdout. This stdout is passed to the Trigger, which then calls the Swapper to switch from the passthrough to a different honey node. Because the timing required to swap to a virtual machine varied depending on the operating system, in addition to the namespace and honey2 VM (TinyCORE) and honey2 VM (Ubuntu 20) used in previous tests, we included 11 additional virtual machines. All VMs are 64-bit operating systems unless otherwise specified.

As discussed in Sect. 5.2, when using the save_state configuration, the time network device activation time gap (roughly 1 s–2 s) is too high to achieve the swap in time, therefore, we only tested using the no_inst and pause_resume configurations. Table 2 shows the results.

CDES was successful in most cases. The most time consuming task is the system calls which are used to control the switch configuration and to VBoxManage, which controls the virtual machines. A note of interest is that when using the T5 template against honey2 VM (TinyCORE), Nmap results indicated a filtered port (as opposed to an open port). This occurred even when scanning it directly, without CDES or any intermediate nodes, and was due to the processing constraints of the VM. As indicated in the Table, with both no_inst and save_state, the swap did occur in time which we validated by analyzing the network traffic on each pathway node.

Looking further into the timings using packet arrival times and recorded timestamps within CDES revealed the following. The time from when a packet is received by the sniffer to when a no_inst swap occurs (when VMs are not instantiated or suspended) is 0.12 s. Within this time, the system call (to the Open vSwitch service) takes 0.10 s to complete. System calls that involve swapping to the honey VMs in the pause_resume case (which includes pausing the previous and resuming the current) varied – we show the total time, from packet arrival through system call in the third column of Table 2. The Ubuntu VMs showed the highest resume times, which are above the 0.3 s threshold before the probes start. One way to alleviate this issue is by using a more capable machine to run the VMs.

Table 2. CDES swap capability against Nmap service probe

Config	Swap from passthrough to	Swap time (seconds)	Win over T4	Win over T5
no_inst	namespace	0.12	Yes	Yes
	Any VM	0.12	Yes	Yes
pause_resume	TinyCORE VM	0.18	Yes	Yes
	Ubuntu 20 VM	0.53	Yes w/defaults	Yes w/defaults
	Alpine 3.11 VM	0.14	Yes	Yes
	CentOS 8.3 VM	0.14	Yes	Yes
	Fedora 3 VM	0.15	Yes	Yes
	FerenOS 2021.01 VM	0.15	Yes	Yes
	Debian 10.7 VM	0.18	Yes	Yes
	Manjaro 21.0 VM	0.19	Yes	Yes
	PopOS 20.04 VM	0.17	Yes	Yes
	Ubuntu 18 VM	0.50	Yes w/defaults	Yes w/defaults
	WinXP 32-bit VM	0.14	Yes	Yes
	Win7 VM	0.16	Yes	Yes
	Win10 VM	0.15	Yes	Yes

When a port is not specified, Nmap will scan the top 1000 most common ports. Using this default behavior, scan completion times ranged from 1.57 s–1.58 s with T4 and 1.56–1.58 with T5. The duration of the Host Discovery phase was the same as when specifying a port (discussed earlier in this section). Chances are higher that CDES will swap before a specific port is probed, resulting in successes when using Ubuntu VMs. This is because ports are not always scanned in the same order.

8   Future Work

We have shown that the open source software, CDES, is a viable solution for employing inline honeynets that can be instantiated and suspended on-the-fly as needed. This solution works well on limited resource devices and with the graphical interface and mechanisms provided by CORE and our adaptations, make this a usable and scalable system. Using this setup, honeynets can range from small-scale (such as using kernel namespaces) to medium-scale (virtual machines) to large-scale external physical machines and networks. Our empirical results show that using CDES has minimal noticeable delay to the connected entities. Finally, we demonstrated that CDES can thwart Nmap probes in real time by redirecting traffic fast enough during an active scan to swap connections before a legitimate node's services are revealed.

The capability demonstrated by this system opens up many possibilities for further improvements, especially in using more sophisticated AI algorithms to decide dynamically which honeynets to activate at any particular time, based on the network monitoring observations. These algorithms can also take into account the available resources and potential impact on load to determine the best course of action. Another direction for research is to test this system using other small-scale systems such as ARM portable devices. We also plan to investigate the feasibility of attaching other software defined networking components such as a controller to synchronize several CDES instances running on multiple devices. Evaluating the performance of the system as well as the effectiveness of different strategies for deploying honeypots in a more complex network setup will also be an important direction for additional experiments.

Acknowledgment. This research was sponsored by the U.S. Army Combat Capabilities Development Command Army Research Laboratory and was accomplished under Cooperative Agreement Number W911NF-13-2-0045 (ARL Cyber Security CRA). The views and conclusions contained in this document are those of the authors and should not be interpreted as representing the official policies, either expressed or implied, of the U.S. Army Combat Capabilities Development Command Army Research Laboratory or the U.S. Government. The U.S. Government is authorized to reproduce and distribute reprints for Government purposes not withstanding any copyright notation here on.

References

1. Acosta, J.C., Basak, A., Kiekintveld, C., Leslie, N., Kamhoua, C.: Cybersecurity deception experimentation system. In: 2020 IEEE Secure Development (SecDev), pp. 34–40. IEEE (2020)
2. Basak, A., Kamhoua, C., Venkatesan, S., Gutierrez, M., Anwar, A.H., Kiekintveld, C.: Identifying stealthy attackers in a game theoretic framework using deception. In: Alpcan, T., Vorobeychik, Y., Baras, J.S., Dán, G. (eds.) GameSec 2019. LNCS, vol. 11836, pp. 21–32. Springer, Cham (2019). https://doi.org/10.1007/978-3-030-32430-8_2
3. dmpayton: Django Admin Honeypot. https://github.com/dmpayton/django-admin-honeypot. Accessed 20 Mar 2021
4. huuck: ADBHoney. https://github.com/huuck/ADBHoney. Accessed 20 Mar 2021
5. Jicha, A., Patton, M., Chen, H.: SCADA honeypots: an in-depth analysis of Conpot. In: 2016 IEEE Conference on Intelligence and Security Informatics (ISI), pp. 196–198. IEEE (2016)
6. KeyFocus: KFSensor. http://www.keyfocus.net/kfsensor/features/. Accessed 20 Mar 2021
7. Sandia National Laboratories: HADES. https://www.osti.gov/servlets/purl/1525940. Accessed 29 Mar 2021
8. Lyon, G.F.: Nmap Network Scanning: The Official Nmap Project Guide to Network Discovery and Security Scanning. Insecure. Com LLC, US (2008)
9. Nazario, J.: Awesome-Honeypots. https://github.com/paralax/awesome-honeypots. Accessed 20 Mar 2021
10. Provos, N.: Honeyd-a virtual honeypot daemon. In: 10th DFN-CERT Workshop, Hamburg, Germany, vol. 2, p. 4 (2003)
11. Razmjoo, A.: OWASP Honeypot. https://github.com/OWASP/Python-Honeypot/wiki. Accessed 20 Mar 2021

12. Cymmetria Research: Struts Honeypot. https://github.com/Cymmetria/StrutsHoneypot. Accessed 20 Mar 2021
13. schmalle: Nodepot. https://github.com/schmalle/Nodepot. Accessed 20 Mar 2021
14. Spitzner, L.: The honeynet project: trapping the hackers. IEEE Secur. Priv. 1(2), 15–23 (2003)
15. Stahn, M.: pypacker. https://gitlab.com/mike01/pypacker. Accessed 20 Mar 2021
16. travisbgreen: AMT Honeypot. https://github.com/travisbgreen/intel_amt_honeypot. Accessed 20 Mar 2021
17. TrendMicro: GasPot. https://github.com/sjhilt/GasPot. Accessed 20 Mar 2021
18. Yadav, T., Rao, A.M.: Technical aspects of cyber kill chain. In: Abawajy, J.H., Mukherjea, S., Thampi, S.M., Ruiz-Martínez, A. (eds.) SSCC 2015. CCIS, vol. 536, pp. 438–452. Springer, Cham (2015). https://doi.org/10.1007/978-3-319-22915-7_40

Gotta Catch'em All! Improving P2P Network Crawling Strategies

Alexander Mühle[✉], Andreas Grüner, and Christoph Meinel

Hasso Plattner Institute, Potsdam, Germany
{alexander.muehle,andreas.gruener,christoph.meinel}@hpi.de

Abstract. Network crawling has been utilised to analyse peer-to-peer systems by academics and industry alike. However, accurately capturing snapshots is highly dependant on the crawlers' speed as the network can be described as a moving target. In this paper, we present improvements based on the example of a newly developed Bitcoin crawler that can be utilised to reduce resource usage/requirements of crawlers and therefore speed up capturing network snapshots. To evaluate the new strategies, we compare our solution, in terms of increased scan-rate and increased hit-rate during crawling, to a popular open-source Bitcoin monitor. Blocking time is reduced on average to 1.52 s, resulting in 94.7% higher scan-rates, while time needed to capture a network snapshot is reduced on average by 9% due to increased hit-rates during network crawling. While we show our improvements at the example of a new Bitcoin crawler, proven concepts can be transferred to other P2P networks as well.

Keywords: Peer-to-peer systems · Blockchain · Network crawling · Internet measurement

1 Introduction

Peer-to-Peer applications have seen a resurgence of popularity in recent years, often in the context of cryptocurrencies such as Bitcoin. Due to this trend, the research community, as well as commercial interests, have undertaken numerous projects to measure these kinds of networks.

Crawling networks is an inherently progressive process, yet the goal is to capture a snapshot of the current network and its participants. Ideally, a snapshot would include all current online nodes exactly. This process, however, is impacted by several factors.

We will describe but also quantify the most prominent of these factors such as churn, NATs, random address responses and lingering offline nodes in Sect. 2.

As main contribution in this paper we further the quest to an accurate network snapshot of large open peer-to-peer systems by improving the strategies used for such crawling. These include:

© ICST Institute for Computer Sciences, Social Informatics and Telecommunications Engineering 2022
Published by Springer Nature Switzerland AG 2022. All Rights Reserved
P. Gladyshev et al. (Eds.): ICDF2C 2021, LNICST 441, pp. 313–327, 2022.
https://doi.org/10.1007/978-3-031-06365-7_19

- Scale-out through a manager/worker architecture
- Optimal timeouts through network measurements of a live network
- Reduction of predictably unsuccessful connections by:
  - Taking into account previous offline time
  - Bogon filtering

We developed a Bitcoin crawling tool incorporating these improvements. We chose the practical example of the Bitcoin network as a current and popular peer-to-peer network and implemented a publicly available monitor of network participants. We utilised the gathered data for other published research on the Bitcoin network, such as characterising proxy usage in the Bitcoin peer-to-peer network [15].

We evaluated the effects of the improvements to the crawling in terms of increased scan rate, the rate at which probes are sent by the crawler, and increased hit rate, the fraction of positive responses by probed peers. Our improvements result in a 94.7% higher scan rate and 9% overall faster snapshot times using the same resources.

2   Motivation

Peer-to-peer network crawlers and recently Bitcoin crawlers are not new and are often utilised for research on the properties of the participants, topology and system behaviours overall. We recognise, however, that improving the speed and resource usage of crawlers is inherent to increased accuracy of such crawlers. This relation between accuracy of crawled snapshots and the speed/resource usage of crawlers is due to properties of peer-to-peer networks and especially privacy aware networks such as Bitcoin. In the following we will discuss these properties and quantify their magnitude in our chosen example network of Bitcoin with a preliminary study.

2.1   Churn

Typically crawlers join a given network and participate in the node discovery protocol, recursively contacting all other discovered peers. Churn, the effect of peers constantly leaving and joining such open networks, is a key contributor to inaccuracies of these measurements. The network can be described as a moving target, during the duration of the crawl, it is already changing, and when finished will not exactly represent the real state of the network. Due to this continuous fluctuation, the speed of a crawl has a direct and significant impact on the accuracy.

There are a few considerations we have to take into account in order to quantify the churn of the Bitcoin system accurately. The measurement of churn itself is impacted by the speed of the crawl and measurement. As we are not doing continuous probing but rather round based measures for our churn analysis, the granularity of the measurements is important. Missing data in between the crawls is an inaccuracy, however we believe that our granularity of roughly 3 min is enough to have an understanding of the magnitude of churn in the network. Not only the granularity of the data but also the duration of the measurement is important as Stutzbach et al. noted in the their seminal paper on understanding churn in peer-to-peer networks [21]. Stutzbach et al. noted that while we can compute the duration of sessions that start and end during our measurement period, this would bias our statistics towards shorter sessions. We therefore chose our measurement duration as 5 days (also eliminating the impact of an diurnal effect), however for our churn statistic we will only take into account sessions that have started in the first 2.5 days. This is the so called "create-based method" used by Saroui et al. [19] in their analysis of the P2P networks Napster and Gnutella. In Fig. 1 a histogram of the observed session lengths during our initial study is shown. The y axis is of logarithmic scale as the session length follows a long tail distribution. Only a small fraction (0.8%) of discovered nodes were online for the complete observation time of 5 days. This is comparable to other previous studies of churn in the Bitcoin network that found the always online nodes to be 2.4% in 2018 at the height of Bitcoin popularity [9]. The median of sessions lengths has stayed the same even through the hype cycle of Bitcoin at one hour.

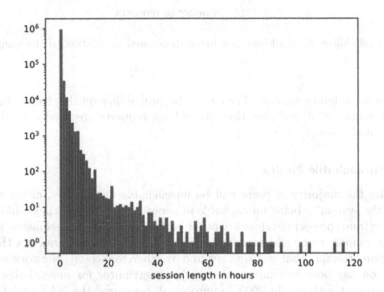

Fig. 1. Histogram of observed session length

2.2 Random Address Responses

For some networks, especially in privacy aware cryptocurrency networks such as Bitcoin, crawling participants in the network is not straight forward in order to minimise the attack surface. The responses to address requests are random and only a portion of the known peers of a contacted peer are returned to avoid revealing information to "network spies" (topology inference, eclipse attacks,

...). This also means repeated crawling is required to increase the likelihood of a more complete view of the network. The reference implementation of Bitcoin[1] randomly chooses 2500 addresses to return for address requests. As the maximum number of peers in the peer database of a client is 20480 we calculate the probability of not receiving a certain address in x requests as $1 - (1/\frac{20480}{2500})^x$. The relation between number of requests and probability of not receiving a certain address is shown in Fig. 2.

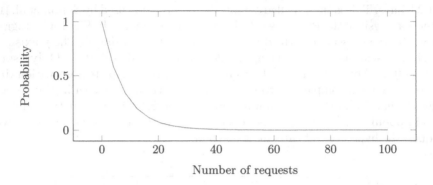

Fig. 2. Probability of an address not being discovered in relation to the number of requests

After a moderate amount of requests the probability quickly trends towards zero, Biryukov et al. estimate that 80 address requests are needed to reliably learn all addresses [1].

2.3 Unreachable Nodes

Generally the majority of peers will be unreachable by crawlers, either due to exiting the system or being unreachable in general. Nonetheless they will be discoverable from the peer databases of other participants. As a consequence, during crawling rounds, these addresses waste resources of potential crawlers through connection attempts that will timeout and are therefore costly. Network address translation has been recognised as a major contributor for unreachable peers in peer-to-peer settings. In 2009 Acunto et al. measured the NAT and firewall characteristics in peer-to-peer systems [6] and concluded that 90% of peers are behind a NAT or firewall with the trend of NATted peers increasing in future years. We confirm this by calculating the fraction of never-online peers in our preliminary Bitcoin study at 94%. Another contributing factor to unreachable nodes is the previously discussed churn. In most peer-to-peer networks, there are no explicit exits from the network, peers simply disconnect from their respective neighbours; this change, however, is not widely propagated. This leads to addresses of such nodes often lingering in the network for a considerable time.

---

[1] github.com/bitcoin.

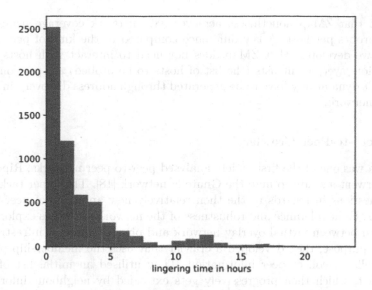

Fig. 3. Histogram of observed lingering time of offline nodes

Figure 3 shows the observed lingering time in the Bitcoin network. It is calculated by observing how long addresses are still included in address request responses after we have found them to be offline. The median lingering time is 1.43 h while the average is considerably longer at 3.7 h while some outliers were lingering for multiple days and as long as our preliminary study ran.

3   Related Work

Since the first large wave of peer-to-peer applications, the exploration of the associated network has been of interest to researchers. In the following, we will hence discuss both efforts from the general peer-to-peer context, often with the use-case of file-sharing, and more recent efforts looking at cryptocurrency networks. However there has also been an interest in network scanners from a more general purpose perspective which some aspects can be applied to peer-to-peer and cryptocurrency crawling.

3.1   Internet-Wide Scanning

Especially for security applications, internet-wide scanning and surveying of open ports has been utilised. The two most prominent examples of such tools are ZMap [5] and NMap [12]. While NMap is a more general purpose tool, ZMap focuses on single-packet probes which drastically increases the scan rate and design decisions such as the lack of state per-connection reduces the required resources for a large scale network scan. An interesting difference between NMap and ZMap design is the choice of no retransmission by ZMap, Durumic et al.

estimate that ZMap nonetheless achieves 98% network coverage using single packet probes per host. A key difference compared to the kind of peer-to-peer crawler we develop is that ZMap does not need to interact with hosts on the application layer, as hit lists (the list of hosts to be probed) are pre-configured and don't dynamically have to be generated through address discovery in a peer-to-peer network.

3.2 Peer-to-Peer Crawler

Gnutella was one of the first widely analysed peer-to-peer networks. Ripeanu et al. underwent a study to map the Gnutella network [18]. The paper tackles two main questions in regards to the then relatively new approach of peer-to-peer networks. Fault tolerance and robustness of the network as well as exploring the mismatch between virtual overlay network and physical internet infrastructure. For this purpose, they developed a crawler that uses the membership protocol of Gnutella to collect peer information. They utilised an initial list of nodes to contact, which then progressively gets extended by neighbour information of newly contacted peers. In order to speed up the crawling process, Ripeanu et al. used a manager/worker architecture where the server was responsible for assigning IPs to clients to contact.

In a very similar fashion, Stutzbach et al. [20] developed *cruiser* which they aimed to be an improved network crawler in order to capture more accurate snapshots of the Gnutella Network. They saw five key areas where this performance increase could be achieved. Inherent to the Gnutella protocol were two areas: handshaking and the two-tier structure of the Gnutella network. Just as Ripeanu before them, they also deployed *cruiser* as a distributed system with manager/worker architecture. Finally, they recognised that appropriate timeouts were essential for a performant crawler as non-responsive peers were a significant percentage (30%–38%) of overall contacts in the Gnutella network.

In addition to the already described approaches, Deschenes et al. [3] also had a running listener in their crawler, which was open to connections. During the membership protocol, the crawler would announce the IP/port of the listener and potentially solicit new connections from unknown peers.

Crawling in the above-described way is not limited to file-sharing networks like Gnutella or eDonkey [22] but has also been employed in VoIP programs such as Skype [7] or IPTV systems [8].

While the previously described crawlers all used a crawling strategy of only going through a queue of available peers, Saroiu et al. [19] followed a different strategy. Rather than crawling through the complete list of available peers, they limited the crawl time per snapshot to two minutes and then restarted the crawling process with the updated list of available peers. This, however, means that they only gather 25%–50% of the total population of peers in the system.

3.3   Bitcoin Crawler

In more recent times the most prominent peer-to-peer network that has been analysed with the use of crawlers has been Bitcoin. The measurement studies had different focuses, from the basic makeup of the network [4,16] to analysis of information propagation [2,10] and inference of topology [14,17] while others focused on deanonymisation of participants [1,11].

Similar to previous peer-to-peer crawlers, these crawlers utilised progressive crawling through available peers. For this purpose, either existing Bitcoin clients were extended for logging capabilities or dedicated crawler software was developed [11,13]. However, to our knowledge, most utilise a single instance approach rather than a distributed manager/worker architecture, and like most previous efforts they stick to a simple crawling strategy contacting all available nodes in each snapshot run.

Some monitors are publicly available such as the KIT DSN Bitcoin monitor[2] and Bitcoinstats.com, yet to our knowledge of the popular currently running monitors only Bitnodes publishes their code[3].

4   Design Considerations

4.1   Architecture

The Bitcoin crawler developed for this project was written as a multi-processing Python3 application. It utilises non-blocking, asynchronous I/O in order to maximise the number of concurrent connection attempts. In order to further increase crawling capacity for a single snapshot, we chose to implement a manager/worker architecture as pictured in Fig. 4. The crawler system, therefore, consists of a central coordinator instance and a variable number of crawling instances. The initial resolution of seed nodes, which are the entry point into the peer-to-peer network, is done at each individual crawling instance, in order to reduce geographic bias in domain resolution. However, all results of address requests are sent to the central coordinator, which then, in turn, gives out new tasks for the crawlers, so a single snapshot is created. Each crawling instance has a local cache of already discovered nodes. The cache minimises network traffic as these nodes do not have to be communicated to the coordinator again. Without the use of such a cache, the central coordinator would quickly become a bottleneck as after the initial discovery in the network. Only new nodes or nodes which had a change in status (online/offline) are sent to the coordinator. The workers themselves are made up of two different subsystems - the active participant in the neighbour discovery protocol and the passive listener. The active connector makes address requests to other peers while at the same time announcing the IP/port of the passive listener. Through this, the addresses of our crawlers are propagated throughout the network. These announcements can lead to unsolicited connection attempts by potentially previously unknown, especially new, peers in the network.

---

[2] dsn.tm.kit.edu/bitcoin.
[3] github.com/ayeowch/bitnodes.

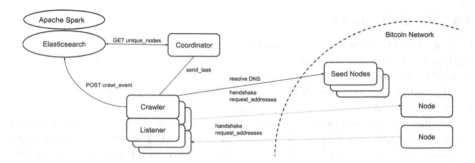

Fig. 4. Architecture overview

4.2   Bogon Filtering

A first approach to improve the hit rate of our crawler is to employ Bogon filtering. The filtering of private or reserved subnets as well as IP space that has not been assigned to an ISP yet is a common practice for firewalls. These are all addresses that should not be reachable on the internet. We utilise bogon IP lists provided by Team Cymru[4]. In regular operation, these should rarely be propagated by Bitcoin peers. However there can be scenarios where they are nonetheless propagated, which we will explain in the following. The Bitcoin reference implementation categorises peers in two categories, *good* and *terrible*. When an address request is received, a random selection of addresses is selected for the answer, but *terrible* nodes are not included. Four different checks characterise these *terrible* nodes: a timestamp more than 10 min in the future, not seen in 30 days, never responded after three attempts or seven separate failures during a week. Even after these checks, there can be instances where unreachable node addresses (i.e. Bogons) get propagated, such as very new addresses (addresses known less than a minute are exempt from the *terrible* rating) or a node might be reachable in a private network and therefore not receive a *terrible* rating yet be unreachable for our crawler from the internet.

4.3   Status Checking

Although there might be some Bogons in the Bitcoin network peer databases, it is much more likely that we encounter valid but unreachable IPs. Network address translation often used for consumer internet connections, firewalls or peers that simply left the network and do not run the peer-to-peer application in question anymore, are typical examples. However, these peers might be only temporarily unreachable, which is why we will have to periodically check their status in subsequent snapshots in order to keep an accurate picture of the network. In our experiments, of the reachable peers most were reachable during our first connection attempt. However, a third of peers that we found to be online at some

---

[4] team-cymru.org.

point during crawling only came online after we started our crawl. Interestingly the number of IPs that re-entered the network after an offline time was relatively low with 3%. We suspect that most residential setups which are more likely to enter and exit the network regularly are already not reachable due to NATs. In Fig. 5 the offline time of peers that either re-entered or came online during our crawl can be observed.

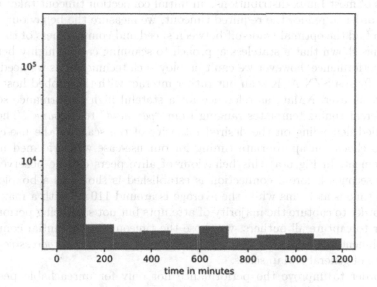

Fig. 5. Histogram of time until successful connection establishment

In order to further improve the performance of our crawler, we will use a kind of "back-off" on our status checks. This is modeled after the observed "dark" times of peers in our measurement. For this purpose, the central coordinator keeps track of the offline time for each participant. The longer a peer has been offline, the less likely it is that it will come back and be reachable. Therefore the coordinator will also be less likely to assign an IP to a crawler if said IP has been offline for a longer time, minimising likely unsuccessful connection attempts. This is implemented by comparing the duration since the *last_checked* date with the *offline_time* at the last check in combination with a backoff factor. In effect it is an implementation of exponential backoff, multiplicatively decreasing the rate at which a node is retried. However we added an upper limit on the decrease so that crawlers hit nodes at least once a day.

4.4   Optimal Timeout

As mentioned before there is a large portion of the network that will never be reachable for our crawlers. This includes already departed peers as well as peers that are unreachable behind a NAT or similar middleboxes. In these cases, the typical behaviour would be to wait for the *tcp_syn_retries* of the kernel to timeout and detect a failed connection establishment attempt. With the default settings of most Linux distributions, an initial connection timeout takes around 45 s. In order to reduce the required timeout, we measure the behaviour of alive peers to find the optimal trade-off between speed and completeness of the crawl. ZMap has shown that a stateless approach to scanning can be highly beneficial to the performance, however we can't employ such techniques as we need to not only perform a SYN-ACK scan but rather interact with the probed host on the application layer. NMap, as reference for a stateful high performance scanner, has different timing templates ranging from *"paranoid"* to *"insane"*. These can be applied depending on the desired intensity of the scan for the use-case. In order to choose an appropriate timing for our use-case we performed network measurement. In Fig. 6(a) this behaviour of alive peers can be observed. The time in seconds before a connection is established is shown as a boxplot. The median time is at 73 ms while the average is around 110 ms with a max of 380 ms. In order to capture the majority of attempts but not sacrificing performance in order to capture all outliers, we chose the timeout for the initial connection establishment as trade-off at 500 ms. This corresponds to the *aggressive* timing template of general NMap scans.

In order to improve the performance not only for unreachable peers but reachable peers as well, in addition to the *tcp_syn_retries*, we consider the TCP connection timeout of already established connections. If there is "silence on the wire", it could take a standard Linux host around 2 h to terminate the connection unless otherwise instructed. Finding a fitting timeout, therefore, is quite beneficial. In contrast to the *tcp_syn_retries* timeout, our idle timeout is considerably longer as it is not dominated by latency but rather the processing/queue at the client of the opposite peer. In Fig. 6(b)/(c) our measured duration of request responses can be seen. In (b) only the minimum measurements of each node are considered while (c) is a representation of all measurements. It shows that as a minimum half of all measurements are below 1.51 s while the upper half of measurements goes up to 13 s. When considering all measurements, however, we observe a considerably higher spread of delays. As these are only outliers and subsequent or previous requests were answered more quickly, we opt to choose the timeout according to the minimum latencies per node not overall. Hence the connection timeout for ongoing connections is set to 13 s.

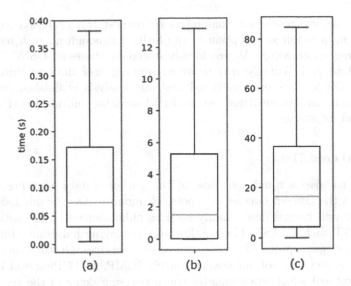

Fig. 6. (a) Time until successful TCP connection establishment (b) Minimum time per node until successful address request response (c) Distribution of all measurements for address request-response

NMap by default attempts to retransmit failed probes 10 times, however as Durumeric et al. have shown, even without retranmission of probes a large coverage of 98% can be achieved. As we will perform continuous crawling rounds we opted to not retransmit probes but rather reattempt the probe later according to the strategy described in the previous subsection.

5   Data Gathering

For the evaluation of the crawler improvements We collected data for 24 h on October 4th 2020. For this, we deployed the central coordinator in Berlin. The crawlers were geographically distributed using a mix of public cloud resources in Ireland, Ohio and Hong Kong as well as resources in Berlin. These regions (EU/NA/Asia) cover the vast majority of participants in the Bitcoin network. The crawlers were connected through IPv4 as well as IPv6 with roughly 250 address requests per second. During this time we connected to 251846 unique addresses of which 6643 were reachable.

5.1   Crawling Etiquette

As we are conducting active network measurements as opposed to less intrusive passive measurements, we have to consider some ethical questions. In order for participants in the network to be able to opt-out of being crawled we include a unique user-agent in our handshakes which includes information on how to contact us. If we receive any complaints or requests for exclusion we add the addresses in question as exception to the hitlist (although no such request was made during our crawling). We use locally stored databases for OSINT (provided by MaxMind and TeamCymru) to avoid sending user data to third parties. After the OSINT has been gathered and our analysis is finished, we replace the IP which can be considered personally identifiable information (PII) with a pseudonym for storage.

5.2   Gathered Data

We will first give a rough overview of the gathered data, showing the functionality of the Bitcoin crawler as a network monitor. On the one hand we are replicating well known functionality such as enhancement of the gathered IPs with OSINT such as ASN, Geolocation and displaying handshake information such as user agent, protocol version and offered services. On the other hand we also offer latency data of our connection via ICMP, as TCPing and inside the Bitcoin protocol which approximates the processing delay of the remote peer. The difference between those latencies is shown in Fig. 7. Especially this extensive latency data which can be extended to include any port desired for a study can be used for interesting insights into to the composition of the network. As we have demonstrated with latency based proxy detection, as well as selective port scanning for proxy detection [15].

6   Evaluation

6.1   Increased Scan Rate

In order to compare the performance of our crawler and specifically the impact of our chosen timeout, we took a popular Bitcoin crawler that is open source as baseline[5]. Bitnodes chooses a single timeout for both the establishment as well as the idle connection, which by default is 30 s, compared with our 1s initial and 13s idle connection timeout. In Table 1 we show in which phase of the connection during our experiment run, connections actually timeout.

It can be observed that the vast majority of peers already fail during the initial TCP connection establishment. This means our improved timeout during this phase gives us a significant performance improvement. Due to the high number of peers behind NATs and firewalls unreachable to our crawler as well as the significant churn in the network, the vast majority (96.2%) of discovered nodes are never reachable and hence timeout. For this majority, our crawler overall (combining all phases and their probability) has an average 1.52 s timeout (94.93% lower compared to Bitnodes). Using the same resources (number of co-routines) this leads to a 94.7% faster scan rate.

---

[5] bitnodes.io.

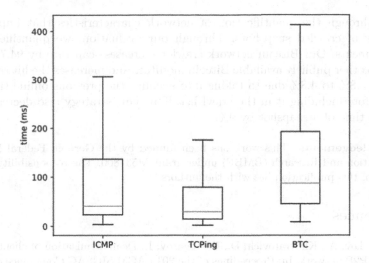

Fig. 7. Latency of reachable nodes measured via ICMP, SYN-ACK and Bitcoin TCP connection

Table 1. Phase of timeout in connection

Phase	Percentage
TCP connection establishment	95.6%
BTC handshake	2.4%
BTC address request	1.7%

6.2   Increased Hit Rate

One of our tactics to increase crawling speed is to not only have lower timeouts but avoid predictable timeouts altogether. The propagation of Bogons in the Bitcoin network seems to be minimal as during a 24 h crawl only 18 Bogons, mainly from private subnets, have been discovered. The increase in hit rate from Bogon filtering is, therefore, negligible. To evaluate the overall effectiveness of our measures, we compare the hit rate as well as discovered new peers of the typical consecutive snapshot strategy with our strategy that takes into account previous offline time. For this purpose, we ran our crawlers with and without the "back-off" strategy for at least 10 consecutive snapshots. The evaluation showed that the back-off strategy indeed increased the hit rate from 3.8% to 4.8% while the amount of discovered new peers stayed consistent with previous efforts. The crawl speed increase due to our back-off strategy was on average 9%.

7   Conclusion

We developed a new Bitcoin crawler that decreases blocking time through optimised timeouts as well as increased hit rate during consecutive network snapshots. The need for optimisation of crawling speed and resource usage has been shown through the quantification of network characteristics that impact the accuracy of crawled snapshots. Through our evaluation, we quantified these improvements. Our Bitcoin network crawler increases scan rate by 94.7% compared to other publicly available Bitcoin monitors and increases the hit rate from roughly 3.8% to 4.8% due to taking into account the previous offline time of a node before including it in the crawl list. This new strategy also decreases the creation time of a snapshot by 9%.

Acknowledgements. This work has been funded by the German Federal Ministry of Education and Research (BMBF) under grant M534800. The responsibility for the content of this publication lies with the authors.

References

1. Biryukov, A., Khovratovich, D., Pustogarov, I.: Deanonymisation of clients in bitcoin P2P network. In: Proceedings of the 2014 ACM SIGSAC Conference on Computer and Communications Security, pp. 15–29 (2014)
2. Decker, C., Wattenhofer, R.: Information propagation in the bitcoin network. In: IEEE P2P 2013 Proceedings, pp. 1–10. IEEE (2013)
3. Deschenes, D.G., Weber, S.D., Davison, B.D.: Crawling gnutella: Lessons learned. Technical report (2004)
4. Donet Donet, J.A., Pérez-Solà, C., Herrera-Joancomartí, J.: The bitcoin P2P network. In: Böhme, R., Brenner, M., Moore, T., Smith, M. (eds.) FC 2014. LNCS, vol. 8438, pp. 87–102. Springer, Heidelberg (2014). https://doi.org/10.1007/978-3-662-44774-1_7
5. Durumeric, Z., Wustrow, E., Halderman, J.A.: ZMap: fast internet-wide scanning and its security applications. In: 22nd {USENIX} Security Symposium ({USENIX} Security 13), pp. 605–620 (2013)
6. D'Acunto, L., Pouwelse, J., Sips, H.: A measurement of nat and firewall characteristics in peer-to-peer systems. In: Proceedings of the 15th ASCI Conference, vol. 5031, pp. 1–5. Citeseer (2009)
7. Guha, S., Daswani, N.: An experimental study of the skype peer-to-peer VoIP system. Cornell University, Technical report (2005)
8. Hei, X., Liang, C., Liang, J., Liu, Y., Ross, K.W.: A measurement study of a large-scale P2P IPTV system. IEEE Trans. Multimedia **9**(8), 1672–1687 (2007)
9. Imtiaz, M.A., Starobinski, D., Trachtenberg, A., Younis, N.: Churn in the bitcoin network: characterization and impact. In: 2019 IEEE International Conference on Blockchain and Cryptocurrency (ICBC), pp. 431–439. IEEE (2019)
10. Kanda, R., Shudo, K.: Estimation of data propagation time on the bitcoin network. In: Proceedings of the Asian Internet Engineering Conference, pp. 47–52 (2019)
11. Koshy, P., Koshy, D., McDaniel, P.: An analysis of anonymity in bitcoin using P2P network traffic. In: Christin, N., Safavi-Naini, R. (eds.) FC 2014. LNCS, vol. 8437, pp. 469–485. Springer, Heidelberg (2014). https://doi.org/10.1007/978-3-662-45472-5_30
12. Lyon, G.F.: Nmap network scanning: The official Nmap project guide to network discovery and security scanning. Insecure (2009)
13. Maesa, D.D.F., Franceschi, M., Guidi, B., Ricci, L.: BITKER: a P2P kernel client for bitcoin. In: 2018 International Conference on High Performance Computing and Simulation (HPCS), pp. 130–137. IEEE (2018)

14. Miller, A., et al.: Discovering bitcoin's public topology and influential nodes (2015)
15. Mühle, A., Grüner, A., Meinel, C.: Characterising proxy usage in the bitcoin peer-to-peer network. In: International Conference on Distributed Computing and Networking 2021, pp. 176–185 (2021)
16. Neudecker, T.: Characterization of the bitcoin peer-to-peer network (2015–2018). Karlsruhe, Technical report, p. 1 (2019)
17. Neudecker, T., Andelfinger, P., Hartenstein, H.: Timing analysis for inferring the topology of the bitcoin peer-to-peer network. In: 2016 Internationl IEEE Conferences on Ubiquitous Intelligence and Computing, Advanced and Trusted Computing, Scalable Computing and Communications, Cloud and Big Data Computing, Internet of People, and Smart World Congress (UIC/ATC/ScalCom/CBDCom/IoP/SmartWorld), pp. 358–367. IEEE (2016)
18. Ripeanu, M., Foster, I., Iamnitchi, A.: Mapping the Gnutella network: Properties of large-scale peer-to-peer systems and implications for system design. arXiv preprint cs/0209028 (2002)
19. Saroiu, S., Gummadi, K.P., Gribble, S.D.: Measuring and analyzing the characteristics of Napster and Gnutella hosts. Multimedia Syst. 9(2), 170–184 (2003)
20. Stutzbach, D., Rejaie, R.: Capturing accurate snapshots of the Gnutella network. In: Proceedings IEEE INFOCOM 2006, 25TH IEEE International Conference on Computer Communications, pp. 1–6. IEEE (2006)
21. Stutzbach, D., Rejaie, R.: Understanding churn in peer-to-peer networks. In: Proceedings of the 6th ACM SIGCOMM Conference on Internet measurement, pp. 189–202 (2006)
22. Yang, J., Ma, H., Song, W., Cui, J., Zhou, C.: Crawling the Edonkey network. In: 2006 Fifth International Conference On grid and Cooperative Computing Workshops, pp. 133–136. IEEE (2006)

Parcae: A Blockchain-Based PRF Service for Everyone

Elizabeth Wyss$^{(\boxtimes)}$ and Drew Davidson

University of Kansas, Lawrence, USA
{elizabethwyss,drewdavidson}@ku.edu

Abstract. Pseudorandom function (PRF) services are utilized to cryptographically harden password hashes against offline brute-force attacks. State-of-the-art implementations of PRF services can additionally offer benefits such as detection of online attacks and practical key rotation, but the cost of doing so in a publicly distributed setting is requiring clients to trust a third party service. These third party services are not incentivized to behave honestly and pose as a single point of failure for Denial of Service (DoS) attacks. A successful DoS attack mounted against a deployed PRF service would prevent its clients from authenticating their users' passwords, thus making it impossible for users to log in to those clients' services.

To address these issues, we design and implement Parcae, the first blockchain-based publicly distributed PRF service. Parcae offers all of the additional benefits provided by state-of-the-art PRF services while also providing DoS attack resilience and service auditing capabilities through use of a permissioned blockchain. Performance analysis shows that our implementation of Parcae is practical and can scale to meet the needs of a dynamically growing client base in a publicly distributed setting.

Keywords: Blockchain · Smart contract · Password · PRF

1 Introduction

The breach of industry password databases continues to be a severe and costly issue. In a data breach investigations report conducted by Verizon in 2019, it was found that out of 1,285 examined data breaches from that year, 35% involved the breach of user credentials–including passwords stored in various formats [11]. Industry standard practices in password management involve storing passwords in a hashed and salted format, but compromised passwords of this form are still vulnerable to offline brute-force attacks. A single modern GPU can calculate over seven billion sha-256 hashes per second [1], and at this rate a typical password hash (derived from a password of length eight containing uppercase letters, lowercase letters, digits, and special characters) can be determined by brute-force in a matter of days. An attacker can parallelize this attack across hundreds or even thousands of GPUs and reduce the time needed to brute-force a password hash to a matter of minutes.

© ICST Institute for Computer Sciences, Social Informatics and Telecommunications Engineering 2022
Published by Springer Nature Switzerland AG 2022. All Rights Reserved
P. Gladyshev et al. (Eds.): ICDF2C 2021, LNICST 441, pp. 328–341, 2022.
https://doi.org/10.1007/978-3-031-06365-7_20

Application of pseudorandom function (PRF) services to passwords is an effective form of password hardening that offers protection against offline brute-force attacks even in case of password database compromisation. Clients using a PRF service send password hashes to a remote server where they are further encrypted under a private key known only to that server. The PRF service then replies with the encrypted password hash that is used by the client for password verification. Because these password hashes are encrypted with a remote key, passwords cannot be guessed in an offline brute force attack unless the remote key is known by the attacker. Companies such as Facebook [9] have internally used privately distributed PRF services to harden their users' password hashes against offline brute force attacks.

Deploying a publicly distributed PRF service would offer these security benefits to any and every password-authenticating client. However, state-of-the-art PRF services pose issues of trust and availability in a publicly distributed setting; clients using such a service must expand their root of trust to contain the PRF service even though it is a third party that is not incentivized to behave robustly and truthfully. The PRF service is incentivized to reduce computational costs by using weak cryptographic algorithms or by behaving dishonestly altogether. Additionally, a publicly distributed PRF service is a single point of failure which must remain constantly functional and online, or clients would lose the ability to perform user authentication. If a PRF service were to experience downtime, all of its clients would be unable to perform user logins for the entire duration of the downtime. Due to this single point of failure, any publicly distributed PRF service would be vulnerable to denial of service (DoS) attacks, and a successfully mounted attack would be costly for all clients using the service.

Our key insight is that **the weaknesses of state-of-the-art publicly distributed PRF services can be addressed through the use of a permissioned blockchain**. This approach poses significant challenges in that PRF services need to protect information to remain secure, and yet blockchains need to expose information to remain verifiable. We find that the inherent privacy conflict between PRF services and blockchains can be overcome through clever applications of cryptography within a permission-delegated blockchain. We demonstrate the effectiveness of this approach through a prototype implementation called Parcae, the first publicly distributed PRF service residing on a blockchain smart contract.

Parcae utilizes partially oblivious PRFs (PO-PRFs) [4] to achieve the security guarantees of existing state-of-the-art PRF services and further solves the root of trust and availability issues of a publicly distributed setting. To ensure faithful execution of the Parcae protocol, clients using Parcae may opt to operate a blockchain auditing peer which allows clients to ensure that Parcae's blockchain peers adhere to the PRF service smart contract honestly, all without the need to expose any private information. To address DoS attack vulnerability, Parcae's blockchain peers operate as separate queryable entities that are automatically scaled up in quantity to be as many as is necessary to meet the PRF service needs of all of Parcae's clients.

We show that Parcae achieves both trustworthiness and continual availability by design and through experimental evaluation. A single blockchain peer is able to process up to 498 Parcae PRF queries per second with an average end-to-end latency of 40 ms per query. This latency is far less than the latency of historical password hardening approaches such as iterated hashing and memory-hard functions. For example, a 2016 iterated hashing scheme deployed by Apple's iTunes user verification process [6] incurs more than six times the latency of a single Parcae query. As more and more clients query Parcae, additional blockchain nodes are dynamically deployed to meet the throughput needs of all of Parcae's clients.

Contributions. In summary, we make the following contributions:

- We design Parcae, the first blockchain-based publicly distributed PRF service protocol enabling any client to harden password hashes against both offline and online brute-force attacks. Parcae further improves on past designs of PRF service protocols by providing innate auditing capabilities and DoS attack resilience.
- We present a prototype implementation of Parcae which utilizes PO-PRFs deployed on a blockchain smart contract to realize our design goals.
- We conduct an evaluation of Parcae both in terms of performance metrics and security guarantees to justify the effectiveness of Parcae.

2   Related Work

PRF services and password hardening schemes have been approached using a wide variety of cryptographic protocols and deployment scenarios [2,4,7,8,10]. Despite this, past implementations fail to sufficiently defend against the adversaries of a publicly distributed setting.

Pythia [4] introduced the notion of a PO-PRF as a cryptographic primitive and designed several PRF service implementations to be used in different deployment scenarios. Most relevant to our work is Pythia's use of PO-PRFs in a publicly distributed PRF service protocol. Under Pythia's PO-PRF protocol, clients request hardened password hashes from the Pythia PRF service by sending a blinded password hash and an unblinded salt value to a Pythia server. By blinding password hashes, the server learns nothing about users' passwords. With unblinded salt values–assumed to be unique to each user–the server can perform rate limiting on a per-user basis to detect and prevent online brute-force attacks on a user's password. Additionally, Pythia clients can request secret key rotations to cryptographically invalidate old hardened password hashes in case of a password database breach. Pythia also introduced zero-knowledge proof verifiability in PO-PRFs, enabling clients to request a proof that a hardened password hash is computed correctly with respect to a public key known by the client. Furthermore, Pythia's PO-PRF protocol is shown to be provably secure in an honest environment. All of these features combined synthesizes past works on PRFs into a standard baseline for future PRF services.

Schneider et al. designed another cryptographic primitive dubbed a partially oblivious commitment (PO-COM) [10] and showed that it achieves the same functional properties as a PO-PRF under a simpler security model. Using PO-COMs, Schneider et al. demonstrated the construction of a password hardening service that achieves the same features as Pythia while also nearly halving the latency required to harden a single password. Under security definitions weaker than those used by Pythia, they also show that honest-adherence to their system's protocol is provably secure.

Phoenix [8] extends upon on the work of Schneider et al. [10] to show that the security definitions used to prove the security of PO-COMs are too weak, leaving room for effective offline guessing attacks against Schneider et al.'s system. To address these issues, Phoenix is introduced as a password hardening service that achieves improved security and efficiency over Schneider et al.'s system while still maintaining all of the features of Pythia. Phoenix achieves slightly improved password hardening latency and nearly 50% better throughput compared to Schneider et al.'s system. Phoenix is also shown to be a provably secure protocol under strong security definitions when executed faithfully.

Lai et al. later revisit Phoenix [8] to design Password-Hardened Encryption Services (PHE) [7], an even more efficient password hardening system that also supports hardening additional user data. They achieve both stronger security guarantees and about 40% better throughput compared to Phoenix. Their improved system is further demonstrated to be provably secure when honestly executed.

Brost et al. design a threshold variant [2] of PHE [7] which seeks to mitigate the single point of failure in password hardening systems. Threshold PHE is a generalization of PHE in which clients can construct a hardened password by combining the outputs of multiple distinct password hardening services. Since the quantity of deployed password hardening services can exceed threshold of distinct services needed to construct a hardened password, clients can still construct hardened passwords even when some password hardening services are not available. With regards to performance, Brost et al.'s system is slower than PHE in terms of throughput and latency within a factor of three. Additionally, Threshold PHE is shown to be provably secure when honestly executed. Despite the increased availability of Threshold PHE, a publicly distributed version of the system would still require clients to expand their root of trust to contain many external third-party password hardening services that are not incentivized to behave honestly.

While past implementations of PRF services and password hardening schemes have been able to achieve high efficiency and numerous security relevant features, none achieve the service auditing capabilities and full DoS attack resilience required to be an effective solution in a publicly distributed setting.

3   Overview

In this section, we show how the design of Parcae overcomes the limitations of past approaches to fully realize a secure publicly distributed PRF service. We first identify the key threats to PRF services in a publicly distributed setting, then describe the system architecture of Parcae, and lastly show how Parcae is used to defeat those threats.

We identify two primary PRF service adversaries unique to the publicly distributed setting: a *disruption adversary* seeking to deny legitimate access to the PRF, and an *impersonation adversary*, seeking to falsify PRF queries, thus invalidating the user authentication process. We assume adversaries have significant resources, including the ability to issue more PRF queries than the entire throughput of any statically-sized PRF service, spoof DNS, and stand up multiple masquerading PRF servers. Although we discuss these adversaries separately, we note that our model considers an adversary with goals of disrupting and impersonating a PRF simultaneously.

High Level Design of Parcae. Parcae is a PRF service constructed using PO-PRFs [4] implemented on a blockchain smart contract. In the Parcae blockchain, two distinct types of peers are defined: cryptographic peers that are centrally operated by Parcae and auditing peers that are decentrally operated by clients. Cryptographic peers handle all incoming transactions and queries, storing cryptographically sensitive information in a private data store accessible only to them. They are only permitted to handle queries and transactions as specified in the Parcae smart contract, and any deviation from the Parcae smart contract is detected and disallowed by the blockchain. Auditing peers receive hashed versions of the read and write sets of every approved transaction handled by the cryptographic peers. This allows auditing peers to verify that transactions sent to the Parcae blockchain are handled in an honest and timely matter. Additionally, if any changes are made to the Parcae smart contract, the blockchain ensures that auditing peers are notified of the changes. In case of an adversary compromising the entire Parcae blockchain, this prevents them from altering the Parcae protocol without first notifying all auditing peers of their alterations.

In Parcae, clients issue API requests that are received by intermediate servers. These intermediate servers house the cryptographic certificates necessary to issue transactions and queries to the Parcae's cryptographic peers. Upon receiving a client's request, an intermediate server will translate the request into a Parcae smart contract transaction or query, issue the smart contract invocation to the Parcae cryptographic peers, and then return its result to the requesting client. Like the Parcae cryptographic peers, intermediate servers support multiple clients using them simultaneously and are dynamically scaled up in size and quantity to meet the needs of all of Parcae's clients.

Using Parcae. When a new client wants to begin hardening passwords using the Parcae PRF service, they simply install a Parcae API library and they can start issuing requests. Figure 1 displays the basic API details of each request available to clients. Before a client can query Parcae for hardened password hashes, they must first register with the Parcae PRF service. The Parcae registration process requires a new client to provide and verify an email address, and upon successful verification the client receives their unique Parcae identity string–used to identify

Command	Description
Register()	Registers a new client with Parcae and returns the client's unique id and public key
Query(id, pass, salt)	Returns Parcae PRF query result
GenAuth(id)	Sends a key rotation authorization token to client out of band
GenUpdate(id, authtoken)	Rotates the client's Parcae secret key and returns an update token
Apply(hash, updatetoken)	Applies update token to hash and returns the newly encrypted hash
Audit()	Registers a new auditing peer and sends the requesting client its required cryptographic certificates

Fig. 1. The Parcae API

them to Parcae–and public key–used to verify query proofs generated by Parcae. Once a new client has successfully registered with Parcae, they can begin to invoke query requests and obtain hardened password hashes from Parcae. If a new client has any existing password hash databases that they want to harden with Parcae, they can query the Parcae PRF service with each password hash in their databases to construct one or more hardened password hash databases. After hardening any existing password hash databases, a client updates their user registration and password verification process by adding one additional function call to perform a Parcae query. Now, the client's password hashes are protected by Parcae from both offline and online brute-force attacks. If a client ever detects that a password hash database breach has occured, they can request a key rotation to cryptographically invalidate all previously stored hardened password hashes. To do this, the client first requests a single-use authorization token that is sent to their verified Parcae email address. The client then sends the authorization token in a key rotation request, and Parcae internally replaces the client's secret encryption key with a new one. After a client rotates their Parcae secret key, they receive both a new Parcae public key and an update token that they can use to update the encryption of existing hardened password hashes to be encrypted under their new Parcae secret key. Parcae implements an entirely offline function that clients can use to apply update tokens to old hardened password hashes. Once a client performs a Parcae key rotation, all breached password hashes become cryptographically invalidated since they are encrypted under a secret key that no longer exists anywhere in Parcae.

If a client requests to operate a service auditing peer, Parcae will register a new auditing peer and send its required cryptographic certificates to the client. These certificates are necessary to validate the auditing peer's role and permissions with respect to Parcae's blockchain. After obtaining the certificates, the client simply installs blockchain operation software and executes a single containerized script to bring up their auditing peer which monitors the Parcae service automatically. While auditing Parcae, clients' auditing peers receive all data blocks distributed on the Parcae blockchain, with private data–such as identity strings and keys–stored in a hashed format. This allows an auditing client to verify their own private data by comparing hashes and furthermore ensures that any change to the Parcae blockchain–such as if the Parcae protocol is altered–is disclosed to all auditors.

4   Parcae Protocol

In this section we give the formal mathematical definitions and security proofs related to the Parcae PRF protocol described in Sects. 3 and 5.

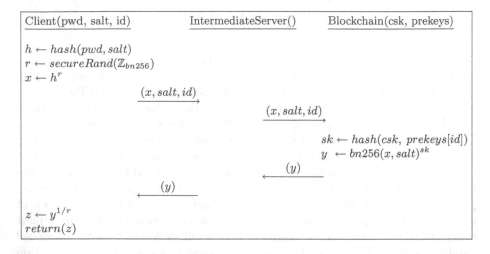

Fig. 2. The Formal Parcae PRF Protocol (Π).

Protocol Definitions. We define the Parcae PRF protocol to be $\Pi = (Client, IntermediateServer, Blockchain)$, with the following specifications: *Client* represents the client-side algorithm that takes a password, salt, and identity string as input, calculates a blinded password hash and uses the remaining algorithms to output a hardened password hash. The *IntermediateServer* algorithm simply forwards data from the *Client* algorithm to the *Blockchain* algorithm and vice versa. *Blockchain* is the algorithm which resides on the Parcae Blockchain. It takes a blinded password hash, salt, identity string, central secret key, and set of prekey values as input, and outputs a hardened blinded password hash. Figure 2 depicts Π in mathematical notation.

Protocol Correctness. Π is correct if and only if it deterministically outputs identical z given identical inputs *pwd, salt, id, csk, prekeys*. The determinicity of the output z follows directly from the determinicity of hashing algorithms, the invertibility of exponentiation, and the exponent-preserving nature of the bn256 elliptic curve bilinear pairing. Hence, the final output z does not depend on the only nondeterministic value present in the protocol, r, implying that z only depends on deterministic operations and is itself deterministic for a given set of inputs. Thus, it is proved that Π is correct.

Protocol Security. We extend upon the proof of PO-PRF security provided in [4] to prove the security of our own scheme, Π. To do this, we define a modified protocol $\Pi' = (Client,\ Blockchain)$ that is identical to the protocol Π detailed in Fig. 2, except the *Client* algorithm is modified to send its intermediate output directly to the *Blockchain* algorithm, and the *Blockchain* algorithm is modified to send its output directly back to the *Client* algorithm, thus foregoing the use of the *IntermediateServer* algorithm entirely. Observe that for a given set of inputs *pwd, salt, id, csk, prekeys*, both Π and Π' output identical z since Π' does not modify any of the functional operations of Π. Assuming that the security of the key generation algorithms used to generate inputs to Π' holds (this is a reasonable assumption because secure key generation algorithms are well-studied) and that the Parcae Blockchain in which the *Blockchain* algorithm resides on securely performs operations honestly (this is a reasonable assumption given the guarantees provided by a private and permissioned blockchain), then the Π' algorithm is functionally and securely identical to the partially oblivious algorithm proved to be secure in [4]. Hence, Π must exhibit the same proved security as Π' if the inclusion of the *IntermediateServer* algorithm does not alter the functionality and security of Π'. This is indeed the case since it was shown above that Π and Π' are functionally identical, and since the *IntermediateServer* algorithm is itself secure given that the servers in which the algorithm is hosted exhibit the same security and availability properties as the rest of the Parcae system. Thus, it is proved that the Parcae PRF protocol, Π, is secure.

5   Implementation Details

Parcae uses a private and permissioned blockchain based on Hyperledger Fabric [5]. From the guarantees of Fabric, cryptographic peers cannot deviate from the protocol defined in the Parcae smart contract. Additionally, Hyperledger Fabric is designed to parallelize transactions and dynamically enroll new peers. This allows Parcae to dynamically scale in size to meet the availability needs of all of its clients.

We opted to require clients to connect to Parcae through intermediate servers so that they do not need to possess cryptographic certificates enabling them to directly submit arbitrary transactions to the Parcae blockchain. The intermediate servers exist to simply transform requests into well-formatted blockchain transactions and queries. Because we host both the Parcae blockchain and intermediate servers on the same local area network, communication costs between the two are minimized. This use of intermediate servers in no way weakens the security model of Parcae since intermediate servers are dynamically scaled just like Parcae cryptographic peers; the intermediate servers simply provide input filtering.

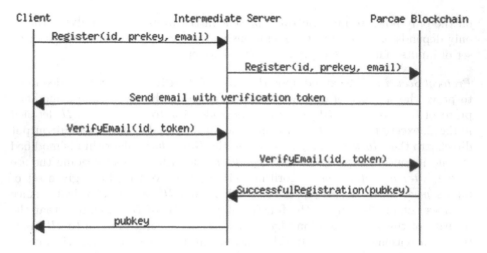

Fig. 3. Parcae client registration protocol diagram.

5.1   Low Level API Details

Parcae Registration. When a new client registers with Parcae, the client first calculates both an identity string and prekey value. Each of these values are computed as secure random integers. Next, the client sends their calculated identity string, prekey value, and an email address to one of many Parcae intermediate servers. The server initiates a blockchain transaction that both records the client's registration information and sends a one-time verification email to the client. Once the client verifies their email, Parcae replies to the client with their unique Parcae public key. Figure 3 depicts the Parcae client registration process as a protocol diagram. Upon successful registration, the client stores both their identity string and Parcae public key in a configuration file needed to identify themselves to Parcae. At this point, the client can begin to query Parcae as a PRF service. Upon successful registration, Parcae's cryptographic peers additionally write the new client's identity string, prekey value, and public key to the Parcae blockchain's private data store. This ensures that Parcae's auditing peers receive a registration block that contains hashed versions of the new client's identity string, prekey value, and public key. With these hashes, the new client can verify that the Parcae blockchain did indeed record all of their registration information correctly.

We note that during registration, Parcae does not need to store a secret key for a newly registered client. This is because Parcae calculates a client's specific secret key as needed by cryptographically combining their identity string and their prekey value with a central secret key known only to Parcae's cryptographic peers.

PRF Queries. To request a PRF query from Parcae, a successfully registered client first hashes the password that they wish to harden and blinds the hash by exponentiating it with a blinding constant–a secure random integer. The client then sends their identity string, the blinded hash, an unblinded salt value, and optionally a proof request to one of many Parcae intermediate servers. The server sends this information to Parcae's cryptographic peers, which calculate a hardened blinded hash by constructing a bilinear pairing of the client's blinded hash and salt value, exponentiated with the calculated client-specific secret key. This hardened blinded hash is then sent back to the client, alongside a verifiable zero-knowledge proof with respect to the client's Parcae public key if requested. Because bilinear pairings preserve exponentiation, the client can then unblind the PRF output by exponentiating it with the inverse of the calculated blinding constant. This use of blinding and unblinding ensures that the final output is deterministic while preventing Parcae from learning anything about passwords passed to it.

Rate Limiting Queries. Rate limiting of PRF queries is performed on a per-user basis, differentiated by the unblinded salt values passed to queries. We assume that salt values are unique to each user since use of unique per-user salts is standard security practice. To perform rate limiting, Parcae records a rate limiting table that is indexed by salt values and stores both a timestamp and count of queries made. Whenever a query is requested, if the rate limiting table shows that for the given salt value, the count of queries exceeds a defined maximum query threshold, the query will be denied and the incident will be reported to the corresponding client. Otherwise, Parcae executes the query as normal and updates the respective timestamp and query count within the rate limiting table. This table is purged on a per-hour basis so that legitimate users should not experience an authentication lockout due to rate limiting.

Generating Authorization Tokens. When a registered client requests a Parcae secret key rotation, they must first obtain an authorization token as to prevent malicious actors from arbitrarily requesting key rotations for legitimate clients. To do this, the client sends their identity string to one of many Parcae intermediate servers. The server then instructs Parcae's cryptographic peers to generate a single-use time-sensitive authorization token and email it to the client's registered email address. The client can then provide this authorization token to request a Parcae secret key rotation.

Generating Update Tokens. After obtaining an authorization token, a client can send their identity string, a freshly calculated prekey value, and their authorization token to one of many Parcae intermediate servers to request a secret key rotation. The server initiates a blockchain transaction that first verifies the client's authorization token. If successful, the cryptographic peers calculate the client's old secret key one last time before replacing their old prekey value with the freshly calculated one. The cryptographic peers then generate the client's new secret key using their new prekey value. From both secret keys, an update token is generated by multiplying the new secret key by the inverse of the old secret key. The cryptographic peers lastly determine the client's new Parcae public key relative to their new secret key, returning both the new public key and update token to the client. The client can utilize this update token to update previously stored hardened password hashes to be encrypted under their new secret key.

Applying Update Tokens. Update tokens can be applied to existing hardened password hashes entirely offline. To do this, a client simply exponentiates a hardened password hash with a Parcae provided update token. Because bilinear pairings preserve exponentiation, this simultaneously undoes the hardened password hash's exponentiation with the client's old secret key and applies an exponentiation with the client's new secret key. This updated hardened hash is now equivalent to the hardened hash obtained by querying Parcae under the client's new secret key.

Auditing Parcae. In Parcae, any actor can request to operate an auditing peer. They need not already be registered as a client since clients should be able to audit and ensure the validity of their own registration. To accomplish this, the auditor sends their request to one of many Parcae intermediate servers, and the server registers a new auditing peer with the Parcae blockchain. The server then distributes the new auditing peer's cryptographic certificates to the auditor. The auditor then installs publicly available Hyperledger Fabric peer images and joins their peer to the Parcae blockchain network. Once the auditing peer joins the network, receives blocks containing the entire Parcae blockchain ledger (with private data stored in a hashed format), and the auditing peer continuously receives all new blocks of data as they are generated. This allows the auditor to both verify the integrity of the Parcae network and validate hashes of transactions which are initiated by them.

6   Performance Evaluation

In order to analyze the performance of Parcae, we deploy both a Parcae blockchain and a set of intermediate servers on Amazon Web Services (AWS) to test the system's latency and throughput. All Parcae components are hosted in the same datacenter region of AWS. The intermediate servers are deployed on an Amazon Elastic Compute Cloud c4.large instance. The Parcae blockchain is deployed on an Amazon Managed Blockchain with a Hyperledger Fabric backend consisting of one to fifteen c5.4xlarge cryptographic peers.

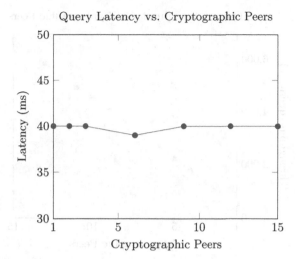

Fig. 4. Parcae query latency vs. number of cryptographic Peers

Latency. To measure the end-to-end latency of a Parcae PRF query, we time the full duration of the Parcae protocol, including client-side blinding and unblinding, checking rate-limiting, performing cryptographic operations, and making all connections between the client, intermediate server, and Parcae blockchain. We find that Parcae achieves an average individual query latency of 40 ms per query with just a single cryptographic peer. Figure 4 shows that as the quantity of cryptographic peers increases, individual query latency remains relatively constant.

Throughput. To measure the total throughput of an individual Parcae cryptographic peer, we measure the total quantity of PRF queries that a peer can process per second while receiving requests parallelized across multiple intermediate servers. From our testing, we find that a single Parcae cryptographic peer can achieve a throughput of up to 498 queries per second. To increase throughput and support more intermediate servers, Parcae dynamically scales its cryptographic peers in quantity to linearly improve the total service throughput. Figure 5 shows our measured linear relationship between the total system throughput and the quantity of cryptographic peers.

Discussion of Performance. Because Parcae strengthens the security measures of past implementations of PRF services and password hardening schemes by using an audited blockchain back-end, Parcae is inherently a slower protocol than past implementations. We find that Parcae's performance metrics are roughly within a factor of two and a half of Pythia's [4] when tested on comparable AWS instances. Despite this, we believe that the performance of Parcae is more than satisfactory to support its use as a practical publicly distributed PRF service. A user incurs only an additional 40 milliseconds between entering their credentials

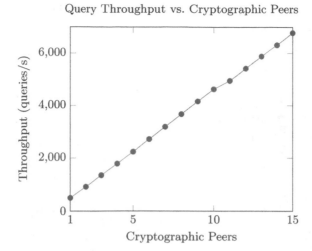

Fig. 5. Parcae total query throughput vs. number of cryptographic peers

and logging in to a client's service; this latency is typically far less than the network latency incurred by connecting to a remote client's service. Additionally, Parcae's throughput is more than reasonable with respect to scalability. With a Parcae blockchain consisting of just a single cryptographic peer that handles 498 queries per second, over 43 million Parcae queries can be processed in a single day. At this throughput, it would take a single Parcae cryptographic peer just over two days to harden the passwords of every one of the 98 million Facebook users that registered new accounts during the second quarter of 2020 [3]. With this level of throughput, it is practical to scale Parcae's cryptographic peers to meet the needs of all of Parcae's clients. For these reasons, we believe that Parcae's performance is both reasonable and practical for deployment in a publicly distributed setting.

7   Conclusions

We proposed the design and implementation of Parcae, a PRF service that fully realizes the needs of a dynamically sized client base in a publicly distributed setting. While past implementations of PRF services have focused on formalizing security definitions and improving efficiency, none have achieved the dynamic scalability and service auditing capabilities required to provide the trust and availability that is needed in a publicly distributed setting. We presented an implementation of Parcae that utilizes the security guarantees of a private permissioned blockchain to create a trustworthy and continually available PRF service. We showed that our system Parcae strengthens the security guarantees of past implementations of PRF services and password hardening schemes to protect against adversaries unique to a publicly distributed deployment scenario.

We lastly showed that our implementation of Parcae is both practical and reasonable in terms of query latency and scalable throughput.

References

1. Binary1985: Gigabyte RTX 2080ti Hashcat benchmarks. GitHub (2018). https:// gist.github.com/binary1985/c8153c8ec44595fdabbf03157562763e
2. Brost, J., Egger, C., Lai, R.W.F., Schmid, F., Schröder, D., Zoppelt, M.: Threshold password-hardened encryption services. In: Proceedings of the 2020 ACM SIGSAC Conference on Computer and Communications Security, CCS 2020, pp. 409–424. Association for Computing Machinery, New York, NY, USA (2020). https://doi.org/10.1145/3372297.3417266
3. Clement, J.: Number of monthly active facebook users worldwide as of 3rd quarter 2020. Brandwatch (2020). https://www.statista.com/statistics/264810/number-of-monthly-active-facebook-users-worldwide/
4. Everspaugh, A., Chaterjee, R., Scott, S., Juels, A., Ristenpart, T.: The pythia PRF service. In: 24th USENIX Security Symposium (USENIX Security 15), pp. 547–562. USENIX Association, Washington, D.C. (2015). https://www.usenix.org/conference/usenixsecurity15/technical-sessions/presentation/everspaugh
5. Fabric, H.: A blockchain platform for the enterprise. Hyperledger-Fabric (2020). https://hyperledger-fabric.readthedocs.io/en/release-2.2/
6. Inc, A.: ios security. Apple (2016). https://www.apple.com/business/docs/iOS_Security_Guide.pdf
7. Lai, R.W.F., Egger, C., Reinert, M., Chow, S.S.M., Maffei, M., Schröder, D.: Simple password-hardened encryption services. In: 27th USENIX Security Symposium (USENIX Security 18), pp. 1405–1421. USENIX Association, Baltimore, MD, August 2018. https://www.usenix.org/conference/usenixsecurity18/presentation/lai
8. Lai, R.W.F., Egger, C., Schröder, D., Chow, S.S.M.: Phoenix: rebirth of a cryptographic password-hardening service. In: 26th USENIX Security Symposium (USENIX Security 17), pp. 899–916. USENIX Association, Vancouver, BC, August 2017. https://www.usenix.org/conference/usenixsecurity17/technical-sessions/presentation/lai
9. Muffet, A.: Facebook: password hashing and authentication. Real World Crypto (2015)
10. Schneider, J., Fleischhacker, N., Schröder, D., Backes, M.: Efficient cryptographic password hardening services from partially oblivious commitments. In: Proceedings of the 2016 ACM SIGSAC Conference on Computer and Communications Security, CCS 2016, pp. 1192–1203. Association for Computing Machinery, New York (2016). https://doi.org/10.1145/2976749.2978375
11. Verizon: Data breach investigations report (2019). https://www.key4biz.it/wp-content/uploads/2019/05/2019-data-breach-investigations-report.pdf

A Hybrid Cloud Deployment Architecture for Privacy-Preserving Collaborative Genome-Wide Association Studies

Fatima-zahra Boujdad[1,3], David Niyitegeka[2], Reda Bellafqira[2],
Gouenou Coatrieux[2], Emmanuelle Genin[4], and Mario Südholt[1,3(✉)]

[1] IMT Atlantique, Nantes, France
{fatima-zahra.boujdad,david.niyitegeka,reda.bellafqira,
gouenou.coatrieux,mario.sudholt}@imt-atlantique.fr
[2] IMT Atlantique, Brest, France
[3] Inria & LS2N, Nantes, France
[4] INSERM, Paris, France

Abstract. The increasing availability of sequenced human genomes is enabling health professionals and genomics researchers to well understand the implication of genetic variants in the development of common diseases, notably by means of genome-wide association studies (GWAS) which are very promising for personalized medicine and diagnostic testing. However, the ever present need to handle genetic data from different sources to conduct large studies entails multiple privacy and security issues. Actually, classical methods of anonymization are inapplicable for genetic data that are now known to be identifying per se. In this paper, we propose a novel framework for privacy-preserving collaborative GWAS performed in the cloud. Indeed, our proposal is the first framework which combines a hybrid cloud deployment with a set of four security mechanisms that are digital watermarking, homomorphic encryption, meta-data de-identification and the Intel Software Guard Extensions technology in order to ensure confidentiality of genetic data as well as their integrity. Furthermore, our approach describes meta-data management which has rarely been considered in state-of-the-art propositions despite their importance to genetic analyses; in addition, the new deployment model we suggest fits with existing infrastructures which makes its integration straightforward. Experimental results of a prototypical implementation on typical data sizes demonstrate that our solution protocol is feasible and that the framework is practical for real-world scenarios.

Keywords: Secure GWAS · Privacy · Data watermarking ·
Homomorphic encryption · Integrity · Intel SGX · Anonymization

1 Introduction

Nowadays, cloud computing services are gaining more and more interest in the field of biomedical analyses and more specifically genetic ones due to its appeal-

Supported by the PrivGen project: https://project.inria.fr/privgen/.

ing characteristics of rapid scalability and low cost. Indeed, cloud computing solutions allow users or data owners to use massive data storage and large computation capabilities while avoiding in-house infrastructure overhead of purchase and maintenance. For instance, cloud computing has greatly contributed to the rapid growth of sequencing data archives (e.g., Sequence Read Archive (SRA) [16]), and genetic data sharing by enabling collaborations on large amounts of data in various genetic projects like the International Cancer Genome Consortium (ICGC) [28].

Despite these benefits, outsourcing genomic private data to environments such as a public cloud platforms exposes it to many security threats ranging from unintentional disclosure (e.g., due to human administrative errors) to on-purpose theft by means of cyber attacks. In fact, human genomes are a very sensitive asset as it allows the unique identification of individuals and contains valuable information, such as their medical condition. Worse, classical anonymization techniques such as identifier deletion or k-anonymity cannot be used for genetic data as information, e.g., about physical appearances, health status can be directly inferred from it. Therefore, cloud services for genetic data storage and/or processing require strong security mechanisms to ensure confidentiality, privacy, and integrity [7].

Several solutions based on homomorphic encryption [5,17,20], secure multiparty computation [4,11] and differential privacy [26,27] have been proposed for securing genetic data during their storage and/or processing on the cloud. Unfortunately, these methods often induce important memory and computation time cost, huge network loads or simply compromise the usability of the data, e.g., because of noise addition, thus making them impractical for analysis of large-scale genetic data in real life scenarios.

Besides, we are recently witnessing the emergence of new hybrid approaches combined of cryptographic software and hardware in order to support privacy-preserving and better-performing security and data protection frameworks. For instance, Canim et al. [8] came up with a framework to secure queries like count and join over genetic data using secure co-processors; Sadat et al. [23] combine Paillier' cryptosystem with SGX in an architecture featuring several distributed data contributors and GWAS computations that are conducted at a central server. Chen et al. [9] consider data querying in addition to data outsourcing problems for which they exploit the enclave sealing feature. Finally, for a distributed genetic analysis, Chen et al. also propose, see [10], secure family-based analyses for Transmission Disequilibrium tests using SGX, AES encryption and compression techniques. However, all these frameworks for secure GWAS still do not specify in their deployments how the meta-data is being accessed in order to select individuals whose genetic data will be used for the analysis. They also often tackle the problem from the confidentiality point of view not considering other vital security features such as integrity. In fact, in all these hardware-based protection methods, confidentiality is guaranteed by secure cryptography hardware and software encryption (e.g., homomorphic encryption) while integrity is ensured by traditional digital signature methods or message authentication codes. However, these integrity control mechanisms add more information to the data [19] which may increase the storage overhead if large-scale data is considered. In order to overcome this inconvenience, solutions based on watermarking have been proposed [15,21] that do not add extra data to the target database. Furthermore, the architectures considered in aforementioned frameworks often rely on in-house infrastructures and public cloud providers seen as a central server for combined-data analyses, thus not supporting more distributed analyses.

In this paper, we propose using a more comprehensive set of security mechanisms for GWAS together with a deployment model for secure GWAS based on hybrid cloud computing. This model supports community and public cloud providers and combines four security mechanisms in order to protect outsourced genetic data during storage and processing. More precisely, we propose three contributions in this paper:

- We present a novel hybrid cloud-based deployment model for secure collaborative GWAS.
- We introduce a framework to secure genetic analyses that provides four security mechanisms: asymmetric/symmetric encryption, watermarking, Intel's SGX and de-identification.
- A proof of concept implementation for a collaborative χ^2 statistical analysis in the context of a GWAS. The implementation is parallelized for time-consuming tasks and has been executed on the proposed deployment model.

The rest of this paper is organized as follows. Section 2 presents the background preliminaries about homomorphic encryption, de-identification, Intel SGX and encrypted data watermarking. The proposed privacy-preserving GWAS framework is detailed in Sect. 3. Experimental results and discussion are given in Sect. 4. Finally, we conclude the paper in Sect. 5.

2   Background Information

In this section, we present background information about genetic association tests and security mechanisms. Concretely, we introduce the GWAS case/control statistical method, SGX technology and metadata anonymization through fragmentation and homomorphic encryption.

2.1   Genetic Association Tests

To find genes related to common diseases, a strategy consists in testing for an association by comparing marker genotype distributions among individuals affected by the disease (case group) and individuals who are not (control group). Markers are usually single nucleotide polymorphisms (SNPs) with two alleles that can be any of the four nucleotides adenine (A), thymine (T), guanine (G) or cytosine (C). Hence, for a SNP with A and C alleles, the three possible genotypes are AA, AC and CC and test data can be summarized in a 2×3 table, cf. Table 1, with the numbers of cases having genotypes AA, AC and

CC respectively in the first row and the numbers of controls with these same genotypes in the second row. To test for an association, a chi-square test can be used that tests the null hypothesis that the genotype distribution is the same in the two groups. This test is a two degrees of freedom test and may lack power. In many genetic studies, a co-dominant model is assumed where the effects of alleles are cumulative and the Cochran-Armitage test for trend [1] is used. This is, in particular, the case in studies where hundred thousands to millions of SNPs spanning the entire genome are tested iteratively.

Table 1. Contingency table with totals.

	AA	AC	CC	Total
Case	o_{11}	o_{12}	o_{13}	T_{l_1}
Control	o_{21}	o_{22}	o_{23}	T_{l_2}
Total	T_{c_1}	T_{c_2}	T_{c_3}	N

Pearson's chi-square test is defined as follows:

$$\tilde{\chi}^2 = \sum_{i=1}^{2} \sum_{j=1}^{3} \frac{(O_{ij} - E_{ij})^2}{E_{ij}} \tag{1}$$

where O_{ij} corresponds to the witnessed count from cell (i,j); E_{ij} is the expected value, defined as: $E_{ij} = \frac{T_{l_i} \times T_{c_j}}{N}$. Here, T_{l_i} and T_{c_j} are the marginal totals of lines and columns respectively, as shown in Table 1, N is the number of individuals in the study.

We use this test, which is commonly used in GWAS inferences [29], for illustration purposes; however, any contingency table based statistical test can be handled using our proposal. Moreover, it is noteworthy to point out that, as we consider the scenario of several data owners that collaboratively analyze all of their data, an additional step is added before deducing the statistical test value. In this additional step the global contingency table is computed: o_{ij}^k being the value from cell (i,j) in a contingency table of the kth data owner among n entities, the global contingency table is calculated by simply summing values from corresponding cells.

2.2 Intel's Software Guard Extensions (SGX)

The recent hardware-based technology for secure remote computations provided by Intel processors which is known under the name SGX (for Software Guard Extensions) appeared for the first time in 2015. The SGX is an architecture extension providing a new set of instructions that allows the creation and management of an isolated environment, called an enclave, at the CPU level. The isolation is implemented in such a way that even the host operating system, the hypervisor and any other privileged software is forbidden from accessing the enclave.

The SGX technology is designed to preserve integrity as well as confidentiality of the computations inside an enclave. Actually, two main features are at the heart of the SGX security model: i) software attestation, that is, the means by which users verify that they are communicating with legitimate hardware that contains their expected program (and data eventually) before they can send their private inputs to the enclave program; ii) data sealing which consists in storing enclave secrets securely at the hard disk level of the host system so that only the enclave that created the sealed data is able to recover it when required. Here, we only harness the attestation process for the provisioning of secret keys to the enclave.

2.3   Data Fragmentation and De-identification

Genetic data is identifying per se, but the process of re-identification is facilitated if the associated meta-data is not well protected. A well-known method to render meta-data, *e.g.*, clinical and demographic attributes, unexploitable to an attacker is de-identification. One de-identification technique consists in dropping any direct or non direct identifiers from the meta-data when they are exposed to a non trusted environment. Such identifiers can be a name or an association of several attributes as the zip code, gender and day of birth, so-called quasi-identifiers [25]. Constraint-based fragmentation techniques have been used as a mechanism for the de-identification of such data. Fragmentation consists primarily in splitting a database to separate identifying features [3,12] and/or in encrypting attributes when necessary: this requires a deployment model involving several servers for data storage and processing so that the splitting constraints can be satisfied.

In the example we consider, only two servers are available for meta-data storage, one of the two being trusted; therefore, the de-identification mechanism we apply on the meta-data consists in keeping singleton identifying attributes, *e.g.*, social security number, along with attributes dropped from each identifying association at the trusted server and outsource the rest. Actually, it is enough to separate only one attribute from each sensitive association for this last to become non-sensitive. To illustrate this, consider the following example: meta-data is abstracted to attributes, those with security-sensitive properties are between parentheses, whether they are singleton or associations:

```
attributes: Id, (SSN), (Zip code, Birth date, Gender), Case/Control
separate    SSN, Birth date
store       SSN, Birth date on the trusted server
outsource   Id, Zip code, Gender, Case/Control
```

The choice of which attributes to separate from association constraints can be driven by the expected information content that represents how much an attribute can help re-identify subjects [13]. Doing so protects the identities of participating subjects in a study but still allows researchers to customize the selection of case/control groups by keeping the phenotype attribute accessible in addition to other non-identifying clinical information. Indeed, we consider keeping the phenotype status attribute accessible to researchers while anonymizing the data on the untrusted side.

2.4 Homomorphic Encryption

Homomorphic encryption (HE) is a security mechanism that enables performing operations on encrypted data without the need for decryption. Decrypted results correspond to the same output that would be achieved when these operations are performed on clear data [2]. In practice, these operations are limited to linear ones, such as additions and multiplications. Formally, let Enc and Dec be the encryption and decryption functions of an HE cryptosystem respectively, and K_p and K_s be its public key and secret key respectively. If m_1 and m_2 are two clear messages, the homomorphism property states:

$$Dec(Enc(m_1, K_p) \star Enc(m_2, K_p), K_s) = m_1 \circ m_2 \qquad (2)$$

where $\star$ and $\circ$ are two operators in the encrypted and the clear domains, respectively.

In this work, we opted for Paillier's HE cryptosystem because of the additive homomorphic property and its simplicity of use [22]. Notice that it is also semantically secure in that the same plain-text has different cipher-texts at each execution. Paillier cryptosystem is additively homomorphic; its utility is straightforward for secure GWAS analyses where computing global tables given contributed contingency tables is done through addition of corresponding values for each SNP.

2.5 Watermarking of Homomorphically Encrypted Genetic Data

In our framework, the integrity control of homomorphically encrypted data is ensured using a database watermarking method recently proposed by Niyitegeka et al. [21].

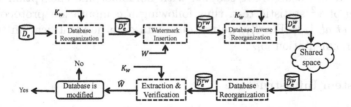

Fig. 1. Steps of watermark embedding and watermark extraction for used watermarking scheme.

Watermark Embedding in Encrypted Databases. As shown in Fig. 1, the watermark embedding process takes as input a homomorphically encrypted database D_e which is first secretly reorganized into a database D_e^r using a secret watermarking key K_w. This reorganization is used in order to ensure that an attacker cannot get access to the secret watermark. To do so, a secret hash is associated to each tuple (line) of the database, and all tuples are reorganized according to their hash values and in ascending order. After reorganizing database tuples, D_e^r is divided into overlapping blocks (see [21]) and one bit of the watermark W is inserted into each block of D_e^r, so as to produce a reorganized and watermarked database D_e^{rw}. Once all blocks are watermarked, the database D_e^{rw} is reorganized back into the encrypted and watermarked database D_e^w. Notice that the watermark W can be randomly generated or generated using the identifier of the user.

Watermark Extraction from Encrypted Database and Integrity Verification. The watermark extraction can be conducted in a similar way as the watermark embedding (see Fig. 1). Indeed, to extract the watermark from a suspicious database $\widehat{D}_e^w$, this database is first reorganized into $\widehat{D}_e^{rw}$ using the secret watermarking key K_w, and $\widehat{D}_e^{rw}$ is divided into blocks. The hash is then computed for each block so as to get access the watermark bit. Once all watermark bits are extracted to form $\widehat{W}$, this information is compared to the original watermark W in order to conduct integrity verification. Any difference between these watermarks will indicate that the database D_e^w was illegally modified.

3   Privacy-Preserving GWAS Hybrid Cloud Deployment

In this section, we introduce a new hybrid model to deploy genetic analyses and handle two major security concerns, confidentiality and integrity of genetic data. We use four security techniques to fulfill the security requirements for data transfer and processing as well as result delivery to researchers. We build a comprehensive framework with a new deployment model for secure genetic data processing of GWAS. Concretely, we use a static version of our scheme for the dynamic watermarking of homomorphic encrypted databases [21]. In addition, we are using SGX coupled with homomorphic encryption for secure processing of χ^2 statistic test, thus following a computation protocol inspired by Sadat *et al.* [23]. Finally, we use our meta-data de-identification techniques through fragmentation [6].

3.1   System Infrastructure

Figure 2 shows a typical system architecture that we are interested in. It represents a collaboration of five types of parties:

- Genetic data owners, (E_i in the Fig. 2). The owners, *e.g.*, research labs, keep genetic data (represented, for instance, by means of VCF files) locally while

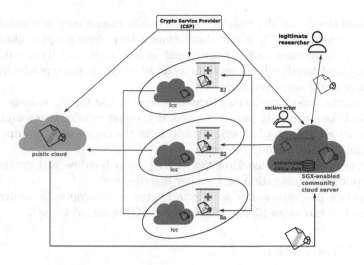

Fig. 2. PrivGen deployment architecture.

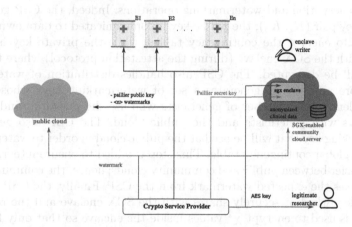

Fig. 3. Key distribution by the CSP.

they outsource the associated de-identified meta-data to a community cloud storage service.

- Local community cloud servers (LCCs). Due to the strong security guarantees of these clouds, they are well adapted to serve as independent providers for compute-intensive operations required by applications of data owners. Such infrastructures are well known to biomedical actors: the French Institute of Bioinformatics[1], for instance, provides a cloud infrastructure providing computing and storage resources for the biomedical and bioinformatics community.

---

[1] https://www.france-bioinformatique.fr/en/infrastructure-0.

- A hybrid cloud provider that provisions two infrastructure domains i) a community cloud (ComC), where data owners keep demographic/clinical data allowing researchers to get transparent access to it and ii) a public cloud (PubC) that handles homomorphic computations on encrypted contingency tables pooled from several owners.
- Researchers, who have authenticated access to the ComC storage platform for meta-data querying purposes. Actually, doing so affords researchers with an accurate selection of genetic data to form the case-control groups which is of main interest in study design.
- A Cryptography Service Provider (CSP), who handles watermarking and encryption key generation and proper distribution.
- An enclave program writer who is in charge of developing a secure module destined to run as an SGX enclave at the SGX-enabled ComC.

3.2 Key Distribution

The cryptography service provider is in charge of key generation and distribution for both encryption and watermarking operations. Indeed, the CSP generates a Paillier key pair (K_s, K_p); the public key is communicated to data owners which they use to encrypt the contingency tables, while the private key is securely shared with the SGX enclave (during the attestation protocol) where the global tables will be decrypted. The CSP also handles distribution of watermarking keys. More precisely, it generates a set of watermarking keys whose number is equivalent to the number of geneticists who use the platform, and it shares these keys with geneticists and the public cloud. The CSP also generates a watermarking key that will be used at the public cloud in order to watermark the resulting global contingency table. This step is added to ensure integrity during data transfer between public and community clouds; hence, the community cloud also receives the expected watermark from the CSP. Finally, the CSP generates an AES key which it securely shares with the SGX enclave and the researcher. This key is used to encrypt χ^2 values inside the enclave so that only legitimate researchers (who hold the decryption key) are able to read the final results. These elements are depicted in Fig. 3.

3.3 Attacker Model

In our secure GWAS application, we aim at protecting the confidentiality and integrity of genetic data and guaranteeing the generation of correct results as well as preventing the re-identification of the participating subjects. Given the key distribution schema presented above, these requirements can be achieved under a semi-honest attacker type for the HCP. Indeed, the HCP provider could straightforwardly insert noise into the data using the Paillier' public key which is inherently available had they been a dishonest party; this would output false results and thus violate the requirement of getting correct results. As to preserving data confidentiality, we need the enclave writer to be independent from the HCP whom we assume not to collude with to get access to Paillier' private key;

hence, as long as it is the CSP (fully trusted) who provisions the SGX enclave with secret keys, data confidentiality is preserved throughout the lifetime of the application; this also means that the SGX technology is fully trusted to meet the security functionalities it does afford. Data integrity might be compromised by the HCP if they ignore cases where integrity check fails, this again would result in generating false results at the last step of the analysis; under a semi-honest attacker model (that is realistic when considering a cloud provider who cares about their commercial reputation), this scenario is excluded.

Besides, we suppose researchers to be honest entities: a malicious or semi-honest researcher with background knowledge on some subjects may still be able to jeopardize their presence in the ComC database and hence infer their health status; such an attack can be countered by techniques like differential privacy and k-anonymity which we have not considered in this work.

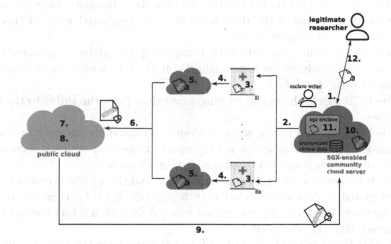

Fig. 4. GWAS workflow.

3.4 Protocol Workflow

We assume the initial state of the architecture is set by outsourcing anonymized clinical data for storage on the community cloud platform and that an authentication system is deployed to allow legitimate researchers to access and query the data. On the other hand, VCF files of genetic data are kept locally at their owners' sites. Hence, linking primary keys should be set so that these files can always be mapped to associated clinical data. This is for researchers who want to select genetic data based on clinical phenotypes and/or demographic attributes. The primary keys can be represented by the anonymous subject identifiers found in VCF files.

Using the architecture of Fig. 2 and assuming the above initial setting, a GWAS analysis can be performed as follows (cf. Fig. 4):

1. The researcher queries ComC for meta-data to form the case-control groups.
2. ComC executes the query, then forwards the primary database keys to the data owners.
3. The owners compute contingency tables from VCF files of involved individuals.
4. They prepare the resulting tables for encryption on their LCC servers.
5. The LCC servers encrypt the contingency tables with the (same) Paillier public key, then they watermark the tables with a secret watermark shared with the PubC.
6. The owners send the encrypted-watermarked tables to the public cloud servers.
7. Upon data reception, PubC first verifies data integrity by verifying the watermark to ensure the data has not been tampered with. If this check fails, a 'resend' request is sent.
8. The public cloud proceeds with computing the global contingency table homomorphically which it watermarks at the end with a secret watermark shared with the ComC.
9. The HCP moves the global contingency tables from the PubC to the ComC server.
10. The SGX-enabled host system of ComC verifies data integrity by ensuring that the inserted watermark is the expected one after which it forwards the rest of the computations to an initiated SGX enclave.
11. Inside the enclave, the tables are decrypted and the χ^2 test is computed after the global table was extended with totals (cf. Table 1), then the resulting values are independently encrypted using AES with a secret encryption key shared with the researchers.
12. Finally, the encrypted χ^2 result values are communicated to researchers who can decrypt the results and infer the p-values.

3.5   Deployment Choices

In this section, we justify the architectural choices advanced in Sect. 3.1. As a reminder, privacy concerns and meta-data storage/access are the major factors defining the architectural elements and the data flows across the infrastructure servers. We discuss our architectural choice with respect to scalability, security, performance and cost criteria. We show, in particular, why simpler architectures like a centralized server are not appropriate for our purposes.

Scalability. The public cloud deployment has been chosen because of the scalability and elasticity properties it affords so that both horizontal and vertical growth can be accommodated with ease. This, in turn, enables arbitrary numbers of data owners to be admitted and large numbers of SNPs to be analyzed.

At the community cloud infrastructure, only vertical scalability has to be supported: the number of global contingency tables to handle depends on the number of considered SNPs and not on that of the contributing entities. For these reasons, we believe the public cloud is the necessary element that guarantees horizontal scalability of the architecture. However, the community cloud is required to perform well even when the number of SNPs becomes huge. Our experimental results below show that our approach meets these requirements and provides a practical solution for scenarios with hundreds of thousands of SNPs.

Unlike the public cloud, the community cloud infrastructure is assumed to have much less computation resources. It is mainly used to permanently store meta-data and handle secure computations thanks to SGX support; the SGX part of the computations has to be strictly minimized. Therefore, we entrust the community cloud host system to check integrity by handling watermark detection operations; only decryption, the χ^2 test, and the final AES encryption are computed inside the enclave. This task allocation is quite realistic as integrity checks do not reveal any secret inputs but they are still very important for correct computation within the enclave.

Security and Privacy. We do not perform the SGX part of the computations on the public cloud (but allocate them to the community cloud) because we would like to avoid side-channel attacks on SGX processors. Since public cloud platforms are multi-tenant, intruders are much more likely to succeed in performing such attacks [14,18]. This arrangement requires (additional) network exchanges between the PubC and the ComC, but we do believe the increased level of security is worth this cost. Furthermore, the introduction of a community cloud allows to envision meta-data management and global access provides stronger guarantees to data owners. They, in turn, can then provide more flexible access to their data to researchers, in particular add data attributes to their shared meta-data that otherwise would not be available to researchers.

Performance. Following the protocol workflow depicted by Fig. 2, the contingency tables' totals are generated inside the enclave just before computing the χ^2 value. This is clearly more efficient than homomorphically generating totals directly in the public cloud or at the geneticists level, because the enclave would then need to perform later six additional decryption operations per SNP in case of a genotype contingency table and five in case of a table with allele counts.

Finally, the watermarking system we chose contributes to enhancing the overall performance of the preprocessing phase: the offline step of homomorphically encrypting contingency tables can result in storing the data for some time before the online process starts. Data integrity can still be checked continuously by data owners thanks to watermark embedding done just after the encryption. If ever the integrity check fails the extracted wrong watermark indicates which block of the data was modified; this means that the data owner can re-encrypt only the modified parts of it and re-watermark it with properly chosen bits (whether the same as in the first watermark or completely new ones). Doing so is much more efficient than with a classical signature whose failure of integrity check leads to re-encryption of all the tables.

Business Model. It is noteworthy to mention that this architecture can be wholly ephemeral: both the global community and public clouds are elastic elements; this is useful in a case where *e.g.,* a project of a couple of months uses a community cloud for the same period but only needs the public cloud occasionally where joint computations are required on private genetic data. In general, such a hybrid cloud improves the security of implementation while leveraging a cost-effective business. In fact, community cloud deployment type tends to be more expensive than a public cloud: using both with markedly differentiated hardware resources permits to couple an affordable budget with an enhanced security level compared to pure public-cloud deployments.

4   Experimental Results

In the following we evaluate an implementation, especially its performance, of a GWAS analysis that executes a χ^2 test using our deployment scheme and framework to secure the analysis.

4.1   Experimental Setup

We have used the following global setup:

- *LCC servers* perform Paillier encryption and watermarking of contingency tables. The encryption uses multiple nodes and all available (in our experiments, 90) cores by splitting the VCF file and assigning each part to a different node for processing. The watermarking operations are executed in a parallel fashion on (in our experiments, 18 cores of) a single node.
- *PubC modules* serve to verify watermarks and compute global tables. Watermark detection is parallelized and the global tables computation uses all of the node's cores.
- *ComC modules* also verify watermarks (by the host system), perform Paillier decryption, compute χ^2 tests and AES encrypt the final results (within the SGX enclave). This part of the application uses one core only.

The VCF file we have worked with contained only 2952 SNPs; for experimental purposes, we have made copies of the available contingency tables to obtain tables of approximate size of 500K. We report execution times on the basis of 1024 bits Paillier keys, 256 bits AES key. The watermark sizes depend on the size of the input file. In order to minimize the number of watermarks to manage, we reorganize the encrypted contingency tables by using bigger chunks so that several tables are contained in a single file of $N \times 6$ entries where N is the number of SNPs of each chunk. In every chunk, each line represents a table of the consecutive values $o_{11} - o_{12} - o_{13} - o_{21} - o_{22} - o_{23}$, cf. Table 1.

Unfortunately, the watermarking algorithm performance was a bottleneck when we chose $N \approx 500$. Therefore, we have split the file with encrypted tables into smaller subfiles, then parallelized the insertion/detection functions. In our case, we chose $N = 5000$, thus, all the data was split into 101 files.

We launched all experiments five times each and report the average time as performance values.

Table 2 presents the hardware infrastructure setup used in our experiments.

Table 2. Experiments' hardware infrastructure.

	Nodes	Processor	Cores/Node
LCC	5	Intel Xeon Gold 5220	18
sgx-en. ComC	1 laptop	Intel Core i7 1.80 GHz	1
PubC	1	Intel Xeon Gold 5220	18

The multi-core servers are part of the French testbed infrastructure Grid5000[2]. We used the cluster "gros" located in the French city Nancy.

4.2 Results

We now present the computation times obtained for each module as previously stated without considering network latency. We report results for two cases: i) contingency tables comprise genotype counts, meaning that six values per table have to be processed, and ii) the contingency tables comprise allele counts, which means that only four values are handled across the lifetime of the application. Though execution times are naturally lower in the second case, real GWAS studies would rather consider contingency tables of genotypes [24], the reason being that testing with allele counts assumes that the two alleles are independent (Hardy-Weinberg principle) which is not always true. However, testing with genotype counts is possible even if one genotype lacks in the table (yielding one degree of freedom less); in the context of our framework this is equivalent to handling four values. In other words, our experiments conducted using allele counts also provides information about the performance of genotype-based scenarios where a genotype might be missing.

The results for genotype counts and allele counts for different numbers of geneticists are, respectively, reported in Tables 3 and 4. The execution times change slightly but significantly with increasing numbers of geneticists at the public cloud level because it homomorphically computes the global contingency table by aggregating tables from an increasing number of entities. At the data owners level, execution times do not change because the experiments were set in such a way that they launch their modules in parallel; a valid assumption for real scenarios given that this part of the solution is performed offline, that is, as

---

[2] https://www.grid5000.fr.

Table 3. Execution times for ∼500K SNPs (genotypes).

Data owners	lcc-crypt	lcc-wat	PubC	ComC
3	110 min	2 min	1 min 52 s	53 min
6	110 min	2 min	3 min 34 s	54 min
9	110 min	2 min	5 min 13 s	54 min
20	110 min	2 min	11 min 23 s	55 min

Table 4. Execution times for ∼500K SNPs (alleles).

Data owners	lcc-crypt	lcc-wat	PubC	ComC
3	75 min	1 min 23 s	1 min 8 s	36 min
6	75 min	1 min 22 s	2 min 6 s	36 min
9	75 min	1 min 22 s	3 min	36 min
20	75 min	1 min 22 s	6 min 45 s	36 min

part of a preprocessing phase. The enclave code also runs in constant time with respect to an increasing number of geneticists because the number of SNPs is fixed which means that the file size (5000×6 for genotype counts and 5000×4 for allele counts) is the same across the three experiments. From the tables above, we infer that the total execution time per SNP including all data flow steps for genotype counts ranges from 20 to 21 ms, while alleles account for approximately 14 ms.

The data flow related to asymmetric operations in our solution is generally the same as in the SAFETY framework [23]. Its authors reported execution times of the SGX enclave module for one genotype contingency table: homomorphic decryption and Fisher's Exact Test (FET) computation take over 7 ms run on an Intel Core i7 3.40 GHz processor. In our framework, Paillier's decryption, chi-square test computation and AES encryption of results take 6.5 ms approximately on the designated hardware (see Table 2). Actually, the chi-square test and FET formulae are different, but as these tests are computed in the clear, we believe the differences in performance is due to the fact that SAFETY delegates all decryption operations to the enclave including the decryption of total values, while we calculate totals in the enclave after the values have been decrypted.

It is very important to mention that the enclave code does not make use of all of the available cores. However, the SGX technology permits multi-threaded code to execute, we leave this extension as a future optimization which should largely enhance the community module performance. In addition, we could also parallelize the watermarking functions themselves so that many threads can insert/detect in/from a single file so that only one (or very few) watermarks have to be managed by the CSP.

5   Conclusion

In this paper, we have presented a new framework that harnesses the use of a hybrid cloud computing deployment model to secure collaborative Genome-Wide Association Studies. We used watermarking, encryption, Intel SGX hardware execution and de-identification in order to ensure integrity as well as confidentiality of genetic data and the associated meta-data. We have also reported results from a proof of concept implementation using the proposed framework. The results show that our approach enables efficient execution of biomedical analyses that can be scaled significantly. Overall, our results show the feasibility of our solution and that it can be used to comprehensively secure real-world biomedical analyses executed on grid-like architectures of already deployed resources.

As future work, we will optimize the three code modules that are part of our architecture, notably, by parallelizing the enclave code. In addition, we will extend our results to accommodate the inference of p-values at the enclave level. Furthermore, we will focus on requiring less resources from geneticists so that most of the heavy computations can be securely outsourced.

Acknowledgments. This work has received a French government support granted to the Labex CominLabs and managed by the ANR in the "Investing for the future" program under reference ANR-10-LABX-07-01, and to the Labex GenMed, ANR-10-LABX-0013, through the project PrivGen.

Experiments presented in this paper were carried out using the Grid'5000 testbed, supported by a scientific interest group hosted by Inria and including CNRS, RENATER and several Universities as well as other organizations (see https://www.grid5000.fr).

References

1. Armitage, P.: Tests for linear trends in proportions and frequencies. Biometrics **11**(3), 375–386 (1955)
2. Bellafqira, R., Coatrieux, G., Bouslimi, D., Quellec, G.: Content-based image retrieval in homomorphic encryption domain. In: 2015 37th Annual International Conference of the IEEE Engineering in Medicine and Biology Society (EMBC), pp. 2944–2947. IEEE (2015)
3. Bkakria, A., Cuppens, F., Cuppens-Boulahia, N., et al.: Preserving multi-relational outsourced databases confidentiality using fragmentation and encryption. JoWUA **4**(2), 39–62 (2013). https://hal.archives-ouvertes.fr/hal-01213956
4. Bogdanov, D., Kamm, L., Laur, S., Sokk, V.: Implementation and evaluation of an algorithm for cryptographically private principal component analysis on genomic data. IEEE/ACM Trans. Comput. Biol. Bioinf. **15**(5), 1427–1432 (2018)
5. Bonte, C., et al.: Privacy-preserving genome-wide association study is practical. In: IACR Cryptology ePrint Archive 2018, p. 955 (2018)
6. Boujdad, F.-z., Südholt, M.: Constructive privacy for shared genetic data. In: CLOSER 2018–8th International Conference on Cloud Computing and Services Science, Proceedings of CLOSER 2018, March 2018

7. Bouslimi, D., Coatrieux, G., Cozic, M., Roux, C.: A telemedicine protocol based on watermarking evidence for identification of liabilities in case of litigation. In: 2012 IEEE 14th International Conference on e-Health Networking, Applications and Services (Healthcom), pp. 506–509. IEEE (2012)

8. Canim, M., Kantarcioglu, M., Malin, B.: Secure management of biomedical data with cryptographic hardware. Trans. Info. Tech. Biomed. **16**(1), 166–175 (2012). https://doi.org/10.1109/TITB.2011.2171701. http://dx.doi.org/10.1109/TITB.2011.2171701. ISSN 1089–7771

9. Chen, F., et al.: Presage: privacy-preserving genetic testing via software guard extension. BMC Med. Genomics **10**(2), 48 (2017)

10. Chen, F., et al.: Princess: privacy-protecting rare disease international network collaboration via encryption through software guard extensions. Bioinformatics (Oxford, England) **33**(6), 871–878 (2017). https://doi.org/10.1093/bioinformatics/btw758. https://www.ncbi.nlm.nih.gov/pubmed/28065902. ISSN 1367–4811

11. Cho, H., Wu, D.J., Berger, B.: Secure genome-wide association analysis using multiparty computation. Nat. Biotechnol. **36**(6), 547 (2018)

12. Ciriani, V., De Capitani, S., Vimercati, D., Foresti, S., et al.: Combining fragmentation and encryption to protect privacy in data storage. ACM Trans. Inf. Syst. Secur. **13**(3), 22:1–22:33 (2010). https://doi.org/10.1145/1805974.1805978. http://doi.acm.org/10.1145/1805974.1805978. ISSN 1094–9224

13. Erlich, Y., Narayanan, A.: Routes for breaching and protecting genetic privacy. Nat. Rev. Genet. **15**(6), 409–421 (2014). https://doi.org/10.1038/nrg3723. ISSN 1471–0064

14. Götzfried, J., Eckert, M., Schinzel, S., Müller, T.: Cache attacks on intel SGX. In: Proceedings of the 10th European Workshop on Systems Security, EuroSec 2017, pp. 2:1–2:6. ACM, New York (2017). https://doi.org/10.1145/3065913.3065915. http://doi.acm.org/10.1145/3065913.3065915. ISBN 978-1-4503-4935-2

15. Khanduja, V., Chakraverty, S.: A generic watermarking model for object relational databases. Multimedia Tools Appl. **78**(19), 28111–28135 (2019). https://doi.org/10.1007/s11042-019-07932-3

16. Langmead, B., Nellore, A.: Cloud computing for genomic data analysis and collaboration. Nat. Rev. Genet. **19**(4), 208 (2018)

17. Lauter, K., López-Alt, A., Naehrig, M.: Private computation on encrypted genomic data. In: Aranha, D.F., Menezes, A. (eds.) LATINCRYPT 2014. LNCS, vol. 8895, pp. 3–27. Springer, Cham (2015). https://doi.org/10.1007/978-3-319-16295-9_1

18. Moghimi, A., Irazoqui, G., Eisenbarth, T.: CacheZoom: how SGX amplifies the power of cache attacks. In: Fischer, W., Homma, N. (eds.) CHES 2017. LNCS, vol. 10529, pp. 69–90. Springer, Cham (2017). https://doi.org/10.1007/978-3-319-66787-4_4

19. Mykletun, E., Narasimha, M., Tsudik, G.: Authentication and integrity in outsourced databases. ACM Trans. Storage (TOS) **2**(2), 107–138 (2006)

20. Nassar, M., Malluhi, Q., Atallah, M., Shikfa, A.: Securing aggregate queries for DNA databases. IEEE Trans. Cloud Comput. **7**(3), 827–837 (2017). https://doi.org/10.1109/TCC.2017.2682860. ISSN 2168–7161

21. Niyitegeka, D., Coatrieux, G., Bellafqira, R., Genin, E., Franco-Contreras, J.: Dynamic watermarking-based integrity protection of homomorphically encrypted databases – application to outsourced genetic data. In: Yoo, C.D., Shi, Y.-Q., Kim, H.J., Piva, A., Kim, G. (eds.) IWDW 2018. LNCS, vol. 11378, pp. 151–166. Springer, Cham (2019). https://doi.org/10.1007/978-3-030-11389-6_12

22. Paillier, P.: Public-key cryptosystems based on composite degree residuosity classes. In: Stern, J. (ed.) EUROCRYPT 1999. LNCS, vol. 1592, pp. 223–238. Springer, Heidelberg (1999). https://doi.org/10.1007/3-540-48910-X_16
23. Sadat, M.N., Al Aziz, M.M., Mohammed, N., Chen, F., Jiang, X., Wang, S.: Safety: secure gwAs in federated environment through a hybrid solution. IEEE/ACM Trans. Comput. Biol. Bioinform. (TCBB) **16**(1), 93–102 (2019)
24. Sasieni, P.D.: From genotypes to genes: doubling the sample size. Biometrics **53**(4), 1253–1261 (1997)
25. Sweenay, L.: Simple demographics often identify people uniquely. Carnegie Mellon. Data Privacy Working Paper 3 (2000). http://dataprivacylab.org/projects/identifiability/
26. Tramèr, F., Huang, Z., Hubaux, J.-P., Ayday, E.: Differential privacy with bounded priors: reconciling utility and privacy in genome-wide association studies. In: Proceedings of the 22nd ACM SIGSAC Conference on Computer and Communications Security, pp. 1286–1297. ACM, New York (2015)
27. Fei, Yu., Ji, Z.: Scalable privacy-preserving data sharing methodology for genome-wide association studies: an application to iDASH healthcare privacy protection challenge. BMC Med. Inform. Decis. Mak. **14**(1), S3 (2014)
28. Yung, C.K., et al.: ICGC in the cloud (2016)
29. Zeng, P., et al.: Statistical analysis for genome-wide association study. J. Biomed. Res. **29**(4), 285–297 (2015). https://doi.org/10.7555/JBR.29.20140007. https://pubmed.ncbi.nlm.nih.gov/26243515. 26243515[pmid]. ISSN 1674–8301

Understanding the Security of Deepfake Detection

Xiaoyu Cao(✉) and Neil Zhenqiang Gong

Duke University, Durham, NC, USA
{xiaoyu.cao,neil.gong}@duke.edu

Abstract. Deepfakes pose growing challenges to the trust of information on the Internet. Thus, detecting deepfakes has attracted increasing attentions from both academia and industry. State-of-the-art deepfake detection methods consist of two key components, i.e., *face extractor* and *face classifier*, which extract the face region in an image and classify it to be real/fake, respectively. Existing studies mainly focused on improving the detection performance in *non-adversarial settings*, leaving security of deepfake detection in *adversarial settings* largely unexplored. In this work, we aim to bridge the gap. In particular, we perform a systematic measurement study to understand the security of the state-of-the-art deepfake detection methods in adversarial settings. We use two large-scale public deepfakes data sources including FaceForensics++ and Facebook Deepfake Detection Challenge, where the deepfakes are fake face images; and we train state-of-the-art deepfake detection methods. These detection methods can achieve 0.94–0.99 accuracies in non-adversarial settings on these datasets. However, our measurement results uncover multiple security limitations of the deepfake detection methods in adversarial settings. First, we find that an attacker can evade a face extractor, i.e., the face extractor fails to extract the correct face regions, via adding small Gaussian noise to its deepfake images. Second, we find that a face classifier trained using deepfakes generated by one method cannot detect deepfakes generated by another method, i.e., an attacker can evade detection via generating deepfakes using a new method. Third, we find that an attacker can leverage *backdoor attacks* developed by the adversarial machine learning community to evade a face classifier. Our results highlight that deepfake detection should consider the adversarial nature of the problem.

Keywords: Deepfake detection · Security

1 Introduction

Deepfakes generally refer to forged media such as images and videos. While forged media has been in existence for decades and was conventionally created by computer graphics methods [1,51], recent progress in deep learning enables automatic, large-scale creation of realistic-looking deepfakes. In particular, many methods (e.g., generative adversarial networks [14,34–36,46]) have been proposed to generate deepfakes, which we call *deepfake generation methods*. Such deepfakes can further be widely

© ICST Institute for Computer Sciences, Social Informatics and Telecommunications Engineering 2022
Published by Springer Nature Switzerland AG 2022. All Rights Reserved
P. Gladyshev et al. (Eds.): ICDF2C 2021, LNICST 441, pp. 360–378, 2022.
https://doi.org/10.1007/978-3-031-06365-7_22

Fig. 1. Illustration of the two key components of a deepfake detection system.

propagated on social medias to spread propaganda, disinformation, and fake news. For instance, comedian Jordan Peele produced a fake video of President Obama criticizing President Trump by altering the lip movements of Obama in a real video [2]. As a result, deepfakes introduce grand challenges to the trust of online information. In this work, we focus on fake faces, a major category of deepfakes, because faces are key components in human communications and their forgeries lead to severe consequences. Therefore, we will use deepfakes and fake faces interchangeably throughout the paper.

Due to the growing concerns of deepfakes, detecting deepfakes has attracted increasing attentions from both academia and industry. For instance, Facebook recently launched a deepfake detection competition [19] to facilitate the development of deepfake detection methods. A deepfake detection system includes two key components, i.e., *face extractor* and *face classifier*, which is illustrated in Fig. 1. Specifically, a face extractor extracts the face region in an image, while a face classifier classifies the extracted face region to be real or fake. As face extraction is a mature technique, existing deepfake detection methods often use state-of-the-art face extractor but adopt different face classifiers. Roughly speaking, existing face classifiers can be grouped into two categories, i.e., *heuristic-based* and *neural-network-based*. Heuristic-based face classifiers [8,22,38,39,42,59] rely on some heuristics to distinguish between fake faces and real faces. For instance, Li et al. [38] designed a face classifier based on the observation that the eyes in fake faces did not blink normally as people do in the real world. However, these heuristic-based face classifiers were soon broken by new fake faces. For instance, the eye-blinking based face classifier was easily broken by fake faces that blink eyes normally [8].

Neural-network-based face classifiers [7,9,17,43,44,47,48,58,62] train deep neural networks to distinguish between fake faces and real faces. Specifically, given a training dataset consisting of both real faces and fake faces generated by some deepfake generation methods, a deep neural network classifier is trained. Then, given a new face, the deep neural network outputs a label that is either "real" or "fake" for it. These deep neural network based face classifiers achieve the state-of-the-art detection accuracy, showing promising applications in detecting fake faces. Existing studies mainly focused on improving the detection performance under *non-adversarial settings*, i.e., they assume the attacker who generates the deepfakes does not adapt to the detectors. Deepfake detection is essentially a security problem, in which an attacker always adapts to defenses. However, the security of the state-of-the-art deepfake detection methods in such adversarial settings remains largely unexplored, except that a few studies [12,21,23,29] showed that face classifiers are vulnerable to *adversarial examples* [13,49]. In particular, an attacker can add carefully crafted perturbations to its fake faces such that a face classifier is highly likely to misclassify them as real faces.

Our Work: In this work, we perform systematic measurement studies to understand the security of deepfake detection. The security of a deepfake detection method relies on the security of both the face extractor and the face classifier. Therefore, we perform measurement studies to understand the security of both components. In particular, we aim to study the following three questions, where Q1 is related to the security of face extractor while Q2 and Q3 are related to the security of face classifier:

– **Q1:** An attacker can easily add perturbations (e.g., Gaussian noise) to its deepfake images. Therefore, the first question we aim to study is: can a face extractor still successfully extract the face region in a deepfake image when an attacker adds a small perturbation to it?
– **Q2:** Existing studies [7,48] often train and test a face classifier using fake faces that are generated by the same deepfake generation methods. However, many different methods have been proposed to generate deepfakes and new methods are continuously developed. Therefore, the second question we aim to study is: can a face classifier trained using fake faces generated by some deepfake generation methods correctly classify fake faces generated by a different method?
– **Q3:** A face classifier is a binary machine learning classifier. The adversarial machine learning community has developed *adversarial examples* and *data poisoning attacks* for machine learning classifiers, which attack classifiers at testing phase and training phase, respectively. Recent studies showed that a face classifier is vulnerable to adversarial examples. The third question we aim to study is: are face classifiers also vulnerable to data poisoning attacks?

Measurement Setup. We extract six deepfakes datasets from two large-scale public sources, i.e., FaceForensics++ [48] and Facebook Deepfake Detection Challenge (DFDC) [19]. We use Dlib [37], an open source face extractor, to extract faces from the images in the datasets. These datasets include 0.9 million to 1.3 million real or fake faces. Among the four datasets extracted from FaceForensics++, each of them contains real faces and their corresponding fake faces that are generated by a specific deepfake generation method. DFDC contains fake faces that are generated by 8 deepfake generation methods. We divide each dataset into three partitions, i.e., *training*, *validation*, and *testing*. Moreover, we train a state-of-the-art neural network based face classifier for each dataset using its training and validation partitions, where the validation partition is used to select the face classifier with the best performance during training. These face classifiers are very accurate in non-adversarial settings, i.e., they achieve 0.94–0.99 accuracies on the testing faces.

Measurement Results. For Q1, we add different amount of random Gaussian noise to an image. Then, we use Dlib to extract the face region from a noisy image. We find that a small Gaussian noise can spoof the face extractor. For instance, when adding noise sampled from a Gaussian distribution with zero mean and standard deviation $\sigma = 0.3$ to images in the DFDC dataset, Dlib fails to extract the face regions for at least 80% of the images. Our results show that face extractor is not secure against small random noise added to an image.

For Q2, we measure the *cross-method generalization* of the face classifiers. Specifically, we assume the face regions are successfully extracted. We use a face classifier trained on one dataset to classify the testing faces in another dataset, where the fake faces in the two datasets are generated by different deepfake generation methods. We find that the face classifiers' accuracies drop to nearly random guessing (i.e., 0.5) in such cross-method setting. Our results show that a face classifier trained on deepfakes generated by one method cannot correctly classify deepfakes generated by another method. Our results imply that the standard evaluation paradigm in previous work [7,48], which trains and tests a face classifier using fake faces generated by the same deepfake generation methods, is insufficient to characterize the security of the face classifier.

For Q3, we measure the security of a face classifier against one simple data poisoning attack called *label flipping attack* and one advanced data poisoning attack called *backdoor attack* [27]. Like Q2, we assume the face regions have been successfully extracted and focus on the security of face classifier. Label flipping attack changes the labels of some training faces such that a trained face classifier is corrupted. We find that the face classifiers are relatively secure against the simple label flipping attacks. For instance, their accuracies only drop by 0.04 when the labels of around 25% of their training faces are flipped. However, the more advanced backdoor attacks can break the face classifiers. In a backdoor attack, an attacker adds a *trigger* (e.g., a chessboard grid in our experiments) to some training faces (e.g., we use 5% of training faces) and changes their labels to be real. Then, a face classifier is trained on the poisoned training faces. We find that the face classifier misclassifies a fake face as real once we inject the same trigger to the fake face.

Security Implications. Our measurement results have several implications for the security of deepfake detection. In particular, our results show that an attacker can evade detection of its deepfakes by adding small Gaussian noise to them to spoof face extraction; an attacker can evade a face classifier by generating deepfakes using a new deepfake generation method; and an attacker can evade detection by exploiting backdoor attacks to face classifiers. Our results highlight that deepfake detection should consider the adversarial nature of the problem and take strategic adaptive attacks into consideration.

We summarize our key contributions as follows:

- We perform the first systematic measurement study to understand the security of the state-of-the-art deepfake detection methods in adversarial settings.
- We find that face extractor is not secure against small perturbation added to an image.
- We find that face classifier is not secure against new deepfake generation methods and backdoor attacks.

2   Background and Related Work

Deepfakes, a combination of "deep learning" and "fake" [3], usually refer to media such as images and videos that are forged by deep learning methods. In this work, we consider deepfakes as faces forged by both deep learning methods and conventional computer graphics methods. Figure 2 shows a taxonomy of deepfakes and their generation methods. Deepfakes for faces roughly include *face synthesis* and *face manipulation*. Face synthesis aims to synthesize faces that do not belong to any persons in the

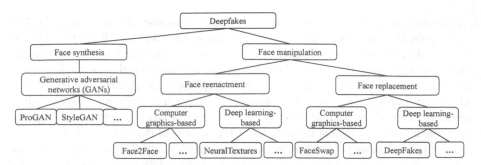

Fig. 2. A taxonomy of deepfakes and their generation methods.

real world, while face manipulation aims to tamper a person's face image to change its facial expression or completely replace it as another person's face. Next, we discuss face synthesis and face manipulation separately.

2.1 Face Synthesis

Most face synthesis methods [14,34–36,46,63] leverage the popular deep learning methods called *generative adversarial networks (GANs)* [26]. A GAN has two main components, i.e., a *generator* and a *discriminator*. Both generator and discriminator are neural networks. The generator takes a random vector (e.g., a vector of random Gaussian noise) as input and aims to generate a fake face that cannot be distinguished from real faces by the discriminator, while the discriminator aims to distinguish between real faces and the fake faces generated by the generator. The two neural networks are trained in turn until convergence, after which the generator wins the race and is able to generate fake faces that cannot be distinguished from real faces by the discriminator. Many GANs have been proposed to synthesize faces. Examples include ProGAN [34], StyleGAN [35], StyleGAN2 [36], StarGAN [14], and CycleGAN [63], etc. For instance, StyleGAN can synthesize fake faces with given styles. StyleGAN2 further improves the fake face quality by redesigning the generator of the StyleGAN. The fake faces synthesized by StyleGAN2 are illustrated on a website [4], refreshing which shows a new synthesized fake face each time.

2.2 Face Manipulation

Based on how the faces are manipulated, face manipulation methods can be divided into two categories, i.e., *face reenactment* and *face replacement*. Given a real face image of one person (called *target face*), face reenactment [45,50,51] aims to change some properties of the target face image as those of another person's face image (called *source face*), e.g., the expressions, accessories, illuminations, or shapes of the face. However, the identity of the target face is preserved. Face replacement [1,5,61] aims to replace the target face with the source face. Figure 3 illustrates the difference between face reenactment and face replacement. In Fig. 3b, the expression and illumination of the

(a) Real   (b) Face reenactment   (c) Face replacement

Fig. 3. Illustration of (a) a real face, (b) a fake face by face reenactment, and (c) a fake face by face replacement.

face are modified by a face reenactment method, while the identity of the face is preserved. However, in Fig. 3c, the face has been totally replaced by another person's face, indicating the identity of the face has changed.

Like face synthesis, many methods have been proposed for face manipulation, including both computer graphics-based methods and deep learning-based methods. Next, we discuss one computer graphics-based method and one representative deep learning-based method for face reenactment and replacement.

Face Reenactment

- **Face2Face.** Face2Face [51] is a computer graphics-based method. Face2Face first builds a target 3D model for the target faces and a source 3D model for the source faces based on a set of face images. Then, given a pair of target face and source face, the attacker transfers the expressions or other properties of the source face to the target face using the two models. Specifically, the attacker computes the parameters (e.g., the expression) of the source face modelled by the source 3D model and uses the target 3D model to generate a fake face with the same parameters.
- **NeuralTextures.** NeuralTextures [50] is a deep learning-based method that jointly learns neural textures and a rendering neural network based on a set of target faces. The neural textures are high-dimensional feature representations of the target faces, which containc important information about the identity. The rendering neural network takes the neural textures and a uv-map, which is a 2D representation of 3D face information, as its input and reconstructs the face images from them. Given a target face and a source face, the attacker first generates the uv-map of the source face carrying the desired information (e.g., the expression). Then the attacker feeds the uv-map together with the neural textures of the target face into the rendering neural network to re-render a fake face with the identity of the target face and the desired properties of the source face.

Face Replacement

- **FaceSwap.** FaceSwap [1] is a computer graphics-based face replacement method. FaceSwap generates a 3D template model with facial landmarks (e.g., noses, mouths, eyes) that are detected in the target face images. Using the 3D model, FaceSwap projects the face region in the target face image to the source face image by minimizing the difference between the projected facial landmarks and the real facial landmarks in the target face image.

- **DeepFakes.** With a little abuse of notations, this method is called DeepFakes [5]. Note that the letter F is capitalized in the method name, while it is not in deepfakes referring to forged media. DeepFakes leverages autoencoders to perform face replacement. Specifically, the attacker trains two autoencoders for the source faces and the target faces, respectively. The two autoencoders share the same encoder but have different decoders. To replace a source face as a target face, an attacker can encode the source face with the shared encoder and decode it with the target face's decoder.

2.3 Detecting Deepfakes

In the past couple of years, many methods have been proposed to detect deepfakes. A deepfake detection system (illustrated in Fig. 1) includes two key components, i.e., *face extractor* and *face classifier*. Most deepfake detection systems adopt off-the-shelf face extractor as it is a mature technique while designing customized face classifiers. Roughly speaking, face classifiers can be grouped into two categories, i.e., *heuristics-based* and *neural-network-based*. Heuristics-based face classifiers [8,22,38,39,42,59] leverage some heuristic differences between fake faces and real faces. For example, Li et al. [39] proposed to capture the face warping artifacts in fake faces. The method is based on the assumption that the quality of the fake faces is lower than that of real faces. Therefore, to match the image quality of the low-resolution fake region and the high-revolution real region, an attacker needs to perform additional face warping, whose artifacts can be used to detect fake faces. However, these face classifiers were soon broken by new fake faces. For instance, deepfake generation methods have been developed to generate high-quality fake faces, breaking the assumption required by [39].

Neural-network-based face classifiers [7,9,17,22,43,44,47,48,58,62] train binary neural network classifiers to detect fake faces. Specifically, given a training dataset including both real faces and fake faces, a neural network classifier is trained. Then, given a new face, the classifier predicts a label "real" or "fake" for it, indicating whether it is a real one or a fake one. While any neural network classifier could be used, state-of-the-art face classifiers [48] leverage the Xception neural network architecture [15] that is pretrained on the ImageNet dataset. Specifically, they fine tune the pretrained Xception neural network using the training faces as a face classifier.

2.4 Security of Deepfake Detection

The adversarial machine learning community showed that classifiers are vulnerable to adversarial examples [13,49]. Since a face classifier is a classifier, it may also be vulnerable to adversarial examples. Indeed, several recent studies showed so [12,21,23,29]. For instance, Gandhi et al. [23] showed that, via adding a small carefully crafted perturbation to a fake face, a face classifier misclassifies it to a real face, where the fake face with perturbation is known as an adversarial example. Carlini et al. [12] proposed

Table 1. Dataset statistics and performance of the face classifier trained for each dataset.

Dataset	Dataset source	Deepfake generation method	#training faces		#validation faces		#testing faces		Detection performance		
			Real	Fake	Real	Fake	Real	Fake	Accuracy	TPR	TNR
F2F	FaceForensics++ [48]	Face2Face [51]	367k	367k	68k	68k	74k	74k	0.98	0.98	0.99
NT	FaceForensics++ [48]	NeuralTextures [50]	367k	292k	68k	55k	74k	60k	0.94	0.90	0.97
FS	FaceForensics++ [48]	FaceSwap [1]	367k	291k	68k	55k	74k	60k	0.99	0.98	0.99
DF	FaceForensics++ [48]	DeepFakes [5]	367k	367k	68k	68k	74k	73k	0.99	0.99	0.99
DFDC	DFDC [19]	8 methods[a]	362k	352k	71k	68k	71k	69k	0.98	0.99	0.98
ALL	FaceForensics++ [48] & DFDC [19]	All methods above	472k	461k	89k	87k	94k	92k	0.96	0.97	0.95

[a] DF-128, DF-256, MM/NN, NTH, FSGAN, etc.

several new attacks to generate adversarial examples against state-of-the-art face classifiers. Hussain et al. [29] considered real-world adversarial examples that are robust to image and video compression codecs. Fernandes et al. [21] leveraged reinforcement learning to generate adversarial examples against face classifiers.

However, existing studies only focused on the security of the face classifier against adversarial examples, leaving the security of face extractor and the security of face classifier against cross-method generalization and data poisoning attacks unexplored.

3 Measurement Setup

3.1 Datasets

We use six datasets from two public large-scale data sources in our experiments, i.e., *F2F*, *NT*, *FS*, *DF*, *DFDC*, and *ALL*. We summarize the statistics of the six datasets in Table 1.

F2F, NT, FS, and DF: These datasets are extracted from the FaceForensics++ dataset [48]. The FaceForensics++ dataset consists of 1,000 real videos from Youtube. Four deepfake generation methods, i.e., Face2Face [51], NeuralTextures [50], FaceSwap [1], and DeepFakes [5], are used to manipulate faces in the real videos, which results in 4,000 fake videos in total. The videos are compressed using H.264 codec and different video qualities are available. We consider the high quality version of the videos, which are compressed with a constant rate quantization parameter 23. We extract the face region in each frame of the videos using the publicly available package Dlib [37], and enlarge the located face regions around the center by a factor of 1.3, following the FaceForensics++ paper [48]. Moreover, we extract the enlarged face regions from the video frames as face images and resize them to 299 × 299 pixels. The pixel values in the face images are then normalized to [−1, 1].

We name the face image dataset consisting of both real faces and fake faces generated by a specific deepfake generation method as the abbreviation of the method. In particular, F2F (NT, FS, or DF) refers to the real faces and the fake faces that are generated by Face2Face (NeuralTextures, FaceSwap, or DeepFakes). For each dataset, we split it to a training set, validation set, and testing set following the FaceForensics++ paper [48]. Specifically, 720 real videos and their manipulated versions are treated as the training set, 140 real videos and their manipulated versions are treated as the validation set, while the remaining 140 real videos and their manipulated versions are treated as the testing set. In our datasets, the face images successfully extracted from the training/validation/testing videos form the training/validation/testing faces.

DFDC: We extracted this dataset from the Facebook Deepfake Detection Challenge dataset [19], which consists of videos from 3,426 paid actors. The released dataset contains 19,154 ten-second real videos as well as 100,000 fake videos generated by 8 deepfake generation methods including DFAE [19], MM/NN [28], NTH [61], and FSGAN [45]. Moreover, some randomly selected videos are post processed to make the fake videos more realistic, e.g., applying a sharpening filter on the blended faces to increase the perceptual quality of the faces. However, it is unknown which method was used to generate each individual fake video. Therefore, unlike the FaceForensics++ dataset, we do not split the dataset based on the deepfake generation methods and treat it as a whole instead. We use 72% of the videos as training videos, 14% as validation videos, and the rest 14% as testing videos. We extract the face images from the frames of a video following the same process as the FaceForensics++ dataset. We extract one face image per 50 frames for fake videos and one face image per 10 frames for real videos, considering the different lengths of fake and real videos. We use the face images successfully extracted from the training/validation/testing videos as the training/validation/testing face images in DFDC. Like the FaceForensics++ dataset, we resize the face images to 299×299 and normalize the pixel values to $[-1,1]$.

ALL: The ALL dataset is a mix-up of the five face datasets above. Specifically, we randomly select 25% of the face images in F2F, NT, FS, DF, and DFDC to form the ALL dataset.

3.2 Training Face Classifiers

As state-of-the-art face classifiers use the Xception neural network [15], we train an Xception neural network classifier for each dataset. Specifically, the Xception neural network was originally designed for image classification on ImageNet and was pre-trained on ImageNet. The last layer is a fully connected layer with 1,000 neurons. Since deepfake detection is a binary classification problem, the last layer of the pretrained Xception neural network is replaced as a fully connected layer with 2 neurons. Moreover, the parameters for the last layer are randomly initialized. We follow [48] to first train the new fully-connected layer for 3 epochs with other layers fixed, and then train the entire network for 15 more epochs. We evaluate the validation accuracy of the model after each epoch and the model with the highest validation accuracy is used as the detector. We use an Adam optimizer with a learning rate 2×10^{-4} to train the model, which is the same as in [48]. We train one Xception neural network for each of the six face image datasets, which results in six face classifiers.

3.3 Evaluation Metrics

We consider three evaluation metrics to measure the effectiveness of the face classifiers. Specifically, we consider testing accuracy, true positive rate, and true negative rate as our metrics. When describing true positive rate and true negative rate, we view fake faces as "positive" and real faces as "negative".

Accuracy: The accuracy of a face classifier is defined as the fraction of the testing face images that are correctly classified by the face classifier. Accuracy is an aggregated metric, which does not distinguish the detection performance of the real faces and fake faces. Therefore, we further consider true positive rate and true negative rate.

True Positive Rate: The true positive rate of a face classifier is defined as the fraction of fake face images that are correctly classified as fake by the face classifier. When an attacker tries to evade detection, its goal is to downgrade the true positive rate.

True Negative Rate: The true negative rate of a face classifier is defined as the fraction of real face images that are correctly classified as real by the face classifier. True negative rate represents a face classifier's ability to recognize real faces.

Table 1 shows the performance of the face classifier for each dataset. We observe that all face classifiers are highly accurate. In particular, they achieve accuracies ranging from 0.94 to 0.99. Note that the performance of our detector for DFDC dataset is higher than those of the winning teams in the Facebook competition because they were evaluated on the private testing dataset, which contains unknown post processing and we do not have access to.

4   Security of Face Extractor

4.1   Experimental Setup

The security of a deepfake detection system relies on the security of both face extractor and face classifier, e.g., if the face region cannot be extracted accurately from an image, deepfake detection fails. In this section, we measure the security of face extractor. A face extractor aims to extract the face region in an image. When the face extractor cannot find an appropriate face region in an image, it outputs NULL. Note that even if the face extractor does not output NULL, its extracted region may not be the correct face region. We consider the open-source face extractor Dlib [37], which was used by previous work on deepfake detection [48].

Recall that each of our datasets includes image frames obtained from real or deepfake videos. We add random Gaussian noise with mean 0 and standard deviation σ to each of the three RGB dimensions of each pixel in an image frame. Then, we use Dlib to extract the face region in the noisy image frame. We repeat this experiment for each image frame in a dataset. Moreover, for a dataset, we define the *face extraction success rate* as the fraction of the image frames in the dataset for which Dlib does not output NULL. Note that our way of defining success rate gives advantages to Dlib, because face extraction may also fail even if Dlib does not output NULL.

4.2   Experimental Results

Figure 4 shows the success rates of face extraction for each dataset except ALL when different amounts of Gaussian noise is added to the image frames. We do not show the

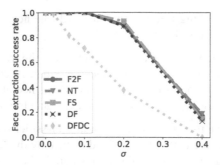

Fig. 4. Face extraction success rate vs. standard deviation of the Gaussian noise added to the image frames.

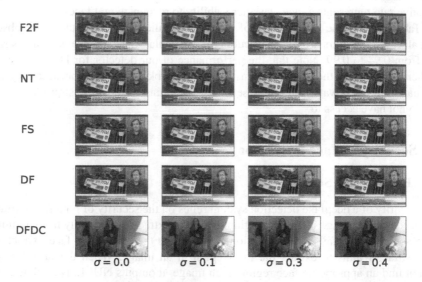

Fig. 5. First column: four deepfake image frames respectively in F2F, NT, FS, and DF generated from the same real image frame and one deepfake image frame in DFDC. Other columns: noisy image frames with different amounts of Gaussian noise.

results for ALL as it is a combination of the other five datasets. We observe that when the noise level σ is very small, the Dlib face extractor can extract the faces in most image frames. However, when σ increases, the success rate drops quickly, indicating that the face extractor fails to extract the faces when a relatively large Gaussian noise is added to the image frames.

For instance, when the standard deviation σ of the Gaussian noise is 0.2, Dlib outputs NULL for 62% of image frames in the dataset DFDC and outputs NULL for about 10% of image frames in the other four datasets; when the standard deviation σ of the Gaussian noise increases to 0.4, Dlib outputs NULL for nearly 100% of image frames in the dataset DFDC and outputs NULL for around 85% of image frames in the other four datasets. Figure 5 shows some examples of image frames with different amounts

Table 2. The accuracy, true positive rate, and true negative rate of each face classifier on the testing face images in each dataset. Each row represents a face classifier trained on a dataset and each column represents a dataset whose testing face images are used for evaluating face classifiers.

(a) Accuracy

	F2F	NT	DF	FS
F2F	0.98	0.56	0.56	0.53
NT	0.52	0.94	0.54	0.61
DF	0.51	0.57	0.99	0.55
FS	0.51	0.55	0.51	0.99

(b) True positive rate

	F2F	NT	DF	FS
F2F	0.98	0.02	0.03	0.06
NT	0.07	0.90	0.01	0.24
DF	0.02	0.05	0.99	0.00
FS	0.02	0.01	0.02	0.98

(c) True negative rate

	F2F	NT	DF	FS
F2F	0.99	0.99	0.99	0.99
NT	0.97	0.97	0.97	0.97
DF	0.99	0.99	0.99	0.99
FS	0.99	0.99	0.99	0.99

of Gaussian noise. We observe that human can hardly notice the noise even if σ is as large as 0.4. In particular, an image frame and its noisy version look the same to human eyes.

We also observe that the face extraction success rate for DFDC drops faster than those for the other four datasets F2F, NT, FS, and DF. We suspect the reason is that the videos in the FaceForensics++ dataset, which is the source of F2F, NT, FS, and DF, were selected such that the faces in them can be extracted easily [48].

Security Implications: Our results imply that an attacker can evade detection of its deepfakes via simply adding random Gaussian noise to them to evade a face extractor.

5 Cross-Method Generalization of Face Classifier

New deepfake generation methods are continuously developed. Therefore, we are interested in understanding whether a face classifier trained on deepfakes generated by one method can detect deepfakes generated by another method.

5.1 Experimental Setup

Recall that each of the four datasets F2F, NT, DF, and FS include fake faces generated by a particular method. DFDC includes fake faces generated by 8 methods, which include some of the four methods. ALL is a combination of all the fake faces. Therefore, we use F2F, NT, DF, and FS to measure cross-method generalization in our experiments as they use different deepfake generation methods. Specifically, we train a face classifier on each of the four datasets as we described in Sect. 3.2. Then, we evaluate each face classifier on the testing face images in each dataset.

5.2 Experimental Results

Table 2 shows the accuracy, true positive rate, and true negative rate of each face classifier on the testing face images in each of the four datasets. We observe the diagonal values in the tables are large. This means that a face classifier trained on deepfakes generated by some method can accurately detect the deepfakes generated by the same

Table 3. The accuracy, true positive rate, and true negative rate of face classifiers on the testing face images in FS. Each row represents a face classifier trained on one or multiple datasets.

(a) Accuracy

	FS
F2F	0.56
F2F + NT	0.55
F2F + NT + DF	0.54

(b) True positive rate

	FS
F2F	0.03
F2F + NT	0.03
F2F + NT + DF	0.02

(c) True negative rate

	FS
F2F	0.99
F2F + NT	0.95
F2F + NT + DF	0.97

method. However, the off-diagonal accuracies are much smaller, e.g., close to 0.5 (random guessing) in many cases. This means that a face classifier trained on deepfakes generated by some method cannot detect deepfakes generated by other methods. We note that the off-diagonal true positive rates are close to 0 in most cases, while the off-diagonal true negative rates are all close to 1, which means that a face classifier classifies almost all testing face images in a different dataset as real. We suspect the reason is that these four datasets share the same real face images.

We also train face classifiers using fake faces generated by multiple deepfake generation methods, e.g., F2F + NT, F2F + NT + DF. Table 3 shows the accuracy, true positive rate, and true negative rate of such face classifiers on the testing face images in FS. We observe that even if a face classifier is trained using fake faces generated by multiple deepfake generation methods, the face classifier still cannot detect fake faces generated by a different method. Note that we did not further include the fake faces in DFDC to train face classifiers, because DFDC may include fake faces that are generated by FS and DFDC does not include information for us to know which method generated a particular fake face.

Security Implications: Our results imply that an attacker can evade detection via generating deepfakes using a new deepfake generation method.

6   Security of Face Classifier Against Data Poisoning Attacks

While adversarial examples attack the testing phase of a classifier, data poisoning attacks aim to attack the training phase by polluting the training data such that a corrupted classifier is learnt. In this section, we measure the security of the face classifier against data poisoning attacks.

6.1   Experimental Setup

We consider a simple data poisoning attack called *label flipping attack* and an advanced attack called *backdoor attack* [27]. For simplicity, we focus on the ALL dataset.

Label Flipping Attack: Label flipping attack, as its name suggests, flips the labels of some training examples. In our deepfake detection, label flipping attack changes the labels of some training real face images to "fake" and the labels of some training fake face images to "real". In particular, we flip the labels of a certain fraction of the training

Real   Face2Face   NeuralTextures   FaceSwap   DeepFakes

(a) Trigger   (b) Face images with trigger embeded

Fig. 6. (a) Trigger used in the backdoor attack. (b) A trigger-embedded real face image and four trigger-embedded fake face images generated by four different deepfake generation methods. The trigger is embedded at the bottom right corner of a face image (highlighted by the red circles). (Color figure online)

face images. Then, we train the face classifier for the ALL dataset on the training face images including the ones with flipped labels. We evaluate the accuracy, true positive rate, and true negative rate of the corrupted face classifier on the testing face images. Note that we do not change the testing face images.

Backdoor Attack: Backdoor attack aims to poison the training examples such that the corrupted classifier predicts an attacker-desired label for any testing example with a *trigger* embedded. In our experiments, we use a chessboard grid as the trigger, which is shown in Fig. 6a. Moreover, we set the attacker-desired label as "real", i.e., the corrupted face classifier classifies any face image with the trigger embedded as real. To perform the backdoor attack, we randomly select a fraction of training face images in the ALL dataset. We embed the chessboard grid trigger to the bottom right corner of each of them and set its label to be "real". Figure 6b shows some face images with the trigger embedded. The size of the trigger is small compared to the size of the face images, i.e., the trigger size is 0.1% of the image size. Then, we train the face classifier using the training face images including the ones with trigger embedded. We also embed the trigger to each testing face image of the ALL dataset and use them to evaluate the accuracy, true positive rate, and true negative rate of the corrupted face classifier.

6.2 Experimental Results

Label Flipping Attack: Figure 7a shows the results for label flipping attack. We observe that the face classifier is relatively secure to label flipping attack. Specifically, the accuracy only drops by 0.07 even when the fraction of flipped labels reaches 37.5%. We suspect this is because of the redundancy in the training dataset. As long as the training face images with correct labels are sufficiently more than the training face images with flipped labels, we can learn an accurate face classifier. When a half of the training face images have flipped labels, the learnt face classifier has true positive rate 0 and true negative rate 1, which indicates that the face classifier classifies all testing face images as real. We suspect this is because the ALL dataset has more real face images in the training set and the face classifier learns to predict every image as real. Note that if the fraction of flipped labels exceeds 0.5, the learnt face classifier is worse than random guessing as more than half of the labels are incorrect.

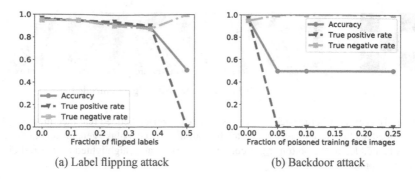

(a) Label flipping attack   (b) Backdoor attack

Fig. 7. Security of face classifier against label flipping attack and backdoor attack. The ALL dataset is used.

Backdoor Attack: Figure 7b shows the performance of backdoor attack to the face classifier. When we do not embed the trigger to any training face images (i.e., the fraction of poisoned training face images is 0), the accuracy, true positive rate, and true negative rate are all close to 1, indicating that the face classifier can still correctly classify the testing face images even if we embed the trigger to them. However, when the trigger is embedded into only 5% of training face images, the true positive rate drops to 0 and the true negative rate becomes 1, indicating that the face classifier classifies all testing face images as real when embedding the trigger to them.

Security Implications: Assume a threat model where an attacker can poison some training face images of a face classifier, e.g., flip their labels and embed a trigger to them. For instance, when the training face images are crowdsourced from social media users, an attacker can provide poisoned face images by acting as social media users. Moreover, the attacker can embed the trigger to its fake faces, which is required by backdoor attack. Our measurement results show that an attacker needs to flip the labels of a large fraction (e.g., >40%) of the training face images in order to attack a face classifier via label flipping attack. However, an attacker can evade detection via backdoor attack that only poisons a small fraction (e.g., 5%) of the training face images.

7   Discussion and Limitations

Leveraging Robust Face Extractor and Face Classifier: Our measurement results show that face extractor and face classifier are not secure against perturbations (e.g., adversarial examples) added to testing images and backdoor attacks. We note that how to defend against adversarial examples and backdoor attacks is still an open challenge, though the adversarial machine learning community has developed multiple methods [11,16,24,40,41,56] to enhance classifiers' robustness against them. Among the different methods, *adversarial training* [41] and *randomized smoothing* [11,16,31] achieve state-of-the-art robustness against adversarial examples, while ensemble methods [30,52] achieve state-of-the-art robustness against backdoor attacks.

In particular, adversarial training adds adversarial examples of the training examples to augment the training dataset, while randomized smoothing builds a smoothed classifier by randomizing an input and provides probabilistic certified robustness guarantee of the smoothed classifier. Randomized smoothing ensures that no adversarial perturbation smaller than a threshold can change the predicted label of a given testing example. However, these methods sacrifice a classifier's accuracy when no perturbation is added to the testing examples [16,41], i.e., a face classifier built by these methods has a lower accuracy even if an attacker does not add any perturbation to its fake faces. Moreover, these methods can only defend against very small perturbations, i.e., an attacker can still evade detection once adding large enough perturbations to its fake faces. Ensemble methods train multiple classifiers and take a majority vote among them to predict the label of a testing example. The predicted label is unaffected by a small number of poisoned training examples. However, a face classifier built by such methods also has a lower accuracy even if an attacker does not perform backdoor attacks.

Neural cleanse [56] was proposed as a defense against backdoor attacks. Specifically, neural cleanse can identify potential backdoors in a classifier and reconstruct the trigger. Neural cleanse is based on an assumption that all testing images embedded with a specific trigger will be predicted as the same target label. Therefore, the trigger can be reverse engineered by searching for the minimum perturbation that can change the classification results of all testing examples to a certain label. Once the trigger is reconstructed, neural cleanse uses input filters, neural pruning, or machine unlearning to eliminate the effect of the backdoor embedded in the classifier. However, neural cleanse cannot detect source-label-specific backdoor attacks, where the backdoor is designed to be effective only for a subset of source testing examples, e.g., face images with blonde hair. In this scenario, the classification results for face images whose hair is not blonde will not be affected by the trigger. Therefore, the assumption that Neural cleanse relies on does not hold and it fails to detect the backdoor [56].

Deepfake Video: In this work, we consider deepfake detection for a static face image. In practice, we may have access to deepfake videos. Therefore, a deepfake detector can consider the statistical information between the image frames in a video to classify it to be real or fake. For instance, one way is to classify each frame of a video as real or fake, and then take a majority vote among the labels of the frames as the label of the entire video. Another intuitive way to deal with videos is to use sequential information of a video. For instance, the detector can track the light source in the video and classify the video as fake if there are inconsistencies in the light source location [33]. Audio information in a video may also be used to aid detection of deepfake videos. However, an attacker does not need to manipulate the audios and one of the leading teams in the Facebook Deepfake Detection Challenge competition found that audio may not necessarily be helpful for deepfake detection [6].

Leveraging Network Security Solutions: Instead of detecting abnormality in the content of an image or video, we can also block the spread of deepfakes from the network security perspective. In particular, deepfakes are often propagated via social media and they may be propagated by fraudulent users such as fake users and compromised users. Therefore, we can detect fraudulent users in social media who propagate deepfakes and limit the impact of deepfakes. Many approaches have been proposed to detect fraudulent users. These approaches leverage user registration information, user behavior, content generated by user, and/or social graphs between users [10, 18, 20, 25, 32, 53–55, 57, 60]. Although these methods cannot detect all fraudulent users, they may increase the bar for attackers to maintain them and spread deepfakes.

8 Conclusion

We evaluated the security of the state-of-the-art deepfake detection methods using six datasets from two large-scale public data sources. Our extensive experiments show that although the detectors can achieve high accuracies in non-adversarial settings, a face extractor is not secure against random Gaussian noise added to the images. Moreover, we found that a face classifier trained using fake faces generated by some deepfake generation methods cannot detect fake faces generated by a different method; and a face classifier is not secure against backdoor attacks. Our results highlight that the major challenge of deepfake detection is to enhance its security in adversarial settings.

Acknowledgements. We thank the anonymous reviewers for insightful reviews. We also thank Xiaohan Wang for discussion and processing datasets for experiments on cross-method generalization. This work was partially supported by NSF grant No.1937786.

References

1. https://github.com/MarekKowalski/FaceSwap
2. https://www.youtube.com/watch?v=cQ54GDm1eL0
3. https://en.wikipedia.org/wiki/Deepfake
4. https://thispersondoesnotexist.com/
5. https://github.com/deepfakes/faceswap
6. https://www.kaggle.com/c/deepfake-detection-challenge/discussion/158506
7. Afchar, D., Nozick, V., Yamagishi, J., Echizen, I.: MesoNet: a compact facial video forgery detection network. In: WIFS (2018)
8. Agarwal, S., Farid, H., Gu, Y., He, M., Nagano, K., Li, H.: Protecting world leaders against deep fakes. In: CVPR Workshops (2019)
9. Bayar, B., Stamm, M.C.: A deep learning approach to universal image manipulation detection using a new convolutional layer. In: IH & MM Security (2016)
10. Cao, Q., Yang, X., Yu, J., Palow, C.: Uncovering large groups of active malicious accounts in online social networks. In: CCS (2014)
11. Cao, X., Gong, N.Z.: Mitigating evasion attacks to deep neural networks via region-based classification. In: ACSAC (2017)
12. Carlini, N., Farid, H.: Evading deepfake-image detectors with white-and black-box attacks. In: CVPR Workshops (2020)
13. Carlini, N., Wagner, D.: Towards evaluating the robustness of neural networks. In: S & P (2017)
14. Choi, Y., Choi, M., Kim, M., Ha, J.W., Kim, S., Choo, J.: StarGAN: unified generative adversarial networks for multi-domain image-to-image translation. In: CVPR (2018)
15. Chollet, F.: Xception: deep learning with depthwise separable convolutions. In: CVPR (2017)
16. Cohen, J., Rosenfeld, E., Kolter, Z.: Certified adversarial robustness via randomized smoothing. In: ICML (2019)

17. Cozzolino, D., Poggi, G., Verdoliva, L.: Recasting residual-based local descriptors as convolutional neural networks: an application to image forgery detection. In: IH & MM Security (2017)
18. Danezis, G., Mittal, P.: Sybilinfer: detecting sybil nodes using social networks. In: NDSS (2009)
19. Dolhansky, B., et al.: The deepfake detection challenge dataset (2020)
20. Egele, M., Stringhini, G., Kruegel, C., Vigna, G.: COMPA: detecting compromised accounts on social networks. In: NDSS (2013)
21. Fernandes, S.L., Jha, S.K.: Adversarial attack on deepfake detection using RL based texture patches. In: Bartoli, A., Fusiello, A. (eds.) ECCV 2020. LNCS, vol. 12535, pp. 220–235. Springer, Cham (2020). https://doi.org/10.1007/978-3-030-66415-2_14
22. Frank, J., Eisenhofer, T., Schönherr, L., Fischer, A., Kolossa, D., Holz, T.: Leveraging frequency analysis for deep fake image recognition. In: ICML (2020)
23. Gandhi, A., Jain, S.: Adversarial perturbations fool deepfake detectors. In: IJCNN (2020)
24. Gao, Y., Xu, C., Wang, D., Chen, S., Ranasinghe, D.C., Nepal, S.: STRIP: a defence against trojan attacks on deep neural networks. In: ACSAC (2019)
25. Gong, N.Z., Frank, M., Mittal, P.: SybilBelief: a semi-supervised learning approach for structure-based sybil detection. IEEE Trans. Inf. Forensics Secur. 9(6), 976–987 (2014)
26. Goodfellow, I., et al.: Generative adversarial nets. In: NeurIPS (2014)
27. Gu, T., Dolan-Gavitt, B., Garg, S.: BadNets: identifying vulnerabilities in the machine learning model supply chain. In: Machine Learning and Computer Security Workshop (2017)
28. Huang, D., De La Torre, F.: Facial action transfer with personalized bilinear regression. In: Fitzgibbon, A., Lazebnik, S., Perona, P., Sato, Y., Schmid, C. (eds.) ECCV 2012. LNCS, vol. 7573, pp. 144–158. Springer, Heidelberg (2012). https://doi.org/10.1007/978-3-642-33709-3_11
29. Hussain, S., Neekhara, P., Jere, M., Koushanfar, F., McAuley, J.: Adversarial deepfakes: evaluating vulnerability of deepfake detectors to adversarial examples. In: WACV (2020)
30. Jia, J., Cao, X., Gong, N.Z.: Intrinsic certified robustness of bagging against data poisoning attacks. In: AAAI (2021)
31. Jia, J., Cao, X., Wang, B., Gong, N.Z.: Certified robustness for top-k predictions against adversarial perturbations via randomized smoothing. In: ICLR (2020)
32. Jia, J., Wang, B., Gong, N.Z.: Random walk based fake account detection in online social networks. In: DSN (2017)
33. Johnson, M.K., Farid, H.: Exposing digital forgeries through specular highlights on the eye. In: Furon, T., Cayre, F., Doërr, G., Bas, P. (eds.) IH 2007. LNCS, vol. 4567, pp. 311–325. Springer, Heidelberg (2007). https://doi.org/10.1007/978-3-540-77370-2_21
34. Karras, T., Aila, T., Laine, S., Lehtinen, J.: Progressive growing of GANs for improved quality, stability, and variation. In: ICLR (2018)
35. Karras, T., Laine, S., Aila, T.: A style-based generator architecture for generative adversarial networks. In: CVPR (2019)
36. Karras, T., Laine, S., Aittala, M., Hellsten, J., Lehtinen, J., Aila, T.: Analyzing and improving the image quality of styleGAN. In: CVPR (2020)
37. King, D.E.: Dlib-ml: A machine learning toolkit. J. Mach. Learn. Res. 10, 1755–1758 (2009)
38. Li, Y., Chang, M.C., Lyu, S.: In Ictu oculi: exposing AI generated fake face videos by detecting eye blinking. arXiv preprint arXiv:1806.02877 (2018)
39. Li, Y., Lyu, S.: Exposing deepfake videos by detecting face warping artifacts. In: CVPR Workshops (2019)
40. Liu, Y., Lee, W.C., Tao, G., Ma, S., Aafer, Y., Zhang, X.: ABS: scanning neural networks for back-doors by artificial brain stimulation. In: CCS (2019)
41. Madry, A., Makelov, A., Schmidt, L., Tsipras, D., Vladu, A.: Towards deep learning models resistant to adversarial attacks. In: ICLR (2018)

42. Matern, F., Riess, C., Stamminger, M.: Exploiting visual artifacts to expose deepfakes and face manipulations. In: WACVW (2019)
43. Nguyen, H.H., Fang, F., Yamagishi, J., Echizen, I.: Multi-task learning for detecting and segmenting manipulated facial images and videos. In: BTAS (2019)
44. Nguyen, H.H., Yamagishi, J., Echizen, I.: Use of a capsule network to detect fake images and videos. arXiv preprint arXiv:1910.12467 (2019)
45. Nirkin, Y., Keller, Y., Hassner, T.: FSGAN: subject agnostic face swapping and reenactment. In: ICCV (2019)
46. Park, T., Liu, M.Y., Wang, T.C., Zhu, J.Y.: Semantic image synthesis with spatially-adaptive normalization. In: CVPR (2019)
47. Rahmouni, N., Nozick, V., Yamagishi, J., Echizen, I.: Distinguishing computer graphics from natural images using convolution neural networks. In: WIFS (2017)
48. Rössler, A., Cozzolino, D., Verdoliva, L., Riess, C., Thies, J., Nießner, M.: FaceForensics++: learning to detect manipulated facial images. In: ICCV (2019)
49. Szegedy, C., et al.: Intriguing properties of neural networks. In: ICLR (2014)
50. Thies, J., Zollhöfer, M., Nießner, M.: Deferred neural rendering: image synthesis using neural textures. ACM Trans. Graph. (TOG) 38(4), 1–12 (2019)
51. Thies, J., Zollhofer, M., Stamminger, M., Theobalt, C., Nießner, M.: Face2Face: real-time face capture and reenactment of RGB videos. In: CVPR (2016)
52. Wang, B., Cao, X., Gong, N.Z., et al.: On certifying robustness against backdoor attacks via randomized smoothing. In: CVPR Workshop on Adversarial Machine Learning in Computer Vision (2020)
53. Wang, B., Gong, N.Z., Fu, H.: GANG: detecting fraudulent users in online social networks via guilt-by-association on directed graphs. In: ICDM (2017)
54. Wang, B., Jia, J., Gong, N.Z.: Graph-based security and privacy analytics via collective classification with joint weight learning and propagation. In: NDSS (2019)
55. Wang, B., Zhang, L., Gong, N.Z.: SybilSCAR: sybil detection in online social networks via local rule based propagation. In: INFOCOM (2017)
56. Wang, B., et al.: Neural cleanse: identifying and mitigating backdoor attacks in neural networks. In: S & P (2019)
57. Wang, G., Konolige, T., Wilson, C., Wang, X., Zheng, H., Zhao, B.Y.: You are how you click: clickstream analysis for sybil detection. In: USENIX Security (2013)
58. Wang, S.Y., Wang, O., Zhang, R., Owens, A., Efros, A.A.: CNN-generated images are surprisingly easy to spot...for now. In: CVPR (2020)
59. Yang, X., Li, Y., Lyu, S.: Exposing deep fakes using inconsistent head poses. In: ICASSP (2019)
60. Yuan, D., et al.: Detecting fake accounts in online social networks at the time of registrations. In: CCS (2019)
61. Zakharov, E., Shysheya, A., Burkov, E., Lempitsky, V.: Few-shot adversarial learning of realistic neural talking head models. In: ICCV (2019)
62. Zhou, P., Han, X., Morariu, V.I., Davis, L.S.: Two-stream neural networks for tampered face detection. In: CVPR Workshops (2017)
63. Zhu, J.Y., Park, T., Isola, P., Efros, A.A.: Unpaired image-to-image translation using cycle-consistent adversarial networks. In: ICCV (2017)

Author Index

Printed in the United States
by Baker & Taylor Publisher Services